From Hope to Hardship

AALDERT
PRINS

FROM HOPE TO HARDSHIP

THE MISSIONARY DREAMS
AND DISAPPOINTMENTS
OF THE BELGIAN GOSPEL MISSION
1918-1962

LEUVEN UNIVERSITY PRESS

This book appears in the peer-reviewed series
KADOC Studies on Religion, Culture & Society

EDITORIAL BOARD

Elena Arigita Maza (Universidad de Granada)
Florian Bock (Ruhr Univesität Bochum)
Timothy Brittain-Catlin (University of Cambridge)
James Chappel (Duke University)
Kim Christiaens (KADOC-KU Leuven)
Kathleen James-Chakraborty (University College Dublin)
James Kennedy (Utrecht University)
Franziska Metzger (PH Luzern)
Patrick Pasture (MoSa-KU Leuven)
Isabelle Saint-Martin (EPHE Paris)
Thijl Sunier (VU Amsterdam)
Árpád von Klimó (Catholic University of America)
Veerle De Laet (Leuven University Press)
Peter Heyrman (KADOC-KU Leuven)

Cover: Pastor Daniël Meijer evangelizing with the *Onze Hoop* magazine in Antwerp, ca. 1928.
[KADOC-KU Leuven: ABEM, 1131]

© 2025 Leuven University Press/Presses universitaires de Louvain/Universitaire Pers Leuven,
Minderbroedersstraat 4, B-3000 Leuven (Belgium)

All rights reserved. Except in those cases expressly determined by law, no part of this publication may be multiplied, saved in an automated data file or made public in any way whatsoever without the express prior written consent of the publishers.

All TDM (text and data mining) rights reserved.

ISBN 978 94 6270 468 8
eISBN 978 94 6166 658 1 (ePDF)
eISBN 978 94 6166 659 8 (ePUB)
https://doi.org/10.11116/9789461666581
D/2025/1869/32
NUR: 712

CONTENTS

Acknowledgments 6

Introduction 9
1. The Desperate Quest for a Mission Field 17
2. Apostles of the Belgian Trenches 27
3. Bridgehead Brussels 47
4. Driven by Dispensational Urgency 61
5. Workers for the Vineyard 79
6. From Formative to Normative: The Structural Development of the BGM 97
7. From Dollar Mission to Beggars Mission, 1926-1936 117
8. New Leadership under the Clouds of War 137
9. The Nazi Occupation 157
10. Cutting the Umbilical Cord, 1945-1962 175
Conclusion 201

Appendices 207

List of Abbreviations 219
Bibliography 220
Index of Persons 237
Colophon 240

ACKNOWLEDGMENTS

This monograph originated in a doctoral dissertation at the Evangelical Theological Faculty in Leuven, Belgium. I am grateful for the education I received over the years from many respected professors from all over the globe, from all kinds of denominational backgrounds, and united under ETF Leuven's motto, *Fides Quaerens Intellectum*. I am particularly grateful to both my promotors, Dr. Klaus Fiedler and Dr. Andreas J. Beck. Both excelled in patiently coaching me in the writing of a dissertation. I can honestly say that all my professors at ETF Leuven's Historical Theology Department did a wonderful job of making their courses alive and relevant for us as students. Also, Dr. Geert W. Lorein and Dr. Jelle Creemers deserve to be mentioned for their feedback and discussions on the Belgian Gospel Mission and Evangelicalism in Belgium. A special word of thanks goes to Dr. Lutz E. von Padberg for his words of encouragement after my initial subject needed to be abandoned just before the finish line. That helped me find the courage to change my focus to a completely different subject.

Barry (d. 2014) and Coreen De Vaal deserve special mention. During the weekends I spent at the Norton House in Brussels as part of my research in the BEM archives, they not only showed tremendous hospitality but also, with their warm display of interest, acted as a sounding board for the discoveries I made while working my way through the extensive archive. I also want to thank my sister, Marjolein Turner-Prins, who translated my dissertation, and her husband, Martin Turner, and Rev. David Turner (d. 2020), for their language input.

As the backbone of my research was done in the archives of the Belgian Evangelical Mission, now Vianova, I want to thank this organization for graciously allowing me to use its extensive archives. Other archives that were most helpful during my research were the Belgian State Archives in Bruges and Brussels, the Boudin-Willems Archives of the United Protestant Church in Belgium, the Archepiscopal Archives of Mechelen-Brussels, the Archives of the Royal Army Museum, Brussels, the Archives of the Institut Biblique de Bruxelles, the Evangelism and Missions Archives at Wheaton College, Wheaton, Illinois, the Special Collections of Dallas Theological Library, the Archives of Moody Bible Institute, and the Zeeuws Archief in Middelburg, the Netherlands.

Further, I couldn't have done the job without consulting the libraries of ETF Leuven, the Faculty for Protestant Theology and Religion Studies, Brussels, and the heritage library collection at KADOC-KU Leuven. The colleagues of the Interlibrary Loan Service of the KU Leuven Libraries deserve credit for handling all my requests. I also spent many hours in the British Library in London, conveniently located next to St. Pancras train station and so easy to reach from Belgium.

Others who deserve mention are my colleagues at KADOC, Documentation and Research Centre on Religion, Culture and Society at KU Leuven. Former director Dr. Jan De Maeyer, Dr. Peter Heyrman, Dr. Godfried Kwanten, the Reading Room Team, Rie Vermeiren, and Jo Luyten all deserve special mention for their practical help and feedback during the research and writing of my dissertation.

When I successfully defended my dissertation in 2015, I intended to publish an edition of my research relatively quickly. However, it took me another nine years to finally accomplish this ambition. I couldn't have done it without the constant support of Dr. Andreas J. Beck, who kept believing in me and boosted me every now and then when the project became dormant. However, most credits during this project phase go to Dr. J.L. Krabbendam, who assisted me in transforming my voluminous dissertation into this coherent monograph.

To my parents, Albert and Rie Prins, I want to say a big thank you for your prayers and support during my studies and this project. It goes without saying that my wife, Ann Roose, and our four children, Jelmer, Nienke, Jildau, and Wiebren, deserve to be mentioned here. Thank you so much for your support and understanding.

As this project has been stretched over so many years, there is a real danger that I have forgotten to mention people who also assisted or encouraged me in some way. Rest assured that I couldn't have done it without you all.

Zeebrugge, December 2024

Headquarters of the Belgian Gospel Mission in Brussels, 1926.
[KADOC-KU Leuven: ABEM, 1141]

INTRODUCTION

In April 1919, just months after the founding of the Belgian Gospel Mission (BGM), Edith Norton wrote in her diary:

> When I die, build me no monument. My monument, it finds itself in Peter, Adolphe, Georgine, Mme. Simonsen, and in others in whom I have had some share in leading them to Christ. They are my joy and my crown. And I do here record, that I see on every side among Christians, so much of the life of the flesh, which manifests itself in self-will and self-aggrandizement and love of the world, that I give myself anew to Him today.[1]

These words capture the essence of the mindset shared by Edith and her husband Ralph, a mindset that shaped the very DNA of the BGM. In a way, the Nortons exemplify the phenomenon George Marsden described: Around the turn of the twentieth century, "enterprising evangelists kept springing up with competing and novel ways to gain a clientele" that saw their work as "simply supplementing the established denominations."[2] Yet the story of the Belgian Gospel Mission stands out as it took on a pioneering role as an early twentieth century, American-based faith mission targeting a Western European country.

This book will explore how the BGM emerged from a specialized faith mission — the British and Allied Soldiers Evangelistic Campaign (BASEC) — and eventually established a new free church denomination in Belgium. Although the BGM continues to exist as VIANOVA, our journey ends in 1962, when eight of

---

1 ABEM, 1122: Diary E. Norton (30 April 1919).
2 Marsden, "The Rise of Fundamentalism," 137.

the mission's church plants were more or less compelled to form an independent denomination, marking the start of a new phase in the BGM's existence. As this book aims at an audience on both sides of the Atlantic, some biographical information in the footnotes may be obvious on one side of the ocean, yet helpful on the other side.

To fully understand the BGM's trajectory and how it navigated the challenges of translating its missionary vision into reality, it is necessary to explore its roots in the Holiness movement and 1920s fundamentalism. The Holiness movement, which can be traced back to John Wesley, emerged in North America in the 1830s. It revived the Methodist doctrine "that all Christians might experience 'Christian perfection' in this life," and thus focused strongly on personal behavior.[3] By the end of the nineteenth century, the Holiness movement had branched into two streams, each with a slightly different understanding of 'holiness.' For this study, the term refers to *Keswick holiness*.

The Keswick Convention is an annual interdenominational conference in North West England since 1875. Its origins go back to the British Moody-Sankey evangelistic campaign of 1873-1874 and to figures such as Robert Pearsall Smith (1827-1898) and his wife Hannah Tatum Whitall Smith (1832-1911), prominent leaders of the American Holiness movement. The first Keswick conference, organized by Anglican Canon T.D. Harford-Battersby and Quaker Robert Wilson, was preceded by several smaller conferences organized by the Smiths. From its inception, the convention endeavored to deepen the attendees' spiritual lives, and advanced missionary work.

Within the Keswick movement, *baptism in the Spirit* led to more intense communion with God, *power for service* in God's Kingdom, and "the active suppression (but not annihilation) of the proclivity to sin."[4] This experience was described as *Victorious Life*, a state of living in victory over sin. This did not imply sinlessness, but sinless tendencies were seen as suppressed by the power of Christ. This state of holiness was not to be taken for granted but had to be maintained and renewed continuously.[5] Unlike the Wesleyan branch, which tended to use the term *holiness*, the Keswick branch preferred the term *sanctification*.[6] Theologically, Keswick holiness aligned with Calvinist traditions by "a fusion of emphasis on piety and correct belief," giving its adherents "an important subjective confirmation of the faith."[7] It was especially popular among Calvinist Baptists, Congregationalists, and Presbyterian Evangelicals.[8] Whereas D.L. Moody and his associates popularized Keswick holiness in the US, Charles G. Trumbull's

3   Kostlevy, *Historical Dictionary of the Holiness Movement*, 1, 5.
4   Carpenter, "Propagating the Faith Once Delivered," 118.
5   Bebbington, *Evangelicalism in Modern Britain*, 173; Marsden, *Fundamentalism and American Culture*, 78, 100-101.
6   Brereton, *Training God's Army*, 5.
7   Marsden, *Fundamentalism and American Culture*, 146.
8   Carpenter, "Propagating the Faith Once Delivered," 118.

adoption of it was important in its further international breakthrough by launching the American Keswick convention in 1913.[9]

Originally, fundamentalism referred to a series of pamphlets entitled *The Fundamentals*. They were published between 1910 and 1915 with the financial backing of Lyman Stewart (1840-1923).[10] It was not until ten years later that the term was coined to describe militant opposition to theological modernism or liberalism.[11] Marsden characterizes this opposition as a 'patchwork.'[12] In 1970, Ernest Sandeen revealed two important roots of this movement: the premillennial prophecy conference movement and the Princeton doctrine of Biblical inerrancy.[13] Marsden convincingly adds two more roots, namely Revivalism and the Holiness movement.[14] Betty DeBerg highlights yet another important aspect, the traditional gender ideology.[15]

Carpenter outlines how fundamentalism took a separatist stance during the interwar period and created its own subculture and infrastructure.[16] It diverged in the 1940s when fundamentalism adopted double separatism under the impulse of Carl McIntire.[17] Double separatism was a distancing not only from modernists and liberals but also from Evangelicals in denominations that made allowances for modernism and liberalism.

Although the Belgian Gospel Mission soon started to refuse all cooperation with the main Protestant denominations in Belgium, as the latter allowed modernists and liberals in their midst, it always remained willing to cooperate with Evangelicals within these denominations.

Therefore, this monograph uses the term '1920s fundamentalism' to specify the initial fundamentalism.[18] This distinction is crucial as the label 'fundamentalism' has emerged since the 1970s in various religious contexts, including Islam and Hinduism. Further, as Marsden indicates, since 9/11, the word 'fundamentalist' has widely been used as a synonym for 'religious extremist,' prompting many conservative American evangelicals to stop naming themselves fundamentalist.[19]

Hutchinson aptly concludes that "[f]or terms such as 'fundamentalist' to remain meaningful, scale, place (context) and time (temporal progression) are critical elements."[20]

9 Ibid., 119.
10 Dixon and Torrey, eds., *The Fundamentals*.
11 Bebbington and Jones, "Introduction," in *Evangelicalism and Fundamentalism in the United Kingdom during the Twentieth Century*, 2; Marsden, *Fundamentalism and American Culture*, 4.
12 Marsden, *Fundamentalism and American Culture*, 4.
13 Sandeen, *The Roots of Fundamentalism*.
14 Marsden, *Fundamentalism and American Culture*, 7, 44.
15 DeBerg, *Ungodly Women*.
16 Carpenter, *Revive Us Again*.
17 See chapter 10, p. 181; Ruotsila, *Fighting Fundamentalist*.
18 Marsden, *Fundamentalism and American Culture* (2022), 304, 306, 341, 429.
19 Ibid., 326.
20 Hutchinson, "Globalized Fundamentalism," 685.

Thus, the label '1920s fundamentalism' in this book stands for single separation from and militant opposition to modernism, coupled with dispensationalism, a literalist interpretation of the Bible, adherence to Biblical inerrancy, and traditional gender ideology, in which women take a secondary position to men, and which is expressed in a severe limitation of opportunities for women in church and missions.

To grasp the significance of the BGM, it's essential to situate it within the broader historical context of missionary activities and the presence of American religious organizations in Europe during that period. When William Carey published his book *An Enquiry into the Obligations of Christians to Use Means for the Conversion of the Heathens* in 1792, he could not have foreseen that it would become an important building block for the unseen explosion of missionary activity around the globe. Other factors that created the momentum were various revivals, spectacular advances in transportation, and conferences such as Keswick.[21] Given the scope of this monograph, we will focus on the development of the American evangelical missionary movement, which began in the late eighteenth and early nineteenth centuries and targeted multiple regions around the globe.[22]

Robert Baird of the Foreign Evangelical Society stands as a pioneer of American missionary activity on the European continent.[23] This society, which merged in 1849 with two other societies into the American Foreign Christian Union (AFCU), focused primarily on Catholic Europe, including Belgium.[24] As Hans Krabbendam points out, parallel to this missionary activity, American holiness preachers and mass evangelists made trips to Europe, and American churches emerged throughout the continent.[25] Following the American Civil War, more and more American denominations, such as Adventists, Baptists, and Methodists, became active in continental Europe.[26] This coincided with the battle cry of converting the world in one generation, in which the Student Volunteer Movement (SVM) played a crucial role. During the interwar period, North America took over the role of Europe as the leading source of missionaries.[27]

Historians like Andrew Walls have pointed out that churches and missionary organizations were, in principle, no different from a voluntary society.[28] Mis-

21 Moreau, "Evangelical Missions Development 1910 to 2010 in the North American Setting," 4; Walls, *The Missionary Movement in Christian History*, 228.
22 Hutchinson and Wolffe, *A Short History of Global Evangelicalism*, 76.
23 Ibid., 81.
24 Eventually, the AFCU left missionary activities to other players on the field. Foreign Evangelical Society, *Fourth Annual Report of the Foreign Evangelical Society*, 64.
25 Krabbendam, *Saving the Overlooked Continent*, 39-40.
26 Religious movements like Jehovah's Witnesses and Mormons also developed missionary activities in Europe. Krabbendam, 40, 45.
27 Walls, *The Missionary Movement in Christian History*, 226.
28 Ibid., 261, 277; Moreau, "Evangelical Missions Development 1910 to 2010 in the North American Setting," 7; Hutchinson and Wolffe, *A Short History of Global Evangelicalism*, 70-71, 75.

sionaries' readiness to leave their own country and culture is a clear example of evangelical volunteering.[29] Americans prioritize individual freedom and decision-making and have a different understanding of space than Europeans. Therefore, they usually had no problem with deploying missionary activities in the Christianized continent of Europe. But where a growing stream of American denominational missionaries from the nineteenth century onwards came to Europe to support Protestant denominations in Catholic or Eastern Orthodox countries, or to establish mission posts on the Continent in the Anglo-Saxon holiness tradition, transatlantic interdenominational and faith missions mostly came on their own initiative after World War I.[30]

Unlike the SVM, YMCA, and other mainline mission-focused organizations, these evangelical missions did not embrace Woodrow Wilson's concept of 'internationalization,' with a focus on establishing world peace and unity.[31] As Brian Stanley succinctly summarizes, "[f]or them, Christian mission was about saving the souls of those who were ... heading for a Christ-less eternity in hell," which David Hollinger describes as "extremely aggressive evangelism.[32] Notably, while American Presbyterians only sent money and missionaries to Europe in the interwar period upon specific requests of European congregations, the BGM entered Belgium without an invitation by Belgian Protestant denominations, driven instead by the personal invitation of a few individuals.

It can be argued that faith missions were part of a broader trend of the global spreading of American evangelical and 1920s fundamentalist organizations during the twentieth century. In a way, the BGM was just one of the dozens of American faith missions founded during the interwar period.[33] But whereas after World War I most of these organizations started targeting Africa and other remote "areas that produced the greatest returns," the European Christian Mission and BGM went against the grain by focusing on a European country.[34] It was only after another World War that others followed their example, making this monograph a valuable complement to Krabbendam's comprehensive overview of American Protestant missions in Europe.[35]

Much like the post-World War II situation of American Protestants in Europe, the BGM, and by extension all faith missions, had a transnational and

29 Hutchinson and Wolffe, *A Short History of Global Evangelicalism*, 75.
30 Krabbendam points out that some American denominational missions only entered Europe on explicit request from European partners and had no intention to set up their own mission stations in the old continent. Walls, *The Missionary Movement in Christian History*, 227; Krabbendam, *Saving the Overlooked Continent*, 11, 46.
31 Moreau, "Evangelical Missions Development 1910 to 2010 in the North American Setting," 6; For an excellent discussion on mainline American Protestantism and Christian Internationalism, see Thompson, *For God and Globe*.
32 Stanley, "Global Mission," 495-496; Hollinger, *Protestants Abroad*, 12.
33 Moreau, "Evangelical Missions Development 1910 to 2010 in the North American Setting," 7.
34 Moreau, 7; Krabbendam, *Saving the Overlooked Continent*, 46.
35 Krabbendam, 13.

trans-denominational character.[36] The BGM serves as an early example of how faith missions contributed to the diversity and expansion of Protestantism in Roman Catholic countries in Western Europe, as well as the distinct and growing trend of American evangelical influence on European Protestantism. Here, we need to define what we mean by 'evangelical.' Melani McAlister rightly states that the category 'evangelical' is broad. But whereas she calls it messy, I prefer to describe it as confusing for outsiders.[37]

Dheedene, Loobuyck, and Oosterlynck struggle to describe the situation of Flemish evangelical Christianity. They confuse the Federal Synod of Protestant and Evangelical Churches in Belgium with a denomination, which it is not.[38] Trans-denominationalism is not limited to Belgian evangelicalism but is a worldwide characteristic of this movement. Since the advance of Modernism or Liberalism within Protestantism, this interchangeability is no longer a given. As the evangelical movement was not limited to evolving *fundamentalism* either, we will use the word *evangelical*. In this book, this refers to David Bebbington's generally accepted quadrilateral, "*conversionism*, the belief that lives need to be changed; *activism*, the expression of the gospel in effort; *Biblicism*, a particular regard for the Bible; and what may be called *crucicentrism*, a stress on the sacrifice of Christ on the cross."[39] We can add to this Harold Ockenga's description of evangelicals as quoted by McAlister, namely that they are being "zealous for practical Christian living."[40]

Dana Robert rightly laments that "[a]ctivistic Evangelicals are notoriously poor at keeping records, especially when their theology predisposes them to look toward an imminent second coming of Christ."[41] The BGM is an exception to this rule, as it has left an extensive archive. Over the past hundred years, it has also founded scores of local faith communities – albeit with varying success – which provide even more records. This makes the BGM an ideal candidate for thorough historical analysis as an evangelical missionary organization.

In conducting this research, Klaus Fiedler's widely accepted theoretical framework for interdenominational or faith missions has been employed as a heuristic research tool. Fiedler states that faith missions had their roots in the Holiness movement, focused on unreached areas and nations, had an individual concept of unity, initially gave women much scope to develop their ministries, had a premillennial eschatology, used a dual baptism policy, had a Calvinist communion theology, and held an underdeveloped view on ecclesiastic offices.[42] Faith missions firmly believed that God would provide the necessary means to support the

36 Stanley, "Global Mission," 500.
37 McAlister, *The Kingdom of God Has No Borders*, 4.
38 Dheedene, Loobuyck, and Oosterlynck, "'Stretched' Postsecular Rapprochement," 120.
39 Bebbington, *Evangelicalism in Modern Britain*, 3.
40 McAlister, *The Kingdom of God Has No Borders*, 5.
41 Robert, "From Missions to Mission to Beyond Missions," 152.
42 Fiedler, *Interdenominational Faith Missions in Africa*; Id., *The Story of Faith Missions*; Id., *Ganz auf Vertrauen*.

missionaries, who often led a sacrificial lifestyle. Such missions are also known for their "flexibility and innovation in mission methods."[43] The BGM can be characterized as a late exponent of the 'second generation' of faith missions, according to Fiedler's framework.[44]

In the following chapters, we will situate the BGM within the broader context of Belgian Protestantism. Although the Reformation significantly resonated during the sixteenth century in the region that now is Belgium, Protestantism became a very small minority due to the Catholic Reformation.[45] Despite substantial growth since the Act of Tolerance by Emperor Joseph II in 1782 – from a handful of local congregations at the start of the nineteenth century to over a thousand today – Protestants still comprise only about 2.5% of the population.[46]

To conclude, it must be said that there is only limited scholarly literature on the history of Evangelicalism in Belgium.[47] Sometimes, the information is not entirely accurate.[48] This monograph contributes to the historiography of Belgian Protestantism by focusing on an important evangelical organization in the twentieth century. Ultimately, by documenting the story of the Belgian Gospel Mission and its founders, Ralph and Edith Norton, *From Hope to Hardship* is an addition to the historiography of faith missions, and an illustration of how American evangelicalism already impacted Protestantism in Catholic Europe during the interwar period. The BGM exemplifies Brian Stanley's conclusion that "it was perhaps inevitable" that faith missions "should give birth to networks of churches overseas that increasingly looked and functioned like mainline denominations."[49]

43 Sauer and Reifler, "The Relevance of Transnational Networking in the Global Ministry of Fredrik Franson," 72.
44 Fiedler, *Interdenominational Faith Missions in Africa*, 48, 52. Id., *The Story of Faith Missions*, 48, 52.
45 Collinet, *Histoire du Protestantisme en Belgique aux xviime et xviiime siècles*; Braekman, *Histoire du Protestantisme en Belgique au XIXme siècle*.
46 The claim that by 2020, Evangelicalism in Belgium had witnessed the fasted growth worldwide is debatable, as the data were incomplete and unreliable. As the Belgian government does not keep statistics on religious affiliation and most Protestant denominations do not publish statistics on membership and church attendance, percentages on Protestantism in Belgium are a kind of educated guesses. Johnson et al., *World Christian Encyclopedia*, Third edition, 20.
47 Scholarly attention for the history of the Evangelical Movement in Belgium is fairly recent. Demaerel, "Tachtig jaar pinksterbeweging in Vlaanderen (1909-1989); Een historisch onderzoek met korte theologische en sociologische analyse;" Brandt-Bessire, "Considérations historiques;" Godwin, "The Recent Growth of Pentecostalism in Belgium," 90-94; Marinello, *New Brethren in Flanders*; Van Marcke, "Het Leger des Heils in België;" Boersema, "De evangelische beweging in de samenleving;" Creemers, "All Together in One Synod?," 275-302; Demart, Tonda, and Tarrius, *Les territoires de la délivrance*; Maskens, "Migration et pentecôtisme à Bruxelles. Expériences croisées," 49-68; Bangura, "African Christian Churches in Flanders," 89-106; Prins, "De protestants-evangelische kerken en de Anglicaanse kerk," 1241-1257.
48 The Baptists and Lutherans never have been part of the United Protestant Church of Belgium as De Volder claims. De Volder, "Belgium and Luxemburg," 81.
49 Stanley, "Global Mission," 505.

Australian Christian World
CHAPMAN - ALEXANDER MISSION
Special Daily Issue

(Registered at the G.P.O., Sydney, for transmission by post as a newspaper.)

No. 10.   AUGUST 2, 1912.   PRICE ONE PENNY.

Mr. and Mrs. R. C. NORTON. Of the Chapman-Alexander Mission Party.

ANNOUNCEMENTS

To-day.   TOWN HALL.   To-day.

1 p.m., Midday Talk;
"THE FACT OF THE FUTURE."

7.30 p.m., EVANGELISTIC SERVICE.
Dr. J. Wilbur Chapman and Mr. C. M. Alexander

SUNDAY, AUGUST 4.

3 p.m., LYCEUM HALL—MEN ONLY.
Overflow Y.M.C.A. Hall.

3 p.m., CONGREGATIONAL CHURCH.
WOMEN ONLY.

Overflow Bathurst Street Baptist Church.

7. p.m., TOWN HALL. EVANGELISTIC SERVICE.

Overflow Meetings. Y.M.C.A. Hall,
And Bathurst Street Baptist Church.
Dr. J. Wilbur Chapman and Mr. C. M. Alexander

The Nortons in Australia in 1912.
[KADOC-KU Leuven: ABEM 894/01]

1
THE DESPERATE QUEST FOR A MISSION FIELD

When Ralph Norton passed away in 1934, the Belgian Gospel Mission lost its founder, director, and principal fundraiser. However, his wife Edith, who played a significant role in his journey, published a biography of her husband the following year by recycling many articles she had written over the years for *The Sunday School Times* (*SST*).[1] Her influence was instrumental in putting Belgium back on the missionary map of their dwindling supporters.[2] At that time, he was still widely known in orthodox evangelical circles in North America for reasons we will discuss later. *Ralph Norton and the Belgian Gospel Mission* is a classic example of a missionary biography written in the first decades of the twentieth century: a one-sided, inspirational chronicle or spiritual portrait of an 'extraordinary' Christian in which evangelism and church planting is seen through the lens of the cosmic battle "between God and the Enemy."[3]

This can be illustrated by how Edith Norton describes her husband's background in the opening chapter. Ralph Caius Norton was born on 10 No-

---

1 The *Sunday School Times* (1859-1966) was an influential periodical that represented the 1920s fundamentalist and holiness branches of American Evangelicalism in the early twentieth century. Harris, *Fundamentalism and Evangelicals*, 24; Reynolds, "Fundamentalist Magazine Publishing," 199.
2 E. Norton, *Ralph Norton and the Belgian Gospel Mission*.
3 By describing her late husband at length as a weak missionary candidate, she intended to inspire her readers not to give up their missionary calling despite numerous setbacks. Sharpe, "Reflections on Missionary Historiography," 76; Sittser, "Protestant Missionary Biography as Written Icon," 309.

vember 1868 in Jonesboro, Indiana, in "pioneer simplicity."[4] His father, a war invalid of the Siege of Vicksburg (1863), is portrayed as someone who raised his son with "many floggings and countless reprimands" and backslid from his faith for some time.[5] By contrast, his mother is described as a devout Christian who had "given her child to God for the ministry, before his birth."[6] This should explain why, despite numerous setbacks, he never rested until he found his mission field. Further, several of Norton's qualities and characteristics, such as his "meticulousness in dress and manner," the "imperative and undeviating demands of duty, and of doing all things with fidelity and scrupulousness," as well as taking advantage of every opportunity for self-progress are traced back to his childhood and upbringing.[7] The sketch is completed with examples of his generosity, resourcefulness, and business instinct as a teenager. Norton's conversion at the age of nineteen is described from a cosmic perspective. When he came forward after the altar call by visiting Holiness Quaker evangelists Harvey Bergman and Allie Pierce Smith, he experienced a mystical manifestation at his conversion.[8]

The biography deliberately mentions that Norton joined the local Methodist Church shortly after his conversion because he believed there was a "more spiritual atmosphere" there "than in his own denomination."[9] By doing so, the habit of accepting people from other Protestant denominations as members of BGM churches for similar reasons is indirectly defended right from the start of the biography. On 30 March 1889, almost a year after his conversion, he received the 'Exhorter's License' for the Methodist Episcopal Church at the Quarterly Conference in Muncie, Indiana.[10] He also signed up for the theological seminary at University DePauw in Greencastle, Indiana. When it became clear that Norton was not adequately prepared for these studies, he first matriculated at the affiliated preparatory school. In 1892, he returned to DePauw to graduate in 1896 with a Bachelor of Arts and joined the Phi Kappa

---

4   E. Norton, *Ralph Norton*, 21.
5   Ibid., 21-22, 25.
6   Ibid., 25.
7   Ibid., 25.
8   Widower Harvey Bergman (1830-1909) married widow Almira Pierce Smith (1838-1909) in 1875. They were originally Methodists but joined the Quakers around the date of their marriage. They operated as evangelists in Indiana and Ohio. Hamm, *The Transformation of American Quakerism*, 103; E. Norton, *Ralph Norton*, 26-29.
9   His father was an Episcopalian, and his mother a Presbyterian. No information is given as to which of these Ralph belonged. E. Norton, *Ralph Norton*, 32; Victorious Life Conference, ed., *The Victorious Life*, 332.
10 Edith Norton here quotes an original document that is not held in the archives. Minutes from 1899 list R.C. Norton as a Licentiate and a local preacher for the Muncie District. E. Norton, *Ralph Norton*, 32-33; Secretary of the Methodist Episcopal Church, ed., *Minutes of the Fifty-Sixth Session of the North Indiana Annual Conference of the Methodist Episcopal Church*, 89.

Psi fraternity and the YMCA, where he was "chairman of Bible Study and Mission Study Committees and the like."[11]

As a DePauw delegate, he attended the first three Student Volunteer Movement for Foreign Missions (SVM) congresses.[12] The SVM was founded in 1886 with the help of Dwight L. Moody during a student conference at Mount Hermon, Massachusetts, and aggressively recruited Protestant missionaries on college campuses at the turn of the twentieth century. SVM's watchword, "the evangelization of the world in this generation," underlined the urgency of foreign missions in light of Jesus Christ's imminent return and in an age of unprecedented opportunities.[13]

Like many other participants, the 1891 conference set Norton "aflame with zeal and conviction" for missions, an implicit reference to his signing the SVM volunteer pledge: "We are willing and desirous, God permitting, to become a foreign missionary."[14] Young Ralph and his fellow delegates fervently tried to pass on the enthusiasm for missions to those enrolled at DePauw. Although many may have signed the pledge, the university's *Alumnal Record* indicates that only a few succeeded in turning their pledge into actual service on the foreign mission field.[15] While some may not have been faithful to their commitment, others were rejected once or multiple times, as was the case with Ralph Norton.

Despite being turned down numerous times, he refused to accept that he was not cut out for a full-time career as an evangelist or missionary.[16] While supporting home and foreign missions with his prayers and the money he earned as a head salesman for educational specialty company Powers, Fowler & Lewis, he felt uncomfortable because he did not realize his SVM pledge. With all doors seemingly closed to his entry into the foreign mission field, people like bishop Joseph S. Key, "a staunch friend of the holiness leaders," encouraged him not to give up his persistent desire to become a foreign mis-

---

11 E. Norton, *Ralph Norton*, 32; ABEM, 1122: "Chronicle of Lives of Ralph C. Norton and Edith Fox Norton;" *Student's Hand-Book 1892-1893*, 6; *Student's Hand-Book 1894-1895*, 7; *Student's Hand-Book 1895-1896*, 7.
12 *Report of the First International Convention of the Student Volunteer Movement for Foreign Missions*, 196; E. Norton, *Ralph Norton*, 34-35; *Students and the Missionary Problem*, 115; Austin, "Blessed Adversity," 54; Broomhall, *The Jubilee Story of the China Inland Mission*.
13 Parker, *The Kingdom of Character*; Harder, "The Student Volunteer Movement for Foreign Missions and Its Contribution to Overall Missionary Service," 145.
14 E. Norton, *Ralph Norton*, 34; *Report of the First International Convention of the Student Volunteer Movement for Foreign Missions*, 26.
15 E. Norton, *Ralph Norton*, 34-35; Weik, ed., *Alumnal Record DePauw University*.
16 Two examples are given in his biography. The Methodist Episcopal Church (South) preferred a candidate who already knew the local language for their missionary work in China. Another mission agency rejected him for missionary work in India for health reasons. E. Norton, *Ralph Norton*, 35, 37.

sionary.[17] Norton quit his job in 1899 and enrolled at Moody Bible Institute (MBI). Here, he met Edith Fox, twelve years his junior; they were married on 16 April 1902.[18]

Edith Blana Fox was born on 6 May 1881 in Manchester, Iowa, and entered Oberlin College in 1899 to study music. When her mother found out her daughter was dreaming of a secular music career, she enlisted family friend Charles M. Alexander, who had Edith accompany him as a pianist on his tour of the Midwest in the summer of 1900.[19] To her mother's great satisfaction, she abandoned her 'worldly' plans under Alexander's influence. He even secured sponsorships for her to study at MBI from 1901 to 1902 to embed her decision firmly.[20]

We only have Edith's account that her husband's choice for a Bible school was motivated by his fear of the growing influence of liberal theology at theological seminaries in the USA. His attendance at numerous revival meetings had undoubtedly fed or initiated this fear. She leaves out the growing resentment towards the Holiness movement within the Methodist Episcopal Church (South), as expressed by the acceptance of 'rule 301' at the annual conference of 1898. Norton's MBI file might have shed more light on this, but unfortunately, it was lost.[21]

Moody Bible Institute was one of the North American religious training or Bible schools that mushroomed in the nineteenth century. The widespread sense of urgency to reap the missionary 'harvest', both in home and foreign missions, opened opportunities for trained laypeople.[22] Bible school graduates – and even those who only followed part of the curriculum – were widely accepted by faith missions like the China Inland Mission (CIM). The Bible

17 E. Norton, *Ralph Norton*, 38; Howard, *A New Invasion of Belgium*, vii-viii; Smith, *Called Unto Holiness*, 35.
18 When Norton enrolled, it was called the *Bible Institute for Home and Foreign Missions*. In 1900, it was renamed *Moody* Bible Institute. For a history and characterization of Bible schools, see Brereton, *Training God's Army*; E. Norton, *Ralph Norton*, 49.
19 Charles McCallon Alexander (1867-1920) was converted during a revival in 1880. From 1892-1894, he studied at Moody Bible Institute, after which he worked as a soloist with evangelists Milan B. Williams (1894-1902), Reuben Archer Torrey (1902-1907), and J. Wilbur Chapman (1907-1918). In 1904, he married British national Helen Cadbury, founder of the Pocket Testament League. Alexander, and Maclean, *Charles M. Alexander: A Romance of Song and Soul-Winning*, 40-41; E. Norton, *Ralph Norton*, 43.
20 E. Norton, *Ralph Norton*, 44-45.
21 This ruling meant that resident ministers could bar outside evangelists from their campuses. As a result, most Holiness evangelists were forced to either adapt their message to what was acceptable to their denomination or to work independently. Phillips, and Baughman, *DePauw: A Pictorial History*, chap. 2, page 7; Synan, *The Holiness-Pentecostal Tradition: Charismatic Movements in the Twentieth Century*, 63; Email communication of Zylstra, Archives Assistant MBI, 24 July 2014.
22 Brereton, *Training God's Army*, 59.
23 ABEM, 877: G. Winston, "History of the BGM," Chapters 1, 2.

schools cultivated the students' missionary enthusiasm in many ways, like inviting missionaries on furlough to give presentations, mission prayer groups, and practical courses such as door-to-door evangelism.[23]

In one of MBI's textbooks on Missiology, *The Evangelization of the World in this Generation*, John Mott "calls for urgent and aggressive action."[24] No wonder Norton again applied to various mission boards. As before, he was refused each time, usually because of his weak constitution. His friends, who had already expressed their doubts when he applied for MBI, seemed to be proved right. Because he was thirty years old already and not a gifted speaker, they felt that "he could best serve God by settling down to make money for the Lord's work."[25] Despite these setbacks, Norton remained determined to pursue his calling. Quite understandable advice, as the average life expectancy in America at that time was forty-seven.

And so, from November 1901 until 1903, he waited in true Holiness style for divine guidance while holding a series of evangelistic meetings in several places in the Midwest as an independent evangelist. He was just one of the many enterprising evangelists that sprang up in America around the turn of the twentieth century. He did not come up with novel ways of evangelism but was "simply supplementing the established denominations."[26] Meanwhile, he made an unsuccessful application to be a missionary to the Philippines. The fact that he kept having health issues, such as "periodical headaches and the physical depression and numbness," justifies the decisions of the various mission boards.[27] Yet Norton himself interpreted these recurring conditions as attacks of the devil. They were related to his "unusually sensitive nature" and the fact that he was very demanding of himself and, at times, intensely self-deprecatory.[28]

In the spring of 1903, he was invited to become a church pastor. This offer was a golden opportunity to end his financial worries as an independent evangelist. Convinced that God had called him to be an evangelist or missionary, Norton declined the offer.[29] A few months later, his poor health forced him to consider a change of ministry. On 19 October 1903, he wrote in his journal, "I am far from well these days & unless the Lord gives me health I fear I will soon be compelled to give up evangelistic work. If so, Lord, lead me into the work

---

24 Mott, *The Evangelization of the World in This Generation*, 14; *Catalogue of the Moody Bible Institute for Home and Foreign Missions*, 25.
25 BEM, 877: G. Winston, "History of the BGM," chap. 1,1-2.
26 Marsden, "The Rise of Fundamentalism," 137.
27 ABEM, 1122: Diary R. Norton (8 Jan. 1902).
28 E. Norton, *Ralph Norton*, 36, 58.
29 The newlyweds spent the summer of 1903 with his mother for lack of funds. With hindsight, the couple decided that this was good preparation for his task as the leader of the faith mission that they founded years later. E. Norton, *Ralph Norton*, 55; ABEM, 1122: Diary R. Norton (17 May 1903).

that will please Thee."[30] Norton's career as an independent itinerant evangelist was now over, and he found himself once more on a dead-end street.

In his diary, Norton wrote that he considered "taking up either YMCA, city or foreign work, or S.S. [Sunday School] work."[31] It was not until August 1904 that he could finally steer his career in this direction. He was hired as Director of the recently reopened Religious Work department of the YMCA in Minneapolis.[32] Being an evangelist in heart and soul, Norton must have had a tough time accepting that, due to a nationwide growing influence of liberal theology, the YMCA had abandoned explicit evangelistic activities.[33]

> There would no longer be any attempt to proselytize. There would still be worship services, Bible study classes, revival meetings, and lectures on the value of religion in one's life. But the new Y would primarily concentrate on offering young men and boys mental and physical recreation to keep them out of trouble and away from the demoralizing effects of vice.[34]

He worked his way around this obstacle by initiating a course in personal evangelism, applying what he had learned at Moody's. Norton invited "strong evangelical leaders" to speak on Sunday afternoons, a method he would later use when he directed the Belgian Gospel Mission in the Interwar Period.[35] In his desire to reach the working classes, he started 'noon meetings' in several factories and railway shops. Norton also initiated Bible lectures for the students at the commercial business colleges and organized several Bible study courses.[36]

In the autumn of 1905, the evangelist J. Wilbur Chapman's team visited the town for an extensive campaign. Chapman (1859-1918), a Moody protégé and Presbyterian premillennialist, was one of the leading evangelists of his day. He developed a new form of urban evangelism in which several evangelistic meetings were held simultaneously in the same town. Chapman organized his evangelistic activities and meetings according to the rational methods of 'big business.'[37] Norton was invited to manage their local personal evangelism

---

30 ABEM, 1122: Diary R. Norton (19 Oct. 1903).
31 Ibid. (21 Oct. 1903).
32 The economic depression of 1893 forced the department to close for several years. Wiley, and Lehmann, *Builders of Men*, 95; BEM, 894: *Minutes Minneapolis YMCA Board of Directors Meeting* (11 March 1904); The Young Men's Christian Association of Minneapolis, *Religious Work Announcement, Season 1904-1905*; E. Norton, *Ralph Norton*, 59.
33 Setran, *The college "Y"*, 118-119.
34 Shepard, *The 150 Year Commemorative Celebration - YMCA of Greater Saint Paul 1856-2006*.
35 Marsden, *Fundamentalism and American Culture*, 132-135.
36 E. Norton, *Ralph Norton*, 60; Lehmann, *Builders of Men*, 95-96; ABEM, 894: *Monthly Meeting of the Board of Directors of the Young Men's Christian Association* (17 Dec. 1904); *Religious Work Announcement, Season 1904-1905*, 4; *Calendar 1905-1906*.
37 Weber, *Living in the Shadow of the Second Coming*, 53; Treloar, *The Disruption of Evangelicalism*, 23; Ottman, *J. Wilbur Chapman, A Biography*.

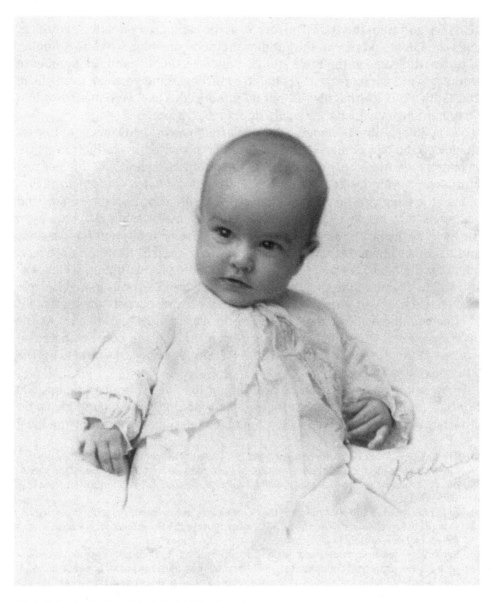

Elisabeth Louise Norton, 6 April 1905-25 March 1906.
[KADOC-KU LEUVEN: ABEM, 1094]

activities and train the staff. The results of the campaign were disappointing. Even though attendance at the Sunday afternoon meetings grew, the number of those who came to the Bible studies only rose slightly, and the number of volunteers did not increase.[38] Yet Ralph's gifts regarding personal evangelism and Edith's musical talents did not go unnoticed. They were invited to join Chapman's team, which they would do six months later.[39]

The intervening period was characterized by a dramatic event that overshadowed the rest of their lives and caused a decisive turn in their lives. On 25 March 1906, their only child, Elisabeth Louise, died shortly before her first birthday.[40] Norton resigned from the YMCA a month later. On top of the loss of his little daughter, he was struggling again with his health once again and was advised by his physician to change jobs. His health issues may have been triggered by the fact that he felt he was hardly given any support for his work, and his department did not grow as much as expected. Norton had several offers on the table, but he chose to accept Chapman's invitation, which was still valid. A month after their daughter had died, the Nortons joined his role model's team.[41] As it turned out, the Nortons became part of "the high point of endeavor and achievement" of pre-World War I global revivalism.[42] As the team's personal work director, Ralph Norton trained the corps of personal workers in the various cities they visited.[43] From 1908 onwards, he also led the 'after meetings.'[44]

As Ralph was still desirous of fulfilling his SVM volunteer pledge, the Nortons continued their search for a foreign mission field where they could minister. Wherever they went, they contacted missionaries to study the local

---

[38] The Religious Work Department reports 337 "professed conversions" for November 1905, largely as a result of the Chapman meetings. "Many of these have already joined the various churches of the city." Lehmann, *Builders of Men*, 96; ABEM, 894: Monthly Meeting (8 Dec. 1905).

[39] In her notebook, Edith Norton writes that it took place in November 1905, but in reality, it took place sometime between 14 and 31 October 1905. JWCP: Scrapbook 1905; ABEM, 1122: Notebook Edith Norton.

[40] Surgery by the world-renowned gynecologist Howard Kelly in December 1907 may explain their further unwanted childlessness. Post-operative complications of an appendectomy may have resulted in female tubal infertility. Prolonged high fever could have been an indication, but unfortunately, this information has not been preserved in the hospital records. Edith Norton mentions Elisabeth's name every year in her diary on her birthday as well as the anniversary of her death. RHKH: The Howard A. Kelly Hospital, Inc. Pathological Laboratory Reports, Oct 1907-Oct 1909; ABEM, 1122: "Chronicle of Lives."

[41] One of his other options was to become Moody Bible Institute's Superintendent of the Men's Department. Wiley, and Lehmann, *Builders of Men*, 95; Norton, "Chronicle of Lives;" Norton, *Ralph Norton*, 60.

[42] Treloar, *The Disruption of Evangelicalism*, 22.

[43] Maclean, "A Week of Wonderful Blessing," 1233-1234.

[44] American revival meetings usually ended with an invitation to come forward in response to the evangelistic sermon. Those who responded were invited to so-called 'after meetings' in the inquiry room where counselors were available to talk and pray with individually.

problems and opportunities.[45] In the autumn of 1913, Chapman and his team traveled to the United Kingdom. Until April 1914, it held several campaigns in Scotland. On 28 February 1914, Edith Norton returned to the US while her husband remained in the United Kingdom with the rest of the team.[46]

While her husband was still in Scotland, Edith attended a lecture by John Mott on "Voluntary Christian Work in Colleges" at Yale and gave a short presentation at an unnamed venue about the "missionary need in Italy and France."[47] Her plea places Edith in the camp of a minority among American mission officials who began propagating reverse missions to ('Papal') Europe at the turn of the twentieth century.[48] Protestant missions in Catholic countries were justified by advocates stating that "the truth is coated over by superstition so thickly that they cannot get down to the saving truth, and it has no effect whatever upon their lives."[49]

Although Ralph Norton was forty-five by now and must have lost count of the times his candidacy was rejected, the couple kept dreaming of joining a missionary organization working in China or any other Asian mission field. They had no ambition whatsoever to become missionaries in Italy, France, or any other country in Catholic Europe. It would take a war to direct them to Belgium, where they would work for another fifteen years.

---

45 In China, they were in contact with Rev Griffith John from the London Missionary Society, pioneer Methodist missionary Dr. H.H. Lowry, and Bishop W.S. Lewis, General Superintendent of the Methodist Episcopalian Mission. In Korea they contacted Presbyterians Dr. James Scarth Gale, Dr. Horace Grant Underwood, Dr. Samuel A. Moffett, as well as Mr. Lee and Pastor Kim. Pastor Kim could be the same person as Pastor Sun-du Kim, who graduated from Sungsil College and taught at Sungsil Middle School. In 1913, the Nortons had a "cherished project" during a campaign in New Zealand: they accompanied the Australian and Methodist missionary William E. Bennett on his travels to Samoa, Tonga, and the Fiji Islands. E. Norton, *Ralph Norton*, 69-70, 78; Email communication of Moon, 27 Oct. 2014.
46 ABEM, 1122: Diary E. Norton (28 Feb. 1914).
47 Ibid. (8 March, 8 April 1914); "Final Meetings of Convention," 3.
48 Stark, "Efforts to Christianize Europe, 400-2000," 117.
49 Smith, "Colombia," 282.

Edith Norton and Peter Van Koeckhoven at the trenches near Ramskapelle in 1916.
[KADOC-KU LEUVEN: ABEM, 1092]

2
APOSTLES OF THE BELGIAN TRENCHES

The outbreak of World War I set in motion a series of events that would ultimately lead the Nortons to their surprising mission field. Like many others, they engaged in evangelism among the Allied soldiers. As we will see, this effort seemed to follow the pattern of his professional career, as they found themselves suddenly in a dead-end street once more.

Shortly after the United Kingdom entered the conflict on 4 August 1914, Chapman was notified that a planned campaign in Scotland had been temporarily canceled.[1] As many young men, mainly from the working class, joined the army, religious organizations and churches entered or intensified army work instead. They realized many of the soldiers probably would not survive on the battlefield.[2] In October 1914, Chapman, Alexander, and Norton assisted the YMCA shortly in their evangelistic work at the British Training Camps on the Salisbury Plains.[3]

When Chapman returned home to America later that month, Norton was granted several months' leave and remained in England. He sent a telegram to his wife, asking her to join him in evangelizing among the British soldiers under the auspices of the YMCA. Norton knew first-hand the importance of moral and spiritual support for the many men who would soon be sent off to

---

1   Ottman, *J. Wilbur Chapman*, 273.
2   Allison, "Free Church Revivalism in the British Army during the First World War," 41.
3   Alexander, and Maclean, *Charles M. Alexander, A Romance of Song and Soul-Winning*, 202; Maclean, and Riddle, *The Y.M.C.A. with the Colours*, 12-13; Yapp, *The Romance of the Red Triangle*, 1918.

the battlefield, as his father and three uncles had served in the Union Army during the Civil War. The conflict took its toll on the Nortons. Ralph's father became a war invalid, and his uncle Harry died as a Prisoner of War.[4]

On 14 December 1914, the Nortons went to France for ten days, looking for opportunities for "further service near the front," again in cooperation with the YMCA.[5] They were confronted with large numbers of refugees and injured soldiers and stated that their revivalist message made the soldiers reflect on sin, God, and eternity.[6] Naively, the Nortons even spread the news that they had "secured permission to visit the trenches of the opposing armies and to talk to the men between battles."[7]

The Nortons' message was in line with that of others. During the first months of World War I, many triumphant reports from army chaplains and evangelists were issued, stating that many soldiers professed conversion. Of course, this fueled the expectation that their combined evangelistic efforts would lead to a revival in the army, affecting the entire country.[8] The openness, however, was not exceptional. It is generally understood that exposure to continuous threats to life, the disruption of social life as they knew it, and being away from their familiar surroundings led to more openness to spiritual matters among all the soldiers. Roman Catholic chaplains and stretcher-bearers also noted a huge revival of spirituality among the recruits.[9]

Shortly after their trip to France, the couple returned to America, confident they finally had found their mission field.[10] Rather than becoming members of the YMCA, they opted to establish their own religious voluntary organization, The British and Allied Soldiers Evangelistic Campaign, or BASEC. Having handed in their notice on 25 March 1915, they immediately started to secure financial backing. Their departure was not without some friction. With his campaigns becoming less and less productive, Chapman was reluctant to let go of two valued crew workers. On top of that, the Nortons were fishing in

---

[4] Whitson, ed., *Centennial History of Grant County, Indiana, 1812 to 1912*, vol. 2, 1215.
[5] E. Norton, *Ralph Norton*, 84.
[6] "Bravery of Atlanta Boys In French Foreign Legion Is Told of by Evangelists," 1; Mrs. Norton, "Why We Are Going Back to England and France," 523; ABEM, 1122: Diary R. Norton (16 Dec. 1914).
[7] Mrs. Norton, "Why We Are Going Back," 523; "American Evangelists Find Rockwell In French Hospital," 3.
[8] E. Norton, *Ralph Norton*, 82-83; R. Norton, "Taking Soldiers Alive for Christ," 218; Allison, "Free Church Revivalism in the British Army during the First World War," 48-49; Treloar, *The Disruption of Evangelicalism*, 136.
[9] Becker, *La guerre et la foie*, 11; Boniface, *Histoire religieuse de la Grande Guerre*, 96; De Schaepdrijver, *De Groote Oorlog*, 198; Laveille, *Au service des blessés, 1914-1918*, 352-353.
[10] R. Norton, "Recruiting for Apostles of the Trenches," 737.

Chapman's pond, soliciting funds for a year's work.[11] With his business instinct, Norton soon succeeded in winning influential people, including MBI's President, James M. Gray, and Henry P. Crowell, for their cause. Like many other American evangelists, they would use a network of wealthy 'laymen' to help fund their organization's projects.[12]

As the Nortons did not limit themselves to a particular denomination and were operating without a financial security system, the new mission can be categorized as a faith mission. They trusted God would provide the necessary means or finances through their supporters in answer to prayer. Their talks in churches and conferences were not meant to bring about prayer support only. They hoped to generate interest in financial support as well. For example, in 1916, Ralph Norton said in one of his many addresses: "We stepped out without a penny, not a cent in view, and we had been receiving comfortable incomes."[13]

By June 1915, they had raised sufficient funds to cover the expected traveling costs, salaries for one year, and 250,000 Gospels and Testaments. As a charity, they knew securing constant publicity via emotive human-interest stories was essential to keep donations going. They created a win-win situation by convincing Charles G. Trumbull to take this voluntary position. Donations for the Nortons could be sent via the establishment of a Protestant weekly, *The Sunday School Times*. In return, the Nortons became the periodical's "personal representatives" in Europe.[14] Thus, the *SST* could regularly publish firsthand observations of the war in Europe, which was regarded as of utmost apocalyptic significance by dispensational premillennialists.[15]

The Nortons now could potentially expand their necessary American network of support with the 80,000 subscribers, to whom they set out their

---

11 ABEM, 1122: Diary E. Norton, n.d.; ABEM, 895: Chapman and Alexander to R. Norton (2 March 1915); Treloar, *The Disruption of Evangelicalism*, 31.
12 Henry P. Crowell (1855-1943), a Presbyterian, was Quaker Oats's Director, a Moody Bible Institute's trustee, and President of the Laymen's Evangelistic Council of Chicago. He was tithing to 65% of his income. James M. Gray (1851-1935) was co-founder of the Boston Bible and Missionary Training School (currently Gordon Divinity School). In the 1890s, he became involved with Dwight L. Moody's evangelistic campaigns. He was an editor for the first edition of the Scofield Reference Bible. He can be categorized as an Evangelical with dispensationalist and premillennialist views. *Catalogue of the Moody Bible Institute*, 18; Marsden, *Fundamentalism and American Culture*, 37, 46-47; Martin, *R.A. Torrey*; "James M. Gray," n.d., accessed 20 Feb. 2014; Walls, "The American Dimension in the History of the Missionary Movement," 13; Day, *Breakfast Table Autocrat*, 129; Marquette, *Brands, Trademarks, and Good Will*, 28-29; ABEM, 1122: Diary E. Norton (17 April, 23 May, 6, 15 June 1915).
13 R. Norton, "Incidents and Experiences," 136.
14 The *SST* assured its readers that "All the money now contributed by readers of the Times will go directly to providing the Scriptures for free distributing among the soldiers of the countries in which the Nortons are able to work." Anon., "Untitled," *Sunday School Times*, 1915, 507; E. Norton, *Ralph Norton*, 86.
15 Evans, "A New Protestantism Has Come," 294.

plans as follows: "As we return, we plan to reach the soldiers, as before, through the meetings held in tents or marquees where they can congregate and listen to a song service, in which they delight to join, and to a message that will endeavor to point them to Christ as a Saviour; after which the opportunity will be given them to make an open confession of Christ."[16]

Upon their arrival in the UK, the Nortons' enthusiasm changed into bitter disappointment. During their stay in the US, some American citizens of German background had been exposed and tried as spies. Therefore, the military authorities ordered that only British citizens could work with the YMCA in the military training camps. Going back was not an option, so Norton became a street colporteur among the "soldiers of many tongues."[17] Norton took his decision as a kind of demotion. During the years with Chapman and Alexander, he often stood in the spotlight. Now, he was one of the many anonymous evangelists on the streets of a big city in a foreign country.[18]

When the ban on non-British citizens from military camps was lifted by the end of September 1915, the Nortons finally could resume their work among the British soldiers. But not for long. Two months later, they decided to focus their activities on the Belgian soldiers whom they had met on the streets of London.[19] As 'poor little Belgium' was a recurring theme of anti-German propaganda in the US, they knew their reports in *The Sunday School Times* would undoubtedly gain attention and generate donations to continue the work as long as deemed necessary.

Already in 1914, Ralph Norton mentioned the "pitiable and heartrending sights" of Belgian refugees in London.[20] A few weeks later, he and Edith handed out free clothing at the Belgian Refugee Headquarters. This was simply one of the many spontaneous creations by the public answering the needs of this humanitarian tragedy.[21] They could not have foreseen that a year later, the Belgian army would become the mission field they were yearning for.

Norton worked more or less to a pattern. Every day, around half past ten, large groups of Belgian soldiers on leave would arrive at Charing Cross Station. He offered them Gospels in French and Dutch as they arrived or left, using the

16 Mrs. Norton, "Why We Are Going Back," 523.
17 Howard, *A New Invasion of Belgium*, 10; Norton, *Ralph Norton*, 88; Editorial, "The Heart of the Belgian Soldier," 597.
18 Mrs. Norton, "Evangelizing the Belgian Soldiers," 36; R. Norton, "Taking Soldiers Alive for Christ," 219; Mrs. Norton, "What the Little Belgian Soldier Told Us," 564.
19 E. Norton, *Ralph Norton*, 90, 92; Mrs. Norton, "Another Milestone in Belgian Evangelization," 155.
20 Mrs. Norton, "Evangelizing the Belgian Soldiers," 36.
21 Cahalan, "The Treatment Of Belgian Refugees In England During The Great War," 178; ABEM, 1122: Diary E. Norton (24 Nov., 4 Dec. 1914).

few phrases for standard situations he had learned from their hotel porter.[22] Whenever a conversation ensued and the soldier did not know English, he would take him to their hotel room and introduce him to his wife. Edith only had rudimentary French language skills, so communicating with their guests was far from obvious.[23]

Having arrived in London, many soldiers aimlessly roamed the streets with very little spending money. It was, therefore, attractive to accept the invitation of a friendly American to join him for some beverages and hospitality in his hotel room, which was only yards away from the station. All the more, as the Nortons stayed at the luxurious Hotel Cecil, with its 800 rooms, the largest resort in Europe.[24] What a contrast that must have been with the barren conditions of the trenches, in which they had to fight and survive at the front.

Depending on the duration of their leave, the soldiers, most of whom were Flemish, came to meet the Nortons once or on several subsequent days. The guests were offered a cup of cocoa; Edith Norton would play the piano and then read in poor French from John 10, a passage that was also a favorite of Roman Catholic chaplains. Then she would kneel and pray for the soldiers, "recounting [...] their miseries, and their isolation from their families in the invaded district, cut off from all communication."[25]

Clearly, not all soldiers understood what the Nortons were trying to say, but their humanitarian aid usually moved them. A Great War veteran later said that he became uneasy when the Nortons locked the door after he had entered their room. He relaxed when they sat on either side of him and did their best to explain the Gospel in English and some French. And when they subsequently prayed and invited him to do the same, he said some prayers he had learned as a Catholic out of politeness.[26] The Nortons knew the man had not been converted to Protestantism. As most of these men would return to the battlefield, the importance of being part of the 'right' church was considered of minor importance. By doing so, the Nortons hoped to remove any reservations the soldiers may have had.

Inspired by Moody's motto, "If you want to win a man to Jesus Christ, you must first win him to himself," they also offered material assistance in the form of using their bathroom, washing and darning socks, and repairing their uniforms.[27] They even gave needy soldiers new socks, rubber boots, or

---

22 Maclean, *Apostles of the Belgian Trenches*, 22; Campbell, *Belgian Soldiers at Home in the United Kingdom*, 22.
23 Through the years, it became clear that Norton had no gift for languages. Had he been selected as a missionary for Asia, this would have been an even higher obstacle. E. Norton, *Ralph Norton*, 94.
24 Campbell, *Belgian Soldiers*, 9; Newnham-Davis, *The Gourmet's Guide to London*, 58–66; Howard, *A New Invasion of Belgium*, 16.
25 ABEM, 877: G. Winston, "History of the BGM," Chapter 2, 6; Norton, *Ralph Norton*, 97.
26 Buunk, "Herinneringen aan Ralph Norton," 1.
27 Mrs. Norton, "The Heart of the Belgian Soldier," 226.

other items whenever necessary. Because of this personal touch, soldiers even started to call them "mother dear" and "father dear."[28] Like similar evangelists among the soldiers, revivalist preaching and practical care were integral parts of holistic evangelism.[29]

Because of their warm welcome, a growing number of soldiers started to correspond with the Nortons. Requests for material aid sometimes led to conversions. One soldier testified that his newfound faith gave him tranquility in the trenches instead of the 'cafard.'[30] Another soldier wrote: "I cannot find words to thank you for having raised me from the mire in which I had fallen and where I know well I should have remained if I had not written to you for a material need. However, when I saw the Holy Scriptures which I had not seen since the beginning of the war, I felt drawn again towards the Saviour of the World, and now I am seeking every means of being pleasing to Him."[31]

At some point, Norton met Peter Van Koeckhoven in front of the Belgian headquarters. Van Koeckhoven asked for a supply of Gospels to hand out to his fellow soldiers. Back in the trenches, he wrote about the openness to the Gospel among the soldiers who read the Gospels in their spare time. Because of his missionary zeal, Edith Norton nicknamed him 'Apostle of the Trenches,' a term that the Roman Catholics also used for new converts who zealously tried to convince their comrades of their newfound faith.[32]

Not long afterward, Van Koeckhoven reported that he and a few other soldiers had dedicated themselves to reading one or two chapters from the Gospels daily.[33] In consultation with the Nortons, this Bible reading club was called *La Ligue des Saintes Ecritures* in French, *De Bond der Heilige Schriften* in Dutch, and *Scripture League* in the communication with the American home front.[34] Members who stated they had read their Gospel were sent a New Testament. The League – possibly without realizing it – shows remarkable similarities with some Roman Catholic initiatives, such as the League of the Sacred Heart, the Living Rosary, and Cyriel Verschaeve's idea for Flemish prayer and

---

28 E. Norton, "A Glimpse of the Norton's at Work," 415; E. Norton, "Taking Jesus in His Fullness," 203; Mrs. Norton, "The Heart of the Belgian Soldier," 226; "The Battle Front," *Sunday School Times*, 195.

29 Allison, "Free Church Revivalism in the British Army during the First World War," 42.

30 'Le cafard' was a condition that would nowadays be described by psychiatrists as depression. It was the term soldiers used to describe the endless waiting and boredom in the trenches. For more on 'le cafard,' see Kahn, *The Neglected Majority*, 73; e-mail communication of Van Daele, 15 Dec. 2017.

31 ABEM, 1061: Paradis, part of a translated letter (23 July 1918).

32 Laveille, *Au service des blessés*, 353–354; Mrs. Norton, "Recruiting for Apostles of the Trenches," 737.

33 Mrs. Norton, "The Apostles of the Trenches at the Belgian Front," 103.

34 Mrs. Norton, "Peter's Bold Plan to Evangelize Belgium's Army," 195; E. Norton, *Ralph Norton*, 101.

study groups. Eugène Laveille claims that almost all members remained true to their commitments and became 'apostles' themselves.[35]

Because of the success of the League, the Nortons received more and more letters, even from soldiers they had never met, requesting Bibles and New Testaments and expressing the desire to recommit their lives to God. And so, a desire grew with the Nortons to visit the front line. Such first-hand impressions, they claimed, would help them better understand the soldiers' material needs and give them the aura of war correspondents for *The Sunday School Times*.[36]

Edith Norton contacted the Belgian socialist leader and Minister of State, Emile Vandervelde, via his wife, Lalla. As the Nortons cooperated with her British Gifts For Belgian Soldiers, she hoped Mrs. Vandervelde would put in a good word for them by her husband to obtain the necessary documents.[37] The plan worked, and Ralph was given an appointment with the Socialist leader on 31 January 1916.[38] Vandervelde contacted Prime Minister and Secretary of War De Broqueville the following day, who granted the favor.[39] Having obtained the necessary papers and invited the soldiers they were in contact with to see them in De Panne, they left London on 1 March 1916.[40]

They arrived in Calais (France), where they found several members of the League and had dinner with Pierre Blommaert, the Protestant Head Chaplain of the Belgian army.[41] The next day, the Nortons took the train to Dunkirk, where they missed the only train to De Panne in Belgium due to extended checks by security personnel.[42] Arriving in De Panne on 5 March 1916, they checked in at Hotel Teirlinck, one of the few hotels that was not used as a

---

35   Laveille, *Au service des blessés*, 349-355; De Schaepdrijver, *De Groote Oorlog*, 205; Vanlandschoot, Van Campenhout, and Fuhrmann, "Verschaeve, Cyriel."
36   E. Norton, "When We Actually Started for the Front," 647.
37   Polasky, *The Democratic Socialism of Emile Vandervelde*, 115; Speyer Vandervelde, *Monarchs and Millionaires*, 114; ABEM, 1122: Diary E. Norton (2 Dec. 1915).
38   Fox Norton, "When We Actually Started for the Front," 647; Mrs. Norton, "The Heart of the Belgian Soldier;" ABEM, 1122: Diary E. Norton (31 Jan. 1916).
39   ABEM, 895: De Broqueville to Vandervelde (18 Feb. 1916).
40   ABEM, 895: Sûreté militaire de l'arrière to R. Norton (24 Feb. 1916); Mrs. Norton, "Peter's Bold Plan to Evangelize Belgium's Army," 95; E. Norton, *Ralph Norton*, 110.
41   Blommaert started in the Service Santé (health care team) as a stretcher-bearer, and he is regarded as the founder of the Protestant chaplaincy in the Belgian army. On 15 September 1914, he was appointed as a voluntary Protestant chaplain for the troops in Antwerp. On 13 May 1915 he was given the job title Aumônier-adjoint de 1e classe chargé du culte protestante dans l'armée Belge. From 23 August 1916 until the end of the war he was Head Chaplain in charge of seven other chaplains. At the start of the war it was assumed there were no Protestants at all in the Belgian army. At the end of the war, Blommaert counted 2,000 Protestants under the Belgian flag. ABEM, 1122: Diary E. Norton; Leconte, *Aumôniers militaires belges de la guerre 1914-1918*, vol. 5, 75-83.
42   Fox Norton, "When We Actually Started for the Front," 647.

hospital. There, they met Captain Thys, for whom they had received a letter of recommendation to grant them an audience with the Queen.[43]

On Thursday, 8 March 1916, they met the Queen and explained what they did for the Belgian soldiers. As not all invited soldiers had been able to meet with the Nortons in De Panne, they also asked her to use her influence to extend their visa. Queen Elisabeth, the driving force behind the organization and coordination of humanitarian aid for Belgian soldiers and civilians, was more than willing to do so.[44] Shortly after their audience, the Nortons received a message that their visas had been extended until 17 March 1916. Many more soldiers visited them in the remaining days, some of whom walked or cycled from far away.[45]

During their stay, Edith Norton visited Jardin Marie José, a school for boys and girls from three to eight in the small town of Vinkem. Its patron was the Belgian Queen, and voluntary donations funded it. She wrote a letter to one of their influential friends, Henry Crowell of Quaker Oats, asking for his support. With Crowell supplying the school with Quaker Oats products throughout the rest of the war, the Nortons had won the trust and support of the Belgian Queen.[46]

The Nortons knew they had to capitalize on the momentum they had achieved. Instead of returning to London, they traveled to Le Havre (France), the seat of the Belgian government in exile. There, they met twice with Blommaert and Vandervelde. Blommaert promised to help the League by handing out evangelistic literature. This was in line with his policy to cooperate with any organization that might assist him in maximizing his ministry, such as the American Council of Christian Churches in America and the Protestant Alliance.[47]

---

43 Thys is probably the same as Captain Robert Thys (1884-1964), a military engineer who was responsible for the sluices at Nieuwpoort. The Nortons do not say who wrote the letter of recommendation, but it may have been Pierre Blommaert. Norton, *Ralph Norton*, 110; ABEM, 895: Autorisation d'entrer dans la Zone des cantonnements de l'armée Belge (12 Feb. 1916).
44 AEPA, 530bis: The King's Orderly Officer's carnet; Norton, *Ralph Norton*, 111-112.
45 ABEM, 895: Captain Thys to Ralph and Edith Norton; Norton, *Ralph Norton*, 114.
46 Unlike most American humanitarian initiatives for Belgium, the Nortons had no Belgian roots E. Norton, "When Service Adjourned to the Wine-Cellar!," 399; AEPA, 653.59: The Nortons to Queen Elisabeth from Belgium (April 1918); Fox Norton, "When We Actually Started for the Front"; Bogaert, and Decoodt, "School van de Koningin;" Trogh, Dendooven and Couttenier, *Amerikanen in Flanders Fields*, 36.
47 Fox Norton, "Our Three Weeks in Paris," 760; ABEM, 1061: Flosse to Ralph and Edith Norton (24 Aug. 1916); Blommaert, "Our Work In Dunkirk," 49; Boudin, "1919 De Opperaalmoezenier van de Protestantse Eredienst Piere Blommaert in opdrecht in de Verenigde Staten van Amerika," 1-32.

Vandervelde had to insist a few times before De Broqueville reluctantly allowed the Nortons to return to visit the trenches.[48] Knowing that many wealthy and influential American businessmen befriended the Nortons, he did not want to offend them. After all, Belgium could use foreign support to alleviate the soldiers' living conditions at the Front.

During the Nortons' second visit to the Belgian sector, Van Koeckhoven accompanied them as their interpreter to first-line trenches near Ramskapelle. They handed out chocolate, encouraged the soldiers, and distributed Gospels. Being one of the few women visitors, Edith was quite an attraction for the soldiers.[49] Being well aware that Mrs. Vandervelde had enabled doors to be opened that would otherwise have remained closed, the Nortons paid her a thank-you visit upon their return to London.[50] By now, the Nortons also received letters from prisoners of war in Germany, interned Belgian soldiers in the Netherlands, and men in the camps for permanently mutilated Belgian soldiers in France.[51]

As the initially planned and budgeted year was over, the Nortons left for New York on 5 July 1916. The summer was used for speaking engagements at conferences and churches, such as the Victorious Life Conference at Princeton and Madison Avenue Presbyterian Church, pastored by Dr. Howard Agnew Johnston. They also called on influential evangelical business people and religious leaders such as Crowell and Torrey.[52]

Material aid for the soldiers was going to be extended. Apart from tracts and Gospels, they would also hand out clothes, and the periodical promised to finance the furloughs of soldiers with whom the Nortons were in contact. According to them, most Belgian soldiers were refused furloughs in London because they had no money for food and lodging.[53] Also, Christmas boxes were to be prepared with presents for the soldiers. They were going to cost about $ 1

---

48   ABEM, 1122: Diary E. Norton (22 March 1916); E. Norton, *Ralph Norton*, 114, 118; ABEM, 895: Vandervelde to E. Norton (5 April 1916), Vandervelde to R. Norton (11 April 1916), Tinant to the Nortons (12 April 1916); Fox Norton, "Taking Jesus in His Fullness," 229.
49   Other American women who visited the frontline were Edith Wharton and Mary Roberts Rinehart. Trogh, Dendooven, and Couttenier, *Amerikanen in Flanders Fields*, 39-40.
50   ABEM, 1122: Diary E. Norton (19-20, 28 April 1916); Norton, "Taking Soldiers Alive for Christ," 231; E. Norton, *Ralph Norton*, 115; Barton, Van Paassen and Verschuuren, *De slagvelden van Wereldoorlog I*, 75.
51   ABEM, 1122: Diary E. Norton (28 April 1916); McQuilkin, *Gospel Heroes of the Belgian Trenches*; Weber, *Living in the Shadow of the Second Coming*, 36.
52   ABEM, 1122: Diary E. Norton (15, 31 Aug. 1916); ABEM, 877: G. Winston, "History of the BGM," chapter 3, 4; Fox Norton, "A Glimpse of the Norton's at Work," 415.
53   In all likelihood, the Nortons were referring to Cabinet Decision B/1778, which restricted the number of furloughs to 300 per day. It was estimated that financing a furlough would cost $ 3.50 per person. Financing these furloughs *Journal Militaire Officiel*, vol. 2, 505; Fox Norton, "Christmas in the Belgian Trenches," 620.

each and were to contain "milk chocolate, a bit of Christmas cake, beef cubes for making bouillon, cocoa cubes for making cocoa in the trenches, a can of condensed milk, perhaps a pound of butter (their most desired luxury)."[54]

Including humanitarian aid to the Belgian soldiers in their mission's budget was a significant change of approach. Until then, all the money from *The Sunday School Times* had been spent on Gospels and New Testaments, and the Nortons personally financed any material aid.[55] Material aid has been used over the centuries as a missionary technique. However, there is a thin line between acceptable and unacceptable behavior. Although the gifts were provided with no strings attached, they were accompanied by religious tracts and proselytizing aims.

Like other humanitarian initiatives, the Nortons benefited from the American public's sympathy for 'poor little Belgium.' In fact, up till 1917, war relief was the primary response to the conflict across the Atlantic. Fundraising efforts generally focused on specific causes and were often based on ethnic solidarity or driven by an ideological agenda. Edith Norton's articles, published in *The Sunday School Times* and other periodicals, and presentations at interdenominational conferences and churches from various denominations followed the general pattern of relief publicity in the United States. First-hand observations and vibrant imagery in public addresses and press articles effectively raised money and created a transatlantic religious alliance.[56]

In September 1916, Edith Norton returned to the United Kingdom "to foster the work on that side," while her husband remained in the US "to create further interest" and raise funds.[57] Upon arriving in London, the work resumed its usual pattern: visits to publishers, recreational activities, devotions with Belgian soldiers, and establishing contacts that could be useful for the mission's development and growth. Two secretaries were hired to correspond with the soldiers, and an office was opened midway between their hotel and Charing Cross Station on 20 November 1916.[58] It was a stone's throw from the Protestant Alliance's office, but there are no indications that the Nortons cooperated with them. The fact that they opened their own office indicates the contrary and aligns with their voluntarism.

That year, 10,000 Christmas boxes were ordered and distributed from 20 December 1916 until the first week of January 1917. Each box contained seven or eight items, depending on the availability of products as the boxes were prepared, as well as an envelope with a gospel, either in French or in Dutch, a

---

54   Fox Norton, "Christmas in the Belgian Trenches," 620.
55   Editorial, "The Heart of the Belgian Soldier," 598.
56   Piller, "American War Relief, Cultural Mobilization, and the Myth of Impartial Humanitarianism,1914-17," 623, 635.
57   E. Norton, *Ralph Norton*, 117; Mrs. Norton, "Another Milestone," 155.
58   Fox Norton, "A Glimpse of the Norton's at Work," 415.

story tract, a brochure in French about the League, a response card that could be returned by soldiers who wanted to become members, and a Christmas card with the following text:

> Your American friends send you their best wishes for Christmas and the New Year. This gift is given to you by the intermediary of Mr. Ralph Norton and Mme. Edith Norton, 15, Strand, London.[59]

As a priority, parcels were sent to the Nortons' nearly five thousand contacts. Over a thousand boxes were sent to Protestants in the Belgian army by a list compiled by Pierre Blommaert. The rest "were dispatched to that number of poor and exceptionally needy soldiers at the front, whose names were supplied by a Belgian committee in London," which did not charge for its part in the Christmas box campaign.[60] In the spring of 1917, several hundreds of raincoats were sent to the soldiers at the front and chocolate to mutilated Belgian soldiers in France.[61]

The number of responses was such that a third secretary was appointed in late February 1917. Belgian Adjutant Odilon Vansteenberghe, strongly influenced by Priscilla Stewart, often came to the office to help translate letters into Dutch.[62] Preachers from several London churches also offered their services.[63] And as the thank-you letters contained many references to the literature in the Christmas parcels, their holistic approach seemed to work. Several soldiers also responded to the gifts by asking, "Teach us of your religion. We have never learned in our old one such love as you have shown to us."[64]

---

59 ABEM, 877: G. Winston, "History of the BGM," Chapter 3, 5.
60 In view of the existing contacts with Lalla Vandervelde it is probable that this committee was British Gifts For Belgian Soldiers. "When 10,000 Soldiers Got Their Christmas Boxes," 96.
61 Mrs. Norton, "The Gospel as Belgium's Hope," 681.
62 Priscilla Livingstone Stewart (1864-1929), a China Inland Mission (CIM) missionary from Ireland, married Charles Thomas Studd (1860-1931), one of the Cambridge Seven and also a CIM missionary, in 1888. In 1913, he founded the Heart of Africa Mission, which is currently called WEC International. Priscilla Stewart had close links with the Holiness movement. Vansteenberghe was converted while recovering in a British hospital, and after his discharge, he worked for the Belgian army in London. From July until November 1915, he stayed with relatives of John Martin Cleaver of the Egypt General Mission. Grubb, *C.T. Studd: Cricketer and Pioneer*; ABEM, 461: Vansteenberghe to Banham (15 June 1938); Thompson, *Firebrand of Flanders*, 21–22.
63 The preachers who can be identified from Edith's diary are: Dupuis, French Church, 29 Oct. 1916; Pastor Lelièvre, 19 Aug. 1917. They were also in contact with Rev. R. Hoffman-de Visme of l'Eglise Suisse de Londres. ABEM, 1122: Diary E. Norton (23 Feb., 22 May 1916).
64 Eventually, they had eight. ABEM, 1122: Diary E. Norton (28 Feb. 1917); ABEM, 877: G. Winston, "History of the BGM," Chapter 3, 5; McQuilkin, *Gospel Heroes of the Belgian Trenches*; Fox Norton, "A Glimpse of the Norton's at Work," 415.

In May 1917, six months later than planned, Ralph Norton returned to London. In communicating with his wife, he justified the delay in religious language.[65] As Norton always connected the news of the world with his devotional reading of the Bible, it is not too difficult to link certain events to his repeatedly postponing his return to London. On 13 December 1916, shortly before he intended to sail to England, *The New York Times* ran an article that Germany and her allies proposed to initiate peace talks.[66] It was quite logical to delay his dangerous transatlantic journey, as their mission would end if the Allies accepted the proposal, which would result in ending the war. In the end, Norton rescheduled his several times before finally sailing on 5 May 1917, about a month after the United States had declared war on Germany.

Norton had used the delay to raise further funding and expand the number of supporters. He anticipated they would raise less support once the United States entered the war as people would donate to causes that served the combatting US troops. Indeed, once the US had officially entered the conflict, their supporters often asked the Nortons why they did not also reach out to American soldiers. They answered that American soldiers had many more possibilities than Belgians to come into contact with the Gospel from an early age. "God has given us to Belgium, and Belgium to us, and we will not turn aside. During the war, our ministry is to the Belgian soldier."[67]

With additional funding secured, office space was expanded in July 1917 by renting the entire first floor of the building. They now had more space for a growing number of secretaries and created a recreational area for the Belgian soldiers on leave in London.[68] The new evangelistic initiative was intended as an alternative for secular and Roman Catholic foyers for soldiers.[69] This is another example of how the Nortons deliberately chose to deploy their own initiatives next to existing alternatives. From the start of the war in 1914, the French-language YMCA foyer in London had been reserved for Belgian military and refugees every Monday evening. As far as we know, the Nortons did not contact this YMCA department to discuss possibly working together or expanding the opening hours for Belgian soldiers.[70]

With operational costs now as high as $ 1,000 per month, excluding the costs of Gospels and New Testaments, and the ambition to triple the number of Christmas boxes, another fundraising tour was imperative. Unlike the previ-

---

65   E. Norton, *Ralph Norton*, 125-126.
66   "Peace Note of Germany and Her Allies, Dec. 12, 1916," 2.
67   Fox Norton, "Under Fire with Belgium's Queen," 589.
68   Howard, *A New Invasion of Belgium*, 43–44; E. Norton, *Ralph Norton*, 129; "Editorial," *Sunday School Times* (7 April 1917), 197.
69   Laveille, *Au service des blessés*, 67–68.
70   Boudin, "Protestantse burger en legeraalmoezeniers ten dienste van Belgische militairen, krijgsgevangenen en geïnterneerden tijdens de wereldoorlog 1914-1918," 26; Snape, *God and the British Soldier*, 210.

ous time, the London office remained open, and the recreation area continued with the help of volunteers. The Nortons sailed for New York on 7 September 1917, about four months after Ralph had returned to London.

Their itinerary shows they established good relations with influential Dispensationalists and Fundamentalists in the USA. In Chicago, the Nortons had several meetings with Crowell and promoted their work again at Moody Bible Institute. They spoke at a Presbyterian church led by Prof. Dr. Cleland Boyd McAfee.[71] They had lunch with the Presbyterian Dr. George L. Robinson and a talk at McCormick Theological Seminary.[72] They gave presentations in Dr. D.M. Stearns' Bible Classes in Philadelphia, Washington DC, Baltimore, and New York.[73] In November, they met with Cyrus I. Scofield and Dr. August H. Strong, and Dr. Howard Kelly.[74] They also seized every opportunity and presented their work at large YMCA and YWCA meetings. Not long before returning to England, the Nortons attended Dr. I.M. Haldeman's First Baptist Church in New York.[75]

By late December 1917, the Nortons returned to London with money "to maintain the newly opened Foyer and keep the stream of Gospel literature going forth" and a budget for thirty-two thousand Christmas boxes.[76] Seven thousand of these were to be sent to Belgian prisoners of war in Germany, and the rest were sent to Le Havre for distribution through military channels. The

---

71 Presbyterian Dr. Cleland Boyd McAfee (1866-1944) seems to have been the first to have coined the acronym TULIP. From 1912-1930 he taught Systematic Theology at McCormick Theological Seminary in Chicago and presided the Presbyterian Board of Foreign Missions from 1930-1936. Vail, "The Five Points of Calvinism Historically Considered," 394; ABEM, 1122: Diary E. Norton (26 Sep., 14, 22 Oct., 30 Nov. 1917).
72 Dr. George L. Robinson (1863-1958), professor of Hebrew and Old Testament at McCormick Theological Seminary, was a delegate at the 1886 Mount Hermon conference, where the Student Volunteer Mission was founded. ABEM, 1122: Diary E. Norton (17 Oct. 1917); Gibson, *A.J. Gordon: American Premillennialist*, 88.
73 ABEM, 1122: Diary E. Norton (26 Sep., 14, 17, 22-23 Oct., 30 Nov. 1917); E. Norton, *Ralph Norton*, 130.
74 Howard A. Kelly (1858-1943), co-founder of Johns Hopkins Hospital, was strongly influenced by Dwight L. Moody and supported Billy Sunday's evangelism crusades. He was a board member of the US Home Council of the CIM, wrote for the *Sunday School Times*, was one of the authors of 'The Fundamentals,' and frequently spoke at the US Keswick conferences. Dr. August H. Strong (1836-1921), presided over the American Baptist Missionary Union (1892-1895), the General Convention of Baptists of North America (1905-1910), and Rochester Theological Seminary (1872-1912). His most important publication, *Systematic Theology*, was first published in 1886, and the last, enlarged edition appeared in 1908. DeRemer, "Thunder in the Pulpit," 34-35; "Guide to the Augustus Hopkins Strong Papers MS 1127."
75 ABEM, 1122: Diary E. Norton (1-4, 11, 15, 25 Nov., 23 Dec. 1917).
76 E. Norton, *Ralph Norton*, 132.

contents were to be similar to those of the previous year, and the tracts to be included were "contributed by different societies and individual friends."[77]

This time, the Nortons were confronted by an unpleasant surprise. The shipment for the soldiers on the front was blocked in Le Havre, as recent military regulations forbade the sending of books as a part of food parcels.[78] When they were notified, the Nortons first tried to resolve the matter by letter and telegram. When this failed, the couple went to Le Havre on 24 January 1918. Several times, they visited Colonel Massinon, the officer overseeing the Christmas boxes. The first time, they went alone; the second time, they took Jules Rambaud, a Protestant chaplain, and the third time, they took a letter of recommendation written by Vandervelde.[79] Massinon could not be swayed. The greeting card with the Nortons' address in London was to stay in each box, but the enclosures with Gospels were to be sent back to London, from where they could send them to all the recipients of packages who replied. They would be allowed to personally hand out two thousand boxes in and around De Panne.[80]

While waiting for the appropriate travel documents to be prepared and the boxes to be sent, the Nortons traveled to Paris, where they were in contact with Pastors Anderson and Arthur Blocher from the *Mission Populaire*.[81] As was his habit, Ralph Norton handed out tracts and Gospels to the soldiers in the streets. Although the *Mission Populaire* had two soldiers' Foyers frequent-

77 Edith Norton's account in *The Christian Workers Magazine* differs from that in *The Sunday School Times* on the details of distribution. Mrs. Norton, "Christmas with the Belgian Soldiers," 176; Fox Norton, "When the Postman Appears at the Belgian Front," 587; E. Norton, *Ralph Norton*, 132–133.
78 According to an article in *The Sword and Trowel*, the Roman Catholic authorities were responsible for this, as they did not want the parcels to hold New Testaments. A more probable explanation would be that the authorities were wary of the Flemish nationalist propaganda and of publications that would demoralize the soldiers. Vandervelde wrote the following letter to the BASEC offices: "I have tried three times to get through to you on the telephone but in vain. I have just had a wire from Le Havre to say that the permission for the Nortons to go to the Front at the New Year is granted. Will you cable them this if you think it is worth while? As I may possibly go to the Belgian Front next week already, would you let me know where the 3000 parcels are, that I am to distribute amongst the soldiers?" "Good Work Among The Belgian Soldiers," 116; ABEM, 895: Vandervelde to Wilson (10 Dec. 1917).
79 ABEM, 1122: Diary E. Norton (25, 26, 28 Jan. 1918).
80 Fox Norton, "God's Hand in a Perplexing Hold-Up," 256.
81 The *Mission Populaire Évangélique* de France [Evangelical Mission to the People of France], also known as the 'McAll Mission,' was founded by Robert Whitaker McAll (1821-1893). He was a Methodist from the United Kingdom who moved to Paris in 1871 to evangelize there, focusing mainly on the working classes. McAll opened preaching halls in Paris and many other French towns and cities. The Nortons were introduced to the mission before the war, when they visited Paris with the Chapman-Alexander Mission. ABEM, 1122: Diary E. Norton (23 March - 17 April 1916); Fath, *Du ghetto au réseau*, 126-127; "Editorial," *c* 1917, 1; "Echoes from Our Relief Work," 19; Bach, "The Soldiers' Foyers," 20-21.

ed by Belgian soldiers, the Nortons also wanted to open their own Foyer in Paris. When they could not find a suitable place near the Gare du Nord, they decided to open a temporary recreational area on the ground floor of Blocher's church, which was within walking distance from the station. It was put under the supervision of Blocher and opened on 22 April 1918 in the presence of a "large crowd," including twenty-five French and Belgian soldiers.[82]

In the meantime, the Nortons traveled to De Panne, where they stayed as guests of the Belgian government and had permission to use the army facilities. Having become trusted partners for the Belgian authorities, they met several Belgian generals and the technocrat and new Belgian Minister of War, Baron Armand L.T. De Ceuninck.[83] The distribution of the food boxes was announced in the army routine order, with the instructions that each recipient had to return the reply slip with some words of thanks. On 22 February 1918, the Nortons handed out 1,500 boxes to "the most necessitous and deserving" of the fifth division, chosen by the General Staff.[84] Army personnel photographed and filmed the parade.[85] The remaining 500 boxes were given to the Protestant Chaplain and three leaders of the League in the trenches, Peter, Arthur, and John, who were to distribute them.[86]

By invitation of the Minister of War, the Nortons traveled to the front lines once more in April 1918. Arriving on Easter Sunday, they attended a church service in the Protestant Chapel. Upon invitation, they subsequently met the Queen in Hotel de l'Océan, where they agreed to have another, more extended meeting in the Jardin Marie José the following day.[87] Well aware of the value of media publicity, the Nortons handed the next day a check to the value of BEF 8,000 to the Queen in the presence of the press. They also gave her a large box with children's clothes, a gift that came with hand-written letters from the American children at Missionary Sunday School of Moody Church, Chicago. The next day, they went to the Jardin once more, this time with sweets they had bought in De Panne for the children.[88]

---

82   ABEM, 1122: Diary E. Norton (22 April 1918); E. Norton, *Ralph Norton*, 137.
83   Baron Armand L.T. De Ceuninck (1858-1935) made his career in the Belgian army. In 1917, he succeeded Charles De Broqueville as Minister of War. After the war, he had another prestigious job in the army, and in 1920, he was part of the Belgian delegation at the League of Nations' disarmament conference. ABEM, 1122: Diary E. Norton (17, 18, 20 Feb. 1918); Ars Moriendi.be, "De CEUNINCK, Baron Armand, L.-T."
84   Fox Norton, "Annexing the Fifth Division of the Belgian Army," 443.
85   The film was located in the BEM archives, poorly preserved. *Koninklijk Belgisch Filmarchief Cinematek* (Cinematek Royal Belgian Film Archive) has since managed to secure three minutes that provide some insight into the parade. Fox Norton, "Annexing the Fifth Division of the Belgian Army," 443-444.
86   E. Norton, *Ralph Norton*, 143.
87   Ibid., "Spending Easter Under Shell Fire at the Front," 503.
88   ABEM, 1122: Diary E. Norton (2 April 1918); Fox Norton, "Under Fire with Belgium's Queen," 589-590; AEPA, 653.59: Nortons to Queen Elisabeth from Belgium (1 April 1918).

Later, they distributed 16,000 Easter parcels to the soldiers, containing greeting cards with the following text:

> We send you to-day with this little gift a joyous message of Easter, from Him whose resurrection from among the dead we celebrate at this time. Christ has risen after having suffered death for every man, and all those who believe on him shall be raised also from the death of sin to live in him a new life. In your exile and loneliness lift your eyes to the Lord.[89]

When the Nortons returned to London from France by the end of April 1918, they prepared to transfer the responsibility for the office and foyer to the secretaries White and Bell.[90] In early June, they returned to the US with Vandervelde's ambitious suggestion that they'd give a Christmas box to each of the 125,000 Belgian soldiers in active service.[91] The Belgian Consul in New York was permitted to transport the shipment from the US to England free of charge. The cost of this operation was budgeted for $ 100,000. Secretary Vandervelde and Commander in Chief Gillain supported the fundraising with a page-size advert in *The Sunday School Times* in which they praised the Nortons and thanked their supporters for their generosity.[92]

This charm offensive should be seen as a way of ensuring continued American support. As much foreign aid was still needed to reconstruct Belgium, a Catholic country, the government tried to stay on the right side of the Protestants in the USA, thereby improving its chances of more financial support. For that same reason, Blommaert visited the USA in the autumn of 1918 for a promotional tour on behalf of the Belgian government in exile. He spoke in churches and parachurch organizations and met with journalists, captains of industry, and representatives of universities.[93]

The Nortons presented their ambitious plan at several Bible conferences that summer and met with their befriended rich and influential evangelical

---

89 At Vandervelde's request, the Nortons handed out envelopes with a voucher and an Easter greeting in French and Dutch in the same wording as the cards in the Easter boxes. The vouchers had a value of $ 0.25 to be used in a government store. E. Norton, "Spending Easter Under Shell Fire at the Front," 503; Ibid., "Satan Sifts a Soldier in Two Warfares," 209; Mrs. Norton, "When I Followed Europe's Finest Orator!," 639.
90 ABEM, 1122: Diary E. Norton (30 April, 1, 7 May 1918).
91 Each soldier was to receive a *bon de magasin* or shopping voucher, to be detached from the Christmas card with its Gospel message. This voucher could be exchanged in a government store for a bar of chocolate, two candles, and a bar of soap. E. Norton, *Ralph Norton*, 146.
92 Fox Norton, "Annexing the Fifth Division of the Belgian Army," 443; "You Will Believe in This New Invasion of a Waiting Belgium," 618; ABEM, 895: Gillain to E. Norton (9 May 1918).
93 Boudin, "L'Aumônier-en-chef du culte protestant Pierre Blommaert en mission aux Etats-Unis d'Amérique," 1, 12-13, 15, 23.

businessmen.[94] They managed to raise the amount needed, but by then, it was clear that the war was nearing its end. This meant the Nortons needed to find a new mission field. Unsurprisingly, during the final year of the Great War, they developed the conviction that they should seize the momentum and set up an evangelical mission in postwar Belgium. The endless stream of letters seemed to suggest a tremendous receptivity to their evangelistic message. Only time would tell how many of the soldiers would continue their interest in Protestantism once they had returned to their everyday lives in a society dominated by Catholicism.

Within three years, they had established contacts with countless Belgian soldiers. By 1918, their London office employed eight secretaries to reply to the endless stream of letters. At the end of the war, the Scripture League reportedly counted 15,000 to 18,000 members, which was around 6% of the Belgian soldiers, including prisoners of war, interned and mutilated soldiers. This was far more than could be expected based on the number of Protestants in prewar Belgium, i.e. ± 0.5%.[95]

Several soldiers even begged the Nortons to come to Belgium once the war ended to share the gospel with their relatives. No wonder the Nortons were convinced "that hearts would be more open for the reception of the Gospel because of the recollection of all that was done for the soldiers during their time of distress."[96] So, on 15 November 1918, just four days after the armistice, the Council of BASEC convened in Philadelphia, PA, "to consider the future of the work for Belgian soldiers."[97]

What started as a two-man mission amongst British and French soldiers had developed into a springboard for missions in postwar Belgium in just a few years. The first signs of this evolution already appeared in 1916, when Trumbull shared his dreams in an editorial that postwar Belgium would be the stage for a large-scale evangelistic campaign.[98] The Nortons waited until 1918 to express themselves publicly, stating they wanted to set up a "strong evangelical Mission" in postwar Belgium.[99] Their primary focus would be the working class people, which can be deduced from the statement that they wanted to do for the Belgian people "what the McAll Mission had done for France."[100] Although they would broaden their focus from the army to the entire popula-

94   E. Norton, "When Service Adjourned to the Wine-Cellar!," 400; ABEM, 1122: Diary E. Norton (19 Oct. 1918); Boyd, "The Bible Conference at Eagles Mere, Pa.;" Putnam, "Missionary Alliance Conference," 36.
95   Howard, "Taking Bread to Belgium," 185; Front page of the *Sunday School Times*, 1919, 709; ABEM, 850: Minutes Board of Trustees (14 Jan. 1920); Anet, "Protestant Churches in Belgium," 33.
96   Howard, *A New Invasion*, 48.
97   This council, launched a year earlier, formalized Norton's relations with their primal advisors and served as a kind of committee of reference. E. Norton, *Ralph Norton*, 147.
98   Editorial, "The Heart of the Belgian Soldier," 598.
99   Fox Norton, "After the War in Belgium – What?," 593.
100 Ibid.

tion, they planned to continue their success formula: "relief work in connection with their evangelistic work."[101]

As we already saw, Roman Catholic countries like Belgium were to them as much of a mission field as countries with a mostly non-Christian population. Like other faith missionaries, they would wholeheartedly agree with Robert Elliot Speer, who believed that missions to these countries were justified "to counter the 'travesty of Christianity' that their churches represented."[102] In the years to come, the Nortons would use this line of argument over and over again. Further, Henry W. Frost, Home Director for North America of the China Inland Mission, considered the Scripture League's members as potential "manhood material for ... evangelizing of the Latin races of Europe, and even of Belgian Congo."[103] Expectations were high on the other side of the Atlantic as well. Ralph was an exceptional fundraiser with an impressive network of wealthy businessmen, and the couple stayed in a luxury hotel. Soldiers and Protestant chaplains must have gotten the impression that teaming up with the Nortons was like landing on a hidden goldmine.[104]

But were the Nortons' expectations realistic? Sociological research has demonstrated that religious receptivity can be caused by being uprooted from one's trusted social environment. Moreover, traumatic experiences are a known contributor to changes in people's religious convictions. Some soldiers left the faith, whereas others found comfort in their faith or started looking for an alternative to the Catholic teachings they had grown up with. A third contributing factor was the warm, parent/child-like relationships that the Nortons developed with the soldiers, who were cut off from their families.[105] Although some converts, such as Odilon Vansteenberghe, could be described as seekers even before the war started, others may have joined the League to receive some literature they could read to pass the time. Only in peacetime would it become apparent how deeply rooted the converts were in their newfound faith and whether the League members would be as vibrant

---

101 ABEM, 850: Minutes Board of Trustees (15 Nov. 1918).
102 Already before World War I, 36 American missionaries served in Catholic Europe. Speer, *South American Problems* 228; Fiedler, *The Story of Faith Missions*, 180; Stark, "Efforts to Christianize Europe, 400-2000," 117.
103 This is in line with John R. Mott, who used the colonial argument by stating that the evangelization of France was of world interest as it "is leading Latin Europe, Latin America, the Balkan States, the Levant, French Moslem Africa, Indo-China, and ... Russia." Fox Norton, "The Soldiers' Christmas in Belgian Trenches," 710; Mott, *The World-Interest in the Evangelization of France*, 15.
104 When Hotel Cecil was requisitioned for the war effort, Edith had to relocate in January 1917. She chose the Waldorf Hotel, another grand hotel. As she didn't like the hotel, she moved to a luxury apartment in the Savoy Mansions the next day. ABEM, 1122: Diary E. Norton (8-9 Jan. 1917).
105 Schweitzer, *The Cross, and the Trenches*, 21, 41, 45.

and evangelistic about their Protestant faith once they had left their miserable conditions and returned to their homes and families. Only time could tell if the civilian population of postwar Belgium would be as receptive as the Nortons hoped. If they succeeded, Ralph Norton could permanently eliminate the label of unsuitability for foreign missions.

Ralph and Edith Norton.
[KADOC-KU Leuven: ABEM, 1406]

3
BRIDGEHEAD BRUSSELS

On 19 November 1918, the Nortons left the United States for Europe. As of 1 January 1919, BASEC would be rebranded to the Belgian Gospel Mission (BGM).[1] Whereas BASEC started without a clear doctrinal basis, the Nortons had done their homework by now. They had studied the constitutions and by-laws of several faith missions and decided to copy the doctrinal basis largely from the China Inland Mission.[2] The mission's base took the shape of an Executive Committee, which, characteristically for faith missions, had an advisory function, would forward means and missionaries to Belgium, and would promote the mission in North America.[3] An important asset for successful fundraising was that Mrs. Lyman Stewart, Mrs. Mary Bordon, and Mrs. Haines Jr., noted philanthropists of the American Keswick Holiness Movement, served as ordinary Committee members.[4]

The close relationship between the Nortons' mission and the *Sunday School Times* continued. With treasurer Charles G. Trumbull, secretary Philip E. Howard Sr., and vice-chairman Howard A. Banks, the *SST* was well represented on the BGM's Board. In the years to come, the periodical would continue regularly publishing articles about the Nortons' mission in Catholic Belgium.

The Nortons knew it would be hard to emulate their success during the Great War. Europe was hardly considered a mission field, and now peace had

---

1 As was customary in faith missions, the name refers to the geographical area where they would work. Fiedler, *Ganz auf Vertrauen*, 275.
2 ABEM, 850: Minutes Board of Trustees (15 Nov. 1918).
3 Ibid. (14 Jan. 1919).
4 Prins, "The History of the Belgian Gospel Mission from 1918 to 1962," 70.

returned to the old continent, the positive sentiment for 'poor little Belgium' was likely to dwindle quickly in the years to come. As the main focus of Western Christian missions still was on Asia and Africa, an uphill battle for media exposure was to be expected once the most dire humanitarian needs had been adequately assessed and met. Based on their experiences of the past few years, they knew they would encounter problems with the language barrier, local customs, and overcoming prejudice. They were well aware that fierce opposition from the Catholic Church was also expected.[5]

But before we delve into the start of the BGM's activities, we need to sketch both the religious and socio-economic landscape in which it would enter. Protestants formed a small minority in Belgian society. At the start of the twentieth century, their number was estimated at some 40,000, most of whom were members of either Presbyterian denominations, the *Union des Églises protestante évangélique du Royaume de Belgique* (UPECB), and the *Église Chrétienne Missionnaire Belge* (ECMB).[6] The UPECB was formed in 1839 by the protestant churches with a government-paid pastor. The ECMB was created in 1849 and has its roots in the Réveil. Most of its local churches were planted in French-speaking Belgium.

Silo, an urban and rural mission organization, was started by a Dutch pastor with Flemish roots, Nicolaas de Jonge. He accepted a post as the minister of the *Vlaams-Hollandse-Evangelische Kerk* in Brussels in 1874. Various evangelistic initiatives focusing on the World Exhibition in Brussels in 1880 led to the separate organization, Silo, for evangelistic activities 'in town and country.' It focused mainly on Flemish people and attempted to have outreach to Flemish people carried out by Flemish believers as much as possible. To this end, De Jonge started a training School for Evangelists in 1876. At the start of World War I, Silo had eight congregations.[7]

The *Exclusive Brethren* came to Belgium partly on the initiative of Dutchman H.C. Voorhoeve, whose activities led to the formation of a congregation in Brussels. Another leading figure was Carl Brockhaus from Elberfeld, Germany, under whose influence a community was established in Verviers by cross-border workers in 1865. In the Flemish town of Ninove, a Brethren church was established around Belgian convert Aloysius Van Der Smissen.[8]

The first *Open Brethren* congregation in Belgium was formed when French evangelist Casimir Gaudibert, who led an ECMB church in Fontaine-l'Evêque,

---

5   E. Norton, *Ralph Norton*, 148–152; Fleming, *In the Wake of the Whirlwind*, 32.
6   According to Houghton, the ECMB had 12,000 registered members in 1914, most of whom belonged to the "laboring and industrial classes." They had 44 (Anet) or 43 (Houghton) congregations and stations, servicing 218 towns and villages, whereas the UPECB had 28 (Houghton) or 29 (Anet) congregations and stations. Anet, "Protestant Churches in Belgium," 33; Seymour Houghton, *Handbook of French and Belgian Protestantism*, 72–73.
7   De Raaf, *Een eeuw Silo*, 126-127.
8   Marinello, *New Brethren in Flanders*, 26-29.

clashed with his denominational leaders about his sympathies with the Open Brethren in England. The congregation sided with its pastor and became the first congregation of Open Brethren in Belgium in 1854. George Müller supported this church. A vital contribution to the growth of the Open Brethren was the arrival of British couple William Nock and Mary Reddish in 1896. William Nock was active in Flanders and Wallonia and cooperated with Casimir's son, George F. Gaudibert.[9]

In 1889, the *Salvation Army* started several corps in Belgium from the Netherlands. Because people were more responsive in French-speaking Belgium, the responsibility for this ministry was handed to the Salvation Army in France in 1902. From then on, Belgium was supervised by Ulysse Cosandey, who later left the Salvation Army but kept visiting Belgium at the invitation of the BGM. From 1939, there was an autonomous Belgian corps.[10] After the war, the Salvation Army deployed its own relief work, entirely in line with its character as an organization. It used foreign funding to hand out soup and blankets on a large scale among all sections of the Belgian population and opened its first 'slum post' in Brussels in 1921. A nurse was permanently present for consultation, and once a week, a hot meal for the elderly was served when food parcels were also handed out in places where research had shown a genuine need.[11]

The *Baptist* denomination entered Belgium via cross-border workers from Wallonia. They had come into contact with the Baptist church in Denain in Northern France and, after their return to their home village of Ougrée, started their own Baptist church there. A Baptist church was also started in Péruwelz (1903) and Mont-sur-Marchienne (1904). These three churches created the Union of Belgian Baptist Churches in 1922. However, the Baptist church Julius Hoffman started in Saint-Gilles (Brussels) in 1906, joined the Evangelical Association of French-language Baptist Churches.[12] The *Gereformeerde Kerken* (Reformed Churches) in Brussels (1894) and Antwerp (1899) resulted from changes in the Dutch ecclesiastical landscape. Conflicts in the Dutch Reformed Church led to the creation of the *Gereformeerde Kerken in Nederland* towards the end of the nineteenth century.[13]

Socio-economically, liberated Belgium had to battle several new battles simultaneously. There was an acute housing shortage as 70,000 homes had been destroyed, and another 200,000 homes were severely damaged. The

9   The Nortons had met Nock already in 1916 and supplied him with New Testaments in Dutch. Tatford, *West European Evangel*, 43-44; ABEM, 895: Nock to E. Norton (1 Dec. 1916).
10 Cosandey, *L'armée du Salut aux pays latins*, 65-69.
11 Dale, "Aperçu sur l'évangélisation en Belgique pendant l'entre-deux-guerres," 10.
12 Hoffmann was a businessman and a lay Baptist preacher. He was involved with creating Tregelle's text-critical edition of the New Testament Textus Receptus. "Het ontwaken van het protestantisme in het Koninkrijk België (1830-1980)," 80-84.
13 "Het ontwaken van het protestantisme in het Koninkrijk België (1830-1980)," 81.

housing problem was made more severe by the return of some 600,000 Belgian refugees and quite a few political prisoners, military internees, and prisoners of war.[14]

A second issue was the severe food shortages. The armistice of 11 November 1918 did not mean Belgium could immediately resume its responsibility for its national food production and import. Many agricultural stockpiles and livestock had been commandeered or destroyed by the occupier. Even before the war, the densely populated and industrialized nation imported large quantities of agricultural products. At the start of 1919, three and a half million Belgians, almost 50% of the population, relied on food aid, and 120,000 hectares of agricultural fields were littered with unexploded bombs and toxic waste.[15] Thanks to the cooperation between the *Comité national de Secours et d'Alimentation* (National Committee for Relief and Food) and the Commission for Relief in Belgium (CRB), no famine erupted in occupied Belgium.[16] The state intervention in food distribution, regulating food import and prices, would last until 1921.[17]

Thirdly, the economy had been decimated. Before August 1914, Belgium was an important industrial power and one of the wealthiest countries in the world. Four years later, the country's infrastructure was almost completely destroyed. Hundreds of bridges and large sections of the national and local rail networks had been destroyed by armies on both sides. Many train engines and most modern factory machines had been taken to Germany. On top of this came the loss of investments in Russia after the Communist revolution. It is estimated that national wealth had dropped by 16 to 20%.[18]

It was quite logical that the BGM would follow in BASEC's footsteps and "continue relief work in connection with … evangelistic work now that peace has come."[19] Moreover, the BGM's intention to cooperate with the existing Protestant churches in Belgium was in line with Charles S. Macfarland's repeated plea that all Protestant agencies interested in France and Belgium unite their efforts.[20] Macfarland was the General Secretary of the Federal Council of Christian Churches in America (FCCC), which started in January 1918 to raise funds

---

14   Dumoulin, "Het ontluiken van de twintigste eeuw, 1905-1918," 838.
15   Demasure, "Het Nationaal Hulp- en Voedingscomité redt de bevolking."
16   Piller, "American War Relief, Cultural Mobilization, and the Myth of Impartial Humanitarianism, 1914-17," 621, 625, 628.
17   After the elections, a new political majority decided to end state intervention, as global food supplies had more or less normalized. Even Wauters had to admit that there no longer was an urgency to assist the population. Bernardo y Garcia, *Le ventre des Belges*, 94, 97, 117.
18   Buyst, "De economische balans van de Eerste Wereldoorlog," 108-111.
19   ABEM, 850: Minutes Board of Trustees (15 Nov. 1918).
20   Committee for Christian Relief in France and Belgium, *An Interchurch Campaign for Protestant Relief in France and Belgium*.

to finance Protestant churches' rebuilding and humanitarian aid to pastors.[21] A *Comité d'Union Protestante* (CUP) would distribute the goods. The Belgian denominations participating in this CUP were the UPECB and the ECMB.[22]

Like the Nortons, Macfarland built extensive contacts with Protestant head chaplain Pierre Blommaert during the war. The Nortons had gained extensive experience with interdenominational cooperation during their years with Chapman. Also, during the war, they collaborated without any known tensions with the Belgian Protestant army chaplains, who were all members of the UPECB or ECMB.

Shortly after 11 November 1918, Protestant army chaplain Armand Marchandise had offered to "examine the situation of the Belgian Churches" when he returned to Belgium.[23] He was determined to help the Nortons with their planned missionary activities. A month later, he reported that not only was there a shortage of food, but he had also received confirmation that the population longed to read the Bible more than ever, which confirmed the Nortons' own impression.[24]

The Nortons wanted to enter Belgium as soon as possible but were not granted access to the devastated country as foreign civilians. They requested a military pass, which was granted, and were allowed to come to Brussels as of 1 December 1918.[25] The Belgian capital was an ideal location for their headquarters, not only for its central location but, more importantly, for their political and military friends would be within reach if needed.[26]

The Nortons arrived in Brussels on 19 December 1918 by a Belgian military limousine and checked in at the Grand Hotel Astoria. Although the German occupier had entirely stripped its interior, they didn't have much choice. Together with the Grand Hotel du Britannique, Astoria was the only hotel allowed to reopen shortly after the Armistice by the authorities.[27] For the next few months, this would be their new headquarters, where they received a constant stream of visitors, all former soldiers with their families, and without delay started with what they described as a "Gospel Ministry."[28]

21 The FCCC consisted of the Presbyterian Church, the United Presbyterian Church, the Methodist Episcopal Church, the National Lutheran Council, the Baptist churches (North), the Congregational Churches, the Reformed Church in America, the Reformed Church in the United States and the Disciples of Christ. Boudin, "L'Aumônier-en-chef du culte protestant Pierre Blommaert en mission aux Etats-Unis d'Amérique 1919," 3.
22 *An Interchurch Campaign for Protestant Relief in France and Belgium*; "Les relations entre Dr. Charles Stedman MACFARLAND Secrétaire-Général du Federal Council of the Churches of Christ in America et le protestantisme belge 1918-1925," 1-29.
23 ABEM, 1073: A. Marchandise to R. Norton (19 Nov. 1918).
24 Ibid. (12 Dec. 1918).
25 ABEM, 895: Grand Quartier Général Belge to R. Norton (28 Nov. 1918).
26 Fleming, *In the Wake of the Whirlwind*, 33; Norton, *Ralph Norton*, 151.
27 Jourdain, "L'hôtellerie bruxelloise 1880-1940," 263.
28 E. Norton, *Ralph Norton*, 155.

The campaign to provide every Belgian soldier with a Christmas parcel was continued after the cease-fire. The Nortons felt that reaching out to soldiers would reach their families and many more of them.[29] Even though their material aid was proselytizing in nature, the Belgian authorities still welcomed the initiative. The need remained high, as explained earlier. A list of permissible items was provided, from which the Nortons chose. The goods were sourced in the United States and shipped to Belgium at the army's expense.

In London, 120,000 Christmas cards were stuffed into envelopes, together with vouchers for chocolate, soap, and candles. The cards were sent via the army in December 1918.[30] Soldiers who were not in a fighting capacity but whom the Nortons had been in contact with during the war were allowed to receive parcels via a Protestant chaplain.[31] Prime Minister Léon Delacroix, from the Catholic party, thanked Ralph Norton on behalf of the Belgian government for his efforts to help the soldiers.

> Your wonderful letters were very comforting to the soldier for the distraction and the sense of well-being they provided to the harsh conditions of his existence. Upon receiving them, the soldier had the joy of knowing someone was thinking of him, seeking to alleviate his suffering and encourage him in his efforts to vanquish the enemy. Dear Sir, you have also provided moments of happiness to thousands of men who were otherwise deprived of the affection and support of their families.
> Now you intend to continue this act of devotion in favour of demobilised soldiers. This is a particularly pleasing thought now that, having only just escaped the danger of war, our soldiers will be grappling with the most serious difficulties. Too often our destroyed factories will not be able to offer immediate work to them, and they need to know that there is an effective help beside them encouraging them to start their lives afresh.[32]

With the help of their secretaries, the Nortons continued their correspondence with the soldiers, mainly in French.[33] The names of soldiers arrested for not returning promptly from leave were passed on to Protestant army chaplains.[34] Just as during the war, not all soldiers understood the Nortons' evangelistic intentions. Some asked for grammar books and dictionaries to help them in

---

29 Mrs. Norton, "The Nortons' Work in Belgium," 806.
30 ABEM, 849: General Workers Letter (Dec. 1928); Norton, *Ralph Norton*, 148.
31 ABEM, 1086: Sanctorum to R. Norton (12 Jan. 1919); BASEC to Sanctorum (4 Feb. 1919).
32 ABEM, 1061: Delacroix to R. Norton (19 July 1919); Mrs. Norton, "Why Jeanne's Face Shone on Christmas Night," 600-601.
33 ABEM, 1077: BASEC to Van Den Bosch (24 May, 5 June 1919).
34 ABEM, 1071: Van den Borght to the Nortons (15 Aug. 1919); ABEM, 1077: Van den Bosch to R. Norton (24 July 1919).

their education. They received what they had requested, with a Gospel of John and a tract.[35]

But how could the BGM assist in alleviating the needs of the civilian population, as the country was still dealing with food shortages? The Nortons appealed to the accumulated goodwill and asked the government for permission to buy food in army stores and hand it out to civilians. After some hesitation, they were allowed to buy "a few tons of Quaker Oats and a few hundred boxes of condensed milk and American chocolate."[36]

Because they had heard that Protestants were receiving less aid than Roman Catholics, the Nortons wanted to be assured that the help they provided would reach the intended receivers.[37] They requested that the government provide trucks with drivers to enable them to organize the distribution themselves. The truck request was refused initially, as there was already a structural dearth of freighters. This prompted Norton to hold a day of prayer on 15 January 1919. Coincidence or not, that same day, they received an unannounced visit from a Colonel with whom they were acquainted and who asked what he could do to express his gratitude for the Nortons' efforts for Belgian soldiers. They asked him to speak to the Army Transport Department on their behalf, and he organized for their request for trucks to be granted. The Liberal Minister of War, Fulgence Masson, then wrote to confirm the arrangement.[38]

The relief work focused on the French-speaking regions of Mons, Charleroi, and Tournai, where the need was the most pressing, and there were relatively many Protestants. At the local level, distribution was primarily carried out by the local spiritual leaders and aimed at its members. Now and then, the Nortons traveled to the regions to help with the distribution.[39] After the first and free distribution, the participating pastors decided it was better for people's self-respect if they paid a small amount for the relief goods. This money was then used to buy more goods, especially footwear. A car journey through Belgium showed a pressing need for food, clothing, and footwear.[40] Goods were also distributed to families and orphans in Brussels. Most families insisted on paying. Only the very poorest and soldiers' families were not required to pay, but the others paid a fraction of the actual value, which enabled the BGM "to help those who are still poorer."[41]

---

35 ABEM, 1071: Van den Borght to R. Norton (8 Aug. 1919), Nortons to Van Den Borght (11 Aug. 1919).
36 This was part of the remaining stock of the Commission for Relief in Belgium. Mrs. Norton, "When Belgians Said 'Thank You' for Gift Boxes," 395; E. Norton, *Ralph Norton*, 157.
37 Whether or not these rumors were true cannot be ascertained.
38 E. Norton, *Ralph Norton*, 157; ABEM, 1061: Masson to R. Norton (6 Aug. 1919).
39 Howard, "Taking Bread to Belgium," 185.
40 E. Norton, *Ralph Norton*, 158; ABEM, 897: R. Norton, *Telegram to Trumbull* (14 Jan. 1919).
41 Mrs. Norton, "When I Told the Belgian Queen a Story," 299.

The end goal was evangelism. The following passage from a thank-you letter for a baby outfit shows that this indirect approach bore at least some fruit: "Touched by all your affection *we are convinced that this can only be prompted by your faith*, your only aim being to serve in all and for all, our Lord Jesus Christ. I hereby promise to bring up my child according to your teachings, that he may be worthy of you, and that he may be always a devoted servant of our Lord Jesus Christ."[42] This indicates that using humanitarian aid to familiarize people with the Evangelical faith was working. The Nortons felt that these people would form the core group for the weekly Gospel services.[43]

Public opinion regarding Protestant relief work was positive during the country's rebuilding when all help was accepted.[44] The BGM and the American Methodist Episcopal Church (South) took advantage of this sentiment. Like the Nortons, they came to Belgium during the aftermath of the war. It focused on material aid, taking an active part in rebuilding the Ypres area and opening a shelter there. In the Brussels area, social activities were also deployed. Acting on the pressing needs of Belgian society fit in with the Methodists' understanding of 'social holiness.'[45]

Military leaders, politicians, and the royal family were also positive about Protestant humanitarian work. Before Ralph Norton traveled back to the United States in August 1919 to raise funds and recruit workers, he received the following letter from Chief-of-Staff General Gillain:

> Your work is finished, it ended with the Victory, but the memory of the good deed you did during a painful time will remain with us all.
> Your friends have demonstrated their altruism with an untiring generosity under the skilled leadership of an elite: though you may demur, as may Madame Norton, I am pleased to pay tribute to what you have done for the sake of our courageous ones.
> Because of you, they have had the feeling that the soul of the family, the soul of friends had come to encourage them, and in the bitterness of separation, they were comforted.
> 'You say you hope to continue!' Consequently, after having so happily served our heroes, do you not think it worthwhile for your Work to consider

42 Ibid.
43 Ibid.
44 The Salvation Army, for example, recorded in 1929: "The slow movement of earlier years has become accelerated since the European War, for service then rendered to Belgian soldiers and refugees revealed more clearly the Army's aims and methods. Consequently, both Government and people are more favourable than formerly." Salvation Army, *The Salvation Army Yearbook*, 63.
45 From the start, the idea was that direct relief work would eventually be discontinued in favor of constructive relief, evangelism, and educational work. To this end, the Methodist Mission was established in 1922, which soon started church planting work. Streiff, *Der Methodismus in Europa im 19. und 20. Jahrhundert*, 169, 218; Schuler, "Crisis, Collapse, and Hope," 9-10; Dale, "Aperçu sur l'évangélisation en Belgique," 13.

the children of the soldiers, the poor children of Belgium, and to spend its energy creating happiness among them, softening the harsh imprint of four long years of German monstrosities.
You have been in our pillaged and destroyed towns, you have crossed [sic] our ravaged, desolate countryside, you have witnessed the sad spectacle of our destitute refugees, you have visited anaemic men, women, and children in our isolation wards, who suffered from too much of privation.
You have given them all clothing, you have distributed food, but you know how great their distress, how numerous their needs remain.[46]

Ralph Norton thought he could profit from this optimistic sentiment and applied for an import tax exemption on civilian clothing destined for demobilized soldiers. The Prime Minister replied that this was impossible for shipments sent in private capacity. In true Belgian fashion, he suggested by way of compromise that they address the shipment to the Central Clothing Depot of the Belgian army in Brussels. This 'formality' would make the Ministry of War the receiver of the shipment. The ministry's office would then clear the shipment through customs in Antwerp free of charge so the BGM could collect it there.

Delacroix also assured Norton that the BGM would be entirely at liberty to decide how to distribute the goods.[47] This approach corresponded with the Belgian government policy of that time, which tried to avoid offending the US, which it viewed as predominantly Protestant. It feared that this might undermine the American willingness to help rebuild Belgium. Similarly, the Belgian diplomatic post in Washington, DC, advised Belgian Cardinal Mercier to tread carefully during public appearances during his planned visit to the US in 1919 to avoid alienating the Protestants and the Jews.[48]

The goods arrived in Antwerp by sea, were transferred into trucks by German prisoners of war, and then driven to Brussels, where the BGM rented a large warehouse from a Christian friend. Edith Norton used the opportunity to share the Gospel with her 'captive audience.' Her story shows that she linked the progress of the war to liberal Protestant theology, which had arrived in the USA from Germany:

---

46   For the original quote, see ABEM, 897: Gillain to R. Norton (1 July 1919).
47   ABEM, 1061: Delacroix to R. Norton (12 June 1920).
48   The trip's aim was two-fold: to thank the Americans for their support and to raise money for the library of the Catholic University of Leuven, which had been destroyed during the war. As the Protestant minority was still regularly persecuted by Roman Catholics in Belgium, these generous gifts by their fellow believers were not at all appreciated by Belgian Protestants. AFPSFA, 347: Emile de Cartier to Paul Hymans, 3 Dec. 1918; AECMB, 2336: Anet and Gautier to 'Our American Friends' (24 March 1923).

> I ventured ...: 'Do you know what caused this war? ... It was the fact that Germany threw the Bible overboard – the precious gift delivered to her by the hand of the faithful servant of God, Martin Luther. She threw it away and followed the mammon of unrighteousness, and see where it has brought her. Shan't we all return to the Bible and to the Christ of the Bible?[49]

In 1920, the BGM still carried out much relief work and evangelism.[50] The Minister of War once more instructed the directors of the Central Clothing Depots in Antwerp and Brussels to give the Nortons and their representatives all the help they would need to clear the goods imported through customs without paying import tax. He also ordered that their men be put at their disposal to load the goods into trucks.[51] On 12 June 1920, Delacroix wrote to the BGM on behalf of the government to thank them for the clothes and other relief goods they had donated and distributed. In this letter, he describes their work as a "mission so useful and very humanitarian."[52] A month later, Joseph Wauters, a Socialist and the Minister of Industry, Employment, and Supplies, wrote in reply to a letter from Ralph Norton that he unofficially "put at your disposition stable no. 13 – and this as much as necessary or possible. I ask you to designate a director who will contact Major Blaise next week, who will be acting on my behalf."[53]

When the Nortons took residence in their Brussels' hotel on 18 December 1918, this was a temporary solution. In April 1919, they permanently closed the BASEC office in London and opened permanent BGM headquarters in Brussels instead. This change is in keeping with the general policy of many faith missions of having their office in their target country.[54] The building was located at Voorlopig Bewindstraat 17, only 150 meters from the hotel. Upstairs, offices and an apartment for the Nortons were created, and at the back of the building, there was "ample space for a book room and storing our merchandise."[55] The ground floor was refurbished as a meeting hall with a capacity of 100 people.

49 This was not a unique position. Their friend A.C. Dixon made similar comments. Glass, "Transatlantic Fundamentalism: Southern Preachers in London's Pulpits during World War I," 173-174; Mrs. Norton, "When I Told the Belgian Queen a Story," 299; ABEM, 1122: Diary E. Norton (22 Jan. 1919).
50 The file on the Nortons, which the Justice Department held in its Public Safety division from September 1919 onwards, has Ralph's occupation down as "Commissionnaire du Relief for Belgium" or "Official of 'Relief for Belgium,'" and Edith's as none. It is unclear whether this entry reflects what the Nortons told the official who wrote the entry, or whether this was his own perception. AJDPS, A1.130.724: File Ralph and Edith Norton.
51 ABEM, 897: Masson to the Directors of the Clothing Depots in Antwerp and Brussels (13 Feb. 1920).
52 For the original quote, see ABEM, 897: Delacroix to R. Norton (12 June 1920).
53 For the original quote, see ABEM, 897: Wauters to R. Norton (17 July 1920).
54 ABEM, 1076: Nortons to Van Den Eede (19 March 1919).
55 "The Nortons in Brussels, Belgium," 297.

As we already said at the end of the previous chapter, the Nortons envisioned following the example of McAll in France, so they pursued a strategy to evangelize the entire population in cooperation with the existing Protestant churches. They dreamed that their befriended soldiers, once demobilized, would "form a nucleus for Bible study in their cities and villages," which would eventually "grow into large assemblies of believers."[56]

However, the Nortons' idea of ecumenism was clearly delineated. They were well aware that this would sooner or later clash with the two main denominations, the UPECB and the ECMB. Already during their Atlantic Crossing in November 1918, Ralph Norton clearly defined his conditions in what can be described as a 1920s fundamentalist impulse. They had to "believe that men are eternally lost without Jesus Christ and are only saved through his precious blood: men likewise who believe that the Bible is God's word to man and final authority in all matters of belief and doctrine."[57]

A month later, while waiting in Folkestone for the ferry to Boulogne, the Nortons were handed a list of leading Evangelicals in Belgium by the Open Brethren pastor Nock, with whom they occasionally had cooperated during the war. The number of names on the list was minimal and probably in line with Marchandise's account, which we discussed earlier. Therefore, the BGM can be described in Stefan Paas' terminology as a confessional mission that targets Catholic territory and distinguishes between orthodox and 'heretic' Protestantism.[58]

It was only a matter of time before the Nortons distanced themselves from the majority of Belgian Protestantism, as demonstrated by their correspondence with soldiers in the Spring of 1919. The Nortons confirm they want to cooperate with "those who love the Lord in truth."[59] In anticipation of when they would start their own services, they worshipped on Sundays at the Baptist and Brethren churches in Saint-Gilles and Brussels, often accompanied by soldiers.[60]

Within a year, on 14 September 1919, the BGM held its first regular church service in its Headquarters. This was in line with Torrey's ideas, who had stated that the established churches "would prove to be an icehouse" to new con-

---

56 Mrs. Norton, "The Nortons' Work in Belgium," 806.
57 E. Norton, *Ralph Norton*, 153; Treloar, *The Disruption of Evangelicalism*, 70.
58 William (1863-1930) and Mary (1859-1929) Nock arrived in Belgium in 1896 with the aim of evangelizing and planting churches. They returned temporarily to the UK during World War I to work among Belgian refugees and Belgian and British soldiers in London and Folkestone, which was their hometown. The Nocks sent New Testaments to believing soldiers, who circulated them among their friends. Paas, "The Making of a Mission Field," 62; Tatford, *West European Evangel*, 43-44; E. Norton, *Ralph Norton*, 150, 156; Mrs. Norton, "Another Milestone in Belgian Evangelization," 155; R. Norton, "Norton's Work in Belgium," 718; ABEM, 895: Nock to E. Norton (1 Dec. 1916); ABEM, 1122: Diary E. Norton (20-21 Dec. 1918).
59 For the original quote, see ABEM, 1082: Nortons to Naert (12 March 1919).
60 ABEM, 1122: Diary E. Norton (5, 19, 26 Jan., 2, 9, 16, 23 Feb., 9, 16 March, 13 April, 11 May, 1, 8, 22 June 1919).

verts and, therefore, "[it] is oftentimes best to have the mission itself organized into a church.[61] It illustrates how Americans emphasize mission organizations' individual and voluntary nature and demonstrates the Fundamentalistic logic that would become the mission's DNA.

Although the BGM had not officially excluded any Protestant church or organization as partners in evangelism, they had experienced during the joint distribution of humanitarian aid that the UPECB and ECMB were heterodox denominations. And so, the Nortons concluded that they could not refer their contacts to these churches. This view was shared by others such as Hoffman and the Dutch theologian Valentijn Hepp. He stated that "[n]early all of the Wallonian part [of the ECMB] has been won over to modernism or at least ultra-left ethics. Scripture criticism is running rampant."[62]

In February 1920, the BGM discussed a field study to redefine the mission's strategy with a select group of friends from Baptist and Open Brethren circles. The BGM's goal would be redefined from aid and evangelism to evangelism, church planting, and apologetics. In evangelism, they would focus on open-air preaching, colportage, personal conversations, child evangelism, and activities for women. The church planting strategy would be starting home meetings and opening small meeting halls in as many small towns as possible. In clear Fundamentalistic language, the mission declared that it should "be ready to defend the faith that we profess against the attacks of rationalists, no matter where they come from, no matter their origin. We will resist attacks made against the Bible, the Word of God; against the facts and miracles therein contained; against the person and the work of Jesus Christ."[63] And so, a head-on collision with the UPECB and ECMB was only a matter of time.

This became apparent in the fall of 1919 during an evangelistic rally with Ruben Saillens from Paris. At the close of these meetings, neither the Brussels' ECMB nor the UPECB parish were mentioned as places in Brussels where the 'sound' Gospel was preached in French.[64] This led to strong criticism by ECMB's Jean Meyhoffer.[65]

In response, BGM's Donald Barnhouse organized a tête-à-tête to discuss their theological views. This was followed by a second meeting, at which Ralph Norton and Odilon Vansteenberghe accompanied him. Both sides confirmed their theological positions and agreed to publish the discussion in a

61 Torrey, *How to Work for Christ*, 266.
62 Hepp, "Synode – Indrukken," 34.
63 For the original quote, see La Mission Belge Evangélique, *La Mission Belge Evangélique*, 2; Howard, *A New Invasion of Belgium*, 68-69, 159; E. Norton, *Ralph Norton*, 161.
64 Mrs. Norton, "When New Shoes Bring Rapture," 715.
65 What some in UPECB and ECMB also found annoying was the 'altar call' and the registration of contact details of those who responded. The first points to a cultural difference, and the second is simply a logistic step to ensure that those who had expressed an interest could be contacted. AECMB, 2226: Aloïs Gautier, "A Grave Fact," 1; Gautier, "Un fait grave," 49-52.

leaflet.[66] Norton intended to expose the theological views of Meyhoffer and his like-minded pastors of the ECMB and the UPECB and claimed that a few of their pastors shared the BGM's position. He hoped that Belgian Protestants would see that, despite their evangelical phraseology, most of these denominations' pastors held liberal views.[67] According to the BGM, the founders of the two denominations would have agreed with the doctrines taught during the campaign with Saillens.[68] This was confirmed by Meyhoffer, who added that he was closer to the Unitarian ideas of the Liberal Protestant church in Brussels. Consequently, lengthy discussions were held at the ECMB Synod in the autumn of 1920 "about the various views on the Holy Scriptures which existed at the heart of the Church, threatening to cause a schism."[69] Despite tough talks, the two parties did not want to risk a split. And so, the motions that had been tabled were withdrawn.

From then on and deep into the twentieth century, the opposing parties fought trench warfare. The BGM repeatedly described the situation in both denominations as alarming and that they contained "only a pitiful minority" of faithful believers.[70] The UPECB and ECMB leadership first branded the BGM as "Mission-d'évangélisation-par-le-Quaker-et-le-Corned-Beef," and later called them narrow-minded.[71] This reaction is in line with the mainline protestant reaction, which labeled the American revivalist wave in post-World War II Europe as "an essentially alien, proselytizing, judgmental, holier-than-thou type of Christianity."[72]

Clearly, the BGM was not interested in further consultation and discussion with denominations or pastors they regarded as liberals. It soon used its evangelical and detailed statement of faith as "a test of fellowship and a base of separation," a faith mission practice and a typically American approach.[73] Driven by premillennial eschatology, the Nortons isolated themselves from most of Belgian Protestantism. The disastrous events in recent years pointed unambiguously to the final stage of world history in the near future. As time was running out, the focus had to be on saving as many souls as possible. There simply was no time for reasoning.[74]

---

66 Before its publication, the text of the leaflet was submitted to the pastor, who confirmed it was a truthful description. ABEM, 889: Barnhouse, "A Conversation...," s.d., 1, 6.
67 Mrs. Norton, "The Norton's Work in Belgium," 718.
68 Printed version Barnhouse, "A Conversation...," [2].
69 For the original quote, see: Winckel, "Buitenland," 3.
70 ABEM, 889: Barnhouse, Manuscript "A Conversation...," 4-5.
71 Delhove, "Histoire du protestantisme belge depuis la création de l'Etat belge jusqu'au début de la seconde guerre mondiale, 1830-1939," 96.
72 Paas, "Mission from Anywhere to Europe," 7.
73 Walls, "The American Dimension in the History of the Missionary Movement," 17.
74 Sutton, *American Apocalypse*, 6.

Tent and Roulotte of the Belgian Gospel Mission, 1928.
[KADOC-KU Leuven: ABEM, 1162]

4
DRIVEN BY DISPENSATIONAL URGENCY

Why did the Nortons, with unwavering commitment, pursue their plans to develop an evangelistic initiative in postwar Belgium, even without a clear-cut strategy, and aware that their fundraising would soon cease to profit from the 'poor little Belgium' sentiment? As fully committed Dispensationalists, the Nortons interpreted recent events on the world stage through the lens of eschatological sections of the Bible. By doing so, the Nortons became convinced there would be a window of five or ten years at most to evangelize in post-World War I-Belgium.[1] By that reasoning, the proclamation of the Gospel was a matter of utmost urgency.[2]

Dispensationalism is a fairly recent school of premillennialism. It emerged in the nineteenth century with John Nelson Darby, who propagated his ideas in evangelical circles in Europe and North America. In the United States, this idea was propagated and refined by authors and leaders such as William E. Blackstone, Adoniram J. Gordon, and James H. Brookes and woven into a tight and

---

1   This timeframe was left out in the published version. ABEM, 886: Guy Fleming, "Manuscript."
2   The Nortons were among many people on whom this premillennial eschatology had a great missionary impact. An example from Belgium is that of Nicolaas de Jonge. He saw himself as an evangelist who would "accept all without distinction in name, denomination, age, outward living conditions, education or past," and who explained his acceptance of his posting to Brussels with an eschatological argument: "With a view of the Second Coming of Christ I felt the need to go there where the masses are." For the original quote, see Valeton Jr., *N. de Jonge in zijn leven en werken*, 5-6; Pocock, "The Influence of Premillennial Eschatology," 129, 131-132.

cohesive system by Cyrus I. Scofield. In 1896, Scofield published *Rightly Dividing the Word of Truth*. His *Reference Bible* (1909), full of annotations and cross-references, was instrumental in globally popularizing Dispensationalism.[3] An important cause for its instant success was that it was published when cultural optimism was about to collapse. This may explain why the Apocalypse was also a dominant theme in Roman Catholicism and Eastern Orthodoxy around that time.[4] The BGM would actively encourage its workers to buy this Bible to use it for their sermon and Bible study preparations and actively disseminate Dispensationalism in Belgian Evangelicalism.

Historic premillennialism has much older roots and goes back to some of the Church Fathers. Both schools interpret *Revelation* 20 quite literally and expect the return of Jesus Christ just before the millennium, a thousand-year earthly reign of Christ with believers from all eras. Premillennialism has a pessimistic and apocalyptic view of the future in which the world will witness a time of unprecedented catastrophes, both man-made and natural, cosmic signs, apostasy, the restoration of Israel, and the emanation of the Antichrist culminating in the imminent return of Jesus Christ. Whereas dispensationalists hold that all 'true believers' will escape this Great Tribulation by suddenly leaving the earth and meeting Jesus Christ in the sky in the 'rapture,' Historic premillennialists believe that the 'true Church' will be heavily persecuted during the 'Great Tribulation'.[5]

In both variants, missions are urgent. Not only may it be the last opportunity to introduce people to the Good News, but the global diffusion of the Gospel is one of the biblical conditions for Jesus' return. Speeding up the missionary efforts might advance His imminent return. Blackstone even predicted that the 'Age of the Gentiles' would end sometime between 1916 and 1934.[6] The Nortons were instructed in dispensationalism during their studies at MBI. After graduation, Norton and his wife associated with outspoken proponents of dispensationalism, such as Sir Robert Anderson, Reuben A. Torrey, and Cyrus I. Scofield.[7]

---

3   Marsden, *Fundamentalism and American Culture*, 37; Robert, "'The Crisis of Missions': Premillennial Mission Theory and the Origins of Independent Evangelical Missions," 44.
4   Jenkins, *The Great and Holy War*, 141-146.
5   Pocock, "The Influence of Premillennial Eschatology," 130; Baker, "Dispensation, Dispensationalism," 343-345; For an overview of the delta of modern Dispensationalism, see Sweetnam, "Defining Dispensationalism," 191-212.
6   Blackstone, "The Times of the Gentiles and the War in the Light of Prophecy," 686-687.
7   Dispensationalism was first mentioned as part of the curriculum in the 1900 catalog. When Ralph Norton started his studies in 1899, the curriculum of the 1898 catalog was still being used. Weber, *Living in the Shadow of the Second Coming*, 45; *Catalogue of the Moody Bible Institute for Home and Foreign Missions*, 18, 20; Fiedler, *The Story of Faith Missions*, 37; Boyer, *When Time Shall Be No More*, 90-91.

Global events seemed to amazingly confirm the dispensational interpretation of the eschatological Bible passages. In the ominous year of 1917, the United States entered the war, Russia witnessed two revolutions, resulting in a Communist takeover, and the Holy Land was liberated from the Ottoman Empire. The world events seemed even more to fit the premillennial doom scenario, so it became an instant best-seller. On top of this came the Spanish Flu of 1918, killing fifty to a hundred million people and affecting to some degree one in three of the world's population. And so, premillennial pessimism was at a height among American Evangelicals, and on both sides of the Atlantic, eschatology was a common issue in Protestantism.[8]

If we zoom in on Europe, the Treaty of Versailles (1919) enforced peace settlement did not bring much-needed political calm. In March 1920, there were riots in the Ruhr Valley, which had just been demilitarized after a foiled coup in Berlin. In August of the same year, a conflict broke out between Poland and the USSR. There was no harmony among the allies, and the United States changed its European policy after President Wilson lost the elections of 1920.[9] When the German government refused to continue paying after an initial payment had been made under the terms of the Treaty, France started a cold war with Germany. Still, the United Kingdom did not follow suit. This cold war led to a temporary French-Belgian occupation of the Rhine Valley in 1923.[10]

A year earlier, in 1922, Mussolini had assumed power in Italy, and from 1925 onward, his reign could be described as dictatorial. Like most Dispensationalists, the Nortons considered 'Il Duce' instrumental in preparing the way for the Antichrist.[11] In 1932, they even had a private meeting with him in Rome.[12] Although their preliminary estimation of the remaining time to evangelize Belgium had been exceeded by then, the Nortons maintained that the End of Times was still imminent.

8   Already in his 1909 edition, he solidified Darby's claim of 1868 on Ezekiel 38 that Russia played a decisive role in the invasion of Israel. But now it seemed even more accurate. Jenkins, *The Great and Holy War*, 177-178; Sutton, *American Apocalypse*, 69-70, 181-182; Koops, "Dutch Calvinist and Catholic War Sermons," 286; Hutchinson, and Wolffe, *A Short History of Global Evangelicalism*, 157.
9   Gerard, "De democratie gedroomd, begrensd en ondermijnd," 945-946.
10 Stevenson, "International Relations," 26-27.
11 The Nortons paid him a personal visit in 1932. During the meeting, Ralph Norton shared his conviction that according to his interpretation of Biblical prophecies, the Roman Empire would be restored before Jesus' return and that he expected this to happen shortly. True to form, Mussolini showed interest and took notes of the Biblical references. The Nortons wrote an influential article on their encounter in the *Sunday School Times*, and the Second Italo-Ethiopian War (1935-1937) seemed to confirm dispensationalist interpretations of Biblical prophecies concerning Italy. R. Norton, "Dreigende rampen," 1-2; R. Norton, "Europe's Impending Disaster," 259; R. and E. Norton, "A Personal Interview with Mussolini," 423, 426; Hankins, *American Evangelicals*, 91; Sutton, *American Apocalypse*, 213-216.
12 R. and E. Norton, "A Personal Interview with Mussolini," 423, 426.

The political upheaval of 1917 in Russia not only reinforced the Nortons' identification of Russia as the great northern kingdom of Biblical eschatology, but it also led to a deep and growing fear of Communism in interwar Europe. This public fear was fed by a communist uprising in the German state of Bavaria and a short reign of Bolsheviks in Hungary. The Netherlands had remained neutral during the war, but in November 1918, a socialist revolution was brewing. The Soviet strategy at the time encouraged division in the capitalist world, and the cooperation between the Soviets and Germany suited this strategy.

In Belgium, two communist parties were founded in 1920 and merged a year later under the impulse of the Komintern. Initially, it had little success as no leading figures from the Socialist Party joined. As part of the opposition, the Socialists found it easy to counter the criticism they received from the Communists.[13] Thus, the communist movement remained small in Belgium.

Even in the absence of a strong communist party, Belgium witnessed a time of political instability. The political landscape changed permanently as the general multiple voting right for men was replaced by a general single voting right for men. From this point onward, nearly all Belgian governments were coalitions. Between 31 May 1918 and 11 May 1926, the country had nine short-lived governments in succession. Now the war was over, and there was no need to continue the *union sacrée* (sacred union) much longer. A climate of mistrust and challenging economic times led to political instability.

When the socialists won the elections of 16 November 1919, Vandervelde's party became almost the same size as the Catholic party. It supplied four ministers to the second Delacroix Government. Cooperation with Vandervelde during World War I had been so positive that Ralph Norton commented, "While we are not putting our trust in princes, it looks as if the Lord has given us three or four Cyruses at Court." The government survived for less than a year.[14]

Around 1923, several factors led to monetary instability in Belgium. Inflation was high, and the Belgian Franc weakened against foreign currencies, which hampered Belgium's economic recovery from the war. For the BGM, this meant that more could be done in Belgium with donations from the US.[15] By early 1924, the Belgian economy had returned to the production levels of 1914.

---

13 Passmore, "Politics," 96; Willequet, "Het politiek en sociaal leven," 19; Gerard, "De democratie gedroomd, begrensd en ondermijnd," 888, 995; Gerard, "De binnenlandse politiek," 80; Stevenson, "International Relations," 27; "Het Politiek en sociaal leven," in: *De dolle jaren in België*.

14 This is a reference to King Cyrus, the Persian king who ended the Babylonian captivity of the Jews and decreed the rebuilding of the temple in Jerusalem. See *Ezra* 1:1-8. ABEM, 850: Minutes Board of Trustees (14 Jan. 1920); Gerard, "De democratie gedroomd," 920.

15 Two main causes of inflation were monetary miscalculations by the government and the fact that Germany failed to make all its payments under the Treaty of Versailles. Veraghtert, "Het economische leven," 62; Gerard, "De democratie gedroomd," 957-958; Blom, Lamberts, and Milis, *Geschiedenis van de Nederlanden*, 347.

Unemployment fell fairly low, and many miners switched to physically less demanding jobs. Mining employers were forced to recruit large numbers of foreigners to continue the production of the coal mines.[16]

Convinced that 'the rapture' could occur any time in the foreseeable future, the BGM Committee in Philadelphia had given the Nortons carte blanche to cooperate with any protestant church in Belgium in evangelism.[17] Of course, the unspoken condition was that these denominations had to be orthodox in theory and practice, as Modernism was considered the apostasy prophesied for the End-Time church.[18] And as we have seen in the previous chapter, the mission decided soon to operate from an almost complete and self-imposed isolation.

For decades, the BGM would only cooperate on a case-by-case basis with individuals from other Protestant churches who passed the mission's test of orthodoxy.[19] It goes without saying that the ECMB and the UPECB did not receive the mission's solo approach well. Mutual recriminations went on for decades, resulting in a fractious relationship between mainline protestants and evangelicals in Belgium that lasts to date. At the same time, it also exemplifies Americans' priority on "individual freedom and the ability to make their decisions on what to do largely as individuals rather than as collective groups."[20]

Nevertheless, the BGM got off to a flying start. They were backed by a favorable exchange rate, Ralph Norton's fundraising capabilities, and the positive image that the Nortons had built up among Belgian soldiers during the war. The mission used several methods – mostly well-tried – to evangelize the entire civilian population.

First of all, it organized multiple evangelistic meetings with befriended international speakers. The first event, which led to the aforementioned row with the ECMB and the UPECB, was held from 13 to 25 January 1920 in the Salle de la Madeleine in Brussels. Large posters, handbills, and people carrying sandwich boards announced Baptist pastor Ruben Saillens from Paris as the main speaker.[21] The Nortons had met him during the war. The mission claimed the meetings attracted between 1,000 and 1,400 people each day. They were all given the tract *The Way to God* by Moody, and after the Gospel was preached, decision cards were handed out with a reply slip. A total of about 200 completed decision cards, roughly 1.5% of the total number of visitors, were sent back to

---

16 More than 40% of the miners in the province of Limburg were foreign-born. Veraghtert, "Het economische leven," 77.
17 ABEM, 850: Minutes Board of Trustees (22 Feb. 1921).
18 Weber, *Living in the Shadow of the Second Coming*, 171.
19 One example is a joint campaign with members of the Methodist Mission and Silo during the Blood Procession in Bruges, a Catholic ritual traditionally attracting large crowds. Together, they distributed 25,000 bilingual tracts paid for by the American Methodist Mission (South). Van Belleghem, "Brugge op 4 mei," 3-4.
20 Moreau, "Evangelical Missions Development 1910 to 2010 in the North American Setting," 7.
21 Mrs. Norton, "Another Milestone in Belgian Evangelization," 155.

headquarters. The senders were invited back a fortnight after the meetings, to which nearly half of them reacted.[22] This response rate was much lower than anticipated, based on their experiences during the war.

Despite this setback, the mission organized a second evangelistic campaign with Saillens in November 1920. This time, it was in Charleroi, some fifty kilometers south of Brussels. The city council allowed them to use the Charleroi Bourse building for free. This rally was also communicated as a success, but no exact numbers were given.[23]

In 1921, meetings were held with Pastor Antonio Antomarchi from Paris, who later joined the BGM, and with Charles Dentan from France.[24] During the following year, Dr. Griffith Thomas, Rowland V. Bingham, Dr. Ralph Atkinson, Philip E. Howard Sr. and Dr. Leon Tucker spoke in various places in Belgium at the invitation of the BGM.[25] In 1923, a campaign was organized in Liège with Charles Inwood.[26] Dutch evangelist Johannes de Heer was invited to special meetings in Dutch- and French-speaking Belgium in several places.[27]

22   Ibid.; Mrs. Norton, "An Old-Fashioned Revival in Belgium's Capital," 287.
23   These were a Baptist church, a Brethren meeting, and a Salvation Army corps. "Another Year in Belgium's Evangelization," 263.
24   Frenchman Antomarchi (1868-1952) worked with the Salvation Army in Europe for some time. He then became a minister in the Reformed Church in France before joining the BGM. Antomarchi was one of the initiators of the Revival Movement *Brigade Missionnaire de la Drôme*. Characteristic of this movement were the use of the imminent return of Christ as an argument for conversion and the strong emphasis on sanctification as well as three-to-four-day campaigns in parishes on the invitation or with the approval of its minister. It also held annual conventions. The movement was active from 1922 until 1940. Dentan (1865-1935) was President of the UCJG in Vigan. Mrs. Norton, "Diplomas for Six Belgian Students," 564; R. Norton, "What Hath God Wrought in Belgium?," 297; E. Norton, *Ralph Norton*, 180; Fath, *Du ghetto au réseau*, 340; Mehl, "Jean Cadier, le matin vient," 401-402; Poujol, *Un féminisme sous tutelle*, 131; Mrs. Norton, "How I Met Aline D'Amour of Poperinghe," 327.
25   Given Antwerp's role as an important port for sea traffic to Africa, it is probable that Bingham made a stopover there on a journey between Canada and Africa. William Henry Griffith Thomas (1861-1924) was an Anglican cleric who was a member of the Resolutions Committee for The World Conference on Christian Fundamentals (1919). Together with Lewis Sperry Chafer, he founded Dallas Theological Seminary. Dr. Ralph Atkinson was a United Presbyterian who worked with Dwight L. Moody, 'Gypsy' Smith, and Wilbur Chapman. Dr. Walter Leon Tucker, editor of *The Wonderful Word*, toured the world as an evangelist. He had good relations with the Christian and Missionary Alliance and taught at Los Angeles Bible Institute from 1910-1913. He often spoke on "prophetic and dispensational subjects." Rowland V. Bingham graduated from Albert B. Simpson's Bible school in New York City and founded Sudan Interior Mission, originally named Africa Industrial Mission. For many years, he edited *The Evangelical Christian*, a conservative evangelical periodical from Toronto that focused on missions. ABEM, 855: R. Norton, *Prayerletter*, (1 Dec. 1922); "The Rev. Dr. Hugh Black, of New York," *The Pittsburgh Gazette Times*, 5 Feb. 1916, 10; "Dr. W. Leon Tucker," 403, 414; Frizen, *75 Years of IFMA*, 119-121.
26   An advertisement appeared in the *Christelijk Volksblad* newspaper describing Inwood as the global representative of the Keswick Convention. *Christelijk Volksblad*, 29 Sep. 1923, [4]; Inwood, "Making Christ Known in Needy Belgium," 523.
27   *Christelijk Volksblad*, 29 Sep. 1923, [4].

The Nortons' friend and mentor, Ulysse Cosandey, regularly came from Switzerland. In 1924, he spoke at meetings in Brussels and Wallonia.[28] A year later, he came over for a campaign in Brussels with the theme "The global crisis, its causes, its effects and its remedy."[29] His compatriot, Salvation Army Colonel Charles Fermaud, was another frequent visitor.[30] In 1925, he was to speak in Antwerp and Liège initially, but additional meetings were organized in Brussels and several BGM churches in Wallonia.[31]

That same year, the mission invited Paul Kanamori, described as the Moody of Japan, to Antwerp, Liège, and Brussels.[32] He was asked to speak about his experiences with Biblical criticism, which was a sideways attack on the UPECB and ECMB and an expression of emerging 1920s fundamentalism within the organization.[33] Lastly, special meetings were held with Pastor Ch. Freundler from Lausanne and American Lewis Sperry Chafer.[34]

All these international speakers were dispensationalists or had links with the Holiness movement, so they shared a DNA with the mission. Initially, the BGM recorded the number of "decisions" made at these meetings, but within a few years, this practice was silently abandoned. One could argue that the figures were good by Belgian standards yet disappointing compared to American figures.

28 Ulysse Cosandey (1864-1949), worked for many years in the Salvation Army. From 1902, until he left the organization, he supervised the Franco-Belgian Territory. Ulysse Cosandey, *L'armée du Salut aux pays latins*, 65-69; "Frappants exaucements de prière en 1924;" ABEM, 1038: "Reports of conversions," 1924.
29 "La Crise Mondiale, ses causes, ses effets, son remède," *Notre Espérance*, 1 Oct. 1925, 1-2.
30 Salvation Army's Lieut.-Colonel Charles Fermaud was raised in a Free Church environment. From 1879 to 1912, he was General Secretary of the World's Alliance of YMCAs and was considered one of the key leaders of the Association in Europe. Muukkonen, *Ecumenism of the Laity*, 254; Steuer, "Key Figures YMCA Secretaries;" R. Norton, "What Hath God Wrought in Belgium?," 296.
31 "Visite du Colonel Fermaud," *Notre Espérance*, 15 Feb. 1926, 33.
32 Tsurin 'Paul' Kanamori (1857-1945) was a Japanese evangelist. His theological position, which was Evangelical to begin with, became influenced by Higher Biblical Criticism from the early 1890s onward, but the death of his wife led him to return to Evangelicalism. From 1915 onwards, he worked as a traveling evangelist. Some called him 'the Dwight L Moody of Japan.' Horner, "Kanamori, Tsurin ('Paul')," 353; "Le Moody du Japon," *Notre Espérance*, 15 Nov. 1925, 3.
33 "Nieuwtjes uit de Zending," *Onder Ons, Maandelijksch bijblad van Onze Hoop* 1, n° 19 (1925), [2].
34 Lewis Sperry Chafer (1871-1952) came from a Congregational background. He graduated from Oberlin College in 1892. From 1901-1914, he worked as a traveling evangelist, keeping close links with Moody Ministries. He participated in the annual Northfield Bible conferences, where he met C.I. Scofield, under whose influence he became a staunch dispensationalist. In 1913, he assisted Scofield in founding the Philadelphia School of the Bible. 1924, he co-founded the Evangelical Theological College in Dallas (currently Dallas Theological Seminary) with W.H. Griffith Thomas. His links with Europe consisted of his friendship with F.B. Meyer and his Th.D. from the Protestant Seminary in Aix-en-Provence (1946). "Frappants exaucements de prière en 1924," 2; Hannah, *An Uncommon Union*; "Gebedsverhooring," 2; *Notre Espérance*, 1 Oct. 1925, sec. Trait d'Union, 2.

However, a more convincing explanation is that the number of decisions was much higher than the number of converts joining the local BGM churches or other churches. This explanation is linked with Belgian politeness, in which people will respond positively to an offer to avoid offending.[35] By omitting the number of decisions, the BGM could still write encouraging reports for its supporters in the United States.

The most substantial focus in evangelism was on colportage and the distribution of free literature. Since the nineteenth century, this method has been tried and tested in transatlantic evangelicalism and revivalism.[36] Most literature, first "simple tracts and booklets," later books and pamphlets, were translated into French and Dutch and published "as the need arose and funds were forthcoming."[37] Titles like Scofield's *Rightly Dividing the Word of Truth* (into French), Blackstone's *Jesus is Coming* (Dutch), Chafer's *Grace* (French), and Sidney Collett's *The Scripture of Truth* (French) confirm the theological position of the Nortons.[38] Evangelical philanthropist Lyman Stewart and his brother Milton largely bore the costs for translating and publishing Torrey's *What the Bible Teaches* (in French) and *How to Work for Christ* (in Dutch).[39] Like the evangelistic meetings, these books were also advertised in *Christelijk Volksblad* (Christian Newspaper for the People), Silo's periodical.[40]

In January 1925, the BGM started its own publication, *Onze Hoop* (Our Hope) in Dutch and *Notre Espérance* (Our Hope) in French. The aim was twofold: evangelism and apologetics: to "fully maintain the spiritual authority of the Bible and rigorously continue to teach its literal meaning."[41]

According to Donald Barnhouse, colportage and literature distribution were helpful because Belgians tended to be curious. However, the BGM's success in literature distribution has more to do with implementing legislation concerning compulsory primary education shortly after the Armistice. As a result,

35 See also Chapter 2, p. 35.
36 The following dissertations give insight into this topic on both sides of the Atlantic. Omon, "Voor het hoogste het beste;" Sagan, "Only a Tract."
37 For a list of the period under research that is as complete as possible, see Appendix 3, 209-215. E. Norton, *Ralph Norton*, 180.
38 Collett is characterized as a "prefundamentalist and essentially late nineteenth-century Evangelical." No copy with bibliographic data has been preserved. E. Norton, "Counting Blessings in Belgium," 390; Blackstone, *Jezus komt*; Chafer, *Le Salut*; ABEM, 850: Minutes Board of Trustees (13 Feb. 1922); E. Norton, "A Place Where His Honor May Dwell," 207; Bassett, "The Theological Identity of the North American Holiness Movement," 108.
39 *How to Work for Christ* had already been published in Dutch in 1907. Whether the Nortons knew this, and whether the book was still available, cannot be ascertained. Torrey, and Ten Broek, *Hoe brengen wij zielen tot Jezus?*; Torrey, *Ce que la Bible enseigne*; Howard, *A New Invasion*, 192.
40 One example of such a book review is the one for *Jezus komt* (Jesus is coming) by W.E. Blackstone. De Jonge also worked hard to make Protestant literature available for Flemish people. *Christelijk Volksblad*, 1 Dec. 1923, 3; 9 Feb. 1924, 3-4.
41 For the original quote, see "Untitled," *Notre Espérance*, 1 Oct. 1925, 1.

Belgium witnessed a rise in literacy in the interwar period. The distributed literature found a ready demand with very few affordable reading materials available, especially in more impoverished areas.[42]

The first supply of 100,000 copies of Gospels, Testaments, and Bibles arrived in Antwerp in May 1919. Shortly after that, the first BGM colporteur started his activities. Gospels and tracts were also given to some unconnected evangelists and colporteurs.[43] Two years later, Norton placed an extra large order of New Testaments because he had "almost a presentiment, that the time was coming when we would see a literal fulfillment of *Amos* 8:11, 'Behold, the day is come, saith the Lord Jehovah, that I will send a famine in the Land, not a famine of bread, nor a thirst for water, but of hearing the words of Jehovah.'" Moreover, he feared that soon "it would be impossible to secure Bibles, Testaments, and Gospels," which were ordered in Russia. Although he was mistaken, he never apologized for his presentiment.[44]

As a result of the colportage activities, people asked for more free literature or a further explanation of the Gospel. In tracts and personal correspondence, the BGM systematically countered Catholic teachings on salvation and eternal life. Some of these contacts had been exposed to Protestantism before.[45] Although the BGM boasted in its transatlantic communication that colportage was a phenomenal success, the reality was more nuanced. Whereas Colporteur Mietes managed to hand out more than 4,000 New Testaments in six months, his colleague Macors complained that only a few people were interested in his evangelistic literature.[46]

A third method the BGM applied was tent meetings. They were usually scheduled in towns or neighborhoods of a large city where the mission intended to plant a new church.[47] The first 'tent campaign,' as it was called, was a joint initiative with the Open Brethren in 1920. It led to a division, as both parties claimed the idea was theirs. And so, the BGM bought their own tents, one for each part of the country. James Hunter, invited as the main speaker for the 1920 initiative, led the tent work in Wallonia for some years.[48] Dutchman Cornelis

---

42 Barnhouse, "Dynamiting Where Tyndale Was Burned," 634; Reynebeau, "Mensen zonder eigenschappen," 39; Goffinet and Van Damme, *Functioneel analfabetisme in België*, 8.
43 Mrs. Norton, "That First Sunday Service in Belgium," 1919, 484.
44 ABEM, 850: Minutes Board of Trustees (13 Feb. 1922).
45 ABEM, 1038: Vanderbeeken, Quaadpeerds [sic], "Report to the American Bible Society" (April 1923).
46 ABEM, 850: Minutes Board of Trustees (13 Feb. 1922).
47 E. Norton, *Ralph Norton*, 166-167; Howard, *A New Invasion*, 128.
48 James Hunter (d. 1947) was from Scotland. After working in Algeria as a missionary for ten years, he went to French-speaking Switzerland, where he lived and worked from 1913 until his death in 1947. During World War I he worked among interned Belgians in the Netherlands. In 1933 he published *Chants Joyeux: Recueil de cantiques pour cultes, réunions d'évangélisation, de sanctification, missions, écoles du dimanche, etc* (Bureau du Réveil, 1933). Dale, *Aperçu*. 15; E. Norton, *Ralph Norton*, 166; Tatford, *West European Evangel*, 45.

Potma led the tent evangelism in Flanders until he was forced out of the BGM for embracing Pentecostalism.[49]

Because it was so accessible, this method of evangelizing was regarded as suitable for Belgium. In the weeks leading up to the tent meetings, colporteurs handed out literature and hung up posters. Once the tent had arrived, the singing of members of nearby evangelical churches inside would also attract people. Some would go in; others would listen from outside.

As in the rallies with international evangelists, those attending were initially asked to sign decision cards during the meetings. As many people signed out of politeness, they soon decided to hand the cards to people as they left. Howard Sr. believed this adapted approach was also imperative in countries where converts would face opposition from their social environment.[50]

Between 1920 and 1925, the tent went in Flanders to places such as Deinze, Eeklo, Kortrijk, Lokeren, Sint-Niklaas, Zele, and Zelzate. In Wallonia, the tent was erected in Ath, Boussu, Braine-le-Comte, Cuesmes, Dour, Huy, Leuze, Liège, Sart, Warquignies, Wasmes, and Wihéries, to name but a few.[51] Some of the more prominent towns and cities were visited for several consecutive years, where the tent would be set up in different parts of town each time. Occasionally, the reports mention the social context of the chosen location, a socialist working-class area or an area characterized by drunkenness and debauchery.[52]

The mission also held evangelistic open-air meetings in town squares and weekly markets from its early years.[53] BGM workers put down a portable organ, stood around it, and sang the opening hymn. Next, the evangelists handed out "sheets containing the hymns" to interested bystanders and, perceiving the audience to be beyond the reach of the BGM churches or posts, "told the Gospel story as directly as possible."[54] In other places, such as Kortrijk, it took some persuasion before local authorities permitted them to preach at the market square. Exceptionally, public interest was so great that police presence was needed to keep the crowds in check. In 1919, this was the case in Sint-Niklaas.[55]

Evangelism among children via Sunday and Thursday Schools was also part of the mission's evangelistic strategy. In the early years, this branch of the

---

49 For Potma, see Van der Laan, and Van der Laan, *Pinksteren in beweging*, 152-153; "Another Year in Belgium's Evangelization," 263.
50 Howard, *A New Invasion*, 131-132.
51 Mrs. Norton, "Diplomas for Six Belgian Students;" ABEM, 899: "Loose notebook leaf;" "Frappants exaucements de prière en 1924;" "Het Evangelisatiewerk in België," 1.
52 "Met de tent door het land," 1.
53 E. Norton, *Ralph Norton*, 164; Dale, *Aperçu*, 25; De Raaf, *Een eeuw Silo*, 19; "Uit het Vlaamsche land," 12; Van Wageningen, *Gedenk de dagen*, 2:97.
54 Howard, *A New Invasion*, 116; "Een en ander over de Missie," 13.
55 ABEM, 1038: Reports of conversions, 1924.

BGM was directed by Philip Howard Jr.[56] He used programs from the American Vacation Bible Schools, which were translated into Dutch and French. The Thursday Schools primarily targeted those who were unable to attend on Sundays. In 1922, fourteen of the twenty-one stations had Sunday School and Children's Meetings. As the children supplied their addresses, BGM workers took the opportunity to visit the parents.[57] Once the nature of these children's activities became apparent and Catholic clergy started to speak out against it, many parents withdrew their children.[58]

Pupils of the regular, i.e., Catholic schools in Belgium who kept attending the Sunday and Thursday Schools usually faced repercussions. To illustrate, the BGM in Lokeren reported that the children were asked at their schools to hand in their Gospels in exchange for a small reward. The teachers then burned the Gospels that were collected this way. The report mentions that despite the prize, some children did not hand in their Gospels.[59] The firmness of these children is explicitly mentioned for fund-raising purposes, but the story is credible as a whole. Most pastors and evangelists claimed that the Sunday and Thursday Schools resulted in conversions, but no exact numbers supported their statements.[60]

Finally, the BGM started to use of evangelistic motorcars in the mid-1920s. Financed by the Methodist Mission, this innovative method was introduced by Silo missionaries in Flanders. It was considered a good way of finding out where it was "necessary and very desirable" to start new local churches.[61] Although the number of registered motorized vehicles rose rapidly between 1922 and 1925 from 49,177 to 115,770, the arrival of a Gospel car would be an attraction in itself in the remote areas where it was intended to be used.[62]

And so, in July 1924, Walter Teeuwissen suggested buying several motor vehicles "with sleeping quarters with room for literature, organ and stereoptical machine, and platform."[63] However, Ralph Norton felt that before making such a significant investment, they would need to explore the possibilities of this evangelistic method. Therefore, a year later, in June 1925, evangelists Duvanel

---

56 Children's work was also carried out as part of tent campaigns. Howard, *A New Invasion*, 149-150, 154-155, 172; Hopkins, "How God's Word Grows and Prevails in Belgium," 471.
57 Howard, *A New Invasion*, 151-152.
58 Ibid., 151; Dale, *Aperçu*, 19.
59 ABEM, 1038: Report to the American Bible Society (April 1923).
60 ABEM, 850: Minutes Board of Trustees (13 Feb. 1922); Howard, *A New Invasion*, 66.
61 De Schepper, "Onze eerste reis met de Evangelisatie-automobiel," [3].
62 Institut national de statistique (Belgium), ed., *Annuaire Statistique de la Belgique et du Congo Belge*, 1925), 234; Ibid (1926), 273; Ibid., (1927), 223; Ibid., (1928), 225.
63 ABEM, 1038: Stories of conversions. In the USA this method was in use as early as in 1917. See: "Carrying the Gospel by Motor," 85; See "Evangelist Touring Country Travels in Unique Auto," 12.

and Golay of the British Open Air Mission (OAM) were invited to Belgium. They campaigned with what they called the "motor wagon" for three months.[64]

Adolphe Max (1869-1939), the Mayor of Brussels and a Liberal, permitted to hold "simple Gospel services in leading squares and boulevards, [...] with a degree of police protection."[65] What the police protection entailed is described in OAM reports to their British supporters. "A constable, sent on purpose to each meeting, discreetly enforces silence on all opposers."[66] A photograph of the vehicle, printed in a leading Belgian newspaper, provided free publicity for the campaign.[67] Norton was now convinced that such a vehicle could reach working-class people in less densely populated areas in a short amount of time. And so, the BGM purchased a "Gospel car" for this region.[68]

Having discussed the various evangelistic methods deployed by the BGM, we will now focus on their church-planting strategy. Although the rapture was expected to occur within a few years, the converts needed a spiritual home until that much-expected moment. Starting their own congregations would allow the BGM to instruct the converts entirely along the lines of their theology.

When the mission installed its headquarters at the Rue du Gouvernement Provisoire in Brussels in the Spring of 1919, it constructed a church hall with a capacity of 100 people on the ground floor. Starting with evangelistic meetings a few months later, it developed into regular church meetings before the end of the year. Soon, the (French-speaking) meetings became overcrowded, and a larger place was found nearby. On 2 October 1921, the new hall, which had a capacity of 400-500 people, was dedicated in the presence of Ruben Saillens, Walther Mouchet (from Switzerland), and J. Kennedy Maclean. Seventy-five percent of those who were present were reported to be regulars.[69] The empty hall at headquarters in the Rue du Gouvernement Provisoire was used as a Dutch-language station from 1923 onward.[70]

Convinced of the imminent rapture, the Nortons initially only wanted to rent suitable places for mission halls. However, almost all contracts were terminated within days as the Catholic clergy pressured landlords not to rent their properties to Protestants.[71] A good example is Antwerp, where the BGM started church services as early as November 1919, even though there were already sev-

---

64 The Open Air Mission started with this evangelistic method in its homeland, the UK, as early as in 1921. "Visite de 'L'Open Air Mission'," 1-2; "Tijdspiegel," 532.
65 "Wonderful Meetings in Brussels with Our Gospel Motor Wagon (From France)," 1.
66 Ibid., 3.
67 Ibid., 6-7.
68 Bolomey, "Through Belgium in a Gospel Motor Car," 581. E. Norton, *Ralph Norton*, 194.
69 Howard, *A New Invasion*, 89.
70 "... pour atteindre, si possible [!], la population flamande des quartiers populeux." "Les Débuts de notre Mission (suite)," 1.
71 The Methodist Mission encountered similar problems. AMCBC, 25: Thonger, Report of the Activities of the French Church at Antwerp, during the Year 1924-1925.

eral Protestant churches.[72] So, the mission's activities relocated from a rented house at Amerikalei 154 to a purchased café nearby. The newly acquired building at Karel Rogierstraat 8 was dedicated on 22 January 1921.[73]

This unforeseen development set the course for the BGM's long-term presence in its mission field. On the other hand, it complicated fundraising. They had to explain in detail why so much of the donated money had to be spent on real estate instead of personnel or evangelistic materials. For their supporters, renting property was deemed far better stewardship in apocalyptic times.[74]

Whereas the first three church plants were strategically chosen: in Brussels, the capital; in Antwerp, the main harbor; and in Bruges (1920), the capital of West Flanders, regular services at other locations were founded at invitations by local Protestants. The case of Liège illustrates this. In 1921, a delegation of dissatisfied members from the local UPECB Church invited the mission to start meetings there. As the BGM deemed the local UPECB and ECMB congregations in this key industrial city to be tinged with Modernism, they accepted the invitation.[75] An interesting historical parallel can be drawn here. During the nineteenth century, the ECMB had started a church in Liège even though there was a local UPECB church already because "the pastor at Liège did not want to spread the Bible" and "did not preach Jesus Christ, and Jesus Christ crucified, who died for our sins and resurrected for our justification."[76] The BGM station in Liège was placed under Henry Bolomey, a Swiss pastor who had led a French-language church in the United States for some years.[77] During the first months, the meetings were held in the parlors of a local businessman. In 1922, a building was purchased.[78]

Already in 1920, meeting halls were opened in smaller cities and rural towns. Tent-evangelism often obtained an entrance to these locations. In 1920, the mission stations in Cuesmes and Leuze were the first direct results of this methodology. After a tent campaign, some of these early church plants were not as promising as initially thought, so the policy to immediately open a hall in such locations was adjusted. Instead, small meetings would be started at the home of one of those who were interested. Only when the meetings outgrew the homes where they were held, the BGM would begin looking for a building.[79]

---

72 During the first few years, the stations were called departments (*afdelingen*), See the stamp on the tract *Een geschiedenis van vier appelen* (Silo: 1919 or 1920). For a list of all known BGM church planting activities, see appendix 4, 215-218.
73 Mrs. Norton, "How I met Aline D'Amour of Poperinghe 327."
74 E. Norton, "Preaching Under Difficulties in Belgium," 60.
75 ABEM, 850: Minutes Board of Trustees (13 Feb. 1922).
76 For the original quote, see Dale, *Aperçu*, 66-67; Anet, *Protestant Churches in Belgium*, 52.
77 ABEM, 850: Minutes Board of Trustees (12 Feb. 1925); Howard, *A New Invasion*, 122.
78 ABEM, 855: R. Norton, Prayer Letter (1 Dec.).
79 Ibid.

Sometimes, the only available place for regular meetings was in an "inconvenient part of the town."[80] A good example is the hall in Eeklo, in the province of East Flanders. The hall was no more than "a remodeled stable. The floor was of earth; a large doorway that had opened out toward the street on the side of the stable had been boarded up and hung with a rough curtain. ...The little meeting hall was separated somewhat from the dwelling house of the property by a dark courtyard."[81] Because of its location and accommodation, it could not be expected to draw people from the middle and higher classes. This was considered a disadvantage, as one of the BGM's objectives was that its locations had to be attractive to all classes of society.

If needed, the BGM worked with go-betweens to rent a property. Such was the case in French-speaking Ath (1922), a town with 12,000 inhabitants. A lady who rented a small place with a capacity of 45 people on behalf of the mission was repeatedly threatened with eviction. A Bible school student led the meetings as part of his practical training. The local population branded everyone who entered the building as Protestant, which made the threshold for those interested quite high.[82]

Occasionally, meeting places were opened due to literature evangelism. A good example is Blauwput, a hamlet now part of Leuven, Flemish-Brabant. Colporteur Michiels met a man who had been in the Netherlands during the war and had read the Bible there.[83] After their return to Belgium, this man and his wife returned to Roman Catholicism because of social pressure.

Nevertheless, he opened his home for BGM meetings. Few people reportedly came in, but some stood outside listening to the meetings.[84] It took three years for the host to break definitively with Catholicism, but he immediately started assisting Michiels. This shows that in the early days, there was no requirement for the hosts of house meetings to be converted. Apparently, interest in the Gospel and willingness to listen were sufficient.

Winterslag is another station whose beginnings can be directly linked to the colportage. It was a part of the fast-growing mining town Genk in the province of Limburg, with inhabitants of many nationalities: Poles, Russians, Germans, Czechs, Italians, Dutch, and, of course, Flemish.[85] The request to start meetings here dates back to 1924. As in Blauwput, the mission began here with house meetings. The lady of the house was a Seventh-Day Adventist, but the colporteur led

---

80   Howard, *A New Invasion*, 111.
81   Ibid., 117-118.
82   ABEM, 850: Minutes Board of Trustees (13 Feb.).
83   It is unclear whether he was interned or a refugee.
84   ABEM, 1038: Stories of conversions.
85   E. Norton, "A Place Where His Honor May Dwell," 207.

her "to see the truth, and [she] walks now in the full liberty of the grace of God."[86] After some time, a meeting hall was opened in the nearby center of Genk.[87]

Occasionally, a church planting pioneer was sent after a thorough survey of a region's political, economic, and religious situation. Such was the case in Manage, La Louvière, and Gosselies in the French-speaking province of Hainaut. Manage emerged as the favorite location, and Herman Quenon was told to find a house that could serve as a home and meeting room.[88] After some difficulties, a suitable building was found, and the inaugural service was held on 15 February 1925. It was followed by a series of evangelistic talks, which was by now becoming a much-used approach for the BGM.[89]

Although the mission sent triumphant reports to its North American backers, several church plants were short-lived. Meetings started in the Flemish cities and towns of Oudenaarde, Vladslo, Blankenberge, and Passendale in 1920 and Ieper in 1921, were quietly abandoned and no longer mentioned in records from 1922 onwards.[90] The reasons for this are known at other locations. The station in Soignies closed only a few months after its opening. The Catholic landlord had terminated the renting contract, and no suitable alternative building was found. The station in La Hulpe closed after three years in April 1923, when only one family, who regularly attended the services with their four children, was left. They were evicted because of their faith and moved to Limal, ten kilometers away, where the BGM had opened a station in October 1923.[91]

By 1925, six years after the first meetings started in Brussels, the BGM had mission posts in eight of the nine provinces of Belgium. A colporteur was active in the sparsely populated province of Luxembourg. Church planting initiatives did not start until 1930.[92]

Most mission posts were planted in Hainaut province, with a relatively strong Protestant presence predating World War I.[93] Although the BGM's humanitarian aid in the immediate aftermath of the hostilities focused on this province, there is no hard data linking this gesture with its church planting activities here. Moreover, five of the ten church plants in Hainaut started sometime after the material relief had ended. The BGM's greater success here compared to other

86 ABEM, 1038: Stories of conversions.
87 In 1917, the coal mine in Winterslag was the first operational mine in the area. ABEM, 1038: Stories of conversions.
88 No details have been preserved on his method of observation. ABEM, 877: Minutes Personnel Committee (18 Sep. 1924).
89 The speaker for this series was Antonio Antomarchi. Ibid. (31 Jan. 1925).
90 ABEM, 855: Prayer letter, n.d. [1920]; Mrs. Norton, "How I met Aline D'Amour," 327.
91 R. Norton, "What Hath God Wrought in Belgium?," 296; *La Mission Belge Evangélique* [1919], 5.
92 This is not to be confused with the neighboring country of Luxembourg. R. Norton, "Is Belgium the Key to Europe's Evangelization?," 121.
93 Overbeeke, *Jaarboek voor de Protestantse Kerken in België 1966*, 40.

BGM mission posts in 1925

Province	Number of stations
West Flanders	5
East Flanders	4
Antwerp	1
Limburg	2
Brabant	5
Hainaut	10
Namur	1
Liège	2
Luxembourg	0

provinces must be seen in the light of the lesser influence of the Roman Catholic church in this region, which had been industrialized at an early stage.[94]

With almost one in three BGM stations planted at locations with a Protestant presence, the existing Protestant churches were rightfully annoyed by the mission's church-planting strategy. The Nortons saw nothing wrong in their approach. As dispensationalists, they were convinced that apostasy was irreversible. This meant that providing an alternative for existing liberal protestant churches was as crucial as planting churches in an area with no Protestant presence at all. That being said, the BGM method also fits nicely in the American way of practicing evangelism, which Europeans perceive as managerial.

But the mission also collided with the other newcomers, the Methodists. In 1923, its station in Hoboken (as of 1983, a southern district of Antwerp) became unstaffed for unknown reasons. While the church activities were temporarily led from nearby Antwerp, the Methodists also began church planting initiatives in Hoboken, probably without consultation. Already in 1921, Methodist William Thonger wrote about the BGM: "It is impossible to say what this Mission is doing at Antwerp as they are only just starting the work in this town."[95] This is far from the truth, as both missions became active in Antwerp in 1919.

Neither party tried to see how they could complement each other. From the side of the BGM, this attitude must be seen in the light of the Nortons' negative experiences with the growing influence of liberalism among the US Methodists. When the BGM found out about the Methodists' church-planting initiatives in Hoboken in February 1924, it immediately, and earlier than planned, sent Jacob Servaas Sr. to restaff the local BGM station. Clearly, the mission feared losing people to a rival church planting mission.[96]

94 Witte, "Vrijdenkersbeweging 1873-1914," 103.
95 AMCBC, 24: Report on Prospects for Evangelistic Activity at Antwerp (26 Feb. 1921).
96 ABEM, 877: Minutes Personnel Committee (19 Feb. 1924).

Having discussed the mission's evangelistic methodology and church planting strategy, we will conclude this chapter by examining the audience it reached. We must bear in mind that the data on the kind of people attending the BGM's activities originates from reports sent to supporters in the United States. On the one hand, the Nortons communicated that most results were achieved among the working classes and the marginalized. This meant, of course, that transatlantic financial support would still be needed for quite some time.

In graphic language, conversions of alcoholics, disabled persons, illiterate people, and laborers were shared with the mission's supporters, just as reports of women being hit by their husbands on account of becoming Protestant. Conversions of people with an occult background were reported with great verve to demonstrate the transforming power of the Gospel.[97]

On the other hand, the mission emphasized in its early years that it also reached the higher classes. The French-language church in Brussels had some prominent members, especially General Emile Galet, former aide-de-camp to King Albert I and President of the Military School, Lieutenant-General Lesaffre of the Military School, and Professor Lagrange.[98] Yet these men are also listed as members of the ECMB in Brussels. This apparent contradiction can be solved by considering that Galet, Lesaffre, and Lagrange frequented the BGM's church services in the capital but remained members of the ECMB. As the BGM had not yet worked out a church order, it could describe any frequent visitor as a member. This was conveniently played out in the mission's international publicity.

Another remarkable link with the higher classes of society was Count Raymond du Val de Beaulieu (1865-1932). The Count was converted to Protestantism in England during the war. After returning to Belgium, he attended several BGM meetings in Brussels and subsequently invited the mission to get involved in his village. He allowed them to start meetings in one of the outbuildings on his estate in Cambron-Casteau.[99]

---

[97] ABEM, 1038: Stories of conversions; E. Norton, "Treasure Seeking in Belgium," 448.
[98] Lesaffre is known to have been baptized in the BGM church in Brussels. After World War II, he became a follower of Frank Buchman's Moral Re-Armament. Charles Lagrange was a Protestant, an eminent mathematician, director of the stellar observatory in Brussels, and lecturer at the Military School. He further developed Belgian Major Brück's 'historical law,' in which human evolution is explained based on the earth's magnetic field and chronology in the Bible. Lagrange extended this teaching by adding ideas taken from the Pyramid of Cheops. He published his ideas in Lagrange, *Leçons sur la Parole de Dieu*. In Lagrange's theory, the history of the world can be divided into periods of five hundred years each, during which particular nations dominate. The last dominating power was a combination of the UK and the USA. Emile Galet was a follower. Jaumotte, "Notice sur Charles Lagrange, membre de l'Académie," *Annuaire* (1992): 37-39; Howard, *A New Invasion*, 98-99; Boudin, "Galet, Emile (1870-1940)," "Lesaffre, André Jules Paul (1882-1982)," 51, 77.
[99] Howard, *A New Invasion*, 125-127.

The workers of the BGM in 1923.
[KADOC-KU LEUVEN: ABEM, 1325]

5
WORKERS FOR THE VINEYARD

In the aftermath of World War I, the Nortons believed the Belgians would be receptive to the Gospel "because of the recollection of all that was done for the soldiers during their time of distress."[1] Aligned with other faith missions, the Nortons embraced a broad spectrum of human resources and prioritized practical skills over theological training. They welcomed individuals from all walks of life, both men and women, Belgian nationals and foreigners, alumni from international Bible schools or people with other relevant training, and workers trained at the BGM's Bible schools.

When the idea of starting a postwar mission in Belgium was taking shape, the Nortons invited the members of the Scripture League to play an essential part in the organization's development.[2] Most of them were low-ranking servicemen but had the advantage of being natives. During their international tours with Chapman and Alexander, the Nortons must have seen the benefits of activating nationals to evangelize among their fellow countrymen and women.

Because the 'trench apostles' could only be deployed after demobilization and most prospective Belgian workers had to be trained in evangelism and church planting, a plan B was needed.[3] The Great Commission had to be fulfilled before time ran out. Therefore, evangelists and pastors had to be attracted, and they could be deployed immediately.

---

1 Howard, *A New Invasion of Belgium*, 48.
2 See Chapter 2, page 44.
3 In the end, only one 'trench apostle,' Cyrille Macors, became a BGM pastor. ABEM, 119: Grandjean to Barbezat (26 Jan. 1926).

An obvious place to recruit was Belgium. Those convinced to join the mission not only had the advantage of being native speakers but were also familiar with the socio-cultural environment and how to address Roman Catholics. Most of the Belgian recruits transferred from existing denominations, such as Silo and the ECMB. Considerably better wages attracted some colporteurs, and one even got promoted to pastor.[4] The mission's headhunting came on top of their words of condemnation of the UPECB and ECMB – no wonder they would rather see the BGM's back.

However, some Belgians with no link to existing protestant churches were also recruited. A good example is Remy Meersman from Oostrozebeke. He had converted to Protestantism during his internment in the Netherlands, where he also came into contact with the Nortons.[5] Back home, Meersman started independent house meetings, and contact was somehow lost for some time. When that was restored, Norton invited him to join the BGM.[6] Meersman first objected by saying that he had no theological training and, therefore, could not work as a pastor. This was no problem for Norton, who had surrounded himself, like other faith missions, with 'neglected forces of Christianity.'[7] Within the eschatological framework, it was natural to have a minimal number of selection criteria.

In another way, Elisée Daumerie is also an example of these 'neglected forces.' He joined the mission as a colporteur in 1924 at the age of 59. A few years later, when the gap between the offer and demand of personnel had narrowed, the personnel policy had changed, and age had become a reason to refuse candidates.[8]

Despite the high hopes and continued efforts to train, hire, and deploy Belgian nationals, their number remained small. For various reasons, most also left the BGM through the back door after a few years. One of the few exceptions to this rule was Odilon Vansteenberghe. As a converted war invalid, he had volunteered with the Nortons in London. He joined the mission on 1 November 1919 and stayed the rest of his life. Within a few years, he became the Nortons' right-hand and co-director after their death.[9]

---

[4] Jan Arnold Monsma, Fernand Castiaux, and August Parmentier came from the ECMB, Karel Blommaert worked for Silo in the Flemish church in Dunkirk (France). ABEM, 850: Minutes Board of Trustees (13 Feb. 1922); AECBM, 1311: Balty to Meyhoffer (11 Feb. 1920).

[5] ABEM, 1039: Tabellen inzake de verspreiding van het aantal Bijbels en Nieuwe Testamenten (1917-1918).

[6] Meersman, ed., *Gods werk gaat door*, 44, 46; Mietes, *Hij reisde zijn weg met blijdschap*, 13-14.

[7] "Welnu, zo kan God u ook gebruiken." Meersman, *Gods werk gaat door*, 44; Cruickshank, Grimshaw, *White Women, Aboriginal Missions and Australian Settler Governments*, 117.

[8] ABEM, 293: Winston Sr. to Van Goethem (9 Jan. 1929); ABEM, 877: Minutes Personnel Committee (19 Feb. 1924, 24 Sep. 1930, 15 Jan., 13 Feb. 1931).

[9] Mrs. Norton, "When New Shoes Bring Rapture," 715.

It was clear to the Nortons that they also needed to recruit missionaries from abroad. Having toured with Chapman and Alexander around the globe, the Nortons knew the disadvantages of speaking with an interpreter. And during their work among Belgian soldiers, it became clear that Edith's skills in French were too limited, and both had no working knowledge of Dutch. Therefore, the BGM preferred native speakers, preferably even bilingual candidates. We will not provide an extensive list here but demonstrate the diversity in nationality and church background of the men and women who joined, which is another characteristic of faith missions.[10]

Alumni from Bible schools in the United States and Canada, such as Henry A. Bolomey, Abraham C. van Puffelen, and Walter Teeuwissen, were recruited.[11] Bolomey was a French-speaking Swiss who pastored a Home Missionary Church in Torrington, Connecticut. His preaching on the Second Coming of Christ had led to problems with some congregation members. Van Puffelen and Teeuwissen had Dutch roots. Teeuwissen worked in a Reformed church in Spring Lake, Michigan. After his return to the US, Van Puffelen ministered in the Presbyterian Church.[12]

Some non-native speakers also admitted. British national H.K. Bentley, Baptist and graduate of Moody Bible Institute, may have had some knowledge of French as the son of a British missionary to Congo.[13] But most were Americans and usually had ties with the Nortons' circle of friends. Donald G. Barnhouse was the first paid worker.[14] John C. Winston Sr. joined in 1922 and soon became the Nortons' right-hand man, like Vansteenberghe. Philip Howard Jr., grandson of Henry Clay Trumbull and the father of Elisabeth Elliott, joined the same year. He had worked for the Pocket Testament League and returned to Philadelphia in 1927 to become the Sunday School Times editor.[15]

---

10   Fiedler, *Ganz auf Vertrauen*, 157.
11   "God continues to wonderfully bless us here and yet our great need is workers. If you have any students there in the school, particularly college men and women, who would like to consider this field, we would be glad to get in touch with them, as we have so many open doors here, and no one to go in. Of course, if they knew French or Flemish they would be all the more acceptable." Mrs. Norton, "A Macedonian Cry from Belgian Cities," 211; ABEM, 1084: Nortons to Dale (27 Feb.); ABEM, 850: Minutes Board of Trustees (20 July 1922); Norton, *Ralph Norton*, 160, 179.
12   ABEM, 850: Minutes Board of Trustees (20 July 1922); Howard, *A New Invasion*, 87.
13   His father, William Holman Bentley went to Congo with the Baptist Missionary Society in 1879. ABEM, 850: Minutes Board of Trustees (13 Feb. 1922).
14   Torrey introduced him to the Nortons after an evangelistic campaign in New York, but no further details are known about this meeting. Torrey knew Donald Barnhouse because he was Dean of the Los Angeles Bible Institute (1912-1924) when he was a student there and knew of the latter's interest in Missions. Hopkins, "What made the man?," 18, 35; Russell, "Donald Grey Barnhouse: Fundamentalist Who Changed," 35.
15   Griffith Thomas, "Speaking 'by Interruption' in Belgium," 592.

Due to the rapid expansion of the work, a Committee for the Examination of Candidates for the Belgian field was created in Philadelphia in 1922 for North American candidates. This would speed up the admission procedure, as the review of candidates could be done without the Nortons.[16] To further improve the recruitment process, the application processes of several older faith missions, including China Inland Mission, Africa Inland Mission, and South-America Missionary Union, were studied.[17]

This led to the writing of a document entitled 'Concerning Candidates,' which was intended to be used for application. Given the interdenominational character of the mission, candidates were not asked about their opinions on church ordinances or church government.[18] The document also throws an interesting light on the BGM's identity in its early years. The profile stipulates that candidates had to be Spirit-filled.[19] This Holiness term was clarified as follows: "This, in its estimation, stands for persons who are strictly evangelical in doctrine, ardent students of the Word, devoted to the person of Christ, prayerful and praiseful in spirit and constantly sane, humble, loving, sacrificial and steadfast and filled with longing for the salvation of the souls of his fellows."[20]

Workers were also recruited from Europe, with varying success. Most of them were French- or Dutch-speaking. Due to the urgency, recruits from various denominational backgrounds were accepted. Now and then, this would lead to severe tensions about baptismal practices, which would drag on for decades. Later, when structural deficits severely affected the BGM, discontent arose among the European workers, who had discovered that their American colleagues benefited from better financial conditions.[21]

Already in 1920, the BGM went to France to recruit recruits for Wallonia and Brussels. They desired Ruben Saillens to join, but he refused as he had a specific calling for France. Instead, he offered to come regularly for evangelistic campaigns, which was gladly accepted.[22] Jean Wälti and Antonio Antomarchi were recruited successfully. The latter was converted in Brussels and had worked with the Salvation Army in Europe for some time. In France, he

---

16 It consisted of the Nortons (ex officio), Mr. Philip E. Howard Sr., Mr. Charles G. Trumbull, and Mrs. J. Harvey Borton. ABEM, 850: Minutes Board of Trustees (13 Feb. 1922).
17 ABEM, 877: Minutes Personnel Committee (4 March 1924).
18 ABEM, 877: Concerning Candidates.
19 Ibid.
20 Ibid.
21 See Chapter 10, page 177ff.
22 ABEM, 850: Minutes Board of Trustees (3 Feb. 1921).

ministered in the Reformed Church and was one of the initiators of the Revival Movement *Brigade Missionnaire de la Drôme*.[23]

In Switzerland, the mission's network played a crucial role in recruitment. Walter Jung applied to the BGM on the advice of Charles Fermaud. Jung had been an evangelist in Russia from 1912 until 1920 and had served as a minister of Reformed churches in Switzerland and France. He initially had problems with the statement of faith, especially with the claim that people cannot be saved after they have died. After a conversation and reading some literature sent to him, he eventually signed the statement of faith, stating that he did this wholeheartedly.[24]

Charles Grandjean responded to an advert in *La Bonne Revue* in which the BGM announced its vacancy for an experienced bookkeeper. During World War I, he had been working in Swiss refugee camps with the YMCA Federation of French-speaking Switzerland. He joined after Frank Cockrem, who worked for Open Air Mission, had encouraged him to present himself to the BGM.[25]

In the Netherlands, workers were recruited for Flanders. Dutch evangelist Johannes de Heer was a vital contact, partly through his conferences and partly through his Christian magazine *Het Zoeklicht* (Search Light), created in 1920.[26] He quoted Barnhouse that the BGM recruited up to 100 evangelists and 250 colporteurs for Belgium. This high ambition reflects his theology of missions. As the BGM was considered to be a part of God's redemptive work in

---

23   This movement's characteristics included using the imminent return of Christ as an argument for conversion and a strong emphasis on sanctification. It also held three to four-day campaigns in parishes on the invitation or with the approval of its minister and annual conventions. The movement was active from 1922 until 1940. Mrs. Norton, "Diplomas for Six Belgian Students," 564; R. Norton, "What Hath God Wrought in Belgium?," 297; E. Norton, *Ralph Norton*, 180; Fath, *Du ghetto au réseau*, 340.
24   Fermaud was Lieutenant-Colonel in the Salvation Army, with a history in the Free Church environment and the YMCA. "Trait d'Union, Supplément mensuel de 'Notre Espérance,'" 15 Feb. 1925, 1; ABEM, 877: Minutes Personnel Committee (9 April, 4 June, 13 July 1925); Muukkonen, *Ecumenism of the Laity*, 254; Steuer, "Key Figures YMCA Secretaries."
25   This evangelical periodical was published in Digne, France, by Mr. and Mrs. H. Contesse-Vernier, who were Closed Brethren. ABEM, 877: Minutes Personnel Committee (1 April 1924).
26   Johannes de Heer was a member of the Dutch Reformed (Nederlands Hervormd) church for his whole life, except for a short spell with the Seventh Day Adventists. He was of great importance to the Evangelical Movement in the Netherlands in the twentieth century, partly because of *Het Zoeklicht*, a dispensationalist periodical he started which focuses heavily on the signs of the times that will precede the return of Jesus Christ. Other achievements were his involvement with the Protestant broadcasting company NCRV, tent evangelism with Nederlandsche Tentzending (Dutch Tent Mission), which he established in 1906, and the songbook named after him. In 1905, he visited Wales to study the revival there. Johannes de Heer established a warm relationship with the Nortons and the BGM. A mutual acquaintance was Charles Alexander, whom De Heer had met in London in 1905. Elsman, *Johannes de Heer*, 39; Slagter, "Heer, Johannes de (1866-1961)."

the crucial years before the 'rapture,' a massive success in evangelism was anticipated.[27] The mission never grew that big, and it soon became more realistic and abstained from setting these kinds of targets. This infinitely optimistic ambition is typically American and was irritating for Europeans who knew from experience that Protestant evangelism in Belgium was challenging and met with countless obstacles.

One of the many Dutch who joined over the years is Jan Knecht Sr. He had a Reformed (*Gereformeerd*) background but joined the Seventh-Day Adventists for some time. Knecht Sr. then switched to the interdenominational organization Jeruël before he applied at the BGM in 1921.[28] Daniël Meijer came to Belgium after being approached by Odilon Vansteenberghe. From 1916, he was an evangelist and local director of the *Vereeniging Nederlandsche Landkolonisatie en Inwendige Zending* (Association of Dutch Land Colonisation and Home Missions) in Houtigehage. Meijer led the Antwerp station until his retirement in 1935.[29] Many of the Dutch who joined had a Baptist or free church background. Others had their roots in the Reformed tradition and introduced paedobaptism in the mission.

Although not openly communicated, avoidable conflicts had occurred in the early years, when foreigners were dropped in pioneering situations without any cultural preparation.[30] Because this had acted as a brake on the growth of the church planting initiatives, newly opened stations were soon run by experienced workers whenever possible. Foreign workers who were new to Belgium were placed in existing stations.[31] To slow down the rapid staff turnover, which was also very cost-ineffective, new workers were told they had to "be ready to do no matter what for the good of the work."[32] They started under supervision, and after some time, depending on their qualities, they would then be given more responsibilities.

---

27 "Evangelisatie in België," 247; Zdanowski, "Protestant Millennialism and Missions at the Turn of the 20th Century," 98.
28 Jeruël was an inter-church city mission established in 1894, which combined evangelism with action against poverty. Van Rijn, *100 Jaar Adventkerk in België*, 7; *Maandblad "Jeruël;"* ABEM, 166: Memoires Knecht Sr.
29 This mission was set up in 1906 by local Dutch Reformed (*Nederlands Hervormd*) pastor J.A. Visscher, who combined evangelism with action against poverty. His initiative continued under *Noord-Jeruël* after he moved to The Hague in 1909. No known dependency links exist with Jeruël Rotterdam, but the name and similar methods indicate that the latter may have been an inspiring example. "Jaarverslag," *Ons Heidewerk* 38; "Houtigehage Ds. Visscherwei 71," accessed 21 March 2013, <http://www.smelneserfskip.nl/monumenten/>; ABEM, 877: Minutes Personnel Committee (4 June 1925); "Nieuwtjes uit de Zending," 1 Dec. 1925, 2.
30 E. Norton, "Exploring for Gospel Centers in the Belgian Ardennes," 81.
31 ABEM, 877: Minutes Personnel Committee (28 July 1927).
32 For the original quote, see: ABEM, 50: Winston Sr. to Charensol (1 Dec. 1928).

Despite their high ambitions to recruit as many Belgians as possible, after fifteen years, the mission – like all other Protestant denominations – still heavily depended on foreign workers. The following chart illustrates this.

	1927	1934
Dutch-language churches and stations		
Belgian pastors	4	4
Non-Belgian pastors	6	11
French-language churches and station		
Belgian pastors	5	6
Non-Belgian pastors	7	12
All Belgian churches and stations		
Belgian pastors	9	10
Non-Belgian pastors	13	23

As prospective Belgian evangelists and pastors had to be trained, Edith Norton already suggested having their own Bible school with a brief, practical, and efficient program in November 1918.[33] Preliminary talks with various pastors and workers in England and France led to exploratory contacts with Ruben Saillens for a joint Bible school for Belgium and France. With too many obstacles, the mission decided to found its own training institute.[34] The idea was to train overseas missionaries, most notably for the Belgian Congo, in addition to its main purpose: preparing new BGM workers.[35]

The *École Biblique de Belge* (a grammatically incorrect name), or Bible Institute of Belgium in English, was Europe's first French-language Bible school.

---

33 ABEM, 850: Minutes Board of Trustees (15 Nov. 1918); Brereton, *Training God's Army*, 12, 62.
34 Saillens was not interested in a dispensationalist school with lecturers solely trained according to Moody Bible Institute's curricula. His advanced age and reported lack of support from his denomination were additional objections against a joint Bible school. The school's location, in Brussels or nearby Paris, was another issue on which both sides disagreed. Blocher, "Tel père, quelle fille?," 173-183; Wargenau-Saillens, *Ruben et Jeanne Saillens*, 89-90; "The Nortons in Brussels, Belgium," 298; ABEM, 889: Reasons Why Brussels is the Logical Place for a Bible Institute for the French and Dutch Speaking People, [1922].
35 Mrs. Norton, "Three Rings at the Convent Door-Bell," 624.

It opened its doors on 9 September 1919 with Barnhouse as its director.[36] The school was also "inseparably linked up with the Victorious Life message," a clear hint to the BGM's Keswick holiness identity.[37] In a later stadium, 1920s fundamentalism became more influential within the curriculum. This can be illustrated with the following quote from its prospectus: "The school does not teach the New Theology but holds on to that which the believers have received 'once and for all.'"[38]

The Bible school started with ten students, which was less than anticipated initially. In April 1919, sixty former Scripture League members intended to enroll. Five months later, only four started their training: Arthur Krik, Peter Van Koeckhoven, Frank Van Den Wyngaert, and Victor Van der Kneipen. The only female student was Miss Valentine Denecker.[39] Krik left during the first term because of family problems. Van der Kneipen also quit; he went to Switzerland for several months. The fact that not all students would complete the entire two-year curriculum was not uncommon in the initial stage of Bible schools. The curriculum was not meant to start a career but to acquire practical skills.[40]

Parallel to the recruitment of evangelists and colporteurs, the eschatological urgency to train as many Belgians as possible in the shortest time impacted the student selection criteria in the early years. Students could enter as early as sixteen years of age.[41] As several students were deemed too young, the minimum age was soon raised to twenty-one, similar to MBI and Biola.[42]

The choice to only offer courses in French was quite logical from an outsider's perspective. At that time, Belgian law prescribed that even in Flanders,

---

36 This contradicts Fiedler's suggestion that the Bible school in Nogent-sur-Marne was Europe's oldest French-language Bible school. Fath recognizes that the BGM Bible school was the first Evangelical and interdenominational French-speaking Bible school in Europe but dismisses it as much smaller than Saillens' Bible school. Fiedler, *Ganz auf Vertrauen*, 432; Fath, *Du ghetto au réseau*, 148; ABEM, 1122: Diary E. Norton (9 Sep. 1919); Howard, *A New Invasion*, 69.

38 For the original quote, see: Prospectus of the Dutch-language BGM Bible school, [2].

39 Denecker, a member of a Silo church in Dunkirk, came from a family affected by alcohol abuse. Mrs. Norton, "When New Shoes Bring Rapture," 715; E. Norton, *Ralph Norton*, 163; Barnhouse, "Training Belgians for Congo Missions," 443; ABEM, 1122: Diary E. Norton (10 Sep. 1919).

40 Mrs. Norton, "When New Shoes Bring Rapture," 715; E. Norton, *Ralph Norton*, 163. ABEM, 1122: Diary E. Norton (10 Sep. 1919); Brereton, *Training God's Army*, 81; Barnhouse, "Training Belgians for Congo Missions," 443.

41 *La Mission Belge Evangélique* [1919], 7; Prospectus of the Dutch-language BGM Bible school [1922].

42 However, North American Bible schools had an opposing tendency. Here, the minimum age dropped from mid-twenty to twenty-one for men and twenty for women. Brereton, *Training God's Army*, 122.

secondary education was in French.[43] That being said, in November or December 1920, there were vague plans to start a Dutch-language Bible school.[44] Only when, in 1921, one alumnus and two students decided to transfer to Silo's reopened Flemish training school for evangelists the plans got a sense of urgency. After four months of preparation, the *Bijbel Instituut België* opened its doors in January 1922. It was led by Van Puffelen, soon to be joined by Jan Knecht Sr.[45]

The Bible schools jointly developed the curricula "with the needs of the people kept prominently in mind."[46] Some courses were written by BGMers; others were taken from American Bible schools and translated with permission, such as *What the Bible Teaches* by Torrey.[47] Like the Moody Bible Institute program, the students had to take time for personal devotions and practical work besides studying.[48]

To better prepare students for independent action on the mission field, it was decided in 1924 to add a third practical year, during which each student would be placed under the supervision of the station leader. These could refuse a student if they lacked competence. Such students received a second chance at a different station. Failure meant dismissal.[49] Students who did not embrace dispensational premillennialism were barred from the third year and did not receive their diplomas.[50]

Although the Bible schools were intended as a training college for future BGM workers, graduates were not guaranteed a place in the organization, even if their results were outstanding. This is not uncommon for faith missions training institutes.[51] By 1927, only eleven BGMers, including nine pas-

---

43 In 1910, a law was adopted that opened the way for introducing Dutch as the language of learning in Flemish secondary education. It would take until 1932 before the language of learning in kindergarten, primary, and secondary education had to be in the main language of the language area: Dutch, French, or German. De Clerck, *Chronologisch Overzicht van de Belgische Onderwijsgeschiedenis 1830-1990*, 67-68, 77, 85, 88-89.

44 Potma, "Revival in Belgium," 3.

45 Silo's founder, Rev. N. de Jonge, had started a training school for evangelists in Laken which counted 19 students between 1876 and 1886. It reopened in 1900 in Schaarbeek, where 12 students were trained until 1911. The third and final training school was situated in Geraardsbergen. Nine students were enrolled between 1921 and 1926. Lutjeharms, *De Vlaamse Opleidingsschool*, 51-52; Howard, *A New Invasion*, 186, 189-190.

46 Bentley had wanted to go to Congo as a missionary, but as his health did not permit it, he chose to train people who were able to go. Howard, *A New Invasion*, 186, 188.

47 ABEM, 50: Bentley to Charensol (1 Oct. 1925).

48 Howard, *A New Invasion*, 190.

49 This is characteristic of faith mission Bible schools; they train but do not provide employment. ABEM, 877: Minutes Personnel Committee (18 Sep., 7 Nov. 1924); ABEM, 228: Bolomey to Howard Jr. (7 Jan. 1927); Van den Berg, "Protestantisme in België," 67.

50 "la Doctrine du Retour Prémillénaire du Seigneur." ABEM, 880: Minutes Commission of Instruction (29 Feb. 1924).

51 ABEM, 877: Minutes Personnel Committee (18 Sep. 1924).

tors, were Bible school graduates. Several graduates had found full-time jobs in other churches or Christian organizations in Belgium or abroad.[52]

That same year, the French-language Bible school was temporarily closed. More new applications and a suitable new director were needed, as Bentley had left the mission. The low interest must have been a blow for the Nortons – perhaps potential students enrolled in other Bible schools, just as with Flemish students in 1921. Miner Stearns' comment at the reopening of the French-language Bible school in 1936 may have hinted at this. As the new principal, he admitted that not all subjects taught were at the desired level but gave his assurances that this was being addressed.[53]

It goes without saying that attention must be paid to the changing position of women in the BGM. In the early 1920s, 1920s fundamentalism was still blended with revivalism and the holiness movement, characterized by egalitarianism. Margaret Bendroth rightly concludes that "[a]ttitudes toward women in the fundamentalist movement were therefore complex, often inconsistent, and tended to defy easy categorization."[54] True, ordination, pastoring a church, and executive leadership were forbidden territory for women, with few exceptions.[55] Still, they could speak at Bible conferences for mixed-sex audiences, be Bible teachers, traveling evangelists, editors of magazines, authors of (devotional) books, articles, and tracts, or (co-) founders of a special-purpose religious organization.[56]

Like other 1920s fundamentalist organizations, the BGM had several female sponsors, such as Mrs. Milton Stewart. Although five of the thirteen members of the US Executive Committee were women, the Board consisted of men only, which is in line with most other faith missions.[57] The Committee for the Examination of Candidates consisted of five persons: three men and two women.[58]

However, in the early days of the BGM, women were also given relatively much more scope in the mission field. Norton's Quaker background, with an

---

52 "Het Bijbelinstituut der Belgische Evangelische Zending," *Onze Hoop*, 1 March 1927, 1.
53 ABEM, 880: Agenda Commission of Instruction (17 Jan. 1931); "Notre Institut Biblique Français," *Notre Espérance*, 15 Feb. 1929, 4; ABEM, 849: General Workers Letter (25 June 1936).
54 Bendroth, "Fundamentalism," 439.
55 A European example is Madeleine Blocher-Saillens, a good friend of the Nortons, who was elected as her husband's successor as pastor of an orthodox Baptist church in Paris. Hamilton, "Women, Public Ministry, and American Fundamentalism," 175–180; Blocher, *Madeleine Blocher-Saillens*.
56 Balmer, "American Fundamentalism," 175.
57 The women were Mrs. J. Mary Borden, Mrs. Lyman Stewart, Mrs. Philip E. Howard Sr., Mrs. R.B. Haines Jr., and Mrs. Charles G. Trumbull. Hamilton, "Women, Public Ministry, and American Fundamentalism," 179.
58 It consisted of the Nortons (ex officio), Mr. Philip E. Howard Sr., Mr. Charles G. Trumbull, and Mrs. J. Harvey Borton. ABEM, 850: Minutes Board of Trustees (13 Feb. 1922).

egalitarian view of women, may have contributed to this, just as the couple's training at Moody Bible Institute. Given the urgency to communicate the Good News, "women students enjoyed considerable educational opportunity and a large measure of equality" at American Bible schools around the turn of the twentieth century.[59] Yet, in the case of the Nortons, the deployment of women had nothing to do with a shortage of male candidates, as with many other faith missions.[60]

By the late 1920s, women became less visible in the BGM, and as of 1934, they were no longer included in the BGM's headcount.[61] By doing so, the mission kept pace with the sociological evolution in Western society. As a result of economic developments and the threat of war, there was a general slowdown in the emancipation of women in Western society.[62] The cutbacks for women corresponded with the changing social values and opinions of a majority of American white middle-class culture. Both society and religious life witnessed a decisive shift from nineteenth-century feminization to twentieth-century masculinization.[63]

More importantly, it is also in line with the general trend in faith missions of gradually limiting the role of women. This can be attributed to the decline of the influence of the holiness movement and the increasing impact of 1920s fundamentalism.[64] We will demonstrate this by discussing Bible school students, pastors' wives, and single women evangelists.

As we have seen before, the mission's Bible school was open for both men and women. The first graduation class of 1921 consisted of four men and two women, Belgian Valentine Denecker and Swiss Deborah Valet.[65] Other women followed in their footsteps. Several were asked to leave before graduation because they were deemed too young and inexperienced to be used among women and girls.[66]

The first signs of the deteriorating situation for female students go back to 1924. Although the school was still open to both men and women, women

---

59 Brereton, *Training God's Army*, 129; Blake Robinson, *A Reporter at Moody's*, 32–33.
60 DeBerg, *Ungodly Women*, 81.
61 As Bendroth concluded, "Attitudes toward women in the fundamentalist movement were ... complex, often inconsistent, and tended to defy easy categorization." Bendroth, "Fundamentalism," 439; ABEM, 51: Winston Sr. to Châtelain (26 March 1934).
62 De Weerdt, *En de vrouwen?*, 135.
63 Fiedler describes the religious change as the re-Calvinization of Calvinism. Fiedler, *The Story of Faith Missions*, 301; Bendroth, "Fundamentalism and Femininity," 228.
64 Fiedler, *The Story of Faith Missions*, 299-301.
65 Denecker did colportage among women outside her study hours. She was joined in the second term by Valet. AIBB: Fiche de Renseignements de l'élève Valet, Mlle Deborah; Barnhouse, "Training Belgians for Congo Missions," 443; Mrs. Norton, "When New Shoes Bring Rapture," 715.
66 AIBB: Fiche de Renseignements de l'élève Willekens-Fischer, Flore, Fiche de Renseignements de l'élève Van Belleghem, Jeanne.

who could not pay for their training from their own means were now refused. The Commission of Instruction argued that it lacked the finances to give them grants. Yet the actual problem was a "lack of opportunity for girls to work in the stations."[67]

By 1929, women were only accepted in some cases.[68] Three years later, there was a complete ban on female students. Again, the fake argument was used, saying that the BGM would not be able to offer them any work.[69] After all, male students were not guaranteed a position in the mission either. Female applicants were referred to other Bible schools, such as *l'Institut Biblique de Nogent* (France), *l'Institut Biblique et Missionnaire d'Emmaüs* (Switzerland), and *l'Ecole d'Evangélistes* run by *Brigade Missionnaire de la Drôme*.[70]

When the ban on female applicants was lifted in 1934, women were still excluded from the final, practical year. Placement in a station or church was considered to be useless, as there was still no room for single women evangelists in the mission. Although this discrimination was clearly communicated, women still applied and were admitted as students.[71]

We have no records about the role of married women in the BGM in the earliest years. The first clear illustration of the role pastors' wives were expected to play dates from 1929. As long as a couple had no children, the wife was to assist her husband. When a BGM couple started a family, her tasks would be primarily the home and the care of the children "to free her husband as much as possible."[72] This means that the pastor's wives lived in the shadow of their husbands.

This was in line not only with faith mission practice but also with the American middle-class ideal. Drawing back from gender equality in the Interwar period was not uncommon for churches and organizations rooted in the holiness movement.[73] This viewpoint was also similar to the expectations generally held in Belgium when Roman Catholicism was still a dominant influence. Contrary to the Liberal and Socialist 'pillars,' Catholicism continued to

---

67   ABEM, 880: Minutes Commission of Instruction (Nov. 1924).
68   "Het Bijbelinstituut der Belgische Evangelische Zending," *Onze Hoop*, 1 March 1927, 1; "Advert," *Onze Hoop*, 1 July 1929, 8.
69   ABEM, 266: Stearns to Metzler (16 March 1933).
70   An exception was made for Jeanne Luc from France. She was admitted because she was planning to go to Africa as a missionary and could not attend the Bible school at Nogent for personal reasons. She only completed the two-year theoretic stage and was therefore not given a diploma but a certificate. ABEM, 34: Stearns to Bertieaux (28 Nov. 1932); ABEM, 183: Luc to "brothers and sisters in the BGM" (11 July 1938); Berrus, "Brigade et Brigadette," 7.
71   ABEM, 98: Stearns to Duez (7 Dec. 1934), Duez to Stearns (14 Dec. 1934).
72   ABEM, 83: Vansteenberghe to Dekker (16 Jan. 1929).
73   Robert, *American Women in Mission*, 219; Marsden, *Reforming Fundamentalism: Fuller Seminary and the New Evangelicalism*, 123; Fiedler, *The Story of Faith Missions*, 299.

oppose women's paid employment outside the home and taught that a woman ought to devote herself to her children, husband, and housework entirely.[74]

The correspondence gives us insight into some of the activities the pastor's wives were involved in. She was usually responsible for the local work among women and children and would accompany her husband on home visits whenever a woman's presence was desirable. When making home visits independently, she would talk about spiritual subjects, everyday issues, and housekeeping. Of course, she was expected to pray for her husband and to encourage him.[75]

When their families became too large, the Personnel Committee allowed several pastors' wives to take on housekeepers to free up some time for home visits and children's and women's work. This was cheaper than replacing them with single female workers, which was a plus in light of the financial situation of the Great Depression. Of course, the underlying argument was the male dominance of first-wave fundamentalism. To avoid jealousy among colleagues, these housekeepers were assigned discretely. However, one wonders how long it took before the colleagues knew.[76]

When, in 1930, Bible school student Miss Lina Rottier informed whether there were opportunities for female pastors in the BGM, Odilon Vansteenberghe wanted to do it by the book and passed her query on to the Personnel Committee. Apart from being a woman, she never would have stood a chance, as she didn't believe in the premillennial Second Coming. Interestingly, the committee determined without further substantiation that it was not qualified to decide.[77] But even without a clear-cut answer, it was evident that women could never lead a local BGM church. This would put them in authority over men, contrary to dispensationalism, which held a permanent subordination of women. And whereas preaching may have been permissible in the start-up of the BGM, ten years later, women were slowly but surely pushed out of the limelight into supportive activities behind the scenes.

However, in the first decade of the BGM, the mission employed single women as evangelists. Under the leadership of Miss May B. White, one of the Nortons' former secretaries during World War I, they were assisting the pastor's wife with local children's and women's work or were deployed as colporteurs or visiting nurses. The way these women were mobilized did not differentiate the BGM from other Protestant churches and missions active in Belgium.[78] Care for the sick at home was a phenomenon that emerged in the

---

74   De Weerdt, *En de vrouwen?*, 141.
75   ABEM, 191: Winston Sr. to L'Hermenault (24 Oct. 1931); Howard, *A New Invasion*, 160.
76   ABEM, 877: Minutes Personnel Committee (15 Jan. 1931).
77   Ibid. (3 May 1930).
78   Dale, *Aperçu*, 36.

twentieth century as a result of growing professionalism and differentiation within the nursing profession.[79]

Their work as visiting nurses or *visiteuses* was often seen to break the ice and create an interest in the Gospel. "Many doors which are closed to us would be open to a nurse," according to Jane Brons, as she explained finding ways to build friendships with and witness to women.[80] In working-class areas, women were often confronted with alcohol abuse and its consequences. Hence, May White's wish to have Henriëtte Hartsen speak at women's meetings in various BGM stations. Hartsen, a member of the lower nobility in the Netherlands, combined evangelism with campaigning against alcohol abuse.[81]

Legitimized by the dispensationalist and inerrantist exegesis of the Bible, the mission became increasingly male-dominated towards the end of the 1920s. The opportunities for single women in the mission were so restricted that White wondered in 1928 if they were needed at all.[82] She left the mission not long afterward. The cases of Anne-Marie De Pooter and Eleanor Scott illustrate her complaint.

De Pooter, an alumnus of the BGM Dutch-language Bible school, had worked for several years without any problems in the area of Ath, Soignies, and Braine-le-Comte until Jules Cailleaux was assigned to Ath as a pastor. The two did not get along very well. She described him as incompetent, disrespectful, and lacking in "wisdom, love, and greatness of soul."[83] De Pooter added that the *visiteuse* was at times regarded as a "stand-in for the leader's wife."[84] After receiving an anonymous complaint that she was visiting people in their homes until 7 or 8 p.m., Cailleaux went along with the complainant. He was very much disturbed when she disagreed with him.[85]

De Pooter addressed Edith Norton on this subject, but in vain. She went along with the masculinization of the BGM and accused De Pooter of being unwilling to submit to "the specific will of the Mission."[86] De Pooter drew her

---

79 The visiting nurses generally nursed the sick, taught families about elementary hygiene, and checked whether health regulations were complied with. In 1921, 'nurse-visitor' as a specialism was introduced in nursing training colleges. Those who specialized in this subject graduated as visiting nurses. The BGM visiteuses combined nursing in the community with evangelism. Baré, *Het Wit-Gele Kruis 1937-2007*, 26-27.
80 ABEM, 31: Report from Miss Brons St. Nicolaas (April 1929).
81 Henriëtte Sarah Hartsen started the Dutch association for teetotalers *Nederlandsche Christen Vrouwen Geheel-Onthouders Unie* in 1898. In the Netherlands she had links with Johannes de Heer, but she was also in contact with revivalists at international level. ABEM, 877: Minutes Personnel Committee (14 Oct. 1926); De Paepe, "Uit het gulden boek: Jonkvrouw Henriëtte Sarah Hartsen, geheelonthoudster en evangeliste," 80-87.
82 ABEM, 248: White to Saucy (18 Jan. 1928).
83 ABEM, 65: De Pooter to the Nortons (15 Sep. 1930).
84 ABEM, 272: Winston Sr. to Teeuwissen (24 Sep. 1937).
85 ABEM, 65: Depooter to E. Norton (12 Nov. 1930).
86 ABEM, 49: Anon. to F. Castiaux (14 Aug. 1926).

conclusions, felt it was time to "put an end to [her] slavery," and resigned.[87] That did not stop her from visiting people in the Ath area, much to the mission's annoyance.

Eleanor Scott was hired as Ralph Norton's personal secretary and was allowed to do spiritual work in her spare time. She took a children's club with 80 children in Stockel under her wing, led a successful Bible Class for girls in the French-language BGM church in Brussels, and took over the women's meeting when May White left. Scott also had plans to do something for teenagers and women in Stockel.[88]

In 1935, several months after Ralph Norton's death, she wanted to expand her work among women to a full-time ministry. Scott claimed Norton had hired her as an evangelist in 1925 but couldn't produce written evidence.[89] She saw the storm coming and feared to be put "in an impossible position, such as I fear some of the other women have been in, and failed."[90]

Her request was refused. When she refused to continue her secretarial position, Scott was fired and accused of having an "intractable spirit" and "outbursts of ill-temper."[91] There simply was no room for a critical attitude toward certain established institutions of the Mission. She accepted the reprimand in typical holiness terminology: "I confess with sorrow that from time to time I lose victory in this way, and I must come to the place where this shall not be."[92]

The gynophobic attitude was not merely imposed from the top down but was also present at the grassroots level. The clearest example is the case of Jeanne Verton, a trilingual saleswoman in the BGM bookshop in Brussels. The leadership's decision to have her 'man' the BGM literature stand at the world expo in Liège in 1930 was met with a severely critical attitude toward certain established institutions of the Mission. The management backed down and decided to send a man to the fair instead.[93] Verton was transferred back to Brussels and had to play second fiddle in the Brussels' side street bookshop.

As a faith mission rooted in the Holiness movement, daily practice and general rule derogations were always possible. Also, as a 1920s fundamentalist organization, it was free "to stretch, or ignore, social conventions if it

87 She added that she would certainly remain submitted to God. For the original quote, see ABEM, 65: Depooter to E. Norton (12 Nov. 1930).
88 This Bible class was also attended by girls from other Protestant denominations, such as the ECMB and the Open Brethren. ABEM, 263: Scott to Personnel Committee (26 Feb. 1935), Scott to Winston Sr. (1 March 1935).
89 ABEM, 263: E. Scott to Winston Sr. (1 March 1935).
90 The underlining is by Edith Norton, who added, "it was this fear which made me so hesitate." [sic] ABEM, 263: Scott to E. Norton; Scott to the BGM Board (16 May 1935).
91 ABEM, 263: Winston Sr. to Scott (28 Feb. 1935).
92 ABEM, 263: Scott to Winston Sr. (1 March 1935).
93 "Onze Zending op de Wereldtentoonstelling te Luik," 5; ABEM, 875: Minutes CAE (4 April 1930, 16 July 1930).

so chose."[94] The most notable exception was a matter of urgency when Edith Norton succeeded her late husband at his express request in 1934. He asked those present on his deathbed to accept his decision and support her as her advisors, which they did.[95]

Against social conventions and the male-oriented policy of the BGM, which he gradually had introduced in the mission, Norton wanted to be succeeded by his wife. Ralph and Edith were not ready to hand over their life work to a new generation. Ralph, who had always been the dreamer, seemed to think returning to the Keswick holiness roots would generate more donations than if someone else succeeded him. Both failed to see that her impact as a publicist and co-founder of the BGM and its predecessor among Anglo-American evangelicals had diminished substantially.

As expected, the American Board of Trustees followed suit. Although the decision was widely supported, not everybody agreed. Somebody told her that God would never bless a church led by a woman. After some reflection, she considered this an evil attempt to "chain her up and prevent her from giving her testimony and that if she would yield on one point, she would need to do so on the other ones."[96]

However, this statement offended the truth. For years, she had allowed women, including herself, to be gradually restricted in addressing a mixed-gender audience. Her appointment as acting director must have been a blow for those who had left the mission because of the increasing gender inequality.

Like other 1920s fundamentalist women, Edith found an outlet to reach both men and women through inspirational and devotional writing. She wrote almost all the articles on the BGM to be published by the Christian press in North America and Great Britain. She published two devotionals, *Opened Windows of Heaven* (1927), *Is He Not Able?* (1934), and the biography *Ralph Norton and the Belgian Gospel Mission* (1935).[97] And behind the scenes, Edith was active as a full member of the mission's executive committee.

When Edith Norton returned to the forefront in the fall of 1934, it was only for a short period. The idea was that associate directors John Winston Sr. and Odilon Vansteenberghe would be presented to the American supporters as the mission's future leaders. It would also buy them some time to take over the helm. No one could foresee that this moment of transition had already come in 1936 when Edith Norton died somewhat unexpectedly due to the complications of an ulcer. But before we delve into the era of Vansteenberghe and

---

94 Hamilton, "Women, Public Ministry, and American Fundamentalism," 187.
95 ABEM, 849: Verslag van een onderhoud met Mr. Norton (14 Sep. 1934).
96 For the original quote, see Blocher-Saillens, and Blocher, *Madeleine Blocher-Saillens*, 87.
97 Edith's biography of her husband is a good example of a 1920s fundamentalist biography. She waived her musical career and chose a religious career at the side of her husband. Hamilton, "Women, Public Ministry, and American Fundamentalism," 174.

Winston Sr., we will first discuss the mission's organizational development under the Nortons' leadership in the next chapter.

Map with most of the churches and stations of the Belgian Gospel Mission in the 1930s.

6
FROM FORMATIVE TO NORMATIVE
THE STRUCTURAL DEVELOPMENT OF THE BGM

As discussed at the end of chapter two, the Nortons had a compelling vision to evangelize Belgium. The period from their arrival in Brussels in December 1919 until February 1926, can be described as the formative phase of the Belgian Gospel Mission. One could say that the organization was in a trial-and-error mode. In this chapter, we will focus on how the mission evolved from an ad hoc directed mission to a formally structured organization, which was partially a missionary organization, and partly an emerging denomination.

In the summer of 1919, the BGM had eight workers: Ralph and Edith Norton, Misses Bell, White, Baert and Walschaert, Donald Barnhouse, and Karel Blommaert.[1] Officially, the tasks and responsibilities were clearly defined. Miss Bell was in charge of the offices and Sunday School. Barnhouse headed up the Bible correspondence course with Scripture League members and the Bible school, which opened in September 1919.[2] Blommaert led the work in Antwerp, and Miss White coordinated the work among women.[3] After his de-

---

1   Mrs. Baert had fled to London with her family at the age of fourteen, at the start of the war. She encountered local Brethren through a business course. Mrs. Norton, "That First Sunday Service in Belgium," 484; Mrs. Norton, "When New Shoes Bring Rapture," 715; *Sunday School Times*, 1919, front page, 709.
2   A total of four lessons were found in the archives. It is unclear whether the course included more than these, nor how long it was used. The subjects covered are: 1) What the Bible teaches about itself; 2) Sin; 3) Salvation; 4) Redemption. ABEM, 1275.
3   Mrs. Norton, "When New Shoes Bring Rapture," 715; Howard, *A New Invasion of Belgium*, 158-159.

mobilization, Odilon Vansteenberghe, who had voluntarily helped the Nortons in London, joined them on 1 November 1919. He assisted Barnhouse in the Bible school and was deployed as a nationwide evangelist.[4]

In reality, it was all hands on deck. People were simply asked to assist the Nortons. By September 1920, the number of co-workers rose to forty-three, most recently converted and still students in the mission's Bible school.[5] At times, it was chaotic. For instance, leases were suddenly terminated with immediate effect. When the Nortons were fundraising in the United States, the mission's day-to-day management was delegated to Barnhouse, Vansteenberghe, and White without clearly defined responsibilities for each of them.[6]

In 1921, the BGM experienced a difficult time with "many resignations" and "others who had to be asked to leave."[7] Despite friction, Ralph Norton did not change his management style. He continued to meet with the heads of departments and station leaders at regular intervals to discuss issues affecting the mission. Yet with the number of workers, called 'members,' rising to fifty and more in 1923, the number of issues to be discussed, and their complexity, a new leadership style was necessary.[8]

The first step in transitioning from a highly informal to a more formal structure was the launch of a 'General Letter.' The idea was to swiftly and effectively share news and decisions with all BGM members.[9] Next, the China Inland Mission, the Africa Inland Mission, and several other faith missions were consulted on how to structure the BGM as a long-term organization. Their advice was a major building block for a committee that had been formed to rethink the organizational structure of the mission.[10] And thirdly, general terms of employment were formulated, which included a probationary period for new workers.[11]

The fact that BGM workers came from various protestant traditions meant that theology could become a divisive issue. And so, the Nortons did their utmost to solidify the BGM's spiritual identity. After prolonged deliberations, a Profession of Faith was accepted in 1925. From then on, the workers were to sign this profession of faith every year, and any refusal to do so "would automatically exclude one from the ranks of the Mission."[12] Although the document was intended to define and defend internal unity, it also led to external separation in practical terms. As a characteristic of a faith mission, this

4 Mrs. Norton, "When New Shoes Bring Rapture," 715.
5 DGBP: Barnhouse to Prentice (24 Aug. 1920), Barnhouse to Hopkins (23 Dec. 1960).
6 DGBP: Barnhouse to Hopkins (23 Dec. 1960).
7 E. Norton, *Ralph Norton*, 171.
8 ABEM, 877: Minutes Personnel Committee (16 Oct. 1924).
9 ABEM, 849: R. Norton, General Letter (6 March 1923).
10 ABEM, 877: Minutes Personnel Committee (4 March 1924).
11 Ibid. (2 Sep. 1924).
12 E. Norton, *Ralph Norton*, 192.

Profession of Faith became the mission's shibboleth for interdenominational cooperation.[13]

Most workers signed the document each year without objection. Others wrote comments or disagreements in the margin, which was allowed within certain limits. Since joining the BGM in 1931, Miner Stearns wrote his dissent to Article 5 in the margin of the English version. The text is as follows:

> I believe that man, having been created pure and in the image of God, is by his own sin *fallen from grace*, and I believe that in consequence all have sinned, are guilty and lost, and absolutely incapable of saving themselves by their own works, being dead in their trespasses and sins; that for those who, in this life, will not repent the result of sin will be eternal punishment of which they will be fully conscious.[14]

Stearns commented: "That's a perfectly good Methodist expression (also borrowed by other denominations), but I think it's unscriptural (in its use here). It is used only in *Galatians* 5:4, so far as I know, and refers to those who seek to be justified by the Law, and *not* to the sin of Adam, or anybody else. It is a question of the distinction between Law and Grace, not between righteousness and sin. In other words, the Galatians fell from Grace, but Adam did not. Adam fell into Grace, if I may say so, for God did not act in Grace toward him until after he sinned, if I understand the meaning of Grace correctly."[15] As the workers were free to sign the document in any of the three languages, Stearns signed the Dutch version without any objections which reads "has fallen from his sinless state."[16]

In February 1926, after lengthy discussions with all workers, a new organizational structure was accepted. The national work was divided into five standing committees: the Business Committee, Personnel Committee, Instruction Committee, Publications Committee, and the Committee of Evangelistic Activities. Membership was limited to three years and could be renewed.

The Personnel Committee also supervised the third-year students at the Bible schools in view of their recruitment. All other students fell under the responsibility of the Instruction Committee, managing the Bible schools. The Committee of Evangelistic Activities was to establish and lead evangelism in areas with no BGM presence yet. BGM pastors and evangelists remained responsible for initiating and coordinating local evangelistic activities.[17]

All workers were now expected to attend quarterly days of prayer at headquarters and assemble twice a year for a General Meeting, called a Conference,

13 Fiedler, *The Story of Faith Missions*, 180.
14 See appendix 1, page 207.
15 ABEM, 266: Stearns to Winston Sr. (11 Jan. 1931).
16 For the original text, see ABEM, 1231.
17 ABEM, 849: General Letter (16 Feb. 1926).

in which progress in the various stations and departments was to be reported. This would also be a time to discuss any complaints or proposals from BGM workers.[18] Two traveling agents would oversee the local churches and mission posts and be authorized to solve urgent problems. During their visits, they assisted the station leaders in interviewing and accepting candidates for church membership. This Presbyterian structure is characteristic of faith missions.

The overall leadership was placed in the hands of an Executive Committee (EC), whose members were appointed indefinitely. Ralph and Edith Norton, G. Collinet, J.C. Winston Sr., and O. Vansteenberghe formed the Committee. It was seconded by the *Conference*, an advisory body consisting of all members of the standing committees.[19] The EC would only intervene in organized churches, i.e., with a pastor and church council, if the conflict could not be solved locally and the EC deemed it necessary. All decisions of the EC and the standing committees had to be made unanimously. If unanimity could not be achieved, this was regarded as a sign from heaven that they should postpone the decision.

In 1932, a final adaptation was made for practical reasons. As most reports were first read out in the CAE and subsequently at the Conference, CAE members heard them twice in one day. And so, these agencies merged into the Committee of Evangelistic Activities and Conference (CAEC). Those who previously had been Conference members only were given an advisory role in the new agency. The Committee was to meet three times a year, which was continued after a one-year trial period.

After the new organizational structure was introduced in 1926, the fieldwork was also restructured. From an early date, BGM activities had been divided into a Flemish and a French-speaking wing. These were now further divided into regions. In each region, monthly meetings were organized for prayer and discussion of local needs.

Initially, Flanders was one region, as the work in this part of the country was still limited. Also, market evangelism was organized by region, albeit Flanders was divided into two sub-regions. Daniël Meijer, minister of the station in Antwerp, requested having a separate subregion for the province of Antwerp to enable a stronger focus on market evangelism. His request was refused because the stations in Lokeren and Sint-Niklaas were deemed to be too weak at the time. He was told that the issue would be reviewed when more meetings had been started in other places, such as Mol and Lier.[20]

The stations were led by BGM workers, who were given free reign when it came to local initiatives. They were assisted by evangelists, evangelistic

---

18 Ibid.
19 Ibid.
20 ABEM, 205: Meijer to Vansteenberghe (22 Feb. 1928), Vansteenberghe to Meijer (29 Feb. 1928).

health visitors or *visiteuses,* and (if available) third-year Bible school students. The latter focused mainly on assisting local ministers and on colportage.

The Personnel Committee arranged transfers. Sometimes, the worker requested the transfer; in other cases, the Committee initiated it. A reason for a transfer could be that it was felt that it was better for the development of a local congregation to have its pastor replaced, that a church elsewhere had lost its leader, or that the Committee felt that the worker's qualities were needed elsewhere.[21]

Before any transfer took place, the BGM worker (or workers) in question would be asked for their opinion. The worker's wishes were usually respected unless the Personnel Committee had urgent reasons to ignore them.[22] The pastors' transfers could cause distress among local believers and, therefore, had to be handled sensitively.[23] Occasionally, a worker disagreed with the Personnel Committee's policies. For instance, Jan Monsma left the Belgian Gospel Mission for Jeruël Church in Rotterdam when the Committee refused his request to promise that the responsibility for the station in Antwerp would be handed to him if Daniël Meijer were to leave.[24]

During its formative years, the mission created a legal status on both sides of the Atlantic. Although the Nortons were convinced that the 'Rapture' was only a matter of years, they were realistic enough to make long-term management plans in case they were wrong. For this reason, in 1921, the Board of Trustees in the United States started researching the advisability of incorporating the BGM.[25]

During that same year, the Belgian government introduced its Charities Act. By transferring properties the Nortons and some close associates had acquired for the mission to a charity, inheritance tax could be avoided, and their successors could not change the theological nature of the organization.[26] The fact that sixty percent of the charities' Executive Committee had to be Belgian nationals was an unforeseen complication for the Nortons.[27] They

21 Berend Hilberinck was promoted from colporteur to BGM station leader, but when the Personnel Committee decided that he was a better colporteur than a pastor, the promotion was reversed. Hilberinck felt disappointed and left. ABEM, 137: Vansteenberghe to Hilberinck (26 Jan. 1935), Vansteenberghe to Guttling (24 Aug. 1935).
22 ABEM, 51: Winston Sr. to Châtelain (4 Sep. 1929).
23 ABEM, 107: Winston Sr. to Dubois (30 Jan. 1931).
24 ABEM, 849: Monsma to Winston Sr. (8 Sep. 1932).
25 ABEM, 850: Minutes Board of Trustees (22 Feb. 1921).
26 "With his wide experience of various missionary societies, which began on a sound evangelical basis, fall into the hands of unfaithful leaders who, through control of the property, had definitely introduced their societies to the ranks of modernism." This remark should be read in the context of the Fundamentalist–Modernist Controversy, which broke out in full during the aftermath of World War I. Norton, *Ralph Norton,* 204.
27 Old Article 26, paragraph 2 of the Belgian Act of 27 June 1921 on *Associations Sans But Lucrative.*

felt this would negatively affect their fundraising in the United States, so they researched other forms of incorporation.

Registering the properties under an American charity was not an option because the charity would have to have its registered office in Belgium. So, the restrictions of Belgian law were accepted. Ralph Norton wrote a tentative copy of the Constitution and By-Laws. After consulting several Christian leaders, a committee fine-tuned the document, which included the BGM's statement of faith.[28] Four years after the introduction of the Belgian Charities Act, the BGM's constitution appeared in the Belgian Bulletin of Acts and Decrees on 29 August 1925.[29] However, behind the scenes, the ultimate authority remained vested with the American Committee. On the other side of the Atlantic, the mission was incorporated in 1927 in Delaware, the state with the cheapest procedure. This allowed the BGM to own assets acquired in the USA through gifts or bequests.[30]

In the meantime, the mission kept purchasing buildings as soon as some money was available for stations where no suitable place was available for rent. Supporters in the United States criticized this. Edith Norton responded with an article in the *Sunday School Times* that explained the problem with using rental accommodation that we discussed earlier. Moreover, she argued, "if we have possession of our own property, with full liberty to preach the Gospel for one year, or even a month, before our Blessed Lord comes back, is that not worth while [sic]? For of what value is the wealth of the Lord's children when he comes, and it is all left behind?"[31] As Jesus' return was not as near as expected, purchasing real estate turned out to be good stewardship after all.

In the second half of the 1920s, the mission also focused on its branding. In 1926, a new logo was introduced. Just like the new headquarters in Brussels, the façade of all BGM buildings needed to contain this logo. The idea was that this would help outsiders to see that these properties, spread throughout the country, belonged to the same national organization.[32] The decision in 1928 to permanently replace the Dutch name *Evangelisatiewerk in België*

---

28 ABEM, 850: Minutes Board of Trustees (20 July 1922).
29 "Annex to Moniteur Belge," 29 Aug. 1925.
30 The State of Delaware is particularly corporate-friendly. For instance, there is no requirement to file or record the transfer of ownership of a corporation that is incorporated in Delaware, and the state imposes no tax on capital stock or assets of incorporations. The Delaware Company, "Formation Information," n.d., accessed 23 June 2013, <http://www.thedelawarecompany.com/llc_corporation_information.aspx>.
31 E. Norton, "Preaching Under Difficulties in Belgium," 60.
32 E. Norton, "When We Dedicated the New Headquarters," 176; "Notes - Personalia, etc," *Notre Espérance*, 1 June 1926, 1.

with *Belgische Evangelische Zending* should be viewed in the light of this same objective.[33]

The initial Dutch version of the mission's name indicates that some of the Nortons' connections were proponents of the Flemish Movement. This movement originated shortly after the Belgian State was created in 1830, and it campaigned against the inferior position of the Dutch language in Belgian society, creating a social divide between the French-speaking middle and upper class and the lower class, which was mostly Dutch-speaking. Although around 1900, legislation slightly improved the position of Dutch, French was still a prerequisite for jobs in the public sector and even in Flanders, the dominant language in education and trade. In Brussels, French had displaced Dutch as the dominant language.

During the war, there was growing resistance – albeit still limited – against the commanders in the army, who all spoke French only. In occupied Flanders, a small section of the Flemish Movement named 'the Activists' co-operated with the German *Flamenpolitik*, the German policy to try and win the sympathy of the Flemish by meeting some of their demands, such as the switch to Dutch as the *lingua franca* at the university of Ghent. In spite of the allegations of undermining national unity, the Flemish Movement became an important phenomenon during the interwar period.

Despite internal divisions in the Flemish Movement, radical Flemish political parties managed to win over a growing number of voters. Meanwhile, many moderate Flemish organizations were founded, which became an ever-stronger influence in Flanders. The Roman Catholic church openly spoke out against the Flemish Movement. It even published a joint statement of Belgian bishops in October 1925. Still, at the grassroots level, many Flemish priests were actively involved in Flemish-minded societies and even contributed to national awareness of the Flemish cause.[34]

The Nortons were aware of cultural tensions between Dutch and French speakers but only saw them as a possible opportunity to make people more willing to listen to the Gospel message.[35] Consequently, they must have underestimated the implications of the word 'Flanders' in the Dutch name of their mission. This became apparent in the conflict with Johannes H. Scheps and Parmentier.

Dutchman Scheps joined the BGM in the Spring of 1923 and was sent to Bruges. Within a few months, a conflict took place as he openly sympathized

33 The English name *Belgian Gospel Mission* had been translated as *La Misson Belge Évangélique* from the very start but was changed to *La Mission Évangélique Belge* in 1931 for grammatical reasons. ABEM, 205: Grandjean to Meijer (2 Oct. 1928); ABEM, 849: General Workers Letter (2 Feb. 1931).
34 Gevers, "Hoogtepunt en einde van een tijdperk," 216; Gerard, "De democratie gedroomd," 1020-1021; Gevers, Willemsen and Witte, "Geschiedenis van de Vlaamse Beweging," 60, 62.
35 ABEM, 850: Prayer letter, n.d. [1920].

with the Flemish nationalists. The BGM Board was displeased and told him, with reference to Philippians 3:20, that they did not take sides in this matter. Scheps transferred to the Reformed Church of Brussels to assist Rev. A. Lauwers, who supported the Flemish nationalists.[36]

Two years later, a similar conflict situation led to a disagreement with Parmentier. The graduate of the Silo Training School, who had built up a prosperous and flourishing church from practically nothing, did not quite fit in.[37] In a sermon on 15 February 1925, he complained "that he was not popular with people in the Mission and that they only wanted him there because he was Flemish."[38] He was summoned to appear before the Personnel Committee and accused of bringing up race and nationality, which was improper in an evangelical movement. Parmentier admitted his wrongdoing. He was now no longer allowed to lead the church in Antwerp but was permitted to stay with the BGM on two conditions: that he publicly withdrew his claim and was reconciled with the individuals he had criticized. He left the BGM within a year after this but remained in Antwerp, where he became a minister of the Methodist Church.[39]

On the one hand, this apolitical viewpoint of the BGM may be typical for faith missions but also demonstrates that the Nortons, in their idealism, did not take the differences between the Dutch- and French-speaking communities in Belgium seriously. Moreover, they may unknowingly have created the illusion that they sympathized with the Flemish Movement by replying to letters from Flemish soldiers in Dutch as much as possible. The incidents with Parmentier and Scheps were not the first signs of cultural tensions between the two language communities in the BGM, and more would follow.[40]

As Jesus' return took longer than initially expected, the mission had to put energy into more formally organizing the churches it had planted and developing a church order. This was a challenge, as its workers came from different church backgrounds. Also, the BGM increasingly had to find a balance between being a foreign church planting organization and a national denomination, a balance between the urgency of evangelism and the urgency to harmonize the organization of the local churches.

In the summer of 1928, John Winston Sr. brought the matter to the forefront. He wrote, "It seems to me that if our churches are to grow and develop

---

36 Here, Scheps also became involved in conflicts and eventually returned to the Netherlands. AJHS, 8: Scheps, "Gesprekken gevoerd door J.H. Scheps met N. Scheps in de periode van januari 1987 tot juni 1988;" Scheps, *Weersta vanaf het begin maar alleen met het geesteszwaard*, 24.
37 *Silo-Vereeniging: stads-evangelisatie in Brussel en lands-evangelisatie in Vlaanderen: na 50 jaren, 1874 - 10 Mei 1924*, [12]; Howard, *A New Invasion*, 146.
38 For the original quote, see ABEM, 877: Minutes Personnel Committee (26 Feb. 1925).
39 Overbeeke, *Jaarboek der evangelische kerken in België* (1963), 15.
40 ABEM, 850: Prayer letter, n.d. [1920].

as they should, they must have a certain amount of self-consciousness; more than they can have when all the direction of the work carried on in them comes from the outside."[41] He also mentioned the need for standard procedures for baptism, communion, weddings, and other church rituals, "so that too divergent customs may not grow up in the several groups and thus cause confusion when they come together."[42]

After this wake-up call, the Commission for the Organization of Churches was formed. Local church membership was on the agenda of the first meeting on 27 December 1928. All participants explained how this was organized in their own denomination.[43] Within a year, the committee published the *Preliminary Stipulations* for the Organization of the churches of the Belgian Gospel Mission.[44] The document discusses membership, the preliminary church council, and communion.

The next step was developing a procedure for electing elders, deacons, treasurers, etc., and their responsibilities.[45] The terminology concerning local congregations and evangelistic stations was also clarified. Until then, stations were sometimes described as 'churches' and sometimes as 'posts,' but the difference had never been made clear. From now on, a BGM station officially became a church when a church council was appointed. In all other cases, the stations were called posts.[46] Three years later, in 1932, a new version of this document was circulated internally. The original three topics, church council, communion, and membership, were discussed in more detail. New topics were church discipline, the church register, and a general description of the universal church.[47]

Most pastors felt that there were no suitable candidate elders in their stations and that they alone should remain responsible for the local church's leadership. We have too little information on the individual church members to conclude whether they were correct or too strict in applying the Biblical requirements for elders and deacons. However, as we will see later, in some cases, an elder or deacon had to be disciplined for severe offenses. The practice of allowing the local pastor to decide by himself whether or not to appoint elders

41 ABEM, 1237: Winston Sr. to R. Norton (28 Aug. 1928).
42 Ibid.
43 Its members were with the Nortons, Vansteenberghe, Winston Sr., and the pastors Jung, van Lierop, Wälti, Teeuwissen, Bentley, Barbezat, and Monsma. ABEM, 1237: Minutes Commission for the Organization of Churches (27 Dec. 1928).
44 ABEM, 1238: Voorloopige bepalingen voor de organisatie der gemeenten van de Belgische Evangelische Zending.
45 ABEM, 219: Winston Sr. to Neusy (2 July 1929).
46 ABEM, 293: Van Goethem to Winston Sr. (2 Jan. 1930).
47 Some of the members in Warquignies struggled with the *Preliminary Stipulations* because most were of the Open Brethren background. The Stipulations were explained during a special meeting and eventually adopted. ABEM, 875: Rapport de l'Agent Itinérant pour la Wallonie fait à la 'Conférence' (10 Jan. 1933).

was open to abuse. Therefore, the *Preliminary Stipulations* from 1929 prescribe the formation of a committee that functioned as a church council where there was none. The committee was to include the local pastor, a representative of the BGM Board, and a pastor from a nearby BGM church who was trusted by both the BGM board and the local pastor. A church council or a temporary committee would counterbalance the pastor, preventing him from acting like a dictator.[48]

In 1932, a sentence about the preliminary church council was added to the paragraph, which stipulates that in a second phase, the church council was to be extended with two elders chosen from the local church membership. Eventually, a third local elder was to be appointed to replace the nearby pastor on the church council. The appointment of elders was to occur in public, and all church council decisions had to be unanimous or consensual, as for the BGM leadership.

After queries were received about problems that had occurred, more details were added to the description of the preliminary church structure. For instance, a stipulation was added that the wife of the candidate elder had to be converted.[49] Issues that were not immediately resolved were the mandate of the elders and whether they had to be inducted by the laying on of hands or by offering the handshake of fellowship.[50]

The preliminary church structure was not always applied consistently. In the bilingual church of Mouscron, pastor Robert Van Goethem had four elders elected in his church, two for the French speakers and two for the Flemish members. He probably did this to maintain an equilibrium between the language communities. As Mouscron was near the language border, maintaining an equilibrium was important, but it went against the explicit instructions of Odilon Vansteenberghe, who had permitted two elders only. He wrote to Van Goethem that if the latter did not rectify the situation, the church of Mouscron might be excluded from the BGM.[51] The elders who had been elected stepped down, and Van Goethem stepped back into line.[52]

The institutionalization of the organization is also traceable in the practice of communion in the local churches. Initially, the decision on whether communion would be served and how often had been taken at a local level. Having a church council was no prerequisite. This all changed with the intro-

48 ABEM, 1238: Preliminary Dispositions in View of the Organization of the Churches of the BGM (1929); ABEM, 693: Vansteenberghe to Van Goethem, (29 Dec. 1933).
49 This was a veiled way of stipulating that the wife also had to be a member of the local BGM church. ABEM, 875: Minutes CAEC (25 Jan. 1934).
50 Some feared that former Catholics would misinterpret the laying on of hands. ABEM, 875: Minutes CAEC (1 Feb. 1935).
51 This sanction was not included in the *Preliminary Stipulations*. ABEM, 693: Van Goethem to Winston Sr. and Vansteenberghe (27 Dec. 1933), Vansteenberghe to Van Goethem (29 Dec. 1933).
52 Ibid.: Van Goethem to Vansteenberghe (30 Dec. 1933).

duction of the *Preliminary Stipulations* in the summer of 1929. From then on, communion was only served in BGM churches with a church council, even if it was preliminary. Only the frequency could be decided locally and varied among congregations.[53] A temporary measure was introduced for stations without a church council that were already holding communion services.[54]

Communion could be taken by anyone who was a member of a BGM church, whereas all others had to ask permission from the local pastor before the start of the service. In preparation for the first local communion service, all interested people were invited to a meeting of the church council or the preliminary church council. Those who wished to take communion were then questioned about "their faith and Christian experience."[55] Although the *Preliminary Stipulations* did not say whether recent converts should partake, John Winston Sr. suggested not to push this but "rather let the Holy Spirit do His work in their hearts."[56]

In exceptional cases, restrictions on communion were imposed on a whole congregation, for instance, by lowering the frequency from weekly to monthly, or in one case, by deferring communion altogether until the problems in a church had been solved.[57] This last measure was eventually revoked when the church was placed under the direct leadership of the mission, which decided that communion should be resumed but with strict controls.[58]

The Belgian Gospel Mission took the classic faith mission stance by accepting believers and infant baptism for its workers. It also allowed its work-

53 Henri Keller, pastor in Warquignies, felt that in view of the spiritual climate, it would be good to have communion once a month instead of every week. ABEM, 164: Keller to Winston Sr., 22 Oct. 1933.
54 The temporary measure remained in place for less than a year. It stipulated that the congregation was allowed to have communion on condition that they would start setting up a church council or a preliminary church council. In May 1930, BGMer Van de Riet apologized for having served communion in Antwerp although there was no church council there. His defending argument was that he did not realize that the temporary measure was no longer in force. One of the places where the temporary measure was used was Warquignies. three elders on the basis of 1 *Timothy* 3:8-13. These three men and the pastor formed the church council. Anyone wishing to take communion had to tell the pastor and would then be visited at home by the elders to be quizzed about their faith and lifestyle. The church council then decided based on this visit's report. The process usually took three to four weeks. Andries was allowed to keep serving communion in this way because this approach guaranteed discipline in the area of communion. ABEM, 4: Andries to Winston Sr. (16 July 1929), Winston Sr. to Andries (26 July 1929); ABEM, 292: Van de Riet to Vansteenberghe (5 May 1930); ABEM, 875: Minutes CAE (4 April 1930); ABEM, 875: Preliminary Stipulations (1929).
55 "leur foi et leurs expériences chrétiennes." ABEM, 51: Winston Sr. to Châtelain (5 Feb. 1930).
56 "mais laissez plutôt le Saint-Esprit travailler Lui-même dans leurs cœurs." Ibid.
57 ABEM, 49: Castiaux to Winston Sr. (1 Aug. 1929); ABEM, 164: Keller to Winston Sr. (22 Oct. 1933).
58 ABEM, 164: Winston Sr. to Keller (13 Nov. 1934).

ers to change sides if they wished.[59] The argument was that baptism was not regarded as needful for salvation. This flexible approach ensured unity and enabled the team to focus on its 'real task' of evangelism.[60] As a faith mission, the BGM was unique because it also implemented this practice in its churches.[61] Believers' baptism by immersion was practiced most widely.[62] Only a few BGMers advocated paedobaptism exclusively, and they all came from Dutch denominations where this was the normative practice. Some French-speaking BGMers came from similar churches, such as the *Église Réformée de France*, but they did not advocate paedobaptism as the preferred option.[63]

The repeated reassurance that there was complete freedom within the mission about the mode of baptism did not mean that all pastors offered both options.[64] Often, the local pastor or evangelist would refer members whose views on baptism differed from their own to those of a colleague of a nearby church.[65] In one instance, evangelist Johannes Elleman asked Vansteenberghe to dedicate his children because his local pastor, Jacob Servaas Sr., was a confirmed paedobaptist who refused to dedicate children.[66]

Daniël Meijer's attitude must have pleased the BGM leadership. He wrote that he believed "not so much in one form of baptism or another — but in the baptism of the spirit — although I happily comply with the wish of believers, either to dedicate their children to the Lord in paedobaptism — or to be baptized as adults."[67]

External circumstances also played a role in the issue of paedobaptism. One couple at the BGM church at Willebroek found that staff at their maternity clinic in Mechelen, which was Catholic, insisted that their child should be baptized in the Catholic tradition. The parents, who did not have a strong view of baptism, felt under pressure from two sides. They contacted BGM pastor Daniel van der Beek, who said he would perform the ritual if paedobaptism proved to be necessary.[68]

59 Fiedler, *The Story of Faith Missions*, 182.
60 ABEM, 248: Winston Sr. to Saucy (13 July 1929); Monsma, "Boekaankondiging," 6.
61 In the Church of Christ in Nigeria, this was only introduced after the mission stations in the far Northeast of Nigeria had transferred from the Anglican Church Missionary Society to the Sudan United Mission. Fiedler, *The Story of Faith Missions*, 338-339.
62 E. Norton, "Finding Peace in a Belgian Gospel Tent," 549.
63 It must be admitted, though, that it is unclear whether they supported paedobaptism when they joined the BGM, like their Dutch colleagues.
64 ABEM, 248: Winston Sr. to Saucy (13 July 1929).
65 People from Antwerp who wished to be baptized by immersion were referred to Brussels, because the church in Antwerp practiced paedobaptism and therefore did not have a baptism tank. ABEM, 205: Meijer to Vansteenberghe (16 May 1932).
66 The first time, Jakob Servaas Sr. explained his refusal by stating that he had never dedicated infants before. The second time, he refused because it was against his convictions as a paedobaptist. ABEM, 111: Elleman to Vansteenberghe (31 July 1932).
67 For the original quote, see ABEM, 205: Meijer to Vansteenberghe (16 May 1932).
68 ABEM, 318: Van der Beek to Vansteenberghe (7 Oct. [1935]).

He had a Reformed background but preferred believers' baptism, although he left the final choice with the parents, as he felt that baptism was a secondary issue.[69] It seems that both baptism practices had fervent proponents in his local church. When Van der Beek had his child dedicated and not baptized, this led to tensions within his local church. Emotions ran so high that some members suggested that he should step down as pastor.[70]

The BGM board transferred him to the church of Sint-Niklaas in 1935, which was a surprising choice, as this church also had a tradition of paedobaptism.[71] As before, he did not baptize infants but referred the parents to pastors of three nearby BGM churches.[72] No one protested until he had another child, whom he also dedicated. Once again, several church members demanded his departure.[73] This time, he was not transferred. He stayed in Sint-Niklaas until 1955.

Although the BGM claimed complete freedom within the mission on the baptism mode, there were regular tensions on this issue. In Antwerp, it started when teenager Elisabeth Lemière was staying with the Châtelain family in Huy for three months, where they practiced baptism by immersion. When she returned home and wished to be baptized this way, her mother was vehemently opposed, whereas her father refused to take sides. As Lemière was still a minor, she decided not to go ahead. She was not baptized by immersion until many years later when she was on the mission field.[74]

Although BGM workers were expected to show mutual respect and forbearance in baptism practice, they only sometimes managed this. Evangelist Jules Michiels, who worked in Blauwput near Leuven, once responded to an invitation to an infant baptism at the Flemish church in Brussels by writing that he did not appreciate "popish infant baptism rubbish."[75]

The do's and don'ts regarding baptism were unclear, especially for new workers. As we saw earlier, the *Preliminary Stipulations* only stated that being

---

69 He added that Solomon's prayer for wisdom was needed regarding baptism in Belgium. He alluded to the pressure that families and maternity clinics applied on young parents to have newborns christened according to Belgian, i.e. Catholic, tradition. The records do not indicate what the parents eventually decided to do. Ibid.

70 Ibid. (30 Aug. 1936).

71 Usually, the BGM leadership tried to ensure a good match between a local church and its new pastor, as we can see from the deliberations about André Vuilleumier. He had been christened but believed in believers' baptism, although he did not want to be 'rebaptized.' His viewpoint was an important factor in his assignment to a local church. The fact that van der Beek was sent to Sint-Niklaas may indicate that the BGM had found no suitable alternatives for the church, nor for Van der Beek, and that they just hoped that tensions such as had arisen in Willebroek could be avoided here. ABEM, 877: Minutes Personnel Committee (19 Sep. 1936).

72 ABEM, 318: Van der Beek to Vansteenberghe (30 Aug. 1936).

73 ABEM, 326: Vanderbeeken to Vansteenberghe and Winston Sr. (30 Aug. 1936).

74 Reich, "Elisabeth Lemière Shannon," 25-26.

75 "Rooms kinderdoopgeknoei." ABEM, 203: Michiels to the BGM board (30 Nov. 1931).

baptized was insufficient grounds for being allowed to take communion. This lack of clarity is remarkable, as there was an obvious need for it.

Jean Quaedpeerds, who had joined from the Baptist church at Ougrée and was now working as an evangelist in Limburg, had been submitting written questions about this from as early as 1927. He asked whether, in cases where infant baptism was practiced, the presence of godparents was required and whether it would be okay to have godparents who were unconverted or Catholic. He also enquired whether BGM pastors needed permission from the BGM board to baptize infants and if a particular qualification was required. His final question was whether both views on baptisms could be advocated and practiced in the same BGM station or church.[76]

This had not been discussed during his application procedure, which again shows that the BGM leadership should have considered the mode of baptism important. Even the more detailed version of the *Preliminary Stipulations* of 1932 needed to clarify agreed practices and views about baptism. The only added stipulation was that dedications and baptisms must be entered into the church register.[77]

In 1933, Henri Keller discussed a lower age limit for believers' baptism. A thirteen-year-old girl had asked to be baptized together with her parents. Keller was convinced that she was genuinely converted, but she had not completed the baptism classes offered to candidates for baptism in Keller's church.[78] As is characteristic of a relatively young organization, the issue was not considered until it presented itself as a practical dilemma. Vansteenberghe and Winston Sr. considered Keller's question. They did not say anything about the lower age limit but advised that the girl could be baptized on the condition that Keller and Winston Sr. would interview her to confirm that she was genuinely converted. "It is clear from the examples that are recounted to us in Holy Scripture," Winston Sr. argued, "that the apostles baptized individuals on the spot."[79]

For a long time, separate services on separate days were held for believers' baptisms for men and women.[80] Baptism services with male and female candidates are not mentioned until as late as 1935.[81] It is unclear why men and women were baptized separately, nor do we know why the practice was eventually given up. No similar practices have been found in neighboring countries or other faith missions.

Because the mission wanted its churches to be as pure as possible, the membership requirements were clearly set out. First, candidates must have had a 'true

76 ABEM, 234: Quaedpeerds to Vansteenberghe (24 Feb. 1927).
77 ABEM, 1238: Preliminary Dispositions (1929).
78 ABEM, 164: Keller to Winston Sr. (n.d.) [1933].
79 For the original quote, see Ibid.: Winston Sr. to Keller (n.d.) [1933].
80 E. Norton, "Finding Peace in a Belgian Gospel Tent," 549.
81 ABEM, 855: USA Newsletter (May 1935).

conversion.' They also had to agree with BGM's statement of faith and stop attending mass. Baptism alone was not sufficient to qualify for membership.[82]

A development is noticeable in the evaluation of candidates for membership. In the preliminary church structure of 1929, the church council only had to ensure that candidates for membership met the prescribed conditions, taking special care that they fully understood the "separation from the world."[83] From 1932 onwards, candidates for membership first had to receive some teaching about the catechism and then have a personal interview with the pastor, in which the latter checked whether the person understood the statement of faith and wholeheartedly agreed with it. If any pastoral issues arose later, the pastor could refer to the teaching the person had received and reprimand members for any behavior that deviated from it.

The sources are insufficient to verify whether the decision-making process for admitting members varied between local BGM churches before the publication of the first church structure. However, judging by the various church backgrounds of the BGMers and John Winston Sr.'s warning letter from 1928, there was likely at least some variation.

Only the membership admission procedure of the church in Tongeren from before 1929 is known from correspondence. The church council would meet after the morning service, and all candidates were discussed individually. After that, the council decided which candidates qualified for membership. Unfortunately, we do not know what conditions the candidates had to meet. Approved candidates were publicly accepted into membership during the evening service of that same Sunday.[84]

The ceremony of the public admission of people into membership was somewhat flexible, as can be seen from a comparison between the churches of Oostrozebeke and Antwerp. In Oostrozebeke, the only question was: "You know you cannot keep company with or marry an unconverted girl; are you willing to follow the Lord in this matter?"[85]

In Antwerp, the candidates had to stand up, raise their right hand, and then agree with a statement about the church's meaning, development, and calling that was read out to them. They then had to answer the following three questions individually:

> Do you confess here in God's presence that you accept Jesus Christ in faith as your only Saviour and Redeemer?
> That he saved you, you have been made His, and you wish to return His love by serving Him?

---

82 ABEM, 1238: Preliminary Dispositions (1929).
83 Ibid.
84 ABEM, 326: Vanderbeeken to Vansteenberghe (5 Dec. 1929).
85 In view of the specific mention of marriage to an unconverted girl, it is probable that there were or had been issues in this area. ABEM, 855: Newsletter USA (21 Jan. 1935).

That you, as witnesses of Jesus Christ, join us to honor His name and detach yourself from anything that may discredit or dishonor Him?[86]

As Samuel Dubois' correspondence to John Winston Sr. shows, not all candidates were accepted. Although this one letter does not provide a strong enough basis for conclusions about the mission in general, nothing indicates that rejecting candidates was unusual. Of the twenty-one candidates, one failed to show up, three were asked to wait, and eleven were accepted. We must assume that the remaining six were rejected because they needed to meet the conditions for membership.[87]

The *Preliminary Stipulations* authorized local church councils to apply church discipline.[88] It is unclear whether this meant stricter supervision of the codes of conduct or simply formalizing what was already practiced. It is interesting to see what situations led to disciplinary measures and what these measures were. Several new converts were cohabiting, and rectifying these arrangements was not always easy.

In some cases, one of the partners (or even both) was still legally married to someone else. In one case, Winston Sr. argued based on *Matthew* 5:32 and 19:9 that divorce on the grounds of adultery was allowed but that the man was wrong in cohabiting without having divorced his wife first. Based on I *Corinthians* 7:12-16, he advised that the man would have to leave his current partner and try to reconcile with his legal wife.[89] On the other hand, Edith Norton argued that these issues required a lot of tact and wisdom. She feared Winston Sr.'s approach would be counterproductive, and the persons concerned would leave the church.[90]

Occasionally, church councilors were also disciplined for sexual misbehavior. One elder stepped down from the church council after committing adultery.[91] He expected to be allowed to resume his task after a public confession of guilt and a plea for forgiveness, but his pastor felt that he should be suspended as an elder for at least several months.[92] Odilon Vansteenberghe

---

86 For the original quote, see ABEM, 205: Meijer to Vansteenberghe (17 April 1930).
87 ABEM, 107: Dubois to Winston Sr. (29 Jan. 1930).
88 ABEM, 1238: Preliminary Dispositions (1929).
89 ABEM, 76: Winston Sr. to Delvigne (18 Jan. 1935).
90 Berend Hilberinck was asked to conduct the wedding of a Protestant Hungarian. The official documents needed for the legal ceremony took a long time; the couple had moved in together, and she was now pregnant. The couple arranged a legal wedding ceremony as soon as the documents arrived, but they also wanted a blessing at church. Hilberinck understood that despite the couple's remorse, he could not bless them in the local BGM church. He asked the BGM leadership for their permission to bless the couple at home. The reply has not been preserved. ABEM, 137: Hilberinck to Vansteenberghe (16 Feb. 1931); E. Norton, "Sunshine and Shadow in Belgium," 617.
91 ABEM, 255: Servaas Sr. to Vansteenberghe (8 Oct. 1935).
92 Ibid. (16 Oct. 1935).

was much stricter in his instructions to the pastor. He wrote that stepping down from his post as an elder was insufficient and that the man should also be barred from taking communion for several months.[93]

Regional leadership meetings were good occasions to discuss issues with discipline. The minutes of these meetings provide some interesting insights. There was some discussion as to whether the church council ought to intervene in marital difficulties, how chatting in church before the start of the service could be discouraged, what to do with a relapsed alcoholic, and what disciplinary measures could be used and when.[94]

Other issues discussed and led to disciplinary actions were short hair for women, domestic violence, and commercial or sports activities on Sundays. Also, a prevalent pastime in Belgium, pigeon keeping, was prohibited because too much alcohol was served at pigeon clubs.[95] The disciplinary measures discussed in the correspondence are barring people from taking communion, excluding them from Sunday meetings, and expulsion from the church.[96]

Although Children's work started as a form of evangelism at a local church, it soon evolved into religious education for the children of the members and visitors. The fact that BGMers complained from time to time that parents did not support the work because they did "not understand the value of religious instruction" seems to illustrate that local workers started to think on a mid-and basis.[97] Yet, whereas children's work flourished, there were no specific activities for young people until the late 1920s.[98] The dominance of the eschatological urgency hampered the development of a long-term vision for the BGM churches. With no youth groups between the Sunday School for children and the church services and Bible studies for adults, it was difficult to retain young people who had grown up in BGM congregations or to attract young people from outside.[99]

This led to tension within the organization. In Ghent, Johan van Lierop complained that his young people were drawn to the local Methodist church,

---

93 This way, Vansteenberghe kept the possibility of further disciplinary measures open. ABEM, 238: Vansteenberghe to Servaas Sr. (25 Oct. 1935).
94 ABEM, 283: Programma voor de Vlaamsche werkers der Belgische Evangelische Zending te Gent (5 July 1937).
95 ABEM, 888: Vansteenberghe, Building in Belgium.
96 ABEM, 875: Vansteenberghe, Rapport de l'agent itinérant des Flandres [30 June 1926]; ABEM, 660: Report from Keller (July 1936); ABEM, 164: Keller to Winston Sr. (23 Dec. 1932); ABEM, 292: Van de Riet to Vansteenberghe (8 April 1935).
97 There are no indications in the archives when the balance shifted from evangelism to religious education. ABEM, 766: Report of Mr. Castiaux.
98 ABEM, 875: Chart of the Children's Schools (May 1925), Ecole des Enfants le Dimanche (Feb. 1926), Rapport sur l'Œuvre parmi les Enfants (4 March 1926); ABEM, 235: Williams to Quenon (23 March 1932).
99 This is the first time people who had grown up in BGM churches were reported to be leaving their churches. ABEM, 855: USA Prayer Letter.

which organized youth meetings.[100] So, in a few locations, a youth group was started, for instance, in the Dutch-speaking church of Brussels. Here, Abraham van Puffelen used Christian Endeavour, the nondenominational youth movement of which he had been an active member in the US, as a model for his work among young adults.[101] His aim was "to teach the young people to express themselves in a discussion of a certain topic, the deepening of their spiritual life and the creating of a missionary spirit."[102] In 1931, a youth association was created for youngsters between fifteen and eighteen.[103]

The BGM's activist approach, with no mid- and long-term plans, is also reflected in the lack of an overall structure for children's and youth work. From 1928 onwards, several national and regional meetings were organized in anticipation of a national youth association.[104] In 1935, the first Flemish BGM youth camp took place in Genk. The following year, there was also a camp for the French-speaking youth in Braine-le-Comte, Wallonia.[105]

The first proposal to combine local youth work from various churches into a national youth association dates from 1926 and came from Liège.[106] Ten years after the initial proposal, the *Belgisch Evangelisch Jeugd Verbond* (Belgian Evangelical Youth Alliance or BEJV) was started in 1936. Odilon Vansteenberghe had opposed the plans for a national youth association for many years. He felt they first needed to find a young and capable married couple to coordinate the work.[107]

Eventually, Abraham Van Puffelen decided not to wait any longer. At the Flemish workers' meeting of 10 February 1935, Van Puffelen's proposal to "establish a youth organization in principle, and to appoint a Committee that would work on this" was accepted.[108] As several committee members had been

100 Van Lierop added that Kerremans also wrote to adults to invite them to join his church. ABEM, 283: Van Lierop to the Nortons (17 Sep. 1929).
101 His association had two types of members: associates and active members. Those who wished to become active members were required to make a fourfold vow based on their confession of Christ. ABEM, 286: Van Puffelen, Report Concerning the Work of the Flemish Post in Brussels (Oct. 1929).
102 One report mentions explicitly the young people at Liège and the fact that they had all quit smoking. Some had also promised to abstain from alcohol. ABEM, 340: Van Puffelen to Winterbottom (20 Feb. 1930).
103 A. van Puffelen, "Jaarvergadering der jonge jeugdvereeniging 'Eben-Haezer' te Brussel," 4; ABEM, 52: Claude to Winston Sr. (2 Oct. 1928).
104 The first was in Brussels on 15 August 1928. Two hundred and sixty-eight French-speaking, and almost two hundred Flemish youths came. A year later, the Youth Day for French-speakers took place on the land of Count du Val de Beaulieu. In 1932, an event was held for Flemish BGM youth in a park in Oudergem. "Naklanken van onze Jeugddag te Brussel," 2; "La Fête du 15 Août," 1.
105 ABEM, 865: Lignier, Quelques souvenirs de l'UJEB; "Het jeugdkamp in Genk," sec. Uit den Arbeid, 2.
106 ABEM, 20: R. Norton to Bolomey (14 Sep. 1926).
107 ABEM, 52: Vansteenberghe to Claude (18 May 1935).
108 ABEM, 286: Van Puffelen to Vansteenberghe (6 March 1936).

part of Christian Endeavour, it is no surprise that the structure and constitution of the BEJV were based on those of this youth movement.[109]

The initiative was communicated to a broader audience through *Onze Hoop* magazine. Even at an early age, evangelism's urgency was fundamental for the BEJV. It aimed to "win young people for Christ and then to make them active in leading others to the same Christ."[110] After the BGM leadership had approved the constitution, 1 May 1936 was chosen as the official launch date.[111] Six months later, the *Union de la Jeunesse Evangélique Belge* (UJEB) was launched, with a constitution almost identical to the BEJV.[112]

---

109 As we saw earlier, Van Puffelen had been involved with Christian Endeavour, while Dutchmen Gerrit van de Riet and Daniël van der Beek had been active in the Dutch branch, the *Bond voor Ernstig Christendom*. G. van de Riet, "Toen ons B.E.J.V. er nog niet was … (3);" Kaastra, *Nederlands Verbond van Jeugdbonden 'Eén in Christus': Christian Endeavour Nederland*, 22.
110 For the original quote, see "Het Belgisch Evangelisch Jeugdverbond B.E.J.V.," 2.
111 This date may have been chosen because it is easy to remember. It closely follows the date on which the constitution was accepted. ABEM, 649: General Workers Letter (23 April 1936).
112 Overbeeke sometimes reports wrong founding dates in his yearbooks. In his first yearbook, he wrongly dates the founding of UJEB to 1937 or 1938. From 1954 onwards, he dates UJEB to 1926, and from 1963 onwards, he dates BEJV to 1935. In his later editions he probably follows the proposal for a national youth organization submitted by French-speakers in 1926 and another one by Dutch-speakers from 1935. Both organizations were founded in 1936. ABEM, 849: General Workers Letter (9 March 1936); "Het Belgisch Evangelisch Jeugd Verbond," 4; Overbeeke, *Jaarboek der evangelische kerken* (1947), 188-189; Ibid., *Jaarboek der evangelische kerken in België 1954*, 175; Ibid., *Jaarboek der evangelische kerken in België 1963*, 172; Ibid., *Jaarboek voor de protestantse kerken in België 1966*, 172-173; Ibid., *Jaarboek van de protestantse kerken in België 1972*, 170-171.

WHY SUPPORT THE BELGIAN GOSPEL MISSION?

Fundraising Brochure, 1930s.
[KADOC-KU Leuven: ABEM, 1277]

7
FROM DOLLAR MISSION TO BEGGARS MISSION, 1926-1936

After successfully implementing the reorganization of February 1926, the prospects appeared suitable for further work expansion. However, within a few years, the Achilles heel of the BEM was painfully exposed. First, the mission was hit hard by the Great Depression. As Ralph Norton had no equal in fundraising skills, his death in 1934 was an additional negative factor in the struggle to generate sufficient means to cover the expenditure.[1] As a faith mission, the Belgian Gospel Mission depended heavily on financial donations from fellow believers and pursued the strict policy of not going into debt.

Resourcefulness was a vital trait of the Nortons, originating from the United States. To secure the majority of donations to the BGM from North America, they undertook numerous transatlantic trips, the first of which was in 1919. Their strategic placement of fundraising adverts, notably in the *Sunday School Times*, and their ability to raise an impressive $ 90,000-100,000 through church visits and conferences testify to their ingenuity and dedication.[2]

Following the war's end, the BGM sent prayer letters to its US supporters in 1920. However, the war's aftermath and the subsequent depression of 1920-21 took a toll on their generosity. Some supporters lost interest, others could

---

1 Like Charles Finney and Dwight L. Moody, Ralph Norton displayed good fundraising skills and the "ability to make easy friends with business leaders." Hambrick-Stowe, "Sanctified Business," 89; ABEM, 850: Minutes Board of Trustees (11 Oct. 1934).
2 ABEM, 850: Minutes Board of Trustees (14 Jan. 1920); Advert, *Sunday School Times*, 1919, 199.

not contribute as before, and sadly, several passed away. This necessitated the Nortons to seek out new supporters in the early 1920s.[3]

The dependency on regular fundraising trips became apparent in 1923. When a scheduled trip was canceled because the Nortons were too busy in Belgium, donations dropped to a third of the usual. So when, in 1925, Ralph Norton had to stay in Brussels to oversee the building of the new headquarters, his wife traveled to the United States by herself for a fundraising trip.[4]

The Nortons faced an uphill battle to convey Belgium, a developed country, as a mission field. They struggled to communicate that people in a developed society may be harder to reach than in supposedly primitive nations, a challenge unique to their mission. The strong influence of Catholic teaching and tradition on the Belgians, a factor often misunderstood by their audience due to the minority position of Roman Catholicism in the USA, further complicated their task. These challenges, coupled with the sharply decreasing funds for humanitarian aid to French and Belgian Protestants from 1922 onwards, painted a bleak picture of their mission.[5] An additional problem for the BGM was that funds had to be raised not only for evangelistic materials but also to finance local pastors and to buy property.

In the late 1920s, the fundraising trips were forced to refocus on small congregations, as the Nortons had already prospected the larger ones in previous years. As these donations were insufficient, the fishing pond had to be expanded. This illustrates the Nortons' struggle to raise enough money for their expanding work in Belgium.[6] The donations of these smaller churches only barely covered their traveling expenses. Despite this, Ralph Norton remained optimistic. He was convinced these visits would generate more income in the long term if these churches included the Belgian Gospel Mission in their annual budgets.

---

3   The Nortons decided to put everyone on their mailing list who had donated a minimum of $ 5. This amounted to 4,000 addresses. ABEM, 850: Minutes Board of Trustees (1 April, 21 Oct. 1920, 20 July 1922).
4   One of the people she met was Henry P. Crowell, who later donated $ 2,000. She also met Canadian Sydney Thomas Smith, a successful businessman and noted lay preacher and Bible teacher, who served as a trustee on the boards of Chicago's Moody Bible Institute, Dallas Theological Seminary, and the Central American Mission. He was director of Pennsylvania's Montrose Bible Conference, became president of the World's Christian Fundamentalist Association in 1925, and was president of the Canadian Bible Society from 1925 until 1947. He served as Vice President of the British and Foreign Bible Society for one term. ABEM, 850: Minutes Board of Trustees (4 March 1926); Norton, *Ralph Norton*, 192; Goldsborough, Howison, "Memorable Manitobans: Sidney Thomas Smith (1878-1947)."
5   ABEM, 887: G. Winston, "History of the BGM," s d.; AUPCB, 602: Minutes of Meeting of the Commission on Relations with France and Belgium (1 Nov. 1922).
6   ABEM, 849: General Workers Letter (Oct. 1927, 6 May 1930, 13 Oct. 1930, Aug. 1933).

Norton's optimism was unsubstantiated. From the 1930s onwards, all American BGMers had to do at least some deputation during their furlough.[7] In an article in the *Sunday School Times,* a few months before the Great Depression hit the US, Edith Norton answered a question they were frequently asked: "Why should we of America support this work in Belgium? There is prosperity in Belgium – can not the work be self-supporting?"[8]

From 1930 onwards, the BGM faced a financial crisis, which turned out to be chronic due to a convergence of developments. First, there was a distinct lack of success in adding a substantial number of new donors and the aging (and dying) group of supporters. Secondly, as we have seen in the introduction, North American churches were confronted with an explosive rise in requests for support from similar missionary organizations. During the interwar period, dozens of new missions were founded, mostly interdenominational faith missions. With so many competitors fishing in the same pond, soliciting for missions in a First World country almost became a mission impossible. Thirdly, due to the Great Depression, many of the BGM's faithful supporters were forced to reduce their donations substantially.[9]

Therefore, fundraising activities to cover monthly costs were also carried out outside the US, even before the Great Depression. As several BGMers were from Switzerland, the mission was promoted here by deputation and speaking engagements.[10] In 1926, Henry Bentley met missionary friends Paul Tissot, H. Mouchet, and Ch. Freundler. Odilon Vansteenberghe represented the BGM at the Keswick-inspired conference of Morges in 1927. Upon invitation, Samuel Dubois promoted the mission at the *Bund Freier Evangelischer Gemeinden in der Schweiz*' federal congress (Association of Free Evangelical Churches in Switzerland) in 1934. During that same year, Henri Keller promoted the Belgian Gospel Mission at the Bible school in Sankt Chrischona.[11]

As for the Netherlands, Ralph Norton encouraged Dutch workers to accept as many invitations as possible to speak in their homeland. These opportuni-

---

7 See ABEM, 293: Van Goethem to Winston Sr. (28 May 1931); ABEM, 849: General Workers Letter (8 Aug. 1933).
8 E. Norton, "Could the Belgians Support Our Mission?," 64.
9 Both traditional and faith missions suffered a severe decline in income. The difference was that traditional missions went into debt to keep their missionaries on the field. As this was no option for faith missions, they had to make tough decisions with regard to their missionaries. Terry, and Gallagher, *Encountering the History of Missions*, 277; Moreau, "Evangelical Missions Development 1910 to 2010 in the North American Setting," 8; R. Norton, "Waarom wij naar Amerika gaan," 2; "Een ernstige mededeeling aan Gods kinderen in en buiten België," 4; ABEM, 849: General Workers letter (6 March 1930).
10 These visits were also used to sign up new workers.
11 Freundler and Tissot were pastors of the Swiss Free Evangelical Churches. "En Suisse," 1; "Zendingsberichten," 1; ABEM, 107: Dubois to Winston Sr. (20 June 1934); ABEM, 164: Keller to Winston Sr. (10 Sep. 1934).

ties were meant to promote the BGM more widely, which could result in more donations.[12]

In the United Kingdom, deputation had been low-key for many years after an unsuccessful attempt to solicit money in 1922.[13] A renewed attempt in 1935 was seconded by the launch of a Council of Reference, which consisted of longtime friend William G. Walters and Rev. Francis C. Brading, both from the Scripture Gift Mission; London businessman and lay evangelist Alexander Lindsay Glegg; John Alfred Kensit, secretary of the Protestant Truth Society, a 1920s fundamentalist and anti-Catholic organization; Rev. E.L. Langston, from the London Society for Promoting Christianity Amongst the Jews, and Rev. Dinsdale T. Young, Superintendent Minister of the Methodist Central Hall at Westminster.[14] The immediate occasion for this UK campaign had been Ralph Norton's death in the Fall of 1934. Despite broadening the fundraising horizon to Europe, most donations still came from the US.

Although the impact of the Great Depression became noticeable in Belgium by the summer of 1930, already in 1929, internal discussions about the BGM's identity as a faith mission intensified.[15] What if the funds were insufficient to pay the salaries? John Winston Sr. reminded Joseph Leprince of the faith mission principle applied by the mission: "We present our needs to the Lord in prayer and we live on voluntary donations by those children of God on whose hearts the Lord has placed this work."[16] As a consequence, the BGMers were actively engaged in prayer for the finances that were needed.[17] It was often repeated to supporters that the BGM, including its workers, had no financial security but depended on donations.[18]

12 They mainly targeted regular church members, as the church councils sending the invitations obviously knew the BGM through their respective missionaries. The underlying motivation for accepting these speaking engagements is that they would receive more individual gifts if they were more widely known. ABEM, 205: Meijer to Vansteenberghe (22 March 1934).
13 In 1931, Peter McRostie of Glasgow Tent Hall organized a deputation trip for O. Vansteenberghe. In 1933, Miss Dickinson went to London for a month to help William Horsburgh prepare for a fundraising tour of several conferences by R. Van Goethem, J. Servaas Sr., and Vansteenberghe. *The Keswick Convention 1931*; ABEM, 850: Minutes Board of Trustees (20 July 1922); ABEM, 850: Personnel Committee Report to CAEC (2 Oct. 1933).
14 Maiden, "Fundamentalism and Anti-Catholicism in Inter-War English Evangelicalism," 156-167; Clifton, Amigo, Friend of the Poor, 136; Superintendent Methodist Central Hall Westminster, "Ministers of Central Hall."
15 The Belgian economy heavily relied on exports. Blom, Lamberts, and Milis, *Geschiedenis van de Nederlanden*, 348.
16 For the original quote, see ABEM, 188: Winston Sr. to Leprince (20 Feb. 1929).
17 ABEM, 849: General Workers Letter (18 Dec. 1926, 31 Aug. 1927).
18 "We take the liberty to declare once more that the work of the Belgian Gospel Mission is a work of faith. That means that there is no person or committee anywhere in the world guaranteeing even the smallest amount of money for our work. The Mission workers are in the same position. They know this and they have accepted that the Mission does not guarantee them any money. This gives us the candor to impress the needs of our work on

In September 1930, the Belgian Gospel Mission experienced liquidity problems for the first time. Ralph Norton shared this with the workers, asking them to pray. He added that he was still determining whether the salaries for the second half of that month could be paid. Until then, the principle of paying salaries only if and to the extent sufficient financial means were available had remained theoretical.

But from now on, the workers would often be paid in part or sometimes not at all. Like most American evangelicals, Norton approached the financial issue from a religious perspective.[19] He was convinced that the BGM was in this precarious situation to be reminded of its total dependency on God.[20]

That didn't rule out rational action. Initially, the BGM tried to counter the misconception that its colporteurs were selling books as a way of living, as was usually the case. The primary goal was spreading the Gospel, not simply selling books.[21] Due to the financial urgency, Ralph Norton now instructed BGMers to sell their existing supply of literature before ordering new supplies. It was felt that this approach would free dormant capital for the purchase of new literature or diversification into general funds. He also called for cost-cutting, saying that free materials should be used locally before ordering new materials.[22]

The financial need was also announced in the local congregations and the BGM magazines *Notre Espérance* and *Onze Hoop*. The believers were encouraged to pray about this and contribute according to their means. The BGMers themselves were also encouraged to give regularly and cheerfully.[23]

On 27 February 1931, the Belgian Gospel Mission held its first day of collective fasting and prayer. Church members who were "advanced the furthest" had been invited too.[24] Shortly after that, Ralph Norton set out on a new fundraising trip to the US. Due to the ongoing crisis, all the hard work

---

all its friends as far as they are children of God. We add to this that the majority of those whose gifts have made the work possible came from 'common', even poor people who can only give small amounts. And the Mission is very grateful for these faithful givers of small amounts." For the original quote, see "Nieuws uit onze posten," *Onze Hoop*, 15 May 1929, 1; ABEM, 49: Castiaux to 'Chers amis' (May 1926).

19 Hutchinson, and Wolffe, *A Short History of Global Evangelicalism*, 171.
20 "I am convinced that the Lord is reducing us to this extreme to make us understand that these gifts are not due to human effort, nor are they provided by any man, but they come from Him directly. I wonder whether we fully appreciate this grace and whether we have thanked the Lord as we should." For the original quote, see ABEM, 849: General Workers Letter (30 Sep. 1930).
21 Omon, "Voor het hoogste het beste," 64; "Nieuws uit den Arbeid – Van een doopfeest en nog wat," 5; ABEM, 10: Winston Sr. to Barbezat (6 March 1929).
22 Apparently significant amounts of materials were left lying around rather than being used or sent back to Brussels. ABEM, 849: General Workers Letter (30 Sep. 1930).
23 Generosity was presented as a means and result of spiritual growth. Ibid. (30 Sep. 1930, 2 Oct. 1930, 17 Feb. 1931).
24 For the original quote, see Ibid. (17 Feb. 1931).

resulted in even less support than before. This must have been a huge disappointment. While he was still in America, Norton repeated his instructions to cut costs, ordered to have salaries frozen, and refused to accept new workers except in exceptional cases.

When the situation deteriorated even further a year later, it was decided to cut salaries by 10%, leading to tithing discussions.[25] Ralph Norton consoled himself by saying that the China Inland Mission did not see its income go down and that "what God is doing for them, He is able to do for us if we walk in fellowship with Him."[26] This kind of reasoning could easily lead to the erroneous conclusion that if revenues remained insufficient, this would be a sign that the BGMers were insufficiently committed to God, either as an organization or individually.

Moreover, his picture of the CIM's financial situation was distorted. CIM had seen a marked drop in middle-range contributions, but some substantial donations had compensated for this.[27] What is more, CIM obtained its income from donations and the sale of a never-ending stream of publications.[28] The Personnel Committee countered Ralph Norton – and rightly so – by pointing out that the China Inland Mission had twenty full-time fundraisers in the US and the UK, and the Belgian Gospel Mission did not have one.[29] The only fundraising by the BGM took place in the form of speaking engagements of workers at conferences or on furlough and of the Nortons' trips.

The BGM had not been prepared for the severe financial setback they encountered now for some time. The policy was that general expenses were paid first, and the remainder was used to pay salaries as much as possible.[30] As a consequence, salaries often were paid out partially. When Jan Monsma asked whether the reduced salaries would be paid at a later stage, he did not get a clear answer. Although some faith missions did this, the final decision had to wait until the Nortons returned from America.[31]

In 1933, the situation worsened once more as the dollar's value fell. The possibility of limiting existing activities was discussed, and after some delib-

25 ABEM, 875: Minutes CAE (5 Jan. 1932).
26 ABEM, 20: R. Norton to Bolomey (10 June 1932).
27 Austin, "No Solicitation," 232.
28 The only comparable BGM initiatives were Howard Sr.'s *A New Invasion of Belgium* and Edith Norton's biography of her husband, *Ralph Norton and the Belgian Gospel Mission*. Ibid., 213.
29 ABEM, 877: Minutes Personnel Committee (7 Oct. 1932).
30 After World War II, this principle became the subject of fierce internal discussions. See Chapter 10. ABEM, 131: Winston Sr. to Georges (29 June 1936).
31 Monsma left sometime later to become an evangelist at Jeruël church in Rotterdam (NL). The reported reason for his departure was his dissatisfaction about not being allowed to become station leader in Antwerp. In light of his query about finances, it is possible that he also had financial reasons. ABEM, 208: Monsma to Winston Sr. (8 Sep. 1932), Winston Sr. to Monsma (15 Sep. 1932); ABEM, 866: Minutes Executive Committee (7 Jan. 1933).

eration, the Personnel Committee decided to tell four workers to look for jobs elsewhere. During that meeting, a resolution was unanimously adopted not to cut support for the Bible schools.[32] A lively discussion within the CAEC ensued about the mission's identity as a faith mission.

As the Personnel Committee had only cited financial reasons for these workers' redundancy, Abraham van Puffelen said that the decision to let them go was an expression of a lack of faith. He also felt that it was high time to "examine ourselves and the mission to see if there are reasons in the mission itself for the lack of funds. ... We will confess our personal sins as well as the sins of the Mission."[33] In this, he followed Ralph Norton's line of thought.

John Winston Sr. responded that God was showing His will by not providing the means needed to continue with the current number of workers.[34] He added that there were additional reasons for terminating the contracts of some BGMers, reasons that would not have been sufficient grounds for dismissal in normal circumstances. The mission promised to support them if they could not find other employment.

As the Belgian Gospel Mission had been modeled on the China Inland Mission, Johan van Lierop suggested asking the CIM for advice before taking any financial measures. John Winston Sr. replied that the BGM needed to find its own way to a solution. Contrary to the CIM, which communicated its needs but did not directly appeal for funds, Ralph Norton believed God wanted him to ask for money explicitly.[35]

Although John Winston Sr. vetoed the suggestion that the Personnel Committee consider reinstating those who had been made redundant by pointing out that "this conference is to give its opinions and counsels," the BGMers were asked to provide feedback by filling out a questionnaire in January 1934.[36]

The first question was whether all suitable candidates should be accepted. Most answered "no." The second question, whether appropriate workers should only be taken if there was an open door and a specific request from a local church, was answered in the affirmative by most, but several people added comments. Answers to the third question, whether all students who had finished the BGM's own Bible schools should be accepted, varied. Some referred to the school rule that completing the course was not guaranteed acceptance as a BGM worker. Others were for this, on condition that there was a need or the means to pay the new workers were available. The fourth and last

32 ABEM, 877: Minutes Personnel Committee (14 July 1933).
33 ABEM, 875: Minutes CAEC (2 Oct. 1933).
34 This is a negative application of CIM's principle that "God's work done in God's way will not lack God's supply." Winston applied it negatively by arguing that if God does not want a work to be done, he will withhold the funds. "History of OFM International."
35 ABEM, 877: Minutes CAEC (2 Oct. 1933).
36 ABEM, 1214: Personnel questionnaire [1934].

question, whether only Belgian nationals trained at the Bible school should be accepted, was largely answered in the negative. Some thought that if there was a choice between two candidates of different nationalities but otherwise equally qualified, preference should be given to the Belgian national.[37]

Shortly after the questionnaires had been returned, the Personnel Committee decided, in line with faith mission practice, that any candidates offering their services should be accepted if they were suitable for a particular vacancy, regardless of whether the means were available.[38] This agrees with most of the answers to the second question but not with what Ralph Norton had said. The Committee further took to heart the suggestion to introduce a probationary period for new workers. From 1935 onwards, new workers were only permanently accepted after a year's probationary period, although exceptions were possible.[39] These decisions by the Personnel Committee illustrate the growing professionalization of the organization as they acted contrary to Ralph Norton's opinion in this matter.

It goes without saying that the financial crisis had a significant impact on the mission's evangelistic activities. Until the worldwide economic recession, the BGM continued to work with many foreign speakers. Some were invited to come over specifically; others were invited to speak as they traveled. This echoes Norton's approach as Religious Work Director with the YMCA in Minneapolis, where he invited "strong evangelical leaders" for evangelistic meetings.[40] When the economic crisis hit the mission, speakers from outside

37 Ibid.
38 ABEM, 877: Minutes Personnel Committee (2 Feb. 1934).
39 Ibid. (18 Oct. 1935).
40 See Chapter 1, page 23. Those who were specifically invited included U. Cosandey, Dr. Ch. Inwood, Johannnes de Heer, Rev. C.J. Hoekendijk, H. Mouchet, Paul Tissot, B. de Perrot, B. Wielenga, Benjamin Eicher, and Jörg Mangold. Speakers who were traveling through included R.V. Bingham, Dr. W.B. Riley, Dr. G. Besselaar, Dr. Samuel D. Gordon, Anna E. McGhie, Dr. John W. Bradbury, W. Krauer, Dr. William E. Houghton, and John Kensit. Also, Clarence E.N. Macartney, who led the conservatives in the Presbyterian church in the US in their debates with modernists, was taken for a tour around BGM stations and churches. René Pache visited Braine-le-Comte to see some of the work of the BGM. Pache, a graduate of the Institut Biblique de Nogent, organized evangelistic training camps for students in the 1930s and played a large part in the establishment of *International Fellowship of Evangelical Students* (IFES) in Switzerland and France. Christiaan Johannes Hoekendijk was a missionary in the Dutch East Indies and, from 1925, served as a pastor of a Free Evangelical church in the Netherlands. Dr. Bastiaan Wielenga was a Reformed minister in the Netherlands; his longest stint was in Amsterdam. Anna E. McGhie worked with the international holiness missionary agency *World Gospel Mission*. Bernard de Perrot was agent of *Mission Intérieure de France*. Willy Krauer was a missionary with *Congo Bolobo Mission* (Regions Beyond Missionary Union), which was led by Grattan Guiness for some time. Dr. William Houghton was a Baptist pastor until he became president of Moody Bible Institute in 1934. Gerrit Besselaar was a professor of South African literature at the University of Natal. He obtained his Doctoral degree at Universiteit Gent. He knew J. van Lierop from newspaper reports. Dr. John W. Bradury was editor of the Baptist weekly *Watchman-Examiner*. Samuel

Belgium were hardly invited anymore, as preference was given to BGM's own workers. The mission also considered having multi-day meetings in fewer places in response to reports that people's interest only grew as the events were nearing the end. It made sense to consider "doing more profound work in the places where we are putting in more work."[41] The reunions were held in their building or a more neutral location and often addressed current issues from a Chiliastic angle, as a bridge to the Gospel, such as *No war, but peace and a way to the perfect state*, or *Current world events and the future we can expect*.[42]

The evangelistic motor car or *roulette* had been a major investment, but the first reports of campaigns in Wallonia were positive. It was claimed that in 1926, over 15,000 people had been reached. The vehicle was used to support local market work or children's meetings. It was also driven to large factories to be parked there during lunch breaks and taken to remote villages.[43] Because of this great success, a second vehicle was bought for the more densely populated Flanders.

To counter the reduction in foreign donations, local congregations were encouraged to organize special collections from 1932 onwards to ensure continued work with the *roulotte*. It didn't help enough, and the *roulottes* were taken off the road in 1933 as a cost-cutting measure. In 1936, when an offer was received for the sponsoring of a new motor car, it was declined because "the gospel cars had not given us the satisfaction that we expected from them due to the difficulties of the upkeep and of using the car and driver all the year around."[44]

Despite the worrying financial situation, an extra push was made in the area of colportage in 1930, on the occasion of Belgium's centenary. A special

---

D. Gordon was a dispensationalist author with a YMCA background and known from the book series 'Quiet Talks'. Benjamin Eicher was a Baptist pastor. Jörg Mangold was a Swiss preacher who held lectures – at the invitation of Gerrit van de Riet – in which he argued that the Protestant church is the true apostolic church. "Annonces," *Notre Espérance*, 15 Oct. 1926, 2; "Annonces," *Notre Espérance*, 15 Nov. 1926, 4; Grandjean, "La Retraite spirituelle de Chexbres, du 3 au 8 May 1926," 1; Personalia," *Onze Hoop*, 1 April 1926, 2; Van Lierop, "De geschiedenis van ons gebouw te Gent," 1; Van de Riet, "Bijzondere samenkomsten in Genk 2 en 3 Febr. 1936," 1-2; ABEM, 49: Castiaux to Winston Sr. (11 April 1927); ABEM, 107: Winston Sr. to Dubois (20 Jan. 1934); ABEM, 283: ABEM, 850: Van Lierop to Winston Sr. (22 March 1932); ABEM, 42: Winston Sr. to Cailleaux (12 Oct. 1932); ABEM, 10: Winston Sr. to Claude (9 March 1934), Winston Sr. to L'Hermenault (19 July 1934), Winston Sr. to Barbezat (30 July 1932, 12 June, 5 Sep. 1936); ABEM, 51: Winston Sr. to Châtelain (10 July 1936); ABEM, 192: Williams to L'Eplattenier (10 April 1931); ABEM, 855: Bulletin USA (9 Sep. 1936); ABEM, 849: General Workers Letter (4 Dec. 1934).

41 For the original quote, see ABEM, 51: Winston Sr. to Châtelain (22 March 1930).
42 For the original quote, see ABEM, 318: Van der Beek to Winston Sr. (4 Dec. 1931); For the original quote, see ABEM,218: J. Overdulve to Vansteenberghe (18 Nov. 1934).
43 *Onze Hoop*, 1 November 1926, sec. Berichten uit het Hoofdkwartier voor de Werkers en Vrienden, 1-2.
44 For the original quote, see ABEM, 656: Vansteenberghe to Winston Sr. (24 Jan. 1936).

edition of *The Reason Why* was sent to those perceived to be part of the privileged classes: doctors, lawyers, army officers, owners of castles and manors, et cetera. Like other Evangelical organizations that had been present in Belgium for some time, the BGM found this section of the population hard to reach. Some responses were received, but they were mostly negative.[45]

This is illustrated in the following quote from a report by colporteur Willem Visée in Leuven. He had, somewhat gingerly, visited the home of a wealthy family that had responded to a BGM tract. The atmosphere turned sour when they realized that the tract in question did not originate from a Catholic but an Evangelical organization. Visée describes the general experience of protestant evangelists on such occasions, "Yet I have learned something during this visit. Everything we say is considered to be good and pure until the name 'Protestant' comes up. Then everything good becomes bad, and what is pure becomes wrong."[46]

A second initiative occasioned by the 100th anniversary of Belgium's independence was the plan to deliver a Gospel or a Bible portion to every home in the country. The workers were asked to carefully report where they had delivered to avoid having some households visited twice and others not. Other churches and denominations were allowed to assist with the distribution, but they seemed not keen. There is only evidence of some Open Brethren doing so.[47]

As colportage and literature evangelism were regarded as the cornerstones of the mission's operations, the BGM was hesitant to reduce these activities.[48] Yet now and then, there was an internal reflection on the pros and cons of colportage. John Winston Sr. argued that the mission should seriously work at spreading the Gospel and edifying literature "in a form that is both within their reach and adapted to their mentality."[49] This means the mission had an open ear for negative feedback insofar as it was on form and wording. He felt they were heading in the right direction and saw the strong Catholic opposition to distributing these materials as evidence. Winston Sr. reasoned that they would not react if the distributed literature had no impact whatsoever on lay people.[50]

One year earlier, Cardinal Jozef Van Roey had gathered the Deans to discuss his concerns about 'apparently systematic Protestant propaganda.'

45 This means that the goal of seeing people from all walks of life turn to Christ was not realized. E. Norton, "A Gospel Booth at a Belgian Exposition," 708-709; Fiedler, *Ganz auf Vertrauen, 297.*
46 For the original quote, see Visée, "Tienen," 2-3.
47 The printed materials were provided and largely financed by the SGM in London. E. Norton, "A Gospel Booth at a Belgian Exposition;" ABEM, 849: General Workers Letter (2 Dec. 1930); ABEM, 219: Winston Sr. to Neusy (31 Oct. 1930).
48 ABEM, 164: Winston Sr. to Keller (4 Feb. 1929).
49 For the original quote, see ABEM, 52: Winston Sr. to Claude (6 March 1931).
50 ABEM, 875: Minutes CAE (23 Sep. 1930).

He ordered the Deans to inventory which Protestants were active in their areas, how they worked, and whether any success they had was temporary or permanent. He also told them to act immediately if they noticed any Protestant activity, either by distributing their own tracts or by speaking out against Protestantism from the pulpit.[51]

The Cardinal's instructions were part of a larger national plan, implementing the worldwide initiative Pope Pius XI had launched under the motto, 'Pax Christi in Regno Christo.' In response to the economic crisis and the rise of totalitarian regimes in several European countries, the Roman Catholic church deployed all kinds of initiatives to strengthen civil society organizations further, organizing political backbone, and by "maintaining and where possible strengthening ecclesiastical practice and moral standards."[52] As the number of places of worship sharply increased during the first decade after World War I, it was clear to everyone that Protestantism had made significant progress in Belgium. For the Catholic church, it was now deemed just as serious a threat as Socialism and Communism.

In 1932, there were concerns about the decline in literature distribution. Looking at the figures between 1926 and 1936 (on the next page), we'll see a picture with more light and shade. Charts 1a and 1b show a declining trend between 1926 and 1934. The figures for 1930 deviate from the trend, but they cannot be compared with those of other years, as special efforts were made during that year on the occasion of Belgium's Centenary. The figures for the evangelistic magazine are more nuanced. The Flemish version steeply increased, with a slight dip in 1929 and 1930, until 1931. The French version is more in line with the trend in charts 1a and 1b.[53]

The downward trend was attributed partly to the crisis but also to Catholic priests instructing their parishioners not to buy or accept anything from BGMers. As the decline for most categories started before 1929, the impact of Cardinal Van Roey's initiative seems to have been smaller than perceived.

Another explanation was found in the increase in colportage by the Jehovah's Witnesses, who reported a sharp rise in the literature they distributed, from just over 13,000 pieces in 1929 to about 150,000 in 1936.[54] This corresponds with Martin Conway's observation that colporteurs throughout Europe noticed that there was now more competition for the people's hearts

51 This instruction was retracted in a subsequent meeting. AAMVR, I, 37,2: Minutes of the Meeting of the Deans (May 1929,1 May 1930, April 1931); De Maeyer, and De Volder, "The Church in Belgium during and after the First World War," 426.
52 For the original quote, see Gevers, "Hoogtepunt en einde van een tijdperk," 195.
53 ABEM, 875: Report to CAEC on colportage in Wallonia (25 April 1932); ABEM, 1055: Scripture Distribution to the End of Dec. 1947.
54 *1929 Yearbook of the International Bible Students Association with Daily Texts and Comments*, 118; *1930 Yearbook of the International Bible Students Association*, 81; *Yearbook of Jehovah's Witnesses for 1937: containing report of activities for the year 1936, together with Daily Texts and Comments*, 141.

Literature distribution by the Belgian Gospel Mission, 1926-1936.

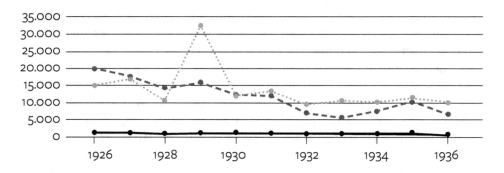

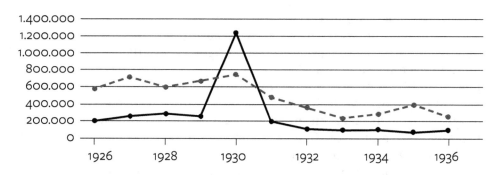

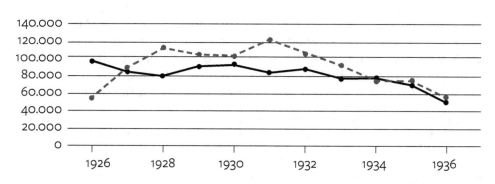

and minds.[55] Finally, in 1934, it was suggested that doing less market evangelism negatively impacted literature distribution.[56] No reason for the decline in market evangelism was offered.

The BGM was not alone in reporting a limited response to the materials it was distributing. In 1935, the British and Foreign Bible Society also noted a downward trend in the figures of the literature they provided for Belgium. The explanation was that fewer people could buy materials because of the economic crises. On top of that, the Methodists and the ECMB were forced by financial reasons to stop colporting.[57] Nevertheless, the Belgian Gospel Mission continued its focus on colportage with Bibles, New Testaments, and Portions. It felt that this was worth doing in a country with so little knowledge of the Bible.[58]

In 1936, Jean Wälti suggested another possible explanation: an unhelpful attitude that had evolved within the mission towards its colporteurs. "We were apt to regard it as an inferior work, and he asked why we had discouraged them."[59] Walter Teeuwissen added that they had made the mistake of turning good colporteurs into pastors.[60] Léon Châtelain suggested remedying the situation by having the pastors join the colporteurs for a day from time to time to enable them to see the value of this ministry.[61]

Wälti's suggestion was indeed the most critical element contributing to the downward trend. The BGM was increasingly evolving into a denomination. As the Rapture was farther off than expected, it was necessary to give more time and energy to developing local churches to keep and nurture the converts. As the mission also distributed many free materials, the Great Depression would have only affected the literature that was to be sold. The other explanations seem to have been of minor importance.

Despite limited financial resources, the mission saw the world fairs of 1930 and 1935 as a cost-effective way to reach many people with the urgent message of conversion in a limited period of time. The Expo of 1930 was organized in Antwerp and Liège. When the BGM learned that the British and Foreign Bible Society would concentrate on the world fair in Antwerp, the mission decided to develop an initiative for the Expo in Liège.

Initial attempts to obtain space on site were unsuccessful. It was then decided to rent a room with a large window near the small entrance to the

---

55 Conway, "The Christian Churches and Politics in Europe," 154.
56 ABEM, 150: Williams to Jongen (24 April 1934).
57 ABEM, 875: Minutes CAEC (1 Feb. 1935); BFBC, *Hundred and Thirty-First Report*, 23-26.
58 ABEM, 150: Winston Sr. to Barbezat (6 March 1929); ABEM, 849: General Workers Letter (15 Feb. 1935).
59 Apparently, he did not consider the weakened purchasing power of the Belgian people as a possible reason for the drop in the number of pieces of literature going out. ABEM, 875: Minutes CAEC (31 Jan. 1936).
60 Ibid.
61 Ibid. (22 Sep. 1936).

Expo site and use the window as a shop window for the Belgian Gospel Mission. Further attempts were also made to find space at the Expo site itself. By the end of February 1930, a printer was found who offered to print 25,000 Gospels per week at a price that was considered to be reasonable. Eventually, a stand was obtained at the Expo site, where materials produced by the newly found printer and materials from the existing BGM stocks were handed out.[62]

In 1935, a world fair was held in Brussels. This time, there were no obstacles to obtaining a stand from which literature was sold or handed out for free. As with regular colportage, the purpose was to use the books, leaflets, Bibles, New Testaments, Gospels, and Bible portions as conversation starters.[63] Since the work at the fairs mainly consisted of brief encounters, the return on the investment in time and budgetary resources could not be measured in conversions. It was, therefore, seen as seed-sowing in faith that some seeds would fall on good soil.

In 1932, the Belgian Gospel Mission showed interest in teaching Religious Education (RE).[64] Although it was presented as a form of evangelism, the underlying reason was the mission's precarious financial situation. Teaching RE caused considerable tension and arguments in the mission after the Second World War, so it is vital to have a clear picture of the BGM's first steps.[65]

The mission envisaged teaching RE in places "where we are the only Protestant organization working there, or where there is no official Protestant church."[66] UPECB Synod President Schyns explained the procedures. The parents of at least ten pupils would have to submit a joint application for a RE teacher for their children. If the application were accepted, the Ministry of Education would ask him, as the official representative of Belgian Protestantism, to put forward a candidate. The condition that the teacher would need to hold no preference for any particular Protestant denomination would not be a problem, the BGM argued, as various denominations were represented within the mission.[67]

---

62 "Onze Zending op de Wereldtentoonstelling te Luik," 5.
63 As a charity, they were given some space free of charge. A Christian architect designed the stand free of charge, the American Bible Society paid the running costs, and SGM donated a significant amount of literature. ABEM, 855: USA Newsletter (18 March 1935); ABEM, 888: Vansteenberghe, "One of Mr. Norton's Posthumous Answers," 2.
64 In Belgian state schools, parents choose in which government-recognized religion their children will be instructed during Religious Education lessons. The first documented Protestant Religious Education lessons were taught in 1925. It was the UPECB's Synod President who assigned the teachers. Braekman, Simons (transl.), and Van den Neste (transl.), "150 jaar protestants leven in België," 17.
65 See Chapter 9.
66 In places with several Protestant churches, the teacher was to be of the denomination representing the majority of the pupils. For the original quote, see ABEM, 849: General Workers Letter (12 Feb. 1932).
67 Ibid.

The eagerness displayed by the BGM is remarkable. It did not insist on the standard requirements concerning the Evangelical beliefs of fellow RE teachers. When questioned, the mission could defend itself by stating that these teaching positions did not involve direct cooperation with RE colleagues whom the BGM would regard as 'modernist.' This financial distress was so urgent that the mission not only accepted that their workers who would be assigned as RE teachers would be paid by the government but also let them free to keep their wages for themselves "or to hand it in for the work of the Mission."[68] Thus, the mission was willing to act contrary to the faith mission principle of total dependency on God and the general rule that workers were expected to support each other with any secondary income they had. As BGMers, more often than not, only received a part of their allowance, taking up RE-positions was accepted as the lesser of two evils.

BGMer Edouard Barbezat informed whether he could also take on other forms of paid employment. John Winston Sr. replied he had written Ralph Norton for advice, but there are no records of his reply.[69] It would have been interesting to see whether he distinguished earnings from teaching Religious Education from secondary incomes from other sources and, if so, on what basis. As we will see in Chapter 10, this inconsistent stance eventually backfired when the directors tried to sanction those workers who refused to transfer their income for RE to central funds.

It goes without saying that the economic crisis also hit the local BGM churches. An aggravating factor was that the Nortons' church planting strategy was based on a short-term plan because of their dispensational eschatology. From the start, local churches or stations had a full-timer to reach as many people as possible. As the signs of the times had been misinterpreted, a situation was created that would hamper the future autonomization of these churches or stations. In 1928, before the onset of the economic crisis, John Winston Sr. already saw the need to develop a financial strategy to encourage local churches to become self-supportive. Only three of the forty-three local churches could pay their fixed costs themselves.[70]

The small congregations would never be able to develop into fully autonomous churches, especially as the actual cost of having a full-timer and a local church building was not communicated. The fear of offending people still prevailed over the need to take responsibility for this. One of the grudges

---

68 For the original quote, see ABEM, 50: Winston Sr. to Charensol (28 Sep. 1932).
69 ABEM, 10: Barbezat to Winston Sr. (16 June 1933), Winston Sr. to Barbezat (23 June 1933).
70 In 1930, the members' meeting at Sint-Niklaas decided to be self-sufficient with the exception of the pastor's salary. In 1934, the French-language church in Brussels tried to do the same and succeeded. Not enough financial data is available from Sint-Niklaas to ascertain whether they, too, succeeded. ABEM, 1237: Winston Sr. to R. Norton (28 Aug. 1928); ABEM, 806: Report from Mr. J. Servaas: St. Niklaas (Jan. 1931); ABEM, 885: Vansteenberghe, "What God hath wrought in fifteen years in Belgium;" ABEM, 875: Minutes CAE (4 Oct. 1928).

people had against Catholicism was the impression that the church was after their money. Based on experiences of Protestant missions in other Catholic countries, the BGM feared offending the local believers, who would then put them on the same level as the Catholic church, namely money-grubbers.

From the moment the mission was hit hard by the effects of the Great Depression, Ralph Norton was less keen to invest in buildings in sparsely populated areas. However, some BGMers argued that more should be done than just having meetings in homes in small towns. A good example is La Ronce, a hamlet of Seneffe where cottage meetings were being held. As some former Catholics felt that the meetings were not church-like enough and stated that others were staying away because they were not meeting in a Protestant church building, the congregation asked for a small chapel. The believers even made a site available to construct their desired chapel. There were requests from other places too for "small halls or temporary huts."[71] Ralph Norton was only willing to grant the requests if these congregations were prepared to carry the cost of a building. Yet these simple structures were never built.[72]

Although only a few BGM churches were financially self-supportive, all churches and stations cared for the poor somehow. In some places there was a special fund for this. In other congregations, care for the poor was financed from local central funds.[73] Because of accusations from Catholic quarters that the Belgian Gospel Mission was persuading people to convert to Protestantism by offering them money, requests for financial aid were considered very carefully.

Financial support was intended for those who testified in word and deed that they were ready to obey the call of the Gospel.[74] There was some concern within the BGM that those who applied for financial support perceived the mission as having unlimited funds and that this could lead to undesired results.[75] On the other hand, it was viewed as a good way of showing church members that their donations were used to help poorer believers.[76]

As American donations had dropped dramatically because of the Great Depression, local church deficits could no longer be compensated without cutting costs elsewhere, i.e., workers' salaries. Therefore, The Belgian Gospel Mission considered having special collections in all congregations for the work in general as a practical way of encouraging people to give.[77] It was also felt that the people who attended regularly should be made aware of the costs

---

71 For the original quote, see ABEM, 235: Winston Sr. to Quenon (16 March 1931).
72 Ibid.
73 ABEM, 243: Rottier to Vansteenberghe (n.d.).
74 "Nieuws van onze posten," (1928); ABEM, 150: Winston Sr. to Jongen (11 April 1927).
75 ABEM, 164: Grandjean to Keller (9 July 1929).
76 ABEM, 283: Van Lierop to R. Norton (18 Feb. 1929).
77 Special collections for other purposes were not allowed unless express permission had been obtained from headquarters. ABEM, 866: Minutes Executive Committee (30 Sep. 1930).

of having a local church. In some places, the income for the care of the poor was higher than that for general funds. This was now described as unfortunate, whereas it had never been pointed out as problematic before.

Whereas Ralph Norton felt the financial struggles were God's way to make Belgian christians realize they needed to contribute more, the reality was that the mission's monetary policy and Norton's qualities as a fundraiser now worked against them. The Belgian Gospel Mission was perceived as a 'Dollar Mission' with seemingly inexhaustible financial back-up in North America. Until then, they had been very reluctant to talk about the actual costs of the local churches out of fear of putting people off. And as the organization seemed to have easy access to money from the US, Belgian Christians saw little reason to donate substantially.[78]

Now, pastors and evangelists were instructed to teach about tithing and to point out to their congregations that contributing to the costs of the local church was a privilege.[79] The idea was to increase the weekly collections, enabling them to finance themselves, including the pastor's salary.

This policy change led to some internal discussions. Jean Wälti reiterated the valid argument that people in Roman Catholic countries were tired of the churches' 'begging' and that this made all extra collections and calls for financial support delicate.[80]

Overall, the new approach bore fruit, at least temporarily. In December 1930, Ralph Norton wrote that donations from within the country had risen since US donations had fallen. In some places, weekly collections doubled in a few months.[81] Belgian gifts dropped again in 1934 and 1935. To combat the persistent misconception the BGM had many wealthy American supporters, an article was published in *Notre Espérance* and *Onze Hoop* in 1936, emphasizing that most US gifts they received were small and given by people with limited incomes.[82]

Many BGMers remained reluctant to communicate about finances. They feared that, in the long run, giving would go down rather than up or that donations for the local church would increase at the expense of offerings for national and international missions, which would receive less. In 1935, the first tensions surfaced as the BGM was simultaneously a faith mission and a denomination.

78   ABEM, 849: General Workers Letter (11 Oct., 2 Dec. 1930).
79   This shows that people were prepared to give for specific causes. Ibid. (2 Oct. 1930); ABEM, 292: Williams to Van de Riet (2 April 1931).
80   ABEM, 875: Minutes CAE (4 April 1930).
81   The total income from collections in 1931 amounted to BEF 225,385.55. In 1932, this rose to BEF 275,473.74, and in 1933, to BEF 293,719.02. In 1934, the total dropped to BEF 284,278.30. ABEM, 849: General Workers Letter (17 Feb. 1931); ABEM, 877: Lybrand, et. al., Report and accounts of La Mission Evangélique Belge, Brussels (7 April 1933, 14 May 1934, and 5 June 1935), Recettes pour le fonds général.
82   "Voor onze Belgische geloovigen," 3.

Whereas the BGM leadership was strongly committed to national evangelism, church members prioritized the local church. This meant they expected the offerings for their pastor would be passed on to him in full. However, the faith mission principle dictated that all incomes, after subtracting local fixed expenses such as gas, water, and electricity, would be integrally transferred to central funds in Brussels. Pastors were paid from what was left after all creditors were satisfied to keep the national activities up and running. This meant a pastor could be paid less than what was explicitly given to him. In 1935, BGMers only received 50-70% of their salaries in some months.[83]

Edith Norton (Ralph Norton had died by this time) called the malcontents "simple minded, ... very limited in their understanding of the workings of the Mission and not far advanced in the Christian life."[84] She wanted to maintain the faith mission principle for all BGM churches to avoid losing the cohesion within the mission. John Winston Sr. also showed no empathy for those who voiced their dissatisfaction. "If they make sacrifices they think that their own pastor should benefit by their sacrifices, and not some unknown person."[85]

Here, we see a conflict of interests between the national leadership and local believers and tension between the BGM being a faith mission and a denomination simultaneously. John Winston Sr. seemed to be aware of this challenging balancing act. He felt the faith mission principle should be maintained for the "evangelistic agency with mission halls" but not for the "group of organized churches come into being."[86] He wrote to Odilon Vansteenberghe to ask for his opinion. He also asked for advice from several leaders of American missionary organizations, "who have doubtless faced, or are facing the same situation."[87]

Vansteenberghe agreed with Edith Norton. He argued that if Winston Sr.'s plan were carried out, the American missionaries would start claiming all donations explicitly sent for them.[88] Furthermore, church members ought to view payments into the central fund as a reimbursement for the investments the BGM has made in their church over the years.

He added another critical dimension to the discussion. The problem was partially because the BGM buildings were more attractive than the average church member was used to. It was a deliberate strategy. Buildings needed to

---

83 Ibid.
84 The term "simple minded" probably refers to the fact that the large majority of church members originated from the working classes. The fact of the matter is that the BGM did not manage to communicate its financial policy to church members in a way they understood. Ibid.
85 ABEM, 655: Winston Sr. to Vansteenberghe (2 Dec. 1935).
86 Ibid.
87 Ibid.
88 ABEM, 656: Vansteenberghe to Winston Sr. (3 Jan. 1936).

appeal not only to the working class but also to the middle and higher classes. For convenience, Vansteenberghe kept silent about this strategy's failure.

He felt that whereas a missionary in Africa could easily take a small part-time job to help their church become self-supporting, in Belgium, the pastor would have to take a full-time job and possibly his wife. Not only would this seriously affect the time available for serving the church, but there was also a limited amount of available jobs.[89]

Vansteenberghe discussed the issue with China Inland Mission's Dr. Archibald E. Glover and concluded that the situation in China could not be compared with the position of missionaries in Belgium.[90] The issue's discussion fell silent because of political developments but resumed after the Second World War. John Winston Sr.'s idea was eventually adopted in 1962 when the first eight local churches started by the BGM were given independent status. We will see in Chapter 10 why this process took so long after the war had ended. But first, we will focus on how Vansteenberghe and Winston Sr. succeeded the Nortons as the mission's directors in 1936 and how Vansteenberghe steered the BGM through the occupation by the Nazis from 1940 to 1944.

---

89   Ibid.
90   The CIM distinguished between churches led by native workers and churches led by missionaries. The former were expected to be self-financing, while central CIM funds supported the latter. ABEM, 321: Vansteenberghe, Report of a conversation with D. Glover of the China Inland Mission.

Odilon Vansteenberghe, John Winston Sr., and Ralph Norton, ca. 1930.
[KADOC- KU LEUVEN: ABEM, 1141]

8
NEW LEADERSHIP UNDER THE CLOUDS OF WAR

In the second half of the 1930s, the clouds of war were gathering over Europe. This would influence not only evangelistic efforts but also church life. The army mobilized several pastors and evangelists, and others decided to return to their motherland. On top of this, the BGM had a change of leadership within two years. In July 1936, Vansteenberghe and Winston Sr. succeeded Edith Norton as joint directors. This was according to her wishes, as expressed at Ralph Norton's deathbed in 1934. Because her death had come rather unexpectedly, the leadership transition was abrupt and could not be planned carefully. Therefore, the Board advised the new directors "to give abundant time to prayer and special study of the general policies of the Mission in the light of the new conditions."[1]

Would the two, who had assisted the Nortons for many years at the helm, hold the same course? How would they deal with the dire financial situation of the mission, and would the political evolution in Belgium and Europe impact the focus of the evangelistic and ecclesiastic activities? The pair took the advice to heart and refused to take any decision that was not necessary for months.[2] In line with the Faith Mission principles, the tasks were assigned based on the qualities the two men displayed, not their nationalities. Winston Sr. would direct the work in Belgium, and Vansteenberghe focused on the relationship with supporters in the USA.[3]

1   ABEM, 850: Minutes Board of Trustees (10 Aug. 1936).
2   ABEM, 875: Minutes CAEC (12 Feb. 1937).
3   ABEM, 864: Minutes Executive Committee (24 July 1936).

The new directors described the challenging circumstances under which they started as ominous and uncertain.[4] Another war in Europe seemed to be more and more unavoidable, and Belgium experienced political insecurity again, this time due to a combination of national and international factors.[5] In Belgium, political tensions erupted over a 'secret' agreement between Rex, the fascist political party for Wallonia, and *Vlaamsch Nationaal Verbond* (Flemish National Alliance), a Flemish nationalist party in the autumn of 1936.[6] Léon Degrelle, party leader of Rex, further aggravated the situation by announcing a March on Brussels, to be held on 25 October 1936.[7] As the BGM considered the possibility that Rexist activists would seize power and establish a dictatorship, it wrote lamentingly to their American backers, "The political outlook in our country is not very encouraging at the time of writing. ... It is to be hoped that the forces that stand for order may win. What an incentive to us, God's children, to seek earnestly to obey the injunction of *Romans* 13:1-7."[8] When the march passed without major incidents, the American supporters were informed that "the political storm that was gathering over our country ... has largely blown over and we do thank God for continual liberty to preach the Word in the open air as well as in our halls."[9]

On the European level, the Spanish Civil War (1936-1939), with the active involvement of Nazi Germany, the Italian invasion of Abyssinia (1935), and the remilitarization of the Rhineland (1936) led in February 1937 to the following observation, "it seems that we are heading irresistibly toward a conflict which will surpass in magnitude and cruelty all the wars of the past."[10] When the BGM accepted the invitation to send Samuel Dubois as a representative to the convention of the *Vereinigung Evangelischer Freikirchen* (Association of Evangelical Free Churches) in Germany in 1937, it could find out firsthand about the difficulties that the church in Germany was experiencing.[11]

---

4   ABEM, 850: Minutes Board of Trustees (23 Oct. 1937).
5   Dujardin and Van den Wijngaert, "1939 - 1950 Land zonder koning," 1080, 1111.
6   The *Vlaamsch Nationaal Verbond* was established in 1933 by Staf De Clercq, and collaborated with the occupiers during World War II.
7   Dujardin and Van den Wijngaert, "1939-1950 Land zonder koning," 1089.
8   ABEM, 855: Bulletin Letter USA (Dec. 1936).
9   Dujardin and Van den Wijngaert, "1939-1950 Land zonder koning," 1091-1092; ABEM, 855: Prayer Letter USA (6 Jan. 1937).
10 Ibid. (10 Feb. 1937).
11 This association organized conventions every other year from 1926 until 1940. At a later stage Dubois was also sent to give presentations on the BGM in some local churches. Dubois' report describes the situation in the Closed Brethren, Seventh Day Adventists, Freie Evangelische Gemeinde, and the Confessing Church. The Closed Brethren were banned by Nazi decree in April 1937. Under pressure from the Gestapo, legal professional Dr. Hans Becker established the *Bund freikirchlicher Christen* (Alliance of Christians in Free Churches), which was joined by two-thirds of the Closed Brethren. Several months later, they were joined by some Open Brethren. John Winston Sr. felt that it was useful for the BGM pastors to be kept abreast of these developments. *Handbuch der deutschen evange-*

Meanwhile, the Belgians, too, grew increasingly anxious under the threat of another war. To make things even worse, the country was hit again by an economic crisis, leading to soaring unemployment rates in 1938. Once more, the circumstances were interpreted eschatologically as "the choicest seed plots for the harvest."[12] Therefore, despite continuing financial worries, the BGM leaders were convinced this was not the time to scale down activities.[13] Yet the mobilization of 1938, prompted by the looming German-Czech conflict about the Sudetenland, impacted the work of the BGM as five of its Belgian pastors were called up for duty. As a result of the Munich Agreement of 30 September 1938, the mobilization was canceled. The men were allowed to return to their churches a few days later, continuing their daily activities.

Like most other citizens, the BGM leadership hoped that, at least for the time, "the danger of a universal conflagration in Europe" had been avoided.[14] This hope was shattered in the Kristallnacht on 9 November 1938. From then on, the Belgian Gospel Mission considered the outbreak of war very shortly a real possibility.[15] When Vansteenberghe was in the USA for deputation during the spring of 1939, Winston Sr. wrote to him, "if hostilities should break out – and it is hard to see how Belgium could really remain neutral in any sort of a general conflict – your presence here would be most important."[16]

Because the new directors expected many conversions under the clouds of war, they decided to continue the financial policy of the Nortons. This meant that maintaining the existing level of activities took precedence over the workers' payment. Edith Norton's death only led to a temporary upturn in American donations, and halving the kitchen staff and reducing the number of secretaries from five to three was not enough. Additional measures had to be taken.[17] Not only had salaries been cut by 40% over six years, but they were also, more often than not, only paid partially. The team was well aware of the hardship this caused for the workers.[18]

When two workers were disciplined in 1938 for moral misconduct, John Winston Sr. repeated his earlier question of whether the BGM's financial difficulties were perhaps the result of secret sin. Relating progress and setbacks

---

lischen Kirchen, 293; Dubois, "Bezoekt de samenkomsten," 2; ABEM, 107: Winston Sr. to Dubois (13 May 1937); ABEM, 164: Keller to Winston Sr. (4 Dec. 1937).

12   ABEM, 855: Bulletin Letter USA (10 Feb. 1937).
13   Ibid. (5 April 1938).
14   Ibid. (1 Nov. 1938).
15   "The international tension at the end of November made us think that perhaps our December Bulletin Letter would have to be written by one of our friends in America. War looked imminent and although Belgium ran a good chance of being spared, at least for the time being, the horrors of an armed conflict, it seemed that our free and easy communication with your friends might become impossible." Ibid. (1 Nov. 1938, Dec. 1938).
16   ABEM, 655: Winston Sr. to Vansteenberghe (25 March 1939).
17   ABEM, 875: Report from the Business Committee (18 Jan. 1938).
18   ABEM, 337: Vansteenberghe to Stephans (9 Dec. 1936).

in the visible world to the metaphysical realm was part and parcel of the faith mission DNA. As the financial difficulties primarily had an economic cause, the immediate disciplinary action had no positive effect on the liquidity gap, and the workers could not be paid their total wages. In September 1938, the situation was so challenging that a donor was asked for permission to use his contribution to pay salaries rather than for the purpose he had indicated. The backer in question agreed.[19]

Despite a structural deficit, new workers continued to be recruited in compliance with the faith mission principle. Even in February 1939, Winston Sr. remained convinced they should continue praying for more workers. The idea was to maximize the evangelistic effort before the doors would be closed. Between 1936 and 1939, the mission welcomed sixteen new workers, more than those who had left for various reasons.[20] Six of them were alumni from the BGM Bible Schools. The ratio of graduates had now risen to a little over one in three. As the schools had been set up expressly for this purpose, the figures were embellished for the North American supporters to "almost half of the workers."[21]

Under the leadership of Vansteenberghe and Winston Sr., the requirements for interdenominational cooperation remained unchanged despite the dire financial situation and the imminent threat of another war. Although for the sake of courtesy, reciprocal invitations were sent to attend celebrations or synods, cooperation on a national level with other protestant denominations in Belgium was out of the question. The following examples will illustrate this:

When called to actively partake in a joint commemoration of 300 years of the *Staten Vertaling* Bible in 1937, the BGM was only willing to participate if the usual requirements were met. This meant that neither the organizing committee nor the speakers could include anyone whom the mission regarded as a 'Modernist,' i.e., someone who did not believe in the plenary inspiration of the Bible. As the other organizers could not guarantee this, the invitation was declined.[22]

---

19   By contrast, when the BGM buildings in Hasselt and Tongeren were sold in 1938, the full amount of the sale was put into the building fund rather than being used to pay workers' salaries. ABEM, 850: Minutes CAEC (23 Sep. 1938, 10 Feb. 1939).
20   Ibid. (10 Feb. 1939).
21   ABEM, 855: Bulletin Letter USA (May 1939), "Personeel en posten van de Belgische Evangelische Zending," 1 Dec. 1938, 8.
22   The anniversary was to be marked by a joint Bible exhibition, evangelistic meetings in the Brussels churches of all partaking denominations, and a closing rally on 3 October 1937. The costs were to be paid from collections in the participating churches, as well as from a collection to be held during the closing rally of 3 October and sponsorship from the *Nederlands Bijbel Genootschap (Dutch Bible Society)*. ABEM, 864: Minutes Executive Committee (14 May 1937).

In the Spring of 1939, the UEPECB invited the BGM to invitation its centenary celebration.[23] In his reply, Winston Sr. described the difficulties that Protestants in Belgium lived through during the seventeenth and eighteenth centuries. The letter finishes with a greeting, "May the church whose flag you bear move forward. May it become a force and a blessing for Belgium and its colony. May the Word of God always find its place in people's hearts, may the life of Christ always manifest itself in the Church, and may the reward that Jesus Christ reserves for faithful churches be granted to you."[24] We can detect a barely veiled criticism here. Later that year, the BGM received an invitation to send a delegation to the ECMB Synod.[25] Winston Sr. and Vansteenberghe declined because no significant changes had occurred since Ralph Norton had decided not to collaborate for doctrinal reasons.[26]

As before, the exclusion of cooperation on the national level because of heterodoxy did not exclude good relations or joint evangelistic initiatives on the local level. A green light was given to several events after assessing the specific situation. Ernest Charensol, pastoring in Warquignies, was informed "that our brother M.R. Pierre is going to Quaregnon ..., to start a work there for the Methodist Mission; he is pleased to be placed so near to you."[27]

In 1937, Van Lierop cooperated with pastor Cornet of the local ECMB in tent evangelism in Ghent.[28] The initiative was repeated the following summer, and North American backers were led to believe that the initiative was a "mighty and visible piece of evidence against the accusation the Catholics love to use, that Protestantism is internally divided."[29] And when the BGM started activities in Oudenaarde, some thirty kilometers south of Ghent, the Silo leaders confirmed they were happy with this. Their local church in Oudenaarde had recently closed, and the Silo leaders felt the Belgian Gospel Mission would provide a good alternative spiritual home for some families.[30]

Finally, to avoid the impression of sheep-stealing, the BGM continued to be cautious about providing a spiritual home for people who were unhappy in their denomination. These could be members of the UPECB, as in Pâturages

---

23 ABEM, 832: Direction Synodale to Winston Sr. (15 March 1939).
24 For the original quote, see Ibid.: Winston Sr. to la Direction Synodale (1 May 1939).
25 ABEM, 823: Harts to Winston Sr. (7 June 1939).
26 Ibid.: Winston Sr. to Harts (21 June 1939).
27 For the original quote, see Charensol worked in Warquignies, less than 7 kilometers from Quaregnon. ABEM, 50: Stearns to Charensol (16 Dec. 1937).
28 Van Lierop, "Tentvergaderingen te Gent," 1.
29 For the original quote, see Van Lierop, "Marktevangelisatie," 2.
30 Buunk, "Post Deynze," 1; ABEM, 35: Buunk to Winston Sr. (5 Dec. 1938), Winston Sr. to Buunk (14 Dec. 1938).

(Hainaut province), the Salvation Army or the ECMB, as in Seraing (Liège province), or even Open Brethren, as in Auvelais (Namur province).[31]

As war loomed in Europe, Odilon Vansteenberghe decided that in the summer of 1937, all of the BGM's efforts would focus on colportage, especially in the villages that BGM colporteurs had never visited. "We must mobilize everyone who can be missed for distribution and colportage."[32] Vansteenberghe meant business, so the evangelistic motor cars or *roulottes* were back on the road during summer.[33] As in the past, they were used for visiting remote villages, drawing the villagers' attention, and serving as a home base for colportage during the daytime. The team would stand around the vehicle to meet people and explain "the Gospel in a calm and quiet way" during the evenings.[34] As before, the cost of use was found to be a problem, even for a few months, so the vehicles were sold in 1939.[35]

Dictated by the imminent threat of war, the plan had not been thought through. The implementation was hampered because only a few colporteurs were left in the mission. Some had been promoted to pastor; others had left because of the uncertain political situation. The main reason for their decline in number was their inferior position in the organization. Colporteurs earned less than pastors, and their work was regarded by several as inferior to church work.[36]

To remedy the shortage, nine colporteurs were recruited in 1937, raising their number to twelve.[37] The stepped-up colporting initiatives, primarily situated in Wallonia, resulted in several new stations and churches.[38] That being said, the response differed from previous years when only the middle and upper classes tended to respond negatively to these BGM activities. Now, the working classes also seemed to lose interest in God. Winston Sr. attributed this to the growing influence of Russian Communism and the ideas that working-class people had about religion.[39] However, these reasons should be

---

31 As for Pâturages, if the people concerned would start an independent church, cooperation and even spiritual and moral support was not ruled out. This group may have been the same as the group that left the UPECB church in Pâturages for the nearby ECMB church in Grand-Wasmes at around that same time. ABEM, 164: Vansteenberghe to Keller (9 Oct. 1936); ABEM, 107: Vansteenberghe to Dubois (12 Aug. 1941); ABEM, 850: Minutes CAEC (18 Jan. 1938); Email communication from Jean-Louis Simonet, 29 May 2014.
32 For the original quote, see ABEM, 850: Minutes CAEC (12 Feb. 1937).
33 Servaas Sr., "De Evangeliewagen," 1.
34 For the original quote, see Ibid.
35 ABEM, 850: Minutes CAEC (23 Sep. 1938); ABEM, 875: Report from the Business Committee (10 Feb. 1939).
36 ABEM, 850: Minutes CAEC (30 Sep. 1937).
37 Ibid. (12 Feb. 1937, 23 Sep. 1938).
38 Ibid. (18 Jan. 1938); Report from Châtelain (Jan. 1938).
39 ABEM, 962: Winston, "The Religious Situation in Europe and Belgium To-Day," *The Fundamentalist*, 2 Aug. 1937.

mentioned in the written reports of the colporteurs themselves. More typical is Vandenbroeck's remark that often Jehovah's Witnesses, Mormons, or other cults had preceded him on his rounds. He urged them to be sensitive in such situations. His approach was to try and "swap" their tracts for BGM tracts and give them copies of *Notre Espérance* each month.[40]

The focus on colportage also led to the translation and publication into French of *Salvation*, and *He is Spiritual* by L.S. Chafer.[41] The translation was funded with an earmarked donation, so the publications were not translated into Dutch. The BGM leaders decided this was fine as they had enough publications in Dutch, albeit not by Chafer.[42] The choice of these books demonstrates that North American Evangelical theology continued its strong presence in the BGM's identity.

The BGM also deployed colporteurs in the German-speaking *Ostkantone*, which was added to Belgium at Germany's expense under the Treaty of Versailles. Since 1930, when this area was opened to non-resident Belgian citizens from outside the region, the BGM had been looking at the possibilities for evangelism there.[43] Finally, and with the consent of Joannes Bivort, the protestant pastor of Eupen, Americans Esther Hoyt and Lulu Sommers were deployed in the Eupen-Malmedy region in 1937. Five thousand copies of a tract entitled *Die Ursachen der Reformation* (The causes of the Reformation) were printed for this project. Hoyt and Sommers had limited success and could not establish a stable BGM core in Eupen or its surrounding towns.[44]

Despite disappointing results, pastors and colporteurs were asked to distribute as much of their stock of Gospel Literature as possible in the spring of 1939. As it became clear that war was unavoidable and would disrupt

---

40 He does not write how he funded this. *Notre Espérance* was a paid-for magazine. It is possible he used back issues that had not been sold. During the tent campaign in Mariakerke near Ghent, the team was hampered by colporteurs from the *Philanthropic Assembly of the Friends of Man*, a group that had broken away from the Jehovah's Witnesses in 1920 and was led by Alexander Freytag from Switzerland. In *Onze Hoop* they are referred to as "Freytag colporteurs." Vandenbroeck to Châtelain, 4 April 1939; "De Tentcampagne, Tentcampagne te Mariakerke Gent," 2; Vernette, and Moncelon, *Dictionnaire des groupes religieux aujourd'hui*, 16; Penton, *Jehovah's Witnesses and the Third Reich*, 137.
41 Chafer, *Le Salut*; Chafer, *L'homme Spirituel*.
42 Both books appeared in 1938, in a run of 2,000 copies each. ABEM, 503: Winston Sr., "Year Report for the American Council of the Belgian Gospel Mission, Inc (1939); ABEM, 850: Minutes CAEC (12 Feb. 1937).
43 Before World War I, only four Lutheran pastors were active in this area, only one of whom was allowed to return by the Belgian authorities as they took charge. The BGM was well aware of the need for German-speaking workers in this area. E. Norton, "Exploring for Gospel Centers in the Belgian Ardennes," 81.
44 Bivort was succeeded by Dr. Karl Hennig, who served in Eupen from 1938 until 1945. Hoyt and Sommers had Bible studies with interested individuals. ABEM, 145: Hoyt to Winston Sr. (21 March 1939); ABEM, 850: Minutes CAEC (12 Feb. 1937); "Personalia," *Onze Hoop*, 1 July 1937, 1.

all evangelistic activities, the idea was that "the Scriptures may continue their lifegiving ministry."[45] The bleak political outlook also prompted Miner Stearns to place the Bible school students at the disposition of the local churches and stations from May until September 1939 to be deployed in colportage. The urgency was so intense that competence in colporting was now of peripheral interest.[46]

The threat of war also prompted renewed efforts in open-air and market evangelism. As experience had shown that it could take a long time for people to pluck up the courage to enter a BGM building, the emphasis on colportage in 1937 was followed by a focus on open-air and market evangelism in 1938.[47]

Although reports from evangelists and pastors indicate few immediate results, the BGM optimistically wrote to its American supporters that after two decades of open-air preaching, "the early prejudice against Protestants is melting. Many Belgians used to group us vaguely with Jews and atheists, but after listening to the street preaching, they are reassured that we believe in God and Christ."[48] Again, the results were essentially glossed over to inflate fund-raising revenues.

In the late 1930s, tent evangelism was also less effective than in the early years, and attendance was often below what was expected based on previous years.[49] Reasons used in the past to explain a lack of interest – the tent was taken to small communities, opposition by the local Catholic church, indifference to religious matters – were now ignored.[50] Even though BGM leadership felt that the tent was not sufficiently attractive to outsiders, it kept organizing tent campaigns. It kept on telling its financial backers they were "an exceedingly important method of preaching the Gospel" to make the gospel more easily accessible to people.[51]

Usually, little discussion occurred about where the tent campaigns would be held. It had become a regular occurrence in some places because they took place in big cities such as Brussels, Antwerp, Ghent, and Liège or because attendance figures were deemed high enough to make a return visit seem worthwhile.[52] Some places were visited for the first time, as field studies

45 ABEM, 855: Bulletin Letter USA (May 1939).
46 ABEM, 503: Winston Sr., Year Report for the American Council of the Belgian Gospel Mission, Inc (4 Dec. 1939); ABEM, 850: Minutes CAEC (10 Feb. 1939).
47 ABEM, 855: Bulletin Letter USA (5 April 1938).
48 Ibid. (May 1939).
49 ABEM, 503: Winston Sr., Year Report for the American Council of the Belgian Gospel Mission, Inc; ABEM, 875: Rapport Tente Française été 1937; Postma, "Eeclo," 2; "Tentcampagne te Moeskroen," 1; ABEM, 875: Rapport Agent itinérant des Flandres (23 Sep. 1938); Van Dam, "Verslag der Tentcampagne te Boom," 1.
50 ABEM, 255: Winston Sr. to Servaas Sr (23 July 1939); Buunk, "Petegem - Deinze," 2.
51 ABEM, 503: Winston Sr., Year Report for the American Council.
52 Brussels, Antwerp, Liège, and Ghent were visited several times because they were big cities. ABEM, 850: Minutes CAEC (21 April 1939).

showed there was a chance the initiative would result in planting a local BGM church. Indeed, the evangelistic tent meetings planted several small local congregations in Wallonia and Flanders. Most of its people had a working-class background; one convert had been with the Antoinists for four years.[53]

Local churches seized the opportunity to organize evangelistic meetings whenever international speakers were available, such as keynote speakers at the BGM conventions or the twentieth anniversary of the mission in 1938. These orators give once more an idea of the BGM's international network. From Switzerland came J.B. Roy-Tophel and René Pache. Ulysse Cosandey addressed the celebratory rally in Brussels on Sunday, 18 December 1938.[54] From France, itinerant Mennonite evangelist Joseph Muller was invited.[55] Americans and personal friends of the Nortons, Dr. Walter L. Wilson and William L. Pettingill, added Belgium to their stops in Europe. Other international speakers were evangelist Leland Wang of the Chinese Missionary Union and Baptist Leonard Sale Harrison from Australia.[56]

From 1937 onwards, the mission received increasing requests for aid for Jewish refugees from Germany.[57] Despite disappointing results with social work as bait for prospective converts, without hesitation or invoking its usual requirements, the mission participated in interdenominational committees in

---

53 Examples of Wallonian church plants are Elouges, Gilly, Auvelais, and Jemelle. Flemish examples are De Panne and Tienen. ABEM, 855: Prayer Letter (17 Sep. 1936, 12 Aug. 1937, 29 July 1938); "De Panne," 1; ABEM, 503: Winston Sr., Year Report for the American Council; ABEM, 875: Rapport Tente Française été 1937, Rapport Tente Flamande (30 Sep. 1937); ABEM, 310: Visée to Vansteenberghe (3, 21 June 1937).
54 ABEM, 875: Winston Sr., Programme des Réunions commémoratives semaine du 18 décembre 1938.
55 Joseph Muller was an itinerant evangelist with the revival movement of the French Mennonites in the 1930s. He was converted after reading a tract by Hugh E. Alexander, and had many contacts in other denominations. ABEM, 875: Châtelain, Report Travelling Agent Wallonia (10 Feb. 1939); Séguy, *Les assemblées anabaptistes-mennonites de Franc*, 587-588.
56 Dr. Walter L. Wilson was pastor of the Central Bible Hall in Kansas City, founder of the Flagstaff Indian Mission to the Navajos, and cofounder of Kansas City Bible College in 1932. William Leroy Pettingill was a Baptist who joined C.I. Scofield in founding Philadelphia College of the Bible, which later became Cairn University. Leland Wang founded the Chinese Foreign Missionary Union in 1928 and was called the 'Moody of China'. His organization focused on "the scattered Chinese in the South Seas of Asia." Leonard Sale Harrison was known for his sermons on end-time prophecies. In the 1930s he toured the world proclaiming the return of Jesus Christ in 1940 or 1941. ABEM, 10: Barbezat to Winston Sr. (21 Feb. 1938); ABEM, 855: Bulletin Letter USA, (2 July, Oct. 6 1938); "Dr. Pettingill te Brussel," 1; Graves, "Walter L. Wilson Converted;" Bruce Gourley, 27 Jan. 2013, e-mail message to author; ABEM, 814: Howard Jr. to Winston Sr. (27 April 1939), Winston Sr. to Howard Jr. (22 May 1939); Wong, "Wang Zai (Leland Wang) 1898-1975."
57 Many refugees who Hitler regarded as non-Arians were Protestants. ABEM, 50: Winston Sr. to Charensol (16 Jan. 1939).

Brussels and Antwerp to provide aid to refugees.[58] This must be seen in the light of the hermeneutics of Scofield and other dispensationalists, resulting in Christian Zionism. The BGM believed that whereas the Church would be temporarily removed from the earth, the Jews would return to the promised land and restore the Eretz Israel.

The committee in Antwerp was soon dissolved because the Protestant churches in the area were uninterested. The Brussels committee remained active until the invasion of May 1940, and the readership of *Onze Hoop* and *Notre Espérance* was encouraged to support this work. The meager support in Belgium for this initiative reflects the international support of evangelicals for the Jewish refugees.[59]

One of the refugees was Messianic Jew and Free Evangelical pastor Otto Samuel. He fled to Belgium in early 1939 and asked the BGM for support to work among Jewish refugees in the country. Samuel showed letters of recommendation from German pastors, some of whom knew the BGM well. He explained that he wanted to meet material needs and evangelize.

As evangelism among Jewish refugees was not viewed as a core activity but had been time-consuming and was now regarded as burdensome, Samuel's request was an attractive proposal. However, the BGM was not ready to put him on the payroll. Therefore, the BGM infrastructure was made available to him only after the American Board of Missions to the Jews confirmed they supported Samuel's plan and would continue to pay his salary. As required by the Belgian authorities, John Winston Sr., as the BGM's Financial Director, stood surety for Samuel, and the BGM was his official employer.[60]

When *Moody Monthly* refused an advertisement from Mission to the Jews and the *Sunday School Times* contemplated doing the same, the BGM was on the horns of a dilemma. As the readership of these periodicals formed the core

---

58 In Brussels this was the *Comité de secours aux réfugiés protestants* (Committee for aid to Protestant Refugees), in Antwerp it was the *Interkerkelijk Comité tot hulp aan Protestantsche Vluchtelingen* (Inter-church Committee for the Aid of Protestant Refugees). Boudin, *La Croix et la Bannière*, 77-78, 84, 222.

59 Ibid., 222; "Comité tot hulp aan Protestantsche vluchtelingen," 3-4; Treloar, *The Disruption of Evangelicalism*, 274.

60 Otto Samuel was Jewish, but had become a Christian through the witness of an injured soldier in a military hospital where they were both recovering during World War I. After the war he spent five years with Dr. Eberhard Arnold. Samuel then became a Free Evangelical pastor in Gelsenkirchen. The increasing persecution of Jews by the Nazi regime prompted him to resign as a pastor and focus on fulltime evangelism among Jewish people. In this he collaborated with Hungarian and Jewish Christian Arnold Frank, minister of the Jerusalem Church in Hamburg. The latter contacted Joseph Hoffman Cohn of the American Board of Missions to the Jews, asking them to take care of Samuel's salary. After the invasion, Samuel was arrested and transported to an internment camp in Perpignan. After being moved to another camp in Vichy-France, he was released and travelled to the USA. ABEM, 814: Winston Sr. to Howard Jr. (10 Aug. 1939); Yaakov, *Evangelizing the Chosen People*, 204-206; Matthäus, *Jewish Responses to Persecution*, 390-391.

of their North American supporters, Vansteenberghe and Winston Sr. feared financial repercussions if its collaboration with Samuel became known in the USA. As *Sunday School Times* director and member of the Board of Trustees, Howard Jr. shied away from giving advice; it was left in the hands of the directors to resolve. Considering aid to Jewish refugees a higher urgency than securing financial support from American evangelical families, they decided to continue their cooperation with Samuel. As it turned out, the directors' concern that this would negatively impact transatlantic donations was without foundation.[61]

In the meantime, Otto Samuel continued his work, spending most of his time in Brussels. After several months, his meetings started to outgrow the small room at the BGM headquarters in the Rue du Moniteur, and he requested the use of the Flemish BGM church in Brussels. By the middle of December 1939, he opened a soup kitchen in Brussels, where over a hundred Jews received a free meal.[62] When Hoyt and Sommers were called back to Brussels because of the dangerous situation at the Eastern borders of Belgium at the start of 1940, they assisted Samuel with his work among the people who were described as "exiled German Jews."[63]

Samuel spent some time in Antwerp, where the local BGM church helped ten Jewish refugees. Antwerp pastor Van de Riet called for the solidarity of other BGM churches to alleviate the pressure on the local diaconate.[64] In the spring of 1939, local believers were also asked to take in Jewish children from Austria, offering "a beautiful opportunity to witness our love for God's chosen people and to bring the message of the Gospel to these children."[65] Seven children out of a convoy of thirty-seven were placed in households that had links with the BGM. The other thirty children were assigned to Catholic fami-

---

61 ABEM, 814: Howard Jr. to Winston Sr. and Vansteenberghe (22 Sep. 1939).
62 ABEM, 180: Winston Sr. to Lloyd (2 March 1940); ABEM, 165: Winston Sr. to Knecht Sr. (17 June 1939).
63 When war broke out, the pair fled to the USA, where they did the same work with the same organization, before returning to Belgium in 1945. ABEM, 886: Fleming, "Manuscript *In the Wake of the Whirlwind*," Chapter 10, 1; ABEM, 850: Personnel Committee Report to CAEC (2 April 1940).
64 It was suggested that every BGM church or station would contribute BEF 10 per month from its fund for relief to the poor, and that individual believers could also contribute. ABEM, 849: Van de Riet, "Het vluchtelingenprobleem van de post van Antwerpen," (Feb. 1940).
65 For the mission to the Jews supported by the Reformed Churches in Antwerp and Brussels, see Maes, *De ster en het kruis*; For the original quote, see ABEM, 849: General Workers Letter (6 March 1939).

lies.[66] The proselytizing activities led both in Antwerp and Brussels to a few (alleged) conversions. Also, Jewish refugees were interested in the Christian faith in other places, such as a chance meeting with a BGM colporteur in the Liège area.[67]

With the clouds of war gathering over Belgium, it was no surprise that the BGM eventually would be involved once more in evangelistic activities in the army. In 1937, the mission was approached by the Belgian army's Head Chaplain for Protestants and a good friend of the BGM, Pierre Blommaert, to collaborate in the military Camp Beverloo. The government was willing to build a Protestant chapel, provided the churches would finance a chaplain. As the UPECB and ECMB had shown little interest, Blommaert turned to the BGM, which supported the idea. Both parties agreed that Maurice Van Doorne, located in Hasselt, was a suitable candidate.[68] As insufficient funds were available to appoint another worker, and attendance was meager in Hasselt, it was decided to close this location and open a new station in Leopoldsburg, close to the Camp.[69] After the chapel had opened and Van Doorne was appointed as an army chaplain, he reported the regular attendance of sixty protestant soldiers. Some twenty soldiers with no protestant background also showed an interest.[70]

Shortly after the Nazi invasion of Poland in September 1939, soldiers' foyers were opened in various BGM churches through local initiatives, and supporters in the USA were reminded of the mission's origins. "This war has made us go back to the soldiers and do among them the kind of work which became the cradle of the Belgian Gospel Mission."[71] The foyer in Eeklo was opened when pastor Willem Postma spoke with a soldier from Wallonia carrying the New Testament his brother had received from the Nortons many years before.[72] He furnished the annex of his church as a foyer. Shortly afterward,

---

66 Reactions have varied. Some pastors reported no positive response at all, others found that some families in their church who had volunteered to take in a child were ignored. One family withdrew at the last minute, explaining they were afraid that the child might be a bad influence on their own child, probably after they had been put under pressure by relatives. ABEM, 10: Barbezat to Winston Sr. (7 June 1939), Winston Sr. to Barbezat (16 June 1939); ABEM, 111: Elleman to Winston Sr. (18 March 1939); ABEM, 218: Overdulve to Winston Sr. (19 June 1939).
67 ABEM, 192: L'Eplattenier to Winston Sr. (1 Feb. 1940).
68 Blommaert had approached Van Doorne with a similar proposal in 1936. ABEM, 281: Van Doorne to Vansteenberghe (8 March 1937).
69 Ibid.: Winston Sr. to Van Doorne (7 Sep. 1937).
70 Twenty-five soldiers came from a BGM church or station. Others belonged to the ECMB, the UPECB, the Reformed (*Gereformeerde*) Church, the Methodists, Silo, the Closed Brethren, the Scottish Church, or came from unnamed denominations. Ibid.: Van Doorne to Vansteenberghe (4 Dec. 1937); ABEM, 556: Vansteenberghe to Trumbull (8 Feb. 1938).
71 ABEM, 855: Bulletin Letter USA (Jan. 1940).
72 The soldier had knocked at the door to ask about service times. He reportedly explained that he had initially kept the New Testament as a memento from the war but was converted after reading it. ABEM, 556: Vansteenberghe to Williams (12 Jan. 1940).

Postma reported that he had welcomed 135 of the roughly 1,000 soldiers from the camp in Eeklo. Most had accepted a New Testament and a 'The Reason Why' tract.[73]

The foyer in Huy was started by the pastor's wife, Mrs. H. Quenon, as an alternative to the Catholic foyer.[74] Although the BGM was a lot less supportive of women in ministry than in its early years, she was encouraged to go ahead and even told that the BGM would help her whenever possible. During its first five weeks, the foyer was visited by 267 soldiers, some of whom were Protestants and some were not.[75]

Based on these and other reports, these initiatives were initially described as a tremendous success, and the foyers were said to attract many non-Christians.[76] But the reasonable amount of interest waned fairly quickly, and the tone became less triumphant: "We are opening our halls to the men in khaki. They do not swarm to them, because they would naturally feel more attracted to the places where dancing, drinking and smoking are indulged in, and of these there is no lack."[77]

It goes without saying that since the start of World War II, the mission has stepped up its efforts to reach as many civilians as possible with the Gospel. The BGM rightly anticipated that little or no evangelism would be possible if Belgium was drawn into the war. At the start of 1940, Open-Air and Market Evangelism was largely abandoned, partly because of the weather and partly because the needed permits were not forthcoming, given the threat of war. The only exception was Brussels, where open-air evangelism was still allowed.[78] Obviously, the plans for tent evangelism that the German invasion thwarted in the summer.

Against the directors' expectations, the increasing threat of war did not increase interest in the message the BGM tried to distribute. Evangelistic methods like tent campaigns and market evangelism started to lose their appeal. Contrary to Ralph Norton, the co-directors were no visionaries. Instead of drawing conclusions and looking for more successful methods to reach the Belgians, they stuck to their traditional practices and repeated the evangelistic topics that had been successful in the early years of the Interbellum.

---

73 ABEM, 226: Postma to Winston Sr. (16 Sep. 1939), Postma to Vansteenberghe (25 Nov. 1939).
74 ABEM, 235: Mrs. Quenon to Winston Sr. (30 Oct. 1939).
75 Ibid. (19 Dec. 1939).
76 ABEM, 457: BGM to Allen (8 Nov. 1939); ABEM, 461: Vansteenberghe to Beesemyer (12 Dec. 1939).
77 ABEM, 855: Bulletin Letter USA (Jan. 1940).
78 Ibid.

The mission's only new initiative was to implement and adapt *Christmas Letters to Prisoners* in November 1939.[79] A month later, the mission took stock of three months of war and, as before, placed events in an eschatological context.

> In spite of all official neutrality Europe is divided into two camps, as far as sympathies are concerned. It is safe to say that Russia and Germany are thrown on their own more and more. Follow the Russian-German frontiers in Europe and you follow almost the frontiers of the Roman Empire. Very small political changes will be needed to make the frontiers conform completely. The scene is thus being prepared for the greatest massacre that the world has ever witnessed.[80]

We conclude this chapter by surveying the situation in the BGM churches and mission posts. In 1937, Sunday services were held at 86 locations. Forty-eight were in French, thirty-four in Dutch, and four were bilingual.[81] Wallonia, less densely populated, had considerably more kitchen meetings than Flanders. By now, a quarter of the churches and stations met in rented accommodation. This seems to indicate that it had become easier to find a place to rent, but insufficient data proves this. The first comprehensive figures about BGM church membership date from 1939, when the 18 Dutch-language churches (i.e. congregations with a church council) had 750 members, and the 20 French-language churches had over 860.[82]

The following year, an open discussion about the BGM's church planting strategy emerged.[83] As seen in Chapter 4, the original plan to only plant church-

---

79 Once the war had started, the evangelistic correspondence with prisoners even came to an abrupt halt, due to the restrictions enforced by the Nazis and the reduction in manpower at the BGM. *Christmas Letters to Prisoners* was established in the United Kingdom in 1880. The letters were written by volunteers, to explain the meaning and purpose of Christmas. ABEM, 476: Winston Sr. to Dimsdale (15 Nov. 1939), Dimsdale to Winston Sr. (24 Nov. 1939); CLP, "A Potted History of Our Work and Ministry."

80 Similarly, Odilon Vansteenberghe wrote a month later, "Little is needed to have Daniel's and Ezekiel's prophecy fulfilled to the letter." Although World War II did not turn out to be the literal and complete fulfillment of the Biblical prophecies of the End Times, tens of millions had perished by the time the Nazi regime unconditionally surrendered on 8 May 1945. ABEM, 855: Prayer Letter Belgian Gospel Mission (7 Dec. 1939); ABEM, 566: Vansteenberghe to Witt (24 Jan. 1940).

81 ABEM, 676: Postes de la Mission Evangélique Belge (Oct. 1937).

82 Another interesting fact from 1939 was that René Dobbelaere, one of the Nortons' many contacts from World War I, with whom they had subsequently lost contact, was now attending the services in Deinze and showed a "renewed interest in the Gospel." ABEM, 503: Winston Sr., Year Report for the American Council; ABEM, 655: Winston Sr. to Vansteenberghe (11 April 1939).

83 ABEM, 875: Report Travelling Agent Flanders;" "Evangelisatie-arbeid in Heyst," 1; Postma, "Maldegem," 3; "Inwijding eener zaal te Gilly," 1.

es in larger towns and hubs had been quietly abandoned.[84] John Winston Sr. now had doubts about the new strategy of starting regular meetings as soon as requests were received from the village or town. The kitchen meetings often had to be abandoned quickly, usually because of interest.[85] He felt it would be better to have people attend an existing church for some time and only start discussing a new church planting project once people had been attending faithfully for some time.[86] For Winston Sr., the urgency of an imminent war seemed to be secondary to the financial issues.

Not so for co-director and Belgian Vansteenberghe. He agreed that starting *byposts* (annex stations) was always risky. Still, he argued that the current strategy was intended to make it less complicated for people to attend a Protestant church, which was hard enough in a society dominated by Catholicism.

Edouard Barbezat suggested varying the church planting strategy in each region depending on the circumstances. He argued that the advantage of the small annex stations was that they would protect new converts against sheep-stealing attempts by other Protestant groups. Moreover, the existing churches did not necessarily provide the teaching that new converts needed. Walter Teeuwissen suggested continuing the kitchen meetings for one or two years in each place before deciding to rent a hall if there was still sufficient interest.[87]

Eventually, in 1938, a majority voted for maintaining the policy of planting churches through small annexes. Shortly afterward, Johannes Elleman in Zele was allowed to rent a house for a few months to see if there would be any lasting interest. He was told to ensure that those interested would be "made to understand their responsibility for the work costs in Zele from the very start. We can't keep financing the home's rent, even if it is low, so the work in Zele will depend on the willingness of the people to make sacrifices."[88]

A similar meaning was used in Binche. After two evangelistic meetings in the *Maison du Peuple*, the local socialist hall, several people requested that the BGM start regular meetings. When a suitable room was found, André Vuilleumier said he was prepared to rent it for several months and to see what would happen. The church at La Louvière was to act as the mother church and requested financial support from Brussels, which was granted.[89] Attendance

---

84 See page 69ff.
85 "Generally speaking, kitchen meetings peter out after a year or two through local jealousies or even worse, and work is reduced to a family or two and finally dies out." ABEM, 457: Vansteenberghe to Ashman.
86 ABEM, 850: Minutes CAEC (23 Sep. 1938).
87 Ibid.
88 For the original quote, see ABEM, 111: Vansteenberghe to Elleman (14 Oct. 1938).
89 ABEM, 323: Vuilleumier to Winston Sr. (25 May 1939).

met expectations even when a room was rented, and the meetings were no longer held in a 'neutral' place.[90]

After twenty years of activity, most local BGM churches were far from self-supporting, which meant that the mission had to finance its pastors. In an attempt to find a solution, John Winston Sr. discussed the thorny problem with Rowland Bingham, co-founder of the Sudan Interior Mission. On the one hand, Winston Sr. underlined that the BGM's desire and goal was definitely that new local churches would eventually become self-supporting, and it encouraged its churches to work towards that goal. On the other hand, he defended the approach of the Nortons, who had always been reluctant to ask churches to be self-supporting.

Winston Sr. said the realization was hampered by "two or three serious considerations of a psychological and material nature."[91] First, no Protestant organization in Belgium was entirely self-supporting. Second, he continued, the people of Belgium were "accustomed to depend on subsidies from the Government granted to the Roman Catholic Church, the Jewish Synagogue and the National Protestant Church." Third, manual workers in Belgium, the majority in BGM congregations, had meager wages.[92]

Winston Sr.'s reasoning did not convince Bingham. He replied that the need for churches to be self-supporting was the only issue on which he differed from the Nortons. He still felt that self-support needed to be high on the agenda from the very start. He added, "Having watched the careers of many others, I know how difficult it is to work towards self-support."[93]

The BGM was limping on two legs, simultaneously wanting everything and its opposite. By covering the financial deficit of the BGM congregations with the help of North American backers, the mission had an instrument to ensure that local leadership remained loyal to the mission's theological identity. But because of this policy, there was less budget for large evangelistic initiatives and fully paying all the workers each month.

There was a pressing need to take action as there was waning support among the backers to use their donations for Belgian congregations instead of evangelists or evangelistic projects. Thus, in the late 1930s, the BGM finally encouraged its local churches to grow towards self-support. First, it was decided that the local congregation had to pay the traveling expenses of visiting preachers. Secondly, congregations meeting in rented accommodation were told that they would have to finance the rent themselves.[94] Thirdly, some local pastors were blamed for not doing enough to make their church members face

90 The annex was closed at the outbreak of World War II. Ibid. (23 June 1939).
91 ABEM, 465: Winston Sr. to Bingham (27 April 1939).
92 Ibid.
93 Ibid.: Bingham to Winston Sr.
94 ABEM, 42: Winston Sr. to Cailleaux (21 April 1938).

their financial responsibilities: "You take part of the truth of the Gospel away from them if you do not teach them to give cheerfully."[95]

In the area of self-governance, the Committee for the Organization of the Churches was deeply divided. Some followed Ralph Norton's view that the churches were best served with an Episcopalian or Presbyterian structure with strict central control. The others, including John Winston Sr., preferred a Congregationalist model in which each church was to form an independent entity "with only a loose and chiefly spiritual connection to the Headquarters."[96] He believed that once the congregations were fully developed and able to function independently, they needed to start their own denomination. This would enable the mission to concentrate "on its aggressive Gospel work fully."[97]

Although the *Preliminary Stipulations* dictated that the Mission always had a "right of inspection" in the churches, Winston Sr. felt that in churches where local elders assisted the pastor, there was no need to have the regional representative present when new members were accepted.[98] Odilon Vansteenberghe was much more cautious. He felt the churches were not ready to form an independent denomination, and the BGM board should maintain some rights over the mission stations. "You will remember how anxious Mr. Norton was to keep the doctrinal basis of the churches pure and sound, and if we let them drift on their own, the danger of their drifting away would be very real."[99] He also very much doubted whether or not the American Board of Trustees would agree.

While outsiders had the impression that the BGM was firmly led from Brussels, several pastors regularly took action or made important decisions without consulting with Headquarters. This suggests these pastors were advocates of the Congregationalist model. For example, when headquarters asked all the churches to send in their membership lists in 1939, as war loomed, it emerged that some pastors had removed members from their lists without prior discussion with the church council.[100] The directors in Brussels had not been notified either, which meant the removals were against the rules. As the intention of a robust and central direction existed, John Winston Sr. reiterated that the *Preliminary Stipulations* must be applied in all its churches and stations.[101]

95 For the original quote, see ABEM, 35: Vansteenberghe to Buunk (6 May 1938).
96 Interestingly, Winston Sr. had turned away from the Presbyterian model because of his experiences with Presbyterian churches in the USA and elsewhere. In contrast, Ralph Norton, who had worked with this denominational for many years, always favored this model. ABEM, 655: Winston Sr. to Vansteenberghe (1 May 1939).
97 Ibid.
98 For the original quote, see ABEM, 850: Minutes CAEC (10 Feb. 1939).
99 Ibid.
100 ABEM, 875: Winston Sr., Rapport Reizende Arbeider (21 April 1939).
101 ABEM, 850: Minutes CAEC (21 April 1939).

Because of this central leadership, local pastors asked Headquarters for advice in many cases involving church discipline. Some cases were also discussed at regional meetings.[102] The starting point in all cases was, "We should not make it too easy for those people, but not treat them harshly either. They must understand how badly they misbehaved, so they must appear before the elders."[103]

Many questions for advice from Headquarters about discipline were linked to marriage. The general rule was that marriages were not blessed if the bride was pregnant. When a couple slipped through the net, and a baby was born way earlier than nine months after the wedding, pastors were advised to refuse communion to them until they had admitted that they had had premarital sex. They were only accepted after a public confession of sin.[104]

Cohabitation was a regular occurrence but not tolerated. The couples in question were told, with reference to the Bible, to rectify the situation, which meant the cohabiting partner, usually the woman, had to move out of the house. When this binding recommendation was followed, it was described as a "victory of the Gospel."[105] Some cohabitating couples chose a different approach. They stayed away from the services until they were legally married and then asked the local pastor to perform a blessing of their marriage.[106] He was prepared to do so, but on condition that the blessing would take place a month after the legal wedding ceremony and not in the church but at the couple's home. Co-director Winston Sr. agreed. "I believe that we must protect the church and not give the impression that everything happens unnoticed; that could lead other brothers and sisters as well as the general public to believe that we are superficial in this respect."[107]

When the third and extended edition of the *Preliminary Stipulations* was published in 1938, it still had no article on baptism. Winston Sr. had suggested including the following text: "*Baptism* The choice of mode of baptism is left to the station leader and his local church, according to their insights and beliefs."[108] As paedobaptism was only practiced in Dutch-speaking congregations, this text was objected to by the Francophones, fearing this would open the door to this type of baptism in Wallonia, too.[109] After much discussion, no consensus was reached, and the proposed text was left out. With no central instructions on the mode of baptism, this issue led to fierce debates in some local congregations now and then.

102 ABEM, 655: Winston Sr. to Vansteenberghe (29 June 1937).
103 For the original quote, see ABEM, 281: Vansteenberghe to Van Doorne (15 Dec. 1943).
104 ABEM, 78: De Smidt to Châtelain (2, 19 Jan. 1939).
105 For the original quote, see ABEM, 35: Buunk to Vansteenberghe (18 June 1936).
106 ABEM, 42: Cailleaux to Châtelain (29 June 1939).
107 For the original quote, see Ibid.: Châtelain to Cailleaux (13 July 1939).
108 For the original quote, see ABEM, 1237: Winston Sr. to the members of the Committee for the Organizing of Churches (15 April 1938).
109 ABEM, 219: Neusy to Winston Sr. (27 April 1938).

Another example that proves the BGM was not as firmly led as assumed is that in 1937, five years after the introduction of the *Preliminary Stipulations*, several congregations still ignored the rule that communion could only be celebrated after a church council had been appointed. Also, the fact that people who had been refused communion in one church were allowed to take communion elsewhere led to friction.[110]

This sacrament's practice also illustrates the mission's ecclesiological development during the past twenty years. Initially, only ordained pastors were allowed to celebrate communion. This was also communicated to the UPECB, ECMB, and other Protestant churches in Belgium as a reassurance that the sacraments were administered according to general reformed practice. However, this principle was gradually and quietly abandoned, and colporteurs had started to celebrate communion from time to time. To provide clarity, the CAEC included this privilege in the regulations for colporteurs in 1939.

110   ABEM, 875: Minutes CAEC (30 Sep. 1937).

The BGM Church in Poperinge was shortly confiscated by the Nazis to be used as a club for the soldiers, 1941.
[KADOC-KU LEUVEN: ABEM, 1180]

9
THE NAZI OCCUPATION

The outbreak of the Second World War in September 1939 added new challenges. The occupation of Belgium in May 1940 led to a forced reorganization and limitation of the activities. It also created an unprecedented financial crisis, as, during the occupation, the BGM was cut off from its leading financial donor, the North American friends. These external circumstances stimulated the first hesitant steps towards compartmentalizing the BGM into a mission and a denomination.

From as early as the spring of 1936, the Belgian Gospel Mission had a contingency plan for the eventuality of the outbreak of war. "If war strikes us … [w]e must get the wives and children out of Brussels by the first train, and places must be made in the Provinces where they can be cared for."[1] Two and a half years later, when Germany made threats in connection with the Sudetenland, the course of action in the eventuality of war was discussed at the workers' conference of September 1938.

The pastors were expected to function as spiritual leaders "… to whom members of our congregations and others will turn in these troubled times. This means that to the extent this will be possible, we want to organize our personal lives and ensure the safety of our family members in such a way that we can help others."[2] After the conference, further instructions were added to maintain contact with headquarters and safeguard the mission's assets. In

---

1   The cause of this strong sense of impending war was the remilitarization of the Rhineland. ABEM, 850: Minutes Board of Trustees (21 April 1936).
2   For the original quote, see ABEM, 1237: Winston Sr., Circular Letter (29 Sep. 1938).

every locality, one or preferably two men were to be appointed to take care of the building should the pastor be forced to leave. The directors had to be notified if a pastor was mobilized, and non-Belgians were to contact the embassy or consulate of their respective countries.[3]

Another precaution was to group churches and stations into clusters based on their geographical locations so that the work could be continued as much as possible should the contact between headquarters and local congregations be permanently disrupted. Each cluster was placed under a pastor who was not likely to be mobilized and who would, therefore, be able to stay.[4] In the spring of 1939, membership lists of local churches (albeit incomplete) and registers maintained by headquarters were sent to the office of the Board of Trustees in Philadelphia as a precautionary measure.[5]

When a staged mobilization took place in Belgium, starting shortly before the German invasion of Poland on 1 September 1939, altogether, seventeen of thirty-six pastors were called up by the armies of their respective countries: eight from Belgium, four from Switzerland, three from France, and two from the Netherlands.[6] For now, mobilized Belgian pastors were allowed to travel back to their churches on Sundays to lead services.[7] Local activities in some places were scaled back to one Sunday service and one weekday activity per week, while the remaining BGMers tried to serve all churches and stations between them.[8]

Several pastors expressed nervousness about the impending war. Samuel Dubois requested to be transferred to an available congregation in case of a forced evacuation of Seraing. Headquarters interpreted his request as a request for immediate transfer and refused because outsiders would regard it as fleeing.[9] He was told to stay in Seraing until a forced evacuation was to take place, but his family was allowed to leave. Dubois replied he did not necessarily want to leave immediately but that allowing his family to go for safety reasons was not an option. This would also lead to criticism.[10]

Despite the added problems, the mission maintained an ambitious tone in its newsletters. Despite the worrying circumstances, the transatlantic supporters were told they wished to extend the work.[11] Even the day before the

3 Ibid.
4 ABEM, 849: General Workers Letter (29 Sep. 1938).
5 ABEM, 875: Winston Sr., Report Travelling Agent Flanders to CAEC (21 April 1939).
6 "Nieuws uit den Arbeid," *Onze Hoop*, 1 Oct. 1939, 3.
7 ABEM, 27: Vansteenberghe to Bouma (8 Nov. 1939).
8 ABEM, 268: Winston Sr. to Stordeur (26 Aug. 1939); ABEM, 281: Vansteenberghe to Van Doorne (28 Nov. 1939).
9 ABEM, 107: Dubois to Winston Sr. (18, 28 Sep. 1939).
10 Ibid.: Winston Sr. to Dubois (3 Oct. 1939), Dubois to Winston Sr. (5 Oct. 1939).
11 ABEM, 855: Bulletin Letter USA (Jan. 1940).

German invasion of Belgium, John Winston Sr. wrote that the planned evangelistic open-air activities would go ahead as usual.[12]

Rumors were flying when Belgium was drawn into the war on 10 May 1940 by a second German invasion in less than thirty years, and people were distressed and needed encouragement. Although most answers were in the circular letter they received in 1938, several pastors asked the BGM directors for their advice now that war had arrived. Gerrit van de Riet, pastoring the church in Antwerp, wrote,

> They say that the enemy, who spares nothing, will lock up all men in camps in Germany, even pastors, like in Poland. Does the mission want us to stay here if our people stay, or should we go? Should all our people leave, it would not make sense if I stay here like a shepherd without sheep and expose myself to all of this ...? Or should I do it for the house? If our people stay, I prefer to stay with them despite the great uncertainty of what the Germans will do with me.[13]

Raoul Claude cycled around the churches as communication was hampered, taking stock of the situation outside Brussels.[14] Most of the buildings were spared. The buildings in Soignies, Braine-le-Comte, and Charleroi sustained minor damage, but the building in Poperinge was badly damaged, and the church in Tournai was destroyed.[15]

During the invasion, the Belgian population, including several BGMers, fled the violence of war en masse.[16] Because no pastor was available, several BGM stations were temporarily closed. Only the church in Marche and its annexes were permanently closed, as their pastor, Jean Wälti, had returned to Switzerland.[17]

---

12 This instruction was based on a Royal Decree issued on 27 April 1940, stipulating that anyone wishing to hold an open-air meeting would have to apply to his local mayor for a permit at least five days in advance. ABEM, 266: Winston Sr. to Stearns (9 May 1940); Ministerie van Binnenlandsche Zaken, "Koninklijk besluit betreffende de samenscholingen in open lucht," 2558.

13 As far as we know, there are no publications as yet about the fate of Protestant clergy in Poland during Nazi occupation. The persecution of Catholic clergy Poland has been extensively documented in Wos, Jacewicz and Akademia teologii katolickiej (Varsovie), *Martyrologium polskiego;* For the original quote, see ABEM, 292:Van de Riet to Winston Sr. and Vansteenberghe (13 May 1940).

14 His wife and children had taken the train back to Switzerland. ABEM, 266: Winston Sr. to Stearns (15 July 1940).

15 ABEM, 503: Winston Sr. to Howard Jr. (10 June 1940).

16 In May and June 1940, an estimated two million Belgian refugees found themselves in France. Herman Quenon and Zéphirin Bertiaux provided pastoral support to the Belgian refugees in Montpellier, under the supervision of head chaplain Pierre Blommaert. Boudin, *La Croix et la Bannière,* 118; ABEM, 266: Winston Sr. to Stearns (15 May 1940).

17 The stations were Binche, Ottignies, Dottignies, Scoumont, De Panne, Boom and Zele. Ibid. (17 Aug. 1940).

Odilon Vansteenberghe was one of the many Belgian refugees who hurriedly left for France. It was feared that the Nazis might turn against him – and with Vansteenberghe against the whole mission – because of his public and open condemnation of the persecution of Jews in Germany. Being a citizen of a neutral country, the BGM leadership did not expect the Germans to be interested in John Winston Sr.[18] He, therefore, remained as director and was assisted by a temporary management team.

By the end of August 1940, most BGMers, including Odilon Vansteenberghe, had returned and resumed their day-to-day activities as far as this was possible.[19] The loss of lives and the number of injured among BGMers and their families were less than had been feared. André Andries' daughter died during a bombardment, and three of Remy Meersman's children were injured by shrapnel.[20] No figures are available for the number of victims among members and regular visitors of BGM meetings.

During the invasion, the mission offered shelter and spiritual sustenance to thousands fleeing the fighting in several places, such as Sint-Niklaas and Willebroek.[21] The church in Ghent was the only official shelter in its street, and pastor Johannes van Lierop met many new people.[22] As Brussels had been declared an 'open city' where no fighting was to take place, and no bombs would be dropped, many Belgians fled to the capital. However, Brussels was bombed on 10 May 1940, and many inhabitants and refugees moved on to France or the Belgian coast. The Belgian coast had remained partly unoccupied during World War I, so they assumed to be safe there.[23]

Other refugees stayed in Brussels, being joined by a new stream of terrified civilians. The building that Otto Samuel had used as a soup kitchen for Jewish refugees was now used as a general shelter.[24] The city council and the Red Cross sent people there, and an average of 50 to 70 people were welcomed each day. Charles Bauwens was in charge and held devotions every evening. As they left, people were handed tracts and a Bible portion while their address was passed on to their nearest BGM pastor.[25] BGM headquarters were also a

---

18 Thompson, *Firebrand of Flanders*, 71-72.
19 The Swiss all ended up staying in Switzerland, while L'Hermenault found work in France. ABEM, 849: General Workers Letter (18 Sep. 1940); ABEM, 78: Winston Sr. to De Smidt (22 Aug. 1940).
20 ABEM, 191: Winston Sr. to L'Hermenault (1 Oct. 1940).
21 Winston Sr. observed that this led to fewer conversions than traditional open-air work, but "on account of the peculiar circumstances and the ability to do personal work, I think our efforts have counted for as much or more in hearts touched and souls reached, for there have been a number of cases of wonderful conversion." ABEM, 503: Winston Sr. to Howard Jr. (10 June 1940); ABEM, 787: Van Dam, Report of Willebroek (1946); ABEM, 758: Van der Beek, Rapport van de werkzaamheden (1946).
22 ABEM, 283: Van Lierop to Winston Sr. (18 April 1938, 1940).
23 Verleyen, *Mei 1940: België op de vlucht*, 104, 116.
24 ABEM, 266: Winston Sr. to Stearns (15 May 1940).

shelter for people "of various walks of life and nationality."[26] They were sent there by the American embassy and consulate, which had been inundated with requests for assistance.

The mission was one of the many agencies actively providing shelter for the estimated half a million people who came to the capital to flee the fighting.[27] By then, the Brussels population had already fled en masse in response to rumors of war.[28] The shelters remained open until they were ordered to close by the German authorities in mid-June.[29]

During the early days of the occupation, several BGMers carried out pastoral work among prisoners of war. John Winston Sr. visited injured British soldiers in a German military hospital in Brussels three times, accompanied by Esther Hoyt and Lulu Sommers. They handed out New Testaments, gospels, books, and magazines. Before Bible school student Offringa could hold church services for the captives, the emergency hospital was closed, and the injured prisoners of war had been taken away.[30]

In Ghent, Johan van Lierop visited at least 400 British soldiers.[31] After several soldiers escaped, restrictions were introduced, making it harder for Van Lierop to see them. Still, by then, he had already successfully passed the names of the prisoners of war to their families in the UK.[32] Jules Neusy tried to visit British and French prisoners of war in the Citadel of Liège. He was denied access but managed to have toiletries and some food passed on to them by a doctor.[33]

Walter Teeuwissen visited British prisoners of war in the Red Cross hospital in Bruges.[34] As early as 1939, Teeuwissen had enquired with the US embassy whether the US government would pay for a possible evacuation if the BGM were to lack sufficient means.[35] Receiving no concrete reply, he waited until March 1940 to hand in his resignation. As the Board of Trustees refused to

---

25 These lists are now in Charles Bauwens' personnel file. ABEM, 15: Charles Bauwens, Rapport du 13 mai au 15 juin 1940.
26 Here too, BGMers used the opportunity to evangelize. ABEM, 503: Winston Sr. to Howard Jr. (10 June 1940).
27 Boudin, *La Croix et la Bannière*, 61-62.
28 Verleyen, *Mei 1940*, 118-119.
29 ABEM, 15: Bauwens to Winston Sr. (18 June 1940).
30 ABEM, 266: Winston Sr. to Stearns (15 May 1940).
31 ABEM, 283: Van Lierop to Winston Sr. (18 July 1940).
32 Ibid. (24 Aug. 1940).
33 ABEM, 219: Neusy to Winston Sr. (1 Aug. 1940).
34 He also offered his services to the USA. ABEM, 876: Minutes Provisional Committee of Activities (26 July 1940).
35 AWT: Merrill to Teeuwissen (30 Oct. 1939).

pay for his journey home, Teeuwissen was still in Belgium during the invasion, raising money to pay for his return to the USA.[36] He left on 17 October 1940, along with the other American BGMers, after the American embassy had ordered all Americans to leave Belgium.[37]

Although he had been determined to stay, John Winston Sr. left that day, too. "I believe that it is better for me to return to America now and be prepared to come back as soon as the situation has calmed rather than staying now and then be forced to leave at a point in time when I would be more useful for the Mission in Belgium."[38] No management team assisted Vansteenberghe. He was at the helm by himself for the rest of the occupation.

During the invasion and early stage of the occupation, the various initiatives demonstrate that the BGM had maintained its holistic view of humankind. Addressing the physical and mental well-being of civilians and prisoners of war was self-evident for the workers in the crisis. Of course, prayers were said that these initiatives would yield some conversions.

This holistic view on the Belgian population also motivated several BGMers and church members to join the resistance, all at their initiative.[39] As the mission had condemned the Nazi regime in Germany well before the occupation, the occupiers were watching the mission closely, which made taking part in the resistance extra risky.[40] When sermons were used to encourage people to hide Jewish people, the occupiers intervened.[41] Yet Jewish people were hidden in several places, in local congregations, the campsite at Limauges, and even at headquarters in Brussels.[42]

Joseph Huyghe deserves to be mentioned as being involved in the arrest of Irma Laplasse. She was sentenced to death and executed for treason immediately after the liberation of Belgium. Her arrest of 1945 was repealed in 1995 after Flemish nationalists had campaigned for her sentence to be quashed, but in the subsequent retrial, she was sentenced to life in prison, and her civil rights were revoked.[43]

---

36   The Board of Trustees asked him to withdraw his resignation. The refusion to finance his return ticked was based on Clause 11 of the China Inland Mission's Principles and Practices, as the Board itself had no rules that applied to this situation. ABEM, 272: Teeuwissen to the Board of the BGM (12 April 1940), Howard Jr. to Teeuwissen (29 March 1940).
37   Ibid., 8 Oct. 1940; ABEM, 877: G. Winston, "History of the BGM," Chapter 9, 3.
38   For the original quote, see ABEM, 849: General Workers Letter (18 Sep. 1940).
39   An exhaustive discussion of this subject would fall outside the scope of this study, and it is possible that some BGMers who were active in the resistance are not listed here.
40   AC, AA1205/32: Van de Riet.
41   AC, AA1205/16: Vandenbroeck.
42   Ibid., AA1205,16,32; Koppel, *Untergetaucht*, 162, 168, 179, 213, 221-222; ABEM, 525: Vansteenberghe to Machlin (2 Dec. 1949, 4 June 1951), Machlin to Vansteenberghe (31 May 1951); ABEM, 333: Winston Sr. to Wolff (2 June 1949); Boudin, *La Croix et la Bannière*, 237-239, 251-252; Email communication from Henk van de Riet, 30 May 2014.
43   See Van Isacker, *De zaak Irma Laplasse*; Pylyser, *Verzwegen schuld*.

Headquarters in Brussels was not only used to hide Jews; it was also a 'rallying center' for Hotton. This resistance group included Théophile De Kerpel, the concierge, and Pierre and Paul Vansteenberghe, sons of Odilon Vansteenberghe.[44] Vansteenberghe himself was actively involved in resistance activity as well, by hiding a Jewish family.[45] According to the postwar version of events, he was not involved and had tried to prevent his sons from getting involved.[46] This distortion of the facts must be placed in the context of the arrest and execution of Pierre Vansteenberghe in 1943. Excerpts from his prison cell letters were used in a fundraising tract, which focused on the young man's faith in dire circumstances.[47] Odilon Vansteenberghe's involvement in the resistance was less heroic. Admitting his participation could have led to criticism that he had taken unjustified risks that had put the interests of the mission at stake.

Pierre Vansteenberghe was not the only BGMer arrested and did not survive the war. Ernest Charensol, pastoring in Warquignies, died in a concentration camp in March 1945.[48] Later, when his widow was asked whether armed resistance was compatible with Christian beliefs, she replied that she and her husband had not regarded it as problematic.[49]

Not all BGMers sympathized with the resistance or were involved in it. Some kept a neutral position, and Désiré Stordeur, the pastor in Mouscron, reportedly even praised Hitler from his pulpit.[50] The meetings in Heist aan Zee were discontinued because the people in whose homes the kitchen meetings were held collaborated with the occupiers. After the war, the BGM church in Bruges split. Some disapproved that after the liberation, pastor Maurice Van Doorne, together with other members of the resistance, went to the homes of collaborators to arrest them at gunpoint.[51]

A notable cooperation between the youth ministries of the main Protestant churches in Antwerp, including the BGM church, started during World War II. Meetings were held quarterly, with each church taking its turn to host

---

44 AC, AA1205/16: Vandenbroeck; Vansteenberghe, "Herinneringen VII," 3.
45 Paldiel, *Churches and the Holocaust*, 161.
46 Thompson, *Firebrand of Flanders*, 75-76.
47 Vansteenberghe, *The Last Night*, 4, 7.
48 Boudin, *La Croix et la Bannière*, 201-202; AC, AA1205/32: Charensol; ABEM, 321: Vansteenberghe, Prayer letter to All Christians in the USA (6 July 1945); Depasse, "Le Pasteur Ernest Charensol (1903-1945)," 33-42. See also "The Righteous Among The Nations: Phebade Family."
49 AC, AA1205/32: Charensol.
50 Boudin bases this assertion on his interview with Jean Dequenne, in which the latter recounted his memories. Dequenne could not remember in which year this happened nor whether Stordeur later changed his opinion with regard to Hitler. Stordeur's personnel file does not contain a reprimand for this, so it is plausible that he did it during the first few years of Hitler's reign when not everyone was aware of Hitler's cruelty. Boudin, *La Croix et la Bannière*, 310-311; Email communication from Boudin, 4 Nov. 2013.
51 ABEM, 281: Van Doorne to Vansteenberghe (9 Dec. 1947).

and lead an evening. Attendance was between 125 and 150 young people per evening.[52]

When some young people were taken to Germany for forced labor, a network for mutual contact was set up. Jean Du Meunier played an essential role in this network. Several German soldiers volunteered to use their account with the army's postal service, thus providing a means to avoid the censoring of correspondence from home to the young men doing forced labor in Germany.[53]

As could be expected, the Nazi occupation worsened the dire financial situation of the mission. Applying the Trading with the Enemy Act, the Federal Reserve Bank no longer let the Board of Trustees transfer money from the US to Brussels.[54] Although the Board still managed to send $ 2,000 early in August 1940, the next transfer, amounting to $ 1,000, was more complicated to achieve.[55] When Winston Sr. heard that funds could still be sent to philanthropic organizations like the Red Cross and the YMCA in Germany, he saw this as a lifeline and hoped that the BGM could be treated similarly. He instructed Miner Stearns to argue that the BGM in Belgium had US citizens among its workers, that it was "an American Organization" that had "been receiving funds regularly from America over a period of more than twenty years," and that this money was needed to continue the work.[56] The request was refused on the grounds that the money was also used for non-Americans. It was not until the liberation that cash transfers from the USA to Belgium could be resumed.[57] The $ 3,000 received from the USA barely covered one month's expenses.

The BGM was forced to cut workers' salaries once more and even sell some buildings to release cash. In some places, such as Arlon, services were continued in a rented room, but other churches, including Tielt and Deinze, were closed.[58] On the other hand, the opportunity was seized to give local churches more financial responsibility. They were charged to pay their pastor

---

52 ABEM, 292: Van de Riet to Vansteenberghe (19 Sep. 1941).
53 "Onze Evangelische Jeugd komt thuis." "Advert," *De Kruisbanier*, 2 June 1945, 4.
54 USC 50: 53. Trading with the enemy, <https://uscode.house.gov/>.
55 The final $ 1,000 was specifically destined for the American BGMers. ABEM, 503: Winston Sr. to Howard Jr. (12, 28 Aug. 1940), Howard Jr. to Winston Sr. (19 Sep. 1940); Boudin, *La Croix et la Bannière*, 254-255.
56 This wording was obviously aimed at the US. In Belgium, the organization's Belgian character was emphasized, especially during the war. ABEM, 266: Winston Sr. to Stearns (11 Aug. 1940).
57 It is unclear whether they were successful or how they proposed to do so as the banks were not allowed to transfer any money. ABEM, 503: Howard Jr. to Winston Sr. (16 Sep. 1940); ABEM, 876: Minutes Provisional Committee of Activities (5 Sep. 1940).
58 The churches in Tielt and Deinze had diminished in size due to people moving house. ABEM, 251: Schmidt to Defraene (3 Nov. 1942); ABEM, 57: Vansteenberghe to De Bruyn (3 April 1941).

from weekly collections and report the difference to headquarters. Colporteurs were allowed to deduct their salaries from the profits of book sales they handed in.[59]

As most churches were too small to afford a pastor's salary from the collections, the workers were asked to explore the possibility of finding paid work outside the mission.[60] This would not be at the expense of the work, as the BGMers had more time on their hands now that they could not carry out several of their usual activities. It was hoped that the measure would enable most Belgian and European workers to stay.[61]

John Winston Sr. was initially optimistic that evangelistic activities could be continued during the occupation. With regard to the possible resumption of open-air meetings, he referred to a Belgian Government decree of 18 July 1940, which stated that "meetings of an exclusively religious character" were now not only permitted but even exempt "from the formality of a special permission."[62] As people only ventured into the streets when necessary for work purposes, urgent family matters, or food shopping and kept their trips as short as possible, it was of no use to resume open-air meetings.[63]

When the Nazis enforced restrictions, such as the temporary ban on colportage in the whole country and a reduction in manpower, as many foreign BGMers left the country, evangelic activities were put on the back burner. In August 1940, some indoor evangelistic meetings for French speakers were held in Brussels, but with little success.[64] BGM magazines, such as *Notre Espérance* and *Onze Hoop*, stopped appearing because there were no funds to print new issues.[65] It was not until 1943 that the Belgian Gospel Mission received permission from German authorities to travel the country for tent evangelism. Still, it was decided not to go ahead as they lacked the workers.[66]

The mobilization of 1939 cut short the studies of some Bible school students.[67] The others continued their training until the invasion abruptly ended the school year. When ten students indicated they wanted to contin-

---

59 Pastors were paid BEF 100 per week, plus BEF 14 for each child they had. ABEM, 876: Minutes Provisional Committee of Activities (5 Sep. 1940); ABEM, 98: Châtelain to Duez (6 Aug. 1940).
60 ABEM, 849: General Workers Letter (11 July 1940).
61 ABEM, 876: Minutes Provisional Committee of Activities (21 June 1940).
62 Militärbefehlshabers in Belgien und Nord-Frankreich, ed., "Verordnungsblatt nr. 8, 25/7/1940" (25 July 1940); ABEM, 855: Winston Sr. to Stephan (3 Aug. 1940).
63 Jacquemyns, *België in de Tweede Wereldoorlog*, vol. 2., 70.
64 ABEM, 266: Winston Sr. to Stearns (11 Aug. 1940); ABEM, 164: Winston Sr. to Keller (16 Aug. 1940).
65 For the policy on the use of magazines of other Protestant churches and organizations, see Boudin, *La Croix et la Bannière*, 71-75; ABEM, 876: Minutes Provisional Committee of Activities (2, 25 June 1940).
66 ABEM, 288: Vansteenberghe to Van Rossum (5 Aug. 1943).
67 ABEM, 855: Bulletin Letter USA (Jan. 1940).

ue their studies and three more students applied by August 1940, the BGM considered reopening the Bible schools in September.[68] Director Miner Stearns was in favor, but the Committee of Instruction decided on financial grounds that the doors would remain closed until further notice. Not only had the financial lifeline with the USA been severed, but it was also unclear whether the Dutch students would have sufficient means to pay for their lodgings if they managed to arrive. Moreover, reopening the school would also raise lighting and heating costs, and travel costs for teaching staff would have to be paid. Furthermore, the practical part of the training – open-air meetings, tract distribution, and pub evangelism – was more or less impossible.[69] The correspondence course was continued as usual throughout the war. The Bible schools would not reopen until 1945/6.

The 1939 mobilization caused some problems for BGM churches in Wallonia. Pastors who had not been mobilized were asked to lead services in the churches whose pastors now served in the army.[70] As there were too few to assist all congregations temporarily deprived of their leader, other scenarios had to be deployed. In some places, local believers kept the church going.[71] In other places, their wives took over some of the responsibilities of absent pastors.

Some did so by their own initiative, such as Mrs. H. Quenon. She wrote: "I did it in the first place for the Lord and also to maintain *in some small part* the church that has been abandoned for the last two and a half months."[72] Others, such as the Van Doornes, asked for instructions from Headquarters. Mrs. Van Doorne was given explicit permission to hold services if no other alternatives were available. She limited herself to organizing prayer meetings.[73] The case of La Louvière is especially striking. Initially, Pastor Jannis De Smidt was made responsible for this congregation in the absence of his colleague André Vuilleumier. But when prayer meetings replaced the Sunday

68 In the best-case scenario, they would have twenty students at the start of the academic year. Ten students had indicated the desire to continue their studies in September. A Dutch student also wanted to continue, but his parents demanded his return home. Four of the students were undecided. ABEM, 272: Winston Sr. to Teeuwissen (26 Aug. 1940); ABEM, 266: Winston Sr. to Stearns (31 Aug. 1940).
69 Already in April 1940, it was decided that the French-language Bible school would temporarily close in the autumn of that same year and that the BGM would no longer subsidize foreign students. ABEM, 875: Executive Committee Report to CAEC (2 April 1940); ABEM, 266: Stearns to Winston Sr. (24 Aug. 1940), Winston Sr. to Stearns (31 Aug. 1940).
70 ABEM, 78: BGM Headquarters to De Smidt (15 Sep. 1939).
71 This situation is documented for Seraing and Leopoldsburg. In Leopoldsburg, a young Russian took responsibility for running the church, and it was reported that the spiritual gifts endowed on him were now manifested. ABEM, 235: Mrs. Quenon to Châtelain (21 Nov. 1939); ABEM, 259: Vansteenberghe to Sikkema (7 Sep. 1939).
72 ABEM, 235: Mrs. Quenon to Châtelain (21 Nov. 1939).
73 ABEM, 281: Winston Sr. to Van Doorne (4 Sep. 1939), Van Doorne to Winston Sr. (12 Sep. 1939).

Mrs. Quenon, second row, third from the left, with allied soldiers in the foyer at Huy, 1944.
[KADOC-KU Leuven: ABEM, 1094]

services in La Louvière, the BGM leadership instructed that De Smidt's wife should lead these, as she possessed the necessary spiritual authority.[74]

As BGM workers still had relative freedom of movement at the beginning of the occupation, church members were reassured that the mission wished to continue its work as usual in as much as this was possible.[75] In terms of attendance, most French-language churches stagnated during the war.[76] Reports about numbers in Flanders are lacking, but in 1943, a new church was started in Schelle, between Antwerp and Brussels. Local baker Verdickt offered to use his bakery for Sunday services and Wednesday Bible studies. The BGM church in Willebroek acted as a mother church for these meetings, which were later moved to a different location.[77]

In some places, and in defiance of German army orders, German soldiers attended regular BGM services.[78] Antwerp's pastor Gerrit van de Riet wrote, "As they were very much against Nazism and came to us in secret, they were respected by our people, even by those who were active in the resistance. These soldiers made their field post numbers available for our clandestine correspondence with our boys in Germany. As a result, these soldiers were summoned to appear before the Gestapo."[79] Pastor Herman Buunk wrote that he regularly received German soldiers at his home in Kortrijk: "Those boys very much need our prayers! I get the feeling that they think our home is a little paradise. My wife and I enjoy doing something for those boys."[80] In Ichtegem, a German pastor preached in the service with translation by pastor Jacob Luteijn.[81]

These soldiers were expected to attend the services organized by the German army chaplains. As of 1941, the occupiers commanded pastor Fernand Castiaux to make the buildings in Soignies and Braine-le-Comte available for church services for German soldiers. Castiaux felt he could not refuse and adapted the times of his services accordingly. The German army made several attempts to take possession of the building in Braine-le-Comte, but Castiaux managed to prevent this by complaining to the local authorities.[82] The church in Poperinge was confiscated by the Germans to be used as a club for off-duty soldiers. Odilon Vansteenberghe successfully contested with the *Ortskomman-*

---

74 ABEM, 78: Directors to De Smidt (15 Sep. 1939).
75 ABEM, 849: Winston Sr., Circulaire aan de gemeenteleden (15 June 1940).
76 ABEM, 51: Châtelain, Report of the Travelling Superintendent of Wallony during the War.
77 De Meyer, "Deze zomer in Schelle een evangelische kerk?," 1.
78 See ABEM, 849: Castiaux to Schmidt (19 Aug. 1941) as an example.
79 For the original quote, see AC, AA1205/32: Van de Riet.
80 For the original quote, see ABEM, 35: Buunk to Vansteenberghe (9 Dec. 1940).
81 For the original quote, see AA1205/32: Luteijn.
82 ABEM, 49: Castiaux to Schmidt (19 Aug. 1941).

dant, arguing that the hall had already been made available to the German field chaplaincy and that the BGM would like it returned.[83]

During World War II, a monthly newsletter for the local youth in Flanders was launched to strengthen mutual ties between young people. Because of the chronic lack of paper, the newsletter was abandoned after some time.[84] Fortunately, the youth camps could continue for both language groups during the occupation. To obtain the support of the State Department of Children's Welfare and *Winterhulp*, they were extended from two weeks to a month in 1943. Accepting state support enabled them to give double rations to the children, but in retrospect, Vansteenberghe regretted that fewer children could come to the camps. Instead of the regular three hundred children in four camps, there were now two camps with only one hundred and fifty.[85] The acceptance of the grant, which went against the spirit of faith missions, was motivated by the acute shortage of food as a result of the war.

Even though large parts of Belgium, including Brussels, were liberated in September 1944, the earliest documents about this period date from as late as 1945. Almost immediately after the liberation, concrete plans were made to resume activities that had been abandoned during the war and even to develop new initiatives.[86] Several problems hampered them. For some time, no money could be wired from the USA to Belgium. Transporting materials from abroad was also difficult because of logistical issues. Thirdly, no visas were granted to foreigners.[87]

The first two reasons caused the delay in resuming on a national scale literature evangelism. *Notre Espérance* and *Onze Hoop* only resumed in 1947 because of the scarcity of paper and the high prices of paper. Therefore, the

---

83 ABEM, 136: Huyghe to Schmidt; ABEM, 738: Vansteenberghe, Draft letter to Ortskommandantur Ypres.
84 J. van Dam, Maandelijkse brief aan alle B.E.J.V.ers, [May 1942]; ABEM, 279: Van Dam to Vansteenberghe.
85 The Belgian State Department of Children's Welfare *(Nationaal Werk voor Kinderwelzijn)* was a continuation of some of the activities of the semi-official *Comité National de Secours et d'Alimentation* (National Committee of Aid and Food), which was established during WWI. Its tasks included hygiene and food for children and child protection. *Winterhulp* (Winter Support) was supervised and protected by the International Red Cross. It coordinated the activities of the Belgian Red Cross, *Vlaams Kruis* (Flemish Cross), *Nationaal Werk voor Kinderwelzijn* (National Work for Child Welfare) and *Nationaal Werk voor Oud Strijders en Oorlogsinvaliden* (National Work for Former Fighters and Disabled War Veterans) during World War II. Kind en Gezin, ed., "Geschiedenis;" Van Dongen, "Winterhulp 1940-1944;" ABEM, 288: Vansteenberghe to Van Rossum (14 Sep. 1943); Van Dam, "Het Belgisch Evangelisch Jeugdverbond, Ons kamp te Limauges," 2.
86 For children's work they wanted to collaborate with International Child Evangelism Fellowship. In view of the differences of opinion on the use of radio for evangelism before World War II, it is remarkable that they now had plans to that effect. "The Belgian Gospel Mission," Sep. 1945.
87 ABEM, 288: Vansteenberghe to Van Rossum (2 Aug. 1945).

Dutch-language BGM church in Brussels published its own magazine, *Opwekking*, between 1945 and 1946.[88] Literature supplies could not be brought in from neutral Switzerland until the capitulation of Nazi Germany. Alternatively, materials could be imported from France, the United Kingdom, and the USA. Still, no orders were placed for several months as the supply lines were poor and no funds were available.[89]

On the local level, allied soldiers attended church services. Among them were several army chaplains and civilian pastors who were allowed to preach.[90] One of them was Robert Laidlaw, a friend of the Nortons and author of *The Reason Why*, a brochure used extensively by the BGM. He arrived in Brussels in October 1944, working under the auspices of the Army Scripture Readers' Association. He was offered an office at BGM's headquarters, and Vansteenberghe encouraged BGMers to give Laidlaw all the support he needed as "one of the Mission's best friends."[91] Services in English were also organized at various places, mainly for the benefit of the soldiers, although civilians were welcome too.[92]

The BGM did not reopen soldiers' foyers, yet. Pastor Daniel van der Beek was approached by former BGMer and Methodist Robert Van Goethem to create a 'Wesley home' for Belgian soldiers at the church's premises. This was forbidden by director Vansteenberghe because Van Goethem should have asked him before approaching Van der Beek. The fact that Van Goethem had left the mission in discord with the leadership will also have been part of the motivation to torpedo this project. It was convenient that, against the BGM policy, smoking would be allowed, which gave Vansteenberghe another argument for the veto. However, should a Wesley home be opened elsewhere in Sint-Niklaas, Van der Beek could lead evening devotions there.[93]

Pastor Van der Beek accepted the decision but felt it was narrow-minded because the soldiers would smoke elsewhere if they were not allowed to smoke at the BGM.[94] His willingness to allow smoking can be explained by the fact that Van der Beek was Dutch, and smoking was usually not an issue for prot-

---

88 ABEM, 231: Poyda to Keller (1 Dec. 1945).
89 ABEM, 235: Vansteenberghe to Quenon.
90 In Charleroi, sermons were given by a Mr. Meima. He remembered Ralph Norton from their days at Moody Bible Institute. ABEM, 10: Barbezat to Vansteenberghe (24 Oct. 1944).
91 Laidlaw was already invited to add Belgium to his European tour in 1939, but that tour was canceled when war broke out in August 1939. ABEM, 656: Vansteenberghe to Winston Sr. (17 March 1939); ABEM, 318: Vansteenberghe to Van der Beek (5 Oct. 1944); "Newsletter Great-Britain," Nov. 1945; ABEM, 50: Vansteenberghe to Mme. Charensol (16 Oct. 1944); ABEM, 219: Vansteenberghe to Neusy (21 Nov. 1944).
92 ABEM, 49: Vansteenberghe to Castiaux (19 Oct. 1944); ABEM, 235: Quenon to Vansteenberghe (30 Oct. 1944), Vansteenberghe to Quenon; ABEM, 659: De Vries, Report of the work in Tienen and Leuven; ABEM, 10: Vansteenberghe to Barbezat (22 Feb. 1945).
93 ABEM, 318: Vansteenberghe to Van der Beek (2 Jan. 1945).
94 Ibid.: Van der Beek to Vansteenberghe (18 Jan. 1945).

estants in the Netherlands. Vansteenberghe, on his part, argued that this type of work rarely led to conversions anyway. He realized that the mission's view on the use of tobacco and also on some other issues deviated from the majority view, adding "that the temptation to be more flexible with the Mission's narrow principles to adapt to modern days" was powerful, but that a change of direction would nevertheless be worldly and therefore wrong.[95] Yet for those unfamiliar with the BGM's Keswick holiness roots, these rules for daily living obtained a legalistic nature.

The liberation also affected interdenominational cooperation. On the national level, Vansteenberghe met with Willem Visser 't Hooft, General Secretary of the provisional committee of the World Council of Churches (WCC) in November 1944. He had come to Brussels to discuss the offer of the World Churches' Department of Reconstruction and Inter-Church Aid to finance the rebuilding and restoration of Protestant churches that had been destroyed or damaged during the war. This offer included BGM churches.

Vansteenberghe declined his friendly offer. They would welcome financial aid for restoring or rebuilding BGM buildings, but not through ecumenical channels, as this would harm the mission's "aggressive and evangelical nature."[96] He was convinced that God would deliver them "in a more complete way and that most of the war damage would be paid for by the Belgian government anyway."[97]

Not long afterward, Rev. Dr. J. Hutchinson Cockburn, Senior Secretary of the Department of Reconstruction and Inter-Church Aid of the WCC, had an appointment with Vansteenberghe. Again, the BGM was unconditionally offered all the financial aid it might need to rebuild and restore its buildings. Vansteenberghe repeated his earlier reply to Visser 't Hooft in what he later described as a painful conversation:

> the BGM wanted to look to the Lord rather than to men and would not accept anything from the Oecumenical Council because of the very out-spoken modernistic tendency in that body. We can feel that much pressure is being exerted to make the mission fall in line with the Protestant organizations working in Belgium. It may be that some of the workers do not fully understand the position which the Directors of the Mission hold with regard to the Geneva Council. From the human standpoint a seemingly unconditional offer of money is very tempting, and after all the years of privation, it would appear foolish on our part to refuse such an offer, but

---

95 A Wesley home was opened at a different location in Sint-Niklaas, but it was unsuccessful. Van der Beek did not offer any explanation for this disappointment, nor did he specify what his expectations had been or what exactly he found disappointing. For the original quote, see ibid.; Vansteenberghe to Van der Beek (29 Jan. 1945), Van der Beek to Vansteenberghe (7 Feb. 1945).
96 ABEM, 235: Vansteenberghe to Quenon (21 Nov. 1944).
97 Ibid.

we would rather walk with the Lord and face privation, if necessary, if only at the end we may be found faithful.[98]

In financial terms, Vansteenberghe's decision to wait for government compensation was a mistake. The first tranche of government compensation for war damage was not paid out until December 1957.[99] In the meantime, the BGM had to cover the restoration costs. As these costs took priority over workers' salaries, the workers suffered, especially those who did not have any other income. Although the "more complete financial deliverance" did not materialize, Vansteenberghe never regretted declining the Council's offer.[100]

In Flanders, the interdenominational *Vereeniging voor Evangelische Uitgaven* (Association for Evangelical Publications or VEU) emerged from the circles of the interchurch cooperation of the Antwerp youth groups.[101] BGMer Gerrit van de Riet was one of the driving forces. Still, several workers, mainly from the provinces of East and West Flanders, objected and wanted to know Vansteenberghe's opinion.[102] He cautiously stated that he sympathized with the organization "in as far as it serves the cause of the Gospel" and that as time went on.[103] The VEU was to publish evangelistic materials; its doctrinal stance would become more explicit.

According to Vansteenberghe, the VEU could "reach all Protestant circles," which had been the original purpose of the BGM itself.[104] He realized it had failed in this respect and that success was not likely. Vansteenberghe hoped that by participating in the VEU, the mission would be able to influence all Flemish Protestants indirectly.[105] But his support had its limits. In 1947, BGMer Herman Buunk was reprimanded for taking up the task of editor of the

---

98 In faith mission terms, one wonders whether the offer had been a 'gift from God.' The refusal had disastrous consequences. Either way, it is clear that the BGM was afraid of being linked in any way with national or international churches or organizations that fell short of its theological standards. If the BGM had accepted this unconditional offer, it would have been able to pay a larger percentage of its workers' wages. ABEM, 874: Vansteenberghe, Report on the year 1945 (13 May 1946).
99 ABEM, 656: Vansteenberghe to Winston Sr. (19 Dec. 1957).
100 ABEM, 874: Vansteenberghe, Report on the year 1945.
101 The last issue appeared in December 2013. "'De Kruisbanier' doorheen 1945," 3.
102 ABEM, 830: Vansteenberghe to Luteijn (27 Oct. 1944); ABEM, 281: Van Doorne to Vansteenberghe (27 Nov. 1944); ABEM, 243: Vansteenberghe to Rottier (12 Feb. 1945); ABEM, 259: Vansteenberghe to Sikkema (7 Feb. 1945).
103 For the original quote, see, ABEM, 281: Vansteenberghe to Van Doorne (8 Dec. 1944).
104 For the original quote, see ABEM, 281: Vansteenberghe to Luteijn.
105 ABEM, 259: Vansteenberghe to Sikkema; ABEM, 243: Vansteenberghe to Rottier (12 Feb. 1945).

VEU's magazine, *De Kruisbanier*. He was allowed to publish in the magazine from time to time, but not regularly.[106]

A priority for the BGM was John Winston Sr.'s swift return to assist Odilon Vansteenberghe with everyday management and supervise the distribution of clothing donated by American supporters to benefit Belgian Protestants.[107] In June 1945, BGM pastor Heinze Sikkema offered to lobby his political contacts to speed up Winston Sr.'s return. Socialist senator Diriken was prepared to take them to see Minister of Foreign Affairs, Paul Henri Spaak, and that the latter might be able to speed up the visa process.[108]

For some reason, Vansteenberghe did not make use of the offer. Instead, on 14 August 1945, he wrote to the Administrator of the Aliens Police in Belgium to request that the American missionaries, including John Winston Sr., be admitted to Belgium.[109] Whether this request advanced John Winston Sr.'s return to Belgium in November 1945 is unclear, but in March 1946, Vansteenberghe made use of his connections. Via F.E. Louwage, Inspector General at the Department of State Security, he tried to hasten the return of John Winston Sr.'s wife, Grace Williams.[110]

---

[106] The first reason for the reprimand was that Buunk had omitted to ask the BGM leadership's permission before proceeding, and he fully admitted this when confronted. Secondly, not everyone in the BGM was happy for him to collaborate with someone from another denomination. This shows that the denominationalizing of the BGM was already a reality. Thirdly, he was told, he should be devoting all his time to the BGM. This last point is inconsistent, as he also taught RE at schools, and no one had ever objected to that. ABEM, 35: Winston Sr. to Buunk, (18 Nov. 1947), Buunk to Winston Sr. (25 Nov. 1947).

[107] The BGM received a request for clothes from the Polish Evangelical church in Glain. BG-Mers were entitled to extra amounts of donated clothing, in compensation for lost earnings during the war. ABEM, 281: Balista et al. to Vansteenberghe (16 July 1945); ABEM, 219: Vansteenberghe to Mme. Neusy (16 May 1945); ABEM, 49: Vansteenberghe to Castiaux (31 May 1945).

[108] ABEM, 281: Sikkema to Vansteenberghe (29 June 1945).

[109] E-mail communication from F. Danis, Secrétaire général Fondation Henri Spaak, 29 Jan. 2013; AJDPS, A1.236.704: Vansteenberghe to l'Administrateur de la Police des Etrangers (14 Aug. 1945).

[110] AJDPS, A.236.704 Louwage to Liekendael (18 March 1946).

George Winston ca. 1960.
[KADOC-KU Leuven: ABEM, 1300]

10
CUTTING THE UMBILICAL CORD, 1945-1962

The aftermath of World War II marked a significant turning point for the BGM congregations. The war's interruption profoundly impacted the mission's activities, raising questions about the future. With Belgium liberated and the administrative and financial ties with the United States restored, the BGM faced a crucial decision. Would it be a return to business as usual, or had the war years left a lasting imprint on the mission's trajectory? This chapter will delve into the painful process of the denominalization of churches planted by the mission. We will place this process into the broader context of the organization as a whole. It will become painfully clear that co-directors Winston Sr. and Vansteenberghe not only struggled to let the mission adapt and evolve in the postwar era but also that they lacked the qualities to steer the organization through a turbulent stage of its existence.

Even with the financial lifeline to the US being restored after World War II, the BGM continued to struggle with severe financial shortages. On the revenue side, the number of non-Belgian donors stabilized more or less, but the average donated amount showed an of trend.[1] Meanwhile, expenses increased due to a sharp rise in living costs. As all expenses passed through central funds, an order of priority had to be introduced. The mission chose to prioritize the payment of bills over its workers' wages "because we must honour our commitments and act fairly towards all men."[2] The impact was that in 1948 and

---

1   ABEM, 849: Winston Sr., General Workers Letter (19 July 1948).
2   For the original quote, see ibid. (6 July 1949).

1949, just under 70% of the salaries were paid out on average. However, only 20 or 30%, or even nothing, was paid out in some months.[3]

Despite the daunting financial situation, Odilon Vansteenberghe saw a glimmer of hope. He believed that the BGM had the potential to become fully self-supporting. "If our Christians here in Belgium were aware of their privileges and accept them, the Mission could be completely independent of any foreign aid." Whether realistic or not, this vision inspired the headquarters to take action. Pastors were instructed to promote giving in their sermons and Bible studies, and church councils were encouraged to scrutinize their expenses. Despite the uncertainty, the mission's determination to achieve self-sufficiency was a beacon of hope for the future.[4]

The cautious approach that the BGM had initially taken in the hope that churches and church members would accept responsibility for their own volition's financial situation had never led to the desired result. As the local Catholic priest received a salary from the Belgian Ministry of Justice, church members were not used to covering a full-time pastor's cost. To avoid giving the impression the BGM was after their money, central funds had structurally cleared local congregations' deficits. This strategy had always enabled the Mission to send full-timers to smaller towns and rural areas, created unrealistic expectations with local believers, and created financial dependency. Other North American evangelical missionary initiatives, which were increasingly parachuted in Catholic Europe in the aftermath of World War II, fell into the same trap in their efforts to create distance from the financial policy of the Catholic Church.[5]

As a result of Headquarters' new instructions and the failure to pay wages in full, the French- and Dutch-language churches of Brussels and the churches of Liège and Charleroi decided in 1947 to become self-supporting. Antwerp's BGM church only followed this example after being reprimanded with reference to I *Timothy* 5:8. The church took action, and from December 1949 onwards, its pastor was paid in full from local church funds. A year later, local offerings covered all expenses.[6]

Paradoxically, this development caused more financial inequality among BGM pastors, as those in self-supporting congregations were not affected when wages could not be paid in full by central funds. When, in June and July

3   Ibid. (2 Dec. 1947, 14 Aug. 1948, 13 Jan. 1949, 25 Jan. 1950); ABEM, 49: Vansteenberghe to Castiaux (26 Feb. 1947); ABEM, 89: Winston Sr. to Delcour (29 Sep. 1949).
4   ABEM, 849: Vansteenberghe to the members of the council of the Flemish church in Brussels (16 Sep. 1948); ABEM, 849: Vansteenberghe and Winston Sr., General Workers Letter (1 Jan., 31 May 1947; ABEM, 849: Vansteenberghe, Circular Letter to the French Speakers (21 Dec. 1951).
5   Krabbendam, *Saving the Overlooked Continent*, 126; ABEM, 866: Winston Sr. to Brown (12 July 1961).
6   Hugens, "Supplement," *Ons Parochieblad*; ABEM, 292: Van de Riet to Vansteenberghe (4 Jan. 1950); ABEM, 874: Annual Report to the Board of Trustees (1952).

1948, no salaries could be paid, some bi-vocational workers spontaneously showed solidarity and helped with financial support. As the situation had not improved by August, the directors now urged the self-supporting churches to assist financially.[7]

As this appeal was in breach of the approved *Preliminary Stipulations for the Churches' Organization*, opposition arose among the BGMers. There were legitimate suspicions that not everyone obtaining income from outside the Mission passed these on to central funds as required by the solidarity principle of faith missions.[8] The directors ignored the objection, stating that this was an extraordinary measure. "We know full well that the ordeal that besets us is severe, but we accept it as coming from God's hand for spiritual reasons that each person needs to discover for himself."[9] Also, it was underlined that local churches had been planted with external funds and that most of these congregations still relied on central funds to remediate their financial deficits. By remaining deaf to the protest, the directors created a growing lack of confidence in their leadership among the mission's workers.[10]

Dissatisfaction was also creeping in on the remuneration structure. Until the invasion of May 1940, the BGM had a system that the Nortons had introduced, with several categories. During the war years, everyone had been paid on a "basis of strict equality of need."[11] After the war, the BGM directors introduced two salary bands: European and American workers. The Americans – married or not – earned $ 100 per month. On the other hand, for Europeans, a distinction was made between single workers – getting $ 50 – and married workers, earning $ 70. European and American families got a children's allowance based on the age of each child.[12] Initially, the wages for Europeans were on the level of the Belgian minimum wage. However, as the BEM did not apply the Belgian automatic wage indexation, and they were more often than not paid partially, BEM families lived in poverty or were forced to look for additional income.[13]

To counter the effect of the partial payment of salaries in combination with a sharp rise in the cost of living, more and more BGMers obtained extra

---

7   Churches that paid more than 40% of their pastor's salary themselves were endorsed to transfer the surplus to central funds so that pastors who received less than 40% of their salaries from their local church could be given an amount that would bring them up to 40%. ABEM, 849: Winston Sr., and Vansteenberghe, General Workers Letter (14 Aug. 1948).
8   ABEM, 292: Van Doorne to the directors of the BGM (20 Aug. 1948).
9   For the original quote, see ABEM, 268: Winston Sr. to Stordeur (27 Aug. 1948).
10 Urech felt that the solution to the financial problems was not to make any further cuts but rather to encourage "confidence, trust and faith in the Mission, among its workers." ABEM, 276: Urech to Winston Sr. (14 Dec. 1950).
11 ABEM, 503: Winston Sr. to Howard Jr. (18 March 1953).
12 Ibid.
13 Dupriez, "Les rémunérations en Belgique de 1936 à 1952," 467.

income through Religious Education (RE) lessons in state schools.[14] The Board of Trustees took a position that seems incongruous. On the one hand, it kept stressing the faith mission principle; on the other hand, it allowed workers to teach RE. These bi-vocational pastors, however, were expected to show solidarity with their less well-off colleagues by passing most of these earnings on to central funds.[15] The complicated interrelationship between the Dutch- and French-speaking workers became even more burdensome as most BGMers teaching RE in Flanders ignored this expectation.

Dissatisfaction was expressed not only by French-speaking workers but also by some American supporters.[16] No wonder the mutual mistrust between French- and Dutch-speaking workers resurged again. Robert Salsac observed, "Real unity, in love and candidness, seems to elude us."[17] Jean Vandenbroeck added: "There is a difference in religious education, a difference in social education which I find hard to explain, given that the majority of the Mission's workers are of modest means, and moreover there is a reluctance to talk to one another about certain fears openly."[18]

The BGM was not the only mission to have two salary levels in Europe. The European Evangelistic Campaign also paid its American workers more than its local employees.[19] To counter objections against this unequal treatment, Winston Sr. stated that the Europeans had free housing, travel expenses, and reimbursement for moving costs. However, the Americans enjoyed these benefits, too.

When European BGMers were refused a reply inquiring about the difference between the pay level and the Americans, it fueled their lack of confidence in the direction. They avoided the danger of overplaying their hand by remaining silent about whether they wanted a rise for themselves or a cut for the Americans.[20] Co-director Winston Sr. preferred to avoid the hot potato. He stressed that the American Board of Trustees should have the final say

---

14 They did this to counter the effect of partial salary payments combined with a sharp rise in the cost of living.
15 They were allowed to keep the income from two hours of teaching to compensate for their professional costs. ABEM, 850: Minutes Board of Trustees (15 Nov. 1950).
16 The reasons cited for this were economic necessity and high medical costs. Especially Flemish RE teachers refused to pass their additional income on to central funds on the basis that other BGMers were not passing on their financial benefits. What these benefits were cannot be ascertained from the available correspondence. Ibid.; ABEM, 876: Provisional Minutes of the Committee for the Organization of the Churches (18 June 1947); ABEM, 318: Van der Beek to Vansteenberghe (23 June 1947).
17 For the original quote, see ABEM, 252: Salsac to Winston Sr. (7 Jan. 1948).
18 For the original quote, see In order to avoid a further escalation, he suggested to limit the joint meetings to Bible study, prayer and sharing. Points of difference would need to be postponed until after unity had been restored. ABEM, 322: Vandenbroeck to Winston Sr. (5 April 1948).
19 ABEM, 655: Winston Sr. to Vansteenberghe (28 May 1954).
20 Ibid. (16 Jan. 1952).

on American missionaries' remuneration. The Belgian local churches should have the final say on their pastors' payment from their own funds.[21] This shows that the China Inland Mission was once more the BGM's role model, where missionaries were financed with foreign funds, and indigenous pastors and evangelists were paid by a self-supporting indigenous church.

In 1954, the Board of Trustees finally came up with a solution to counter the effects of the reduced payment of wages for the American BGMers. It allowed American churches to supplement the wages of the missionaries they supported by sending personal donations.[22] The fact that donations earmarked for them were used for other purposes while the BGM was recruiting Europeans "for whom there was no provision for support" caused considerable dissatisfaction among the American missionaries who had built up full financial support.[23] What annoyed them especially was that some of the BGM churches who paid their pastor's salary themselves categorically refused to show solidarity by putting money into the BGM's central funds in times of hardship.[24]

Meanwhile, the European workers had to find their own solution to counter the partial payment of salaries, limited reimbursement of expenses, and the sharp rise in living costs. Supported by their church councils, even more BGMers taught RE in state schools. This strategy was met with incomprehension and reprimands from the directors, who claimed that the workers were too materialistic and greedy. However, as the BGM was four and a half months behind with the payment of salaries in November 1956, additional and regular funding was necessary for many workers to feed their families.[25]

And so, the bi-vocation of a growing number of BGMers as RE teachers in state schools became more and more of a Gordian knot for the mission. On the one hand, the directors complained that the RE lessons distracted the pastors from their church work. On the other hand, the BGM could not fully pay their workers, nor did it want these lessons to be taught by people with different theological opinions. Sometimes, a worker was ordered to move to another city to prevent the classes from being assigned to "a liberal teacher."[26]

---

21 Ibid.
22 ABEM, 850: BGM, Inc. Minutes (29 June 1954).
23 ABEM, 655: Winston Sr. to Vansteenberghe (18 Dec. 1957).
24 It is unclear whether the initiative for this refusal came from the members or the local pastor. ABEM, 1237: Winston Sr. to the Board of Trustees; ABEM, 145: Hoyt to Winston Sr. (31 Oct. 1957).
25 ABEM, 849: Winston Sr., General Workers Letter (15 Nov., 19 Dec. 1956); ABEM, 1237: L. Winston to the Board of Trustees.
26 ABEM, 318: Vansteenberghe to Van der Beek (18 Oct. 1952), Van der Beek to Vansteenberghe (26 Oct. 1952); ABEM, 272: Winston Sr. to Teeuwissen (12 May 1953); ABEM, 850: Vansteenberghe, Annual Report to the Board of Trustees (1955); ABEM, 56: Vansteenberghe to De Backer (12 July 1957).

In its internal communication, the directors accused bi-vocational workers of often only teaching their own children. Yet, in its external communications, the BGM claimed this was a way of reaching families who would never attend a BGM church.[27] The latter argument became even more convincing with the introduction in 1959 of a new law, which resulted from the *Schoolpact* from November 1958. Pupils in all state schools now had the right to receive RE lessons in their choice religion.[28]

Concurrently, the BGMers who taught RE indicated that they were prepared to cut down on their lessons in exchange for a post as a mission's local church pastor, guaranteeing full payment of their pastor's salary.[29] Apart from the legal issues, this would also be impractical. There were not enough local churches that would be able to guarantee their pastor's total payment. Eventually, the directors resigned themselves to the fact that a growing number of BGMers were supplementing their meager salaries with an income through teaching RE. "While we are not pleased with the amount of time and effort which these religious instruction classes require, yet as we see the matter at present, there is no choice but to go ahead with it."[30]

In 1958, the American missionaries tried to minimize the tensions with their European colleagues by suggesting that all workers be paid the American salary level. The idea was dismissed as financially unviable. In 1961, the Europeans discovered that John Winston Sr. and Miner Stearns had private money in the USA, as the Nortons had at the time, strengthening suspicions even further.[31]

The financial difficulties impacted those already working with the BGM and led to a change in British and North American missionaries' recruitment policy. Candidates were not allowed to leave for Belgium until full support for their first year had been received or pledged. Although this was a sensible decision in financial terms, it harmed the recruitment of new missionaries. For

---

27 ABEM, 318: Vansteenberghe to Van der Beek (18 Oct. 1952); ABEM, 118: Winston Sr. to Fontaine (26 Sep. 1956).
28 This right applied to the religions that were recognized by the Belgian government. At that point in time, the choice was between Roman Catholicism, Protestantism, and Judaism. Although Humanism was not recognized as a religious conviction that could be taught in schools until 1981, pupils could choose nondenominational moral instruction during their Religious Education lessons from the start of the school year of 1959. Later on, Eastern Orthodoxy (1985), Islam (1974), and Anglicanism (1991) were added as well. Van Rompaey, *Strijd voor waardering*, 225; ABEM, 850: Annual Report to the Board of Trustees (1960).
29 ABEM, 318: Vansteenberghe to Van der Beek (18 Oct. 1952), Van der Beek to Vansteenberghe (26 Oct. 1952).
30 The number of workers teaching Religious Education in state schools had risen to 20 by 1958, and to 25 by 1960. ABEM, 874: Annual Report to the Board of Trustees (1961); ABEM, 849: Vansteenberghe, General Workers Letter (23 Jan. 1958).
31 ABEM, 1237: Winston Sr. to the Board of Trustees; ABEM, 866: Winston Sr. to Brown (12 July 1961).

instance, it took Stanley and Freda Dawe five years before their support had been arranged, and they were allowed to go.[32]

The rules were made even stricter in 1959. From then on, candidates were only accepted once their full support had been pledged and received in the bank. Once more, the Belgian Gospel Mission followed rather than set the trend. After World War II, most faith missions had changed to this practice already.[33] The stricter policy was also applied to European applicants. The only exceptions were Belgians because the new policy was deemed unfeasible. One of the few Belgians who applied after World War II and was accepted was Bible school graduate Jules De Backer (1911-1979). He joined from the Open Brethren in 1953 as a colporteur.[34]

In sum, the post-World War II years were characterized by mounting tensions between the directors and the other BGMers, American and European workers, and French and Dutch speakers. These tensions were rooted in the structural imbalance between the BGM's income and expenses. Different languages, cultures, and salary bands added extra layers to an increasing mutual distrust.

As the revenues of Belgian origin were far from covering all the costs, international fundraising was still necessary. Yet in North America, where the source of the bulk of international donations was, this became even more complicated in the post-World War II era. Not only had the sentiment of compassion with 'poor little Belgium' long gone, but American evangelicals became largely divided between two challenging umbrella organizations: the American Association of Christian Churches (ACCC) and the National Association of Evangelicals (NAE).

Whereas both aimed at interdenominational cooperation and shared a growing concern about the ecumenical movement and the increasing influence of modernism in American Protestantism, the two became fierce rivals. Founded in 1941 by Carl McIntire, the ACCC described itself as "separatist and fundamentalist."[35] Their policy strengthened the militant and anti-intellectual meaning of the term 'fundamentalist.' On the other hand, the NAE (1942) did not take an isolationist, anti-intellectual and anti-cultural stance. Those adhering to the NAE were soon labeled as Neo-Evangelicals.[36] Krabbendam aptly describes how an intense rivalry developed between both organizations, spilling over American borders as both platforms actively recruited new mem-

---

32   ABEM, 5: Winston Sr. to Dawe (16 Aug. 1951), Dawe to Vansteenberghe (28 Dec. 1951); Dawe to Horsburgh (14 Oct. 1951).
33   ABEM, 503: Winston Sr. to Howard Jr. (13 Feb. 1959).
34   ABEM, 849: Vansteenberghe and Winston Sr., General Workers Letter (30 April 1953).
35   McIntire also founded the International Council of Christian Churches (ICCC). McIntire, *What Is the Difference between Fundamentalism and New Evangelicalism*; "History of the International Council of Christian Churches," 217-223.
36   Matthews, *Standing Up, Standing Together*; National Association of Evangelicals, "History."

bers outside the US.[37] Visits by both the ICCC and the NAE to the Mission in 1950 should be seen in the light of this rivalry.

Out of concern that the American divisions between NAE and ICCC would overspill into Europe, the *Centre Evangélique d'Information et d'Action* (CEIA, Evangelical Information and Action Center) was founded in 1948 in France. The organization promoted unity among French-speaking Evangelicals in Europe. The scope of this unity became apparent when the organization decided that local churches and individual members of the *Église Réformée de France* (Reformed Church of France) and the French-language Lutheran church were allowed to join, but representatives of the Pentecostal movement were not. The founders feared that any contribution of the latter would have a polarizing rather than a converging effect because of their strong emphasis on the spiritual gifts. The BGM accepted the invitation to participate. The Belgian Mennonites and Open Brethren, invited at the request of Winston Sr., as well as the Belgian branch of the Bible League, followed their example.[38]

The BGM directors chose to take the route of benevolent neutrality, primarily for financial reasons. Its American support base is still a significant source of income, partly sympathized with the ACCC and partly with the NAE, so a clear preference for either would undoubtedly have financial consequences.[39] However, refraining from taking a clear stand also closed the door to several independent congregations sympathizing with the ICCC.[40]

Although the BGM regularly sent observers to congresses and conferences of both organizations, the BGM had the closest ties with the NAE, as illustrated by the acceptance of a donation from the NAE's War Relief Commission in 1947, which was not made widely public.[41] In 1955, ICCC ultimately attempted to win the BGM's express support. The mission repeated that it re-

---

37 Krabbendam, *Saving the Overlooked Continent*, 92-99.
38 Ibid., 92-113; ABEM, 850: Minutes Board of Trustees (15 Feb. 1951); ABEM, 963: Winston Sr. to Serr (14 May 1948), Serr to Winston Sr. (25 June 1948), Minutes of the Meeting (1-2 July 1948), Centre Evangélique d'Information et d'Action Minutes (Jan. 1955).
39 According to John Winston Sr., the rivalry between the two organizations was so strong that "whoever shows sympathy for one risks incurring the antipathy of the other." For the original quote, see ABEM, 963: Winston Sr. to Nicole (17 June 1948); ABEM, 850: Minutes Board of Trustees (15 Feb. 1951).
40 Faith missions did not advocate double separation, whereas the ICCC did. For that reason, McIntire and his adherents despised them almost as much as they despised Neo-Evangelicals. ABEM, 655: Winston Sr. to Vansteenberghe (5 April 1952); "Associated Gospel Churches," in *Melton's Encyclopedia of American Religions*, 559.
41 It also underlines the weakness of the argument that the government would reimburse the BGM for most of the war damage it had incurred, an argument used to defend the BGM's decision in 1944 to refuse financial support from ecumenical quarters. ABEM, 874: Annual Field Report to the Board of Trustees; Howard, *The dream that would not die, 1846-1986*, 26-29; ABEM, 1226: Winston Sr. and Vansteenberghe to the ICCC (30 June 1950); ABEM, 874: Winston Sr. and Vansteenberghe, General Workers Letter (28 July 1951); REA, 338-13-8: List of Participants International Conference of Evangelicals (1951).

mained "in sympathy with their struggle against modernism and the ecumenical movement" but could not go any further.[42] It was only prepared to stay in fellowship with the ICCC as far as possible.

In the meantime, the Interdenominational Foreign Mission Association (IFMA) was gaining a reputation in the USA as an 'accrediting agent.' By becoming an Associate Member in 1951, the BGM hoped this would lead to an upturn in donations from the USA to keep the work going in Belgium. Several pastors had already left the BGM as salaries were low and often not paid in full. Although donations did not increase substantially, the financial argument remained the main reason for maintaining membership.[43]

Moreover, the mission used traditional channels to communicate internationally about its need for financial support and personnel: deputizing and attending synods and conferences outside Belgium. The BGM consistently positioned itself as independent of all denominations in the countries concerned.[44] Despite this neutral position, obtaining invitations to speak in denominational churches became increasingly difficult, as these were now focusing more and more on their own missionary organizations. Furthermore, churches were inundated with requests from missionaries who wished to return to the mission field as soon as possible and who wanted to give presentations. A general complaint was heard all over the USA that "deputation opportunities for faith missions had about reached the saturation point."[45] A third problem for the BGM was that from the 1950s onwards, Americans were starting to see Europe more and more as one mission field, giving less scope for organizations such as the Belgian Gospel Mission that focused on one country only.[46]

Despite the precarious financial situation, high evangelism expenses were hardly questioned. The growing tensions of the Cold War became the dominant urgency to maximize efforts to reach Belgians in places without any Evangelical presence before a hostile communist change of regime would prohibit such activities. As lending money was against faith mission principles, the pastors and evangelists pulled the short straw. Systematically, the budget

---

42 ABEM, 655: Winston Sr. to Vansteenberghe (14 Oct. 1955).
43 Ibid.: Winston Sr. to Vansteenberghe (20 Nov. 1951); ABEM, 503: Winston Sr. to Howard Jr. (1 July 1959).
44 Some examples are Buunk's attendance at a conference of the Free Evangelical Church in West Germany, Winston Sr's attendance at the *Union des Eglises réformées évangéliques'* Synod in France, and Castiaux's representation of the BGM at the Synod of the French *Union des Eglises Evangéliques Libres*. The American BGMers and Odilon Vansteenberghe regularly toured the USA. ABEM, 10: Winston Sr. to Barbezat (19 Aug. 1948); ABEM, 35: Buunk to Winston Sr. (27 June 1949); ABEM, 49: Winston Sr. to Castiaux (27 July, 14 Sep. 1949).
45 John Winston Sr., approvingly quoting Dr. Ralph Davis, General Secretary of the American Branch of the African Inland Mission. ABEM, 655: Winston Sr. to Vansteenberghe (13 Nov. 1954); Reich, "Elisabeth Lemière Shannon, " 174.
46 Krabbendam, *Saving the Overlooked Continent*, 123.

deficit was 'solved' by the partial payment of the workers we discussed earlier in this chapter. The following overview will discuss the various methods the BGM deployed to reach the Belgians.

After the liberation, the classic forms of evangelism were resumed as soon as possible: colportage, open-air meetings, and tent evangelism. However, these classic methods proved less fruitful than in the interwar period. After World War I, there was a remarkable receptivity for Protestant evangelistic initiatives, but this did not repeat itself after the Second World War.

In fact, more and more Belgians regarded colportage as obtrusive, mainly because the Jehovah's Witnesses also used this method. When some BGMers dared to question this method, Vansteenberghe strongly disagreed. He blamed the disappointing figures of literature distribution on the lack of full-time colporteurs, the growing number of places where Christian literature could be obtained, and the fact that pastors had less time available for literature distribution.[47]

Tent campaigns were also relentlessly resumed despite dredging much smaller crowds than in the interwar period. This was masked for the supporters by including those who listened outside the tent in the publicity numbers. That way, results could still be described as encouraging.[48]

By the middle of the 1950s, the tents were worn out. They were replaced by a modern but expensive alternative: a 'mobile church.'[49] The 'church on wheels' was custom-made from a truck with a trailer and intended for smaller places. It had the advantage of being easier to move from one place to the next than a tent.

Not long after the inauguration on 10 December 1953, it emerged that the high cost of use was a problem, as it had been for the *roulottes* during the interwar period. Driven by the scare of an imminent communist takeover, the mobile church continued to be used. Although it was communicated that "the opportunities are so great that we must use them now while we still have the chance," the visible results were far from spectacular.[50] Small groups of Chris-

[47] In 1957, the number of printed copies per issue of *De Wachttoren* (The Watch Tower), the magazine of the Jehovah's Witnesses, rose from around 350,000 to nearly 600,000. By 1960, the number had risen to just over a million copies. ABEM, 830: Van der Linde to Vansteenberghe (4, 10 Aug. 1959), Vansteenberghe to Van der Linde (10 Aug. 1959); Watch Tower Bible and Tract Society, "1958 Yearbook," 96.

[48] Jean Vandenbroeck bought an old army tent for small-scale tent campaigns in the area of Auvelais, in remote villages that would not usually be covered by the 'normal' BGM tent campaigns. ABEM, 874: Annual Field Report to the Board of Trustees (1948, 1955, 1956); ABEM, 850: Report at Annual Meeting BGM Inc. (9 May 1949).

[49] John Winston Jr. introduced this novelty, developed by Assemblies of God pastor J.M. Ruthven in America. ABEM, 652: Winston Sr. to Elliott (18 Feb. 1953); ABEM, 567: Winston Sr. to Williams (8 Jan. 1953); ABEM, 537: Winston Sr. to Petersen (4 March 1955); Ruthven, "New Folding Church Trailer," 10.

[50] ABEM, 652: Vansteenberghe to Elliott (28 May 1954); ABEM, 1012: De Smidt, Verslag van het werk met de rijdende kerk in 1956 (30 Jan. 1957).

tians were started only in four locations. In most other places, the measurable results were rather disappointing.[51]

This deterred local churches, who had to pay as of 1956 to invite the mobile church to their area, from investing much manpower and money. By 1959, the mobile church was used only sporadically, and it eventually disappeared from view.[52] Blinded by urgency, rational financial arguments had been brushed aside. And so, the structural partial payment of the workers was caused by disappointing donations and excessive evangelistic expenditure.

Also, evangelistic meetings resumed after the war. Some savings were made by inviting fewer evangelists and speakers from outside Belgium.[53] The exception to the rule was an interdenominational campaign in 1959 featuring British evangelist Eric Hutchings.[54] Despite negative experiences from the past, an altar call was held, which had a great response. One hundred and twenty-six of the roughly seven hundred people who attended the final meeting were reported to have converted. Just as with the first campaign with Ruben Saillens, shortly after World War I, most had responded out of cultural politeness and did not abide by their decision. This fact was swept under the carpet, and reports on the campaign were unisono lyrical. In fact, Hutchings was invited once more to Belgium in 1960. This campaign led to thirty new contacts for the BGM, but again, most proved less keen than initially thought.[55]

A few years earlier, Winston Sr. invited the rising star of American Evangelicalism, Billy Graham, to Belgium as part of his European tour.[56] He had met the evangelist when Graham visited Belgium in 1946 as part of a new American evangelistic organization, Youth for Christ. The Youth for Christ team must have reminded him of the early days of the BGM, months after World War I had ended.[57] Odilon Vansteenberghe was less keen. He felt that one meeting could only lead to short-lived interest and that a several-day campaign would be more effective. He also struggled with Graham's requirement that all Protestant churches in Belgium be invited to participate in the campaign. Other

---

51   Saint-Hubert, Neufchâteau, Florennes and Montignies-sur-Roc. Only Saint-Hubert had been visited with the tent and the mobile church, with varying results. ABEM, 861: UK Newsletter (1 Oct. 1954); Rapport moral sur les activités de la Mission en 1956, 1957; ABEM, 1012: De Smidt, Verslag van het werk met de rijdende kerk in 1956.
52   ABEM, 879: Minutes Workers Conference (16 Oct. 1959).
53   Some of the international speakers were Fleming H. Revell Sr. (1953), Gaston Racine (1955), and George Brucks (1957). ABEM, 461: Barbour to Winston Sr. (2 Nov. 1953); ABEM, 190: Vansteenberghe to Lecerf (Aug. 1956); "Bijzonder week-end in de Bethelkerk," 1.
54   ABEM, 887: G. Winston, "History of the BGM," Chapter 14, 2.
55   The campaign was described as "the most memorable event in the history of Belgian Protestantism since the days of the Reformation." Social and ecclesiastical backgrounds were not recorded. Haesevoets, "Evangelisatie-Kruistocht te Luik met het team Eric Hutchings," 4, ABEM, 1011: Minutes Eric Hutchings Crusade (20 Nov. 1959).
56   ABEM, 485: Winston Sr. to Graham (4 May 1955).
57   Krabbendam, *Saving the Overlooked Continent*, 91.

BGMers were unsure about Billy Graham because of his connections with the WCC and with individuals whom the BGM deemed to be modernists.[58]

Vansteenberghe was relieved when it turned out that a stop in Brussels did not fit in Graham's schedule. He rightly feared that going ahead with a Billy Graham campaign would make it harder for the BGM to explain its rejection of the WCC. The Board of Trustees more or less agreed with the Belgian co-director.[59]

It was not until 1975 that a Billy Graham crusade held in Belgium at the Heysel stadium for multiple days was titled Eurofest 75. This time, the BGM participated, as Graham had by now become the greatest evangelist of the twentieth century. The results were meagre compared to those of other European cities the American evangelist visited that year.[60] One could say that the BGM was a precursor of the invasion of the many American evangelical organizations that would flood Europe after World War II.[61]

That being said, the mission was not blind to the unsatisfying results of the prewar forms of evangelism and worked hard to find new ways to transmit their message to the population. One of these new methods was radio. Loyal to its self-imposed isolation, the BGM declined the offer to participate in interdenominational programs on Belgian public radio. Some participants were regarded as "unsaved," and the rest might proclaim theological views that contradicted their own.[62]

Instead, the mission fully supported its worker, Miner Stearns, who set up *La Bonne Nouvelle par les Ondes* (The Good News through the (Radio) Waves or BNO) in 1946. The BNO had obtained air time on Radio Luxembourg for a weekly program.[63] Addresses of listeners who wrote to express an interest

58   If the plan were to go ahead, he would have preferred to organize it as a BGM event, in spite of the heavy financial costs. ABEM, 655: Vansteenberghe to Winston Sr. (5, 11, 19 April 1955), Winston Sr. to Vansteenberghe (12, 16 April 1955).
59   Ibid.: Vansteenberghe to Winston Sr. (22 April 1955), ABEM, 503: Howard Jr. to Winston Sr. (5 Sep. 1958).
60   Five years before Eurofest '75 took place, Billy Graham's Euro '70 campaign, which ran from 5-12 April 1970 in Dortmund (Germany) was projected live on a screen in a sports hall in Deurne (Antwerp) via a closed-circuit TV link and translated into Dutch. Neither the Executive Committee, nor the Board of Reference included a representative of the BGM. However, the *Vereniging van Vrije Evangelische Kerken van de B.E.Z.*, the association of free churches founded in 1962 by autonomized BGM churches, was represented in the Board of Reference in the person of George Winston. "Advert," *De Kruisbanier*, 9 Dec. 1969, 2; "Foto's van de Euro '70 Billy Graham kruistocht in Deurne bij Antwerpen," *De Kruisbanier*, 21 April 1970, 3.
61   Krabbendam, *Saving the Overlooked Continent*.
62   ABEM, 321: Vandenbroeck, Circular Letter Regarding Radio Transmissions (23 Feb. 1950); ABEM, 849: Vansteenberghe, General Workers Letter (27 Feb. 1950); ABEM, 318: Vandenbroeck to Winston Sr. (28 Sep. 1949); APRT, 4: Minutes Commission de la Radiodiffusion (2 March 1950).
63   The programs were in French but contained advertising for the Dutch-language *Onze Hoop* magazine. ABEM, 266: Stearns to Winston Sr. and Vansteenberghe (12 Dec. 1952); Advert, *Onze Hoop*, Jan. 1947, 4.

in the Gospel were passed on to BGM pastors as much as possible. The mission considered the BNO part of the BGM, but Stearns had a different opinion. He acknowledged a close spiritual affiliation but initiated a complete separation of the two organizations in 1952.[64] The rift between the BGM directors and Miner Stearns became so deep that the latter was asked to step down as Principal of the mission's Bible schools. He obliged but also stressed his willingness to continue his cooperation with the BGM.[65]

Another novelty was evangelistic films. In 1948, there was still some unease about the suitability of this medium. The Nortons had condemned cinema-going as worldly entertainment, but church members became increasingly opposed to outright banning cinema-going. This shifting attitude among church members indirectly reflects the 1950s as the golden age of cinema.

As more Christian and evangelistic films were made in the USA and Christian opinion of films changed, the BGM trod carefully. After consulting its pastors, evangelists, and colporteurs, the mission reluctantly decided to ban cinema-going no longer. Church members were now allowed to use their conscience, and the door was opened to the use of evangelistic films.[66]

A final novelty was an evangelistic telephone line set up in 1961. A short evangelistic message on an answering machine was played to all who rang the number. The idea came from the USA via Jacques Blocher of the Bible Institute at Nogent-sur-Marne (France). It was hailed as a great success, with 14,000 calls in only a few months, and a separate charity was set up for this work, which was carried out jointly with the Open Brethren. The incomplete project file in the mission's archives does not indicate whether anyone was converted and, if so, how many conversions took place as a result of this work.[67]

In addition to the continuing evangelistic activities, we must discuss the project during the 1958 World Expo in Brussels. Already in 1955, the Scripture

64 ABEM, 266: Stearns to Winston Sr. and Vansteenberghe (12 Dec. 1952); ABEM, 503: Vansteenberghe to Howard Jr. (10 April 1953), Winston Sr. to Howard Jr. (1 April 1953); ABEM, 266: Stearns to Howard Jr. (8 May 1953).
65 ABEM, 266: Winston Sr. to Stearns (6 March 1954), Stearns to Winston Sr. (31 March 1954).
66 The argument was that a 'real Christian' would intuitively know that cinema-going was inappropriate. ABEM, 292: Winston Sr. to Van Doorne (12 March 1948); ABEM, 133: Haesevoets to Vansteenberghe (4 Dec. 1958).
67 Other 'Evangelical groups' were invited to join the initiative. The charity's working title was *De Blijde Boodschap per Telefoon* (The Gospel by Telephone). The eventual name of the charity established in 1962 was *Bonne Nouvelle par Téléphone / Goed Nieuws per Telefoon* (Good News by Telephone). In 1962, the number of calls registered was 74,574 over 11 months. In 1963, there were 80,683 registered calls. Whenever a caller supplied their address, evangelistic reading materials would be sent to them. By the middle of 1962 an average of two such mailings went out weekly. ABEM, 654: Winston Sr. to Dickinson (28 Nov. 1961); "Telefoondienst in Brussel," 2; Minutes Asbl La Bonne Nouvelle par Téléphone, 10 Jan. 1962; ABEM, 1026: Winston Sr., Rapport statistique sur La Bonne Nouvelle par Téléphone (5 March 1963), ASBL Bonne Nouvelle par Téléphone, Minutes Administrative Council (28 June 1962).

Gift Mission (SGM) suggested that the BGM have some presence at Expo '58. Because of the delicate financial situation, the mission naively hoped for a place in the national pavilion of Belgium or the USA. Of course, this plan did not materialize. The Federation of Protestant Churches in Belgium held out a hand to join their project. This was refused on the grounds that its other partners had links with the World Council of Churches.

Instead, the BGM hesitantly applied for thirty square meters of commercial concession. They were not the only ones. The Belgian Bible Society (BBS) also wanted a stand but lacked the finances. The United Bible Societies (UBS) was prepared to help them on condition that the BBS join in with the Federation of Protestant Churches in Belgium's project. The BBS Board declined the UBS's offer, as Odilon Vansteenberghe and some other members objected.[68]

Despite insufficient financial resources, the BBS Board decided to have their own pavilion named *De Lichtende Bijbel* (The Bible that spreads light). It had a large Bible, 15 meters high and 10 meters wide, to which a strip with 800 lights had been fixed. It showed Bible texts in eight languages.[69] The BGM abandoned its own project to join this one with the Open and Closed Brethren, the Mennonites, and the Salvation Army. The SGM joined by providing Scripture portions and a financial donation.[70]

The Belgian Minister of Economic Affairs, Jean Rey, of Protestant origin, helped to secure an option at a top location near the main entrance.[71] Despite a $ 15,000 deficit in the budget, the decision was made in July 1957 to exercise the option. The BGM acted as an intermediary to obtain $ 25,000 from Henry Parsons Crowell's trust fund, which was used to close the budgeted deficit. When the project had made a small profit at the close of the Expo, the BGM was permitted to decide how it should be used. The money was transferred to its general funds, which were said to have suffered from the fundraising for the pavilion at the Expo.[72]

Even though the evangelism budget took priority over paying salaries in times of structural financial shortages, the mix of trusted and new evangelistic

68   ABEM, 655: Winston Sr. to Vansteenberghe (18 Aug., 5 Sep. 1955); ABEM, 548: Winston Sr. to Smith, SGM, 25 June 1956; ABEM, 656: Vansteenberghe to Winston Sr. (18 Aug. 1955); ABEM, 503: Vansteenberghe to Howard Jr. (2 Feb. 1957).
69   To remove their objections, the BBS proposed creating a separate association with no official links to the WCC. ABEM, 503: Vansteenberghe to Howard Jr. (24 April 1957); ABEM, 548: Winston Sr. to Smith (6 May 1957).
70   The cover of John's Gospel had a photograph of the Atomium, which had become a famous landmark by then. ABEM, 903: Caufriez, The Participation of the Belgian Bible Society in the Universal and International Exhibition of Brussels (1958); ABEM, 503: Vansteenberghe to Howard Jr.; ABEM, 649: Caufriez to Vansteenberghe (15 Dec. 1956).
71   ABEM, 855: USA Prayer Letter (24 April 1958); ABEM, 461: Winston Sr. to Becker (22 April 1958).
72   ABEM, 478: Vansteenberghe to Crowell (11 Nov. 1957), Crowell to Vansteenberghe (3 Aug. 1957), Winston Sr. to Crowell (26 Dec. 1958), Crowell to Winston Sr. (16 Jan. 1959).

methods did not result in much numerical growth. As a result, attendance at BGM services plateaued. If the substantial financial sacrifices had produced many converts, perhaps the almost structural partial payment of salaries would have been reluctantly accepted. Instead, support for the budgetary priorities crumbled steadily.

To put things in context, the BGM was not the only one dealing with disappointing results. Based on the few available data, Protestantism as a whole had come to a temporary standstill. When the Second Vatican Council (1962-1965) opened the door for improved relationships with Protestants and Catholics, who were encouraged to read the Bible daily, Protestants seized this window of opportunity for their evangelistic initiatives. Protestantism in Belgium resumed its growth, both in existing denominations and by the entrance of new players on the field.[73]

From the mid-1950s, the process of stimulating BGM churches to independence more or less coincided with the transition of leadership of the mission. This was a complicating factor in the snail's pace process of denominization. In 1954, at the age of 67, Odilon Vansteenberghe decided for the first time to step down as a co-director. He said he felt he no longer had the strength to lead an organization constantly battling internal unrest and dissatisfaction because of its continual financial difficulties.[74] However, he withdrew his resignation at John Winston Sr. and the Board of Trustees' request. Three years later, he resigned again, stating he no longer wished to be a trustee or deputize in the USA.[75]

Clearly, no lessons had been learned from the death of Ralph Norton and the ensuing leadership crisis thirty years earlier. As the co-directors had continuously been preoccupied with short-term projects, fundraising, and conflict management, no time had been set aside to develop a succession plan. So, Vansteenberghe was pressed for a second time to stay on. He agreed to postpone his retirement but explained to his co-director that his resignation could not be delayed indefinitely. Winston Sr. also hoped to step down shortly, preferably at the same time as Vansteenberghe. He feared that any other course of action might widen the rift between Europeans and Americans and strengthen the "rivalry between French- and Flemish-speaking elements," causing the BGM to fall apart.[76]

When Vansteenberghe saw in 1959 that no solution was imminent, he stepped down as a co-director after all. A year later, he also left all BGM committees in which he was still involved. To give the BGM some financial relief,

---

73 Overbeeke, *Jaarboek ... 1950, 1954, 1963, 1966,* and *1972*.
74 His strength had badly deteriorated due to the failing health and subsequent death of his wife. ABEM, 656: Vansteenberghe to Winston Sr. (4 Nov. 1954).
75 ABEM, 1237: Vansteenberghe to the Board of Trustees (16 Sep. 1957).
76 ABEM, 503: Howard Jr. to Vansteenberghe (30 Sep. 1957); ABEM, 656: Vansteenberghe to Winston Sr. (26 Nov. 1957); ABEM, 850: Minutes Board of Trustees (1 June, 26 Sep. 1957).

he resigned as a worker in 1961 but remained involved in the background. A year later, he died unexpectedly at the age of 75 while visiting Switzerland and was buried there.[77]

As no successor had been found for Vansteenberghe, the American Board of Trustees asked John Winston Sr. to remain the sole director for the time being.[78] Only at this stage was a planning committee set up to find successors for Winston Sr. and Vansteenberghe. The fruitless search for an internal candidate dragged on for two years.

In 1961, the Belgian Executive Committee and the American Board of Trustees jointly proposed John Winston Jr. as the new director in a fresh attempt to resolve the deadlock. His candidacy, however, did not gain the required two-thirds majority of votes in the Conference, an administrative body consisting of all BGM workers.[79] A new committee was formed and instructed to look for a director and an assistant director or two co-directors, preferably an American and a European.

Behind the scenes, an important decision had been made. As the process of forming an independent denomination of BGM churches was in a crucial stage, the Board decided that it would be unwise "to change (trade) horses during crossing a stream."[80] Therefore, Winston Sr.'s succession was delayed until after the autonomization of the first BGM churches. Also, candidates were now allowed to be recruited from outside the Mission.

Finally, a viable applicant was found: Homer Payne. The fact that he was an American with a PhD from Dallas Theological Seminary was good news in the communication to the North American backers. Having worked at the Swiss *Institut Biblique et Missionnaire Emmaüs* since 1948, made Payne's candidacy acceptable for the Europeans. It meant that he was familiar with European culture. He was accepted by the US Board of Trustees and the workers in Belgium in the fall of 1962 and started his new job on 1 April 1963. Nine years

---

77 To avoid spending money on repatriation that could be spent more usefully elsewhere, Vansteenberghe had stated several times that if he were to die outside Belgium, he wanted to be buried locally. ABEM, 321: Vansteenberghe to the BGM Governing Board (11 April 1960), Vansteenberghe to the Executive Committee (5 May 1960), Vansteenberghe to the Personnel Committee (18 Oct. 1960); ABEM, 655: Winston Sr. to Vansteenberghe (20 May 1960); ABEM, 503: Winston Sr. to Howard Jr. (29 Aug. 1962); Thompson, *Firebrand of Flanders*, 117.

78 ABEM, 655: Minutes Board of Trustees (5 Nov. 1959).

79 The Executive Council was established in 1960 to supervise all BGM activities. It consisted of five members: a director to represent the Board of Trustees, two members representing the French-speaking workers, and two members representing the Dutch-speakers. ABEM, 849: De Smidt, General Workers Letter (19 Sep. 1961); ABEM, 879: Minutes Workers Conference (30 Sep. 1961); ABEM, 850: Minutes Board of Trustees (2 Nov. 1961); ABEM, 866: Brown to Winston Sr. (20 Nov. 1961), Winston Sr. to Brown (12 Oct. 1962).

80 ABEM, 222: Stearns to Payne (n.d.), Brown to Payne (23 July, 26 Oct. 1962), Circular Letter of the Nominating Committee (24 May 1962); ABEM, 866: Winston Sr. to Brown (8 March, 22 Oct. 1962).

after Vansteenberghe first announced he wanted to step down, and one year after the first BGM churches had been autonomized into a new denomination, the BGM was ready for a new episode.

The indigenization process of the local churches that the BGM had planted, was slowed down considerably by World War II. Although the churches were forced to survive without financial aid from the US, it was impossible to discuss their organizational development. The first meeting after the war of the Committee for the Organization of the Churches took place on 18 June 1947.[81] Vansteenberghe insisted that the local churches urgently needed to be guided toward financial and administrative autonomy.[82] The urgency was not only driven by the financial difficulties. With the Iron Curtain down and the start of the Cold War, it was feared that Belgium soon, in one way or another, would come under communist rule. As this would almost certainly put an end to the transatlantic financial lifeline, indigenization plans were now considered to be urgent.[83] Despite this urgency, the process would drag on for another fifteen years.

To realize the autonomy of the local churches, pastors were given several guidelines in line with the *Preliminary Stipulations for the Organization of the churches of the Belgian Gospel Mission* of 1938, such as the appointment of one or two elders where this had not yet taken place.[84] Yet pastors complained that it was often difficult to find men in the local churches who displayed the "real qualities that would make of them established elders."[85] However, this complaint was not new and goes back as far as 1929, when the first version of the *Preliminary Stipulations* was distributed. Although elders could only be appointed after approval from the headquarters, pastors were hardly given any suggestions for remedying this problem. As we lack sufficient data on the issues, we remain in the dark about whether or not the standard was set too high in applying the Apostle Paul's profile of elders and deacons.

As we have seen earlier in this chapter, church councils had to go over their expenses with a fine-tooth comb, and pastors were told to educate their parishioners in generosity. In the early 1950s, further measures were taken to unburden the overall budget of the mission. Each local congregation was instructed to put together its own entire budget progressively. A quantifiable objective was to increase donations for the pastor's salary by 10% each year until it was fully realized. Additional support from central funds would be negotia-

---

81 ABEM, 1237: Invitation (14 June 1947).
82 ABEM, 876: Provisional Minutes of the Committee of the Organization of the Churches (18 June 1947).
83 Judt, *Postwar: a History of Europe since 1945*, 124.
84 ABEM, 1238: Preliminary Dispositions in View of the Organization of the Churches of the BGM (1938); ABEM, 849: Vansteenberghe, Circular Letter (20 July 1947).
85 ABEM, 320: C. Vansteenberghe to Winston Sr. (14 May 1952).

ble if real income was below budget.[86] As most BGM churches were located in smaller towns, primarily with members from the lower classes, becoming self-supportive would be quite a challenge. Merging several small churches into one larger, self-sufficient church might have done the trick, especially now that transport became more available, but this was never considered.

And while several churches and kitchen meetings were closed shortly after the war because interest had faded, the BGM continued to deploy new church planting initiatives in other locations.[87] This contradictory move in times of chronic underfunding must be seen in light of urgency. The mission was convinced that either the rapture of the church or a Communist occupation was at hand. Therefore, even with a structural financial deficit, church planting expenditures were considered to be absolutely necessary. And so, financially autonomous churches were encouraged to create a structural financial surplus, which would be transferred into central funds to start new churches.[88]

It seems naive of the Committee to expect the local churches to display such financial solidarity. No preliminary study was carried out into the feasibility of the plan. To what extent were church members able – and willing – to give more? Furthermore, the plan did not include any sanctioning measures. What would the BGM do if churches were unable or unwilling to realize the desired increase in income?

The committee members realized that this was an ambitious plan and that the church councils would need to use the necessary tact when presenting their budgets to their churches and discussing these with them.[89] Divergent positions in an intense debate about whether income from any Religious Education teaching job should be transferred to central funds halted the autonomization of churches. The Committee for the Organization of the Churches did not meet for several years.[90]

In 1955, pastors in the region of Charleroi formulated a suggestion to break the impasse and offer a solution for the growing dissatisfaction among the workers. The plan included the workers' participation in management affairs and greater financial autonomy for the local churches.[91] The idea was to group the churches into six clusters, each of which would be led by one of the already self-supporting churches, i.e., the Dutch-language church in Brussels, the French-language church in Brussels, and the churches in Ghent, Antwerp,

---

86 Evangelistic stations without church council were exempt. ABEM, 849: Vansteenberghe, Circular Letter.
87 ABEM, 874: Annual Field Report to the Board of Trustees (1947, 1952).
88 ABEM, 849: Vansteenberghe, Circular Letter.
89 Ibid.
90 ABEM, 841: Vuilleumier to C. Vansteenberghe (21 Nov. 1951).
91 ABEM, 1237: Circulaire Colloque de Charleroi (20 July 1955).

Liège, and Charleroi.[92] Each of these churches was to financially assist the other churches in its cluster wherever possible. Only if they ran out of funds, the remaining deficit would be bridged from central funds.[93]

Although the Headquarters' objective was that local churches would soon become self-governing, self-supporting, and self-propagating – entirely free from foreign aid, it reprimanded the architects of the plan for breaching the procedure.[94] The plan was formulated during an extra item on the regional meeting agenda, which the directors had not been notified of. According to the rules, no items could be added to the agenda without the directors' permission.[95] Even in desperate financial circumstances, the chain of command had to be strictly observed. Although this did not improve the relationship between the initiators and the directors, they accepted the reprimand, apologized, and underlined their good intentions.[96]

Despite the procedural error, the plan was discussed at length at the national workers' conference of 26 October 1955. Although everyone agreed that something should change in the BGM, the response to the proposal was varied. The old fault line between Dutch- and French-speaking workers now deepened as bi-vocational pastors on both sides of the language border responded differently. Dutch-speaking RE-teachers disagreed with the plan, seeing it as an attempt to force them to share their additional income with the others. They claimed that the way in which the disparity in individual incomes had been handled in the last few years had cultivated a deep-rooted suspicious attitude. The heated discussion took so long that the meeting was adjourned without a vote as many had to leave to take their last train home.[97]

The proposal was amended in a small study group. Churches would gradually become autonomous and then unite into a denomination. The newly formed affiliation would maintain the BGM's 'Principles and Practices,' and the BGM remained responsible for transfers and appointments of pastors. Under certain conditions, pastors were allowed to combine their jobs with teaching RE. Workers unable or unwilling to become bi-vocational to close the local deficit were offered three options. They would be linked to several churches raising the required salary jointly; they would be supported by a financially

---

92 In Wallonia, Soignies, Enghien, Sart, Braine-le-Comte, Warquignies, Tournai, Ath, and Mouscron were to be clustered with Brussels. La Louvière, Chatelineau, Auvelais, Quiévrain, and Céroux-Mousty were to be clustered with Charleroi, and Seraing, Huy, Saint-Mard, Arlon, and Jemelle with Liège. The French speakers wisely abstained from making suggestions about how the churches in Flanders were to be clustered. ABEM, 879: Minutes Workers Conference (26 Oct. 1956).
93 ABEM, 1237: Circulaire Colloque de Charleroi.
94 ABEM, 850: Winston Sr., Remarks at the Board of Trustees (7 Dec. 1954).
95 ABEM, 1237: Winston Sr. to Knecht Jr., Lecerf et al. (30 July 1955).
96 ABEM, 318: Vandenbroeck to Winston Sr. (1 Aug. 1955).
97 ABEM, 879: Minutes Workers Conference (26 Oct. 1955).

stronger church out of solidarity or remain paid from central funds as an evangelist in a new program.[98]

A few months later, twenty-nine-year-old George Winston devised a similar plan. His idea was to form a Congregationalist denomination within five years "for fellowship and united action (a) in evangelism (b) in discussion of common problems (c) in support of smaller churches (d) in exerting of stabilizing and corrective spiritual influence on each other."[99]

Unlike the American Board, his motives were not inspired by the Cold War. He regarded financial support from outside Belgium "in the long run, a detriment rather than a help," as local churches would become addicted to external funding; it kept the pastor responsible for the mission and not for his church and fueled discontent as policy decisions were imposed from the top.[100] He noticed that financial support from the US was declining despite prosperity and was convinced this downward spiral could be broken if donations were spent for what they were earmarked.

Although his father was open to the idea that the BGM would become obsolete in the distant future, the directors openly rejected George's radical and rapid route. The main points of dissension were properties, rents, and salaries. In this proposal, each local church was to be run as a separate charity "which would own the local church property, to which the Mission would turn over the building in due time, perhaps based on a reimbursement by the local group of a nominal cost of their building over twenty-five years."[101]

The fact that most properties were bought with US donations as a bulwark against liberal Protestantism in Belgium made the idea of handing over the property unacceptable. Vansteenberghe was especially explicit in his objections. He was convinced that by remaining owner of the buildings, the BGM could prevent congregations from joining "existing Belgian Protestant Organizations which are affiliated with the World Council of Churches."[102] It would

98 If the income exceeded a predetermined amount, the surplus minus professional expenses would have to be transferred into central funds. In consultation with the directors, the worker transferring the money was to choose what it would be spent on. ABEM, 849: Regional Workers' Meeting of Charleroi to the Members of the Executive Committee (12 Oct. 1956).
99 ABEM, 503: Winston Sr. to Howard Jr. (8 May 1957), Howard Jr. to Winston Sr. (8 May 1957).
100 ABEM, 460: G. Winston, Memorandum.
101 In a letter to his son George, John Winston Sr. describes his report as "disparaging and dismal," and expresses the view that it would have been better if George had brought this up in a candid discussion with the directors. "If we are to get anywhere except a deadly impasse, we must approach these things with a spirit of mutual understanding and respect and a willingness to yield to one another." At an earlier stage, Odilon Vansteenberghe had already spoken out against an enforced reduction of support from Headquarters within a set time span. ABEM, 656: Vansteenberghe to Winston Sr. (22 April 1955); ABEM, 503: Winston Sr. to Howard Jr. (8 May 1957); ABEM, 338: Winston Sr. to G. Winston (4 May 1957).
102 It was not until the 1980s that the buildings were handed over to the local churches. ABEM, 656: Vansteenberghe to Winston Sr. (22 April 1955).

also give the BGM "a certain power of veto," especially in decisions about the appointment and salary of a pastor.[103]

George Winston was summoned to appear before the directors to explain his memorandum. He said that he understood that realizing his proposal would cause some 'casualties' in terms of churches and pastors, but this would be a refining process revealing the true spiritual state of those involved. He also admitted that his plan would not cure all ills but felt it was necessary. He thought that it was unbiblical for the Belgian churches to be ultimately subordinate to the Board of Trustees in Philadelphia.[104] Despite their vehement objections against this proposal, the directors admitted they had only been paying lip service to the idea of the indigenous church, and no progress had been made under their leadership.[105]

The transatlantic response to George Winston's plan was positive, as this was also what the Board of Trustees aimed for. Key trustees Philip and Catherine Howard Jr. and chairman Harry Jaeger found his arguments "rather convincing" and would discuss it with the others.[106] In their defense, the directors stated that George's memorandum contained many inaccuracies, misstatements, misrepresentations, and serious accusations. Young Winston admitted that his document did not present all the data correctly but insisted that the correct figures would lead to the same conclusions. He felt that the directors' response was too much aimed at his person rather than his argument, and that this was only deepening the crisis unnecessarily.[107]

While the Board did not wholly adopt George's memorandum, he persuaded them to increase their demand for the self-supporting BGM churches to become autonomous. They also followed his reasoning that the denomination to be formed had to emphasize fellowship more than administrative links.[108] Taking this stand was a thinly veiled criticism of the directors in Belgium, who seemed unable to make any progress in critical issues and wanted to remain in control over the emerging denomination. In this context, Vansteenberghe's second announcement that he wanted to step down must be seen.

---

103 Ibid.
104 ABEM, 338: G. Winston to Winston Sr. and Vansteenberghe (9 May 1957).
105 ABEM, 879: Proposed Statement to the Council of Workers; ABEM, 460: Minutes of the Special Meeting for American BGM Workers (10 May 1957).
106 ABEM, 503: Howard Jr. to Winston Sr. (14 March 1957).
107 ABEM, 1237: Winston Sr. to the Board of Trustees (29 April 1957); ABEM, 338: G. Winston to Winston Sr. and Vansteenberghe (9 May 1957).
108 He informed the Board that most BGMers would not be happy with Carlos Vansteenberghe, John C. Winston Jr., or George Winston as possible new leaders of the Mission. ABEM, 850: Minutes Board of Trustees (17 April 1957).

To speed up the autonomization of the churches, Jaeger drafted a working paper and gave the directors until 1 September 1957 to reply.[109] All the directors did was pass the paper on to the American BGMers for their response, as the Europeans had indicated several times that they were not particularly interested in cutting the ties between the BGM and the churches. Their primal concern was a decent income paid in full each month.

The American missionaries trod carefully. On the one hand, they confirmed that George Winston's memorandum contained some "unfortunate inaccuracies and discrepancies;" conversely, they pointed out that it expressed the essence of the unease among the BGMers.[110] However, to ensure a successful autonomization, the churches would need to demonstrate that they had the required stability, continuity, and capacity. Therefore, the US missionaries suggested that the BGM consult other faith missions – as it had done in the past – to find out how they applied the indigenous principle. In the meantime, the Committee for the Organization of the Churches should resume its activities.[111]

Nevertheless, it took a year before the named committee met again on 22 May 1958, almost eleven years after its previous meeting. Co-director Winston Sr. wanted them to form advice on the existing proposals to found the new denomination.[112] The Committee had to choose between George Winston's proposal and a plan devised by Jan Knecht Sr. based on the Charleroi proposal. Although most local congregations had a financial deficit each year, somehow, and without going into detail, both projects were confident financial autonomy was within reach. They also agreed that the main obstacle to independence was the lack of suitable candidates for the office of elder. As internal documents, the authors leave out the causes of what they call the church members' spiritual immaturity. As most members came from the lower strata of society, this seems to be an indirect referral to low education levels.

As the Committee members were hopelessly divided, the dossier was again in a deadlock.[113] This division reflected the situation of the mission as a whole, which was described as "widespread discontent among energetic workers and pastors, and bewilderment among others."[114] John Winston Jr. hit the nail on the head that the tremendous mutual mistrust was caused by the unsuccessful effort of the organization to simultaneously be "an American

---

109 ABEM, 460: Jaeger, Suggestions for Discussion at Some Early Meeting of the Belgian Gospel Mission (25 April 1957), Winston Sr. to Vansteenberghe, Palmberg, Shanley, Sommers, Hoyt, D. Winston, G. Winston, L. Winston, Winston Jr., and G. Winston (7 February 1958).
110 ABEM, 850: Stearns et al., Resolution (10 May 1957).
111 ABEM, 503: Minutes of the Meeting of US Missionaries about the Jaeger Letter (8 July 1957).
112 ABEM, 1237: Minutes Committee for the Organization of the Churches (22 May 1958).
113 Ibid. (2 July 1958); ABEM, 879: Minutes of the French-speaking part of the Workers' Conference (23 Oct. 1958).
114 ABEM, 1237: Winston Jr. to the Board of Trustees (31 Oct. 1957).

Mission, a group of workers of many nationalities, and an informal association of churches and posts."[115]

Once again, the decision was postponed by forming a subcommittee to create wording about the autonomization to be included in the *Preliminary Stipulations*. They came up with the following:

> The churches, when reaching maturity, i.e., having a complete church council, capable of self-governance, and able to fully meet their material needs, have the liberty to manage and administer their finances. They can choose their spiritual leader. However, his election will not take place without the approval of the Personnel Committee, and his salary level will be determined by said Committee.[116]

As the full committee did not reach a consensus about this wording, the fact that the BGM still held to Ralph Norton's principle to only implement decisions that had been made unanimously threw a spanner in the works. This made the Board of Trustees nervous. The success of the Sputnik project, as part of the nuclear arms race between the USA and the USSR, was in full swing. Assuming that France strongly influenced Belgium, it was firmly believed that a democratic takeover by the Communists in France would immediately be felt in Belgium. As the French Communist Party had attracted roughly 20% of the voters in recent elections, such a scenario was deemed plausible. Therefore, the Board told the BGM churches to be prepared for communist rule in which the Americans would not be welcome.[117]

In February 1959, George Winston intensified the pressure by saying that he would quit the meetings if no proposal were drafted for the Workers Conference to be held in the spring. It is unknown whether the Cuban revolution played a part in the deliberations, but his threat had the desired effect. The already financially self-sufficient congregations were to be invited "to form an association of free evangelical churches, born from the BGM, that other churches could join and in which each church keeps its own character."[118] The Statement of Faith and the *Preliminary Stipulations* were to form the basis of the denomination.

---

115 Ibid.
116 For the original quote, see ABEM, 1237: Minutes Committee for the Organization of the Churches (4 Sep. 1958).
117 ABEM, 879: Proposed Statement to the Council of Workers.
118 The addition "born from the BGM" had been proposed by Gerrit van de Riet. This specification was extensively discussed once again several months later. Some committee members felt that in the future this would be found too exclusive. However, no consensus about the wording was reached and it was therefore maintained. For the original quote, see ABEM, 1237: Minutes of the Committee for the Organization of the Churches (26 Feb., 21 May 1959).

The next hurdle was drafting the conditions for joining. Some committee members felt these should not be too strict, which might deter some churches. Others went further and proposed minimal requirements enabling the smaller rural churches to join. Eventually, a consensus was reached. To become autonomous, a church would need to have a church council with at least four elders and a balanced budget.

To avoid reinventing the wheel, the Committee studied the church orders of the denomination of Free Evangelical Churches in Germany, the Netherlands, France, and Switzerland for inspiration.[119] This aligns with the general practice in the BGM and other faith missions. Without minuting why, the Committee decided to use the constitution of the *Églises Evangéliques Libres* (Free Evangelical Churches) in France as a starting point.[120] The new denomination was given the organizational form of a Belgian *association sans but lucratif* (not-for-profit association), whose General Assembly was to appoint an Executive Committee that was given the title *Commission de l'Assemblée Générale* (Committee of the General Assembly).[121]

As many congregations could not be financially fully autonomous, the requirements for joining were somewhat relaxed. The local churches could cover their costs however they liked except by appealing to the BGM's central funds.[122] Whether to organize itself as a non-profit or a "factual association" was left to the local church to decide.[123]

The Board of Trustees initially aimed to launch the denomination in 1958. That turned out to be impossible due to unfruitful internal discussions, which slowed down the Committee for the Organization of the Churches' work considerably. Frustrated about the slow pace, the Board applied pressure in November 1959 by demanding a progress report immediately and copies of the minutes of Committee meetings in the future.[124] This measure proved successful. In the Spring of 1960, the draft text about the denomination to be founded was ready for discussion during the regional meetings.[125]

119　Ibid. (26 Feb. 1959).
120　The documents from the other countries were now only consulted for comparison. ABEM, 1237: Minutes Committee for the Organization of the Churches (23 March 1959).
121　"La Commission de l'Assemblée Générale." It was given authority to call general meetings, write and circulate annual reports, approve callings on pastors, supervise compliance with the Statement of Faith and the constitution, represent the denomination at the national and international level, handle applications for membership, and organize the visitation of the churches that joined. Every church that joined would be entitled to two representatives. Ibid. (21 May 1959).
122　Ibid. (23 March 1959).
123　An asbl/vzw is similar to an incorporation, whereas a 'factual organization' does not have a legal personality in Belgian law. Ibid.: (21 May 1959).
124　ABEM, 503: Howard Jr. to Winston Sr. (20 Nov. 1959).
125　These took place on 21 Jan. 1960 in Seraing, 2 Feb. in Charleroi, 3 March in Ath, and 7 April in Ghent. ABEM, 1237: G. Winston, Circular Letter (1960).

Interestingly, some decisions were made with a simple majority.[126] This indicates that the Committee was internally divided and that the consensus model had been abandoned to save time and meet the expectations of the Board of Trustees. Only seven or eight of the fifty-two churches met the requirements for joining the denomination, so the option to relax the requirements in the future was left open.[127]

As the proposal did not gain the required support of 75% of the BGMers, there was a hitch once more. The workers were encouraged to submit amendments to help obtain the necessary votes. The fact that only two people gave feedback illustrates the despondency in this dossier.

Their input was included in a new proposal discussed at the Workers Conference on 8 January 1961. The main changes were lowering the number of required elders from four to three and linking the pastor's salaries to those of BGM pastors.[128] The text was adopted after a lengthy debate, but many were reported to have voted "half-heartedly, without conviction."[129]

According to John Winston Sr., this was because many doubted the viability of the new denomination and the governing capabilities of the local church councils.[130] The real reason was that many strongly suspected that the BGM would maintain a strong influence. Therefore, in September 1961, a new amendment was proposed after consultation with church councils and church meetings. It stated that the BGM Personnel Committee would no longer have a say in appointing pastors.[131] The workers showed little enthusiasm for the autonomization project. The text was adopted with slightly more support but still in an atmosphere of resignation.

All obstacles now seemed to have been removed, and the target date for the launch of the *Vereniging van Vrije Kerken van de BEZ.* (Association of Free Churches of the BGM) was set for 1 January 1962.[132] The denomination was to include the following eight local churches: Brussels (French language), Brussels (Dutch language), Antwerp, Liège, Charleroi, Kortrijk, Bruges, and Auvelais.[133]

---

126   Ibid.: Winston Sr., Accompanying letter [1960].
127   Ibid.
128   ABEM, 866: Proposal by the Committee for the Organization of the Churches (8 Jan. 1961).
129   The vote on the proposal took place in two rounds. In the first round, 35 of the 36 who were present agreed in principle with the autonomization of local churches. In the second round, the draft text was accepted with only 3 votes against. ABEM, 879: Minutes Workers Conference (2 April 1961); ABEM, 866: Winston Sr. to Brown (12 Aug. 1961).
130   Ibid.
131   ABEM, 879: Minutes Workers Conference (30 Sep. 1961).
132   The pastors in question were invited to a preparatory meeting on 13 Dec. 1961. ABEM, 850: Winston Sr. to the pastors of the churches that will form the new denomination (30 Nov. 1961).
133   ABEM, 879: Minutes Workers Conference (30 Sep. 1961).

But the launch had to be postponed once again, as it took more time than expected to persuade the elders and members of the churches involved.[134] In Antwerp, the church meeting only agreed "for the sake of, and out of love for, the Belgian Gospel Mission."[135] In Auvelais, establishing the new denomination was viewed as a step toward the autonomy of all churches, which the BGM started but again within the BGM framework.[136] Bruges agreed, "if it is necessary."[137] Charleroi pointed out that churches should only be allowed to join if they obtained the finances they needed from their collections and contributions.[138] Eventually, all eight church meetings reluctantly agreed.

The Board of Trustees responded with disappointment, writing that "it seems that the BGM is about the only faith mission with headquarters in America that does not have an active indigenous church program, and after 40 years in Belgium, we should really be showing missions in primitive lands how to do it."[139] Finally, on 3 March 1962, the new denomination was officially founded in a meeting led by interim chairman John Winston Sr.[140] A Board of Governors was elected, which was granted the authority to allow exceptions to the requirements for joining and even to adapt them.[141] Ralph Norton's aim, the indigenization of the churches started by the BGM, had finally been realized, albeit only in part and without much enthusiasm.[142]

---

134 ABEM, 866: Winston Sr. to Brown (13 Jan. 1962).
135 For the original quote, see ABEM, 292: Van de Riet to Winston Sr. (26 Feb. 1962).
136 ABEM, 850: Auvelais Elders to Winston Sr. (26 Feb. 1962).
137 For the original quote, see ABEM, 318: Van der Beek to Winston Sr. (19 Feb. 1962).
138 ABEM, 325: Vuilleumier to Winston Sr. (19 Feb. 1962).
139 ABEM, 879: Proposed Statement to the Council of Workers.
140 Antwerp was represented by its pastor Gerrit van de Riet and elders G. Coeck and H. Hugens; Auvelais by pastor Jean Vandenbroeck and elders D. Léger and J. Guillaume; Bruges by pastor Daniël van der Beek and elders L. Gilbert and A. Van den Eynde; the Dutch-language church in Brussels by pastor Leendert Knecht and elder A. Vercauteren; the French-language church in Brussels by pastor Jannis de Smidt and elders A. Dobbelaere and F. Van den Bemden; Charleroi by pastor Georges Vuilleumier and elders A. Grassart and A. Baudouin; Liège by pastor Jean Knecht Jr. (1911-1995), and elders A. Basti, F. Vanderwouwer. ABEM, 850: Agenda (3 March 1962).
141 ABEM, 866: Winston Sr. to Brown (8 March 1962).
142 The BGM (now VIANOVA) currently has 6 churches. The large majority gradually joined the new denomination over the years.

CONCLUSION

When Ralph Norton took the SVM pledge in 1891, Belgium was surely not the mission field he had in mind. When he enrolled in Moody Bible Institute (1899-1901), he thought it to be a shortcut to the foreign mission fields. Here, he met his wife, Edith Fox, was taught Dispensationalism, received practical training in many forms of evangelism, and was repeatedly reminded of the urgency of missions. Despite the pressing need, the couple was confined to the waiting room for many years. It would take twenty-three years and numerous failed attempts for Asian mission fields to become a foreign missionary in a first-world country, Belgium.

At the age of 50, and after an unexpectedly successful mission to Belgian soldiers during World War I, Norton and his wife arrived in Brussels in December 1918 to start the work of the Belgian Gospel Mission. Here, they would serve for another two decades, leaving the organization in the hands of their much-appreciated and trusted wingmen, John C. Winston Sr. and Odilon Vansteenberghe.

Starting as an American interdenominational evangelistic organization intending to work closely with the Belgian protestant churches, the BGM evolved into a church-planting mission within a year. Its self-imposed isolation in the Belgian protestant landscape fitted their eschatological framework. Its intentional or unintentional headhunting in Belgian Protestantism also contributed to strained relationships with other denominations. Fully convinced that they were living in the end times, the Nortons considered evangelism to be the most urgent and applied tried-and-tested methods to reach as many people as possible. The BGM's impact on the Belgian Protestant landscape was profound, shaping the religious landscape in ways that are still felt today.

Given the Nortons' intention to work primarily with Belgians, the establishment of their own Bible school became inevitable. The eagerness to train Belgian students was evident. In the end, the schools' impact on the mission's personnel remained limited as not all graduates applied or were accepted. As the mission also needed personnel already before the first students graduated, the BGM recruited workers proficient in Dutch or French, both in Europe and North America.

Logically, the number of Belgian pastors did not keep pace with the increase in local churches and stations. This reinforced the perception that Protestantism was a foreign form of Christianity. Together with social pressure, this affected the response to their evangelistic efforts in difficult-to-quantify ways.

The gradual shift in BGM's emphasis from holiness to 1920s fundamentalism significantly influenced the role of women in the organization. As evangelistic initiatives became more male-dominated, single women missionaries left the BGM and reinforced the supporting role of pastors' wives. However, accepting Edith Norton as her husband's successor exemplifies the organization's flexibility in gender policy when necessary. This change had no impact in the area of cooperation. Institutional cooperation was consistently withheld unless the BGM was in complete theological agreement with the other party. By contrast, incidental collaboration at a local or individual level was always possible and took place fairly regularly.

The Great Depression's financial strain profoundly affected all elements of the BGM. The mission's unwavering reliance on North American donations underscored its financial vulnerability and dependency, ultimately shaping its evangelistic strategies and organizational sustainability during this period. Despite these challenges, elements of Keswick holiness persisted, demonstrated by the continued recruitment of new workers even amidst chronic financial shortages.

The policy of staffing each church plant with a full-timer backfired; transatlantic funds were no longer enough to pay its staff and operating costs as well as supplement local church budgets. As the organization had been reluctant, for understandable reasons, to encourage church members and regular visitors to take financial responsibility for their congregations, they had developed a complacent attitude towards church finances.

Under the encouragement of John Winston Sr., the first steps toward the autonomization of BGM churches were taken, modeled after the New Testament primitive church. In 1929, the first constitution was drafted. Despite efforts to appoint elders and deacons, local leaders frequently indicated a shortage of suitable candidates, yet headquarters provided little guidance to address this issue. The church structure remained fluid, as various procedures outlined in the *Preliminary Stipulations* were not consistently applied across all BGM churches. The formation of a national youth organization as an umbrella for local youth groups indicated the emergence of a new denomination within the BGM.

When Vansteenberghe and Winston Sr. were appointed as the organization's new co-directors in 1936, the mission had already developed into a significant entity within Belgian Protestantism. The mission's relations with the major Protestant denominations remained icy as they continued the BGM's isolated course in interdenominational cooperation. Despite ongoing financial difficulties and disappointing visible or direct results, the mission determinedly applied its traditional evangelistic methods. New evangelistic initiatives, such as soldiers' foyers and missions among Jewish refugees, only emerged due to the external factor of the clouds of war. To reassure financial backers and encourage continued or increased donations, the mission often exaggerated the results of its evangelistic initiatives. As budget shortages persisted, the BGM attributed financial difficulties to spiritual causes and prioritized workers last when allocating available funds, which is consistent with its faith mission identity.

From September 1939 until the invasion in May 1940, the BGM once again – with limited success – utilized humanitarian aid as a vehicle for evangelism, as it had during World War I and the immediate post-Armistice years. During the mobilization, the mission's Faith mission identity facilitated a return to its previous Holiness stance on the role of women. In places where BGM workers were recalled to serve in the armed forces, the necessity to maintain church activities temporarily allowed pastors' wives to assume some responsibilities of their absent husbands. As could be expected, the occupation's restrictions led to the near-total cessation of direct evangelistic activities. The mission's congregations were now confronted with forced financial autonomy as the BGM was cut off from foreign financial support. Thus, the organization had no choice but to permit its workers to take on second jobs to supplement their income. This turned out to be one of the main factors contributing to the prolonged tensions and conflicts leading up to the autonomization of some BGM church plants in 1962.

From 1945 to 1962, the BGM grappled with significant challenges, such as financial instability, leadership transitions, and the complex denominational process. The mission was plagued by a pervasive sense of unease, which was exacerbated by mutual distrust among various groups within the organization. This unease dragged on for many years, primarily due to two key factors.

Firstly, Vansteenberghe and Winston Sr. responded inadequately to the mission's financial challenges. They failed to respond to the workers' demands for full salary payments amid rising living costs and criticized efforts by workers and congregations to supplement their inadequate BGM payments through part-time RE teaching. Consequently, they lacked the authority to enforce financial solidarity between bi-vocational and other workers.

Secondly, the mission's American Board of Trustees perpetuated unequal treatment of Europeans during the prolonged budget crisis, making decisions solely for American missionaries while neglecting European counterparts. This inequality fostered unity among Europeans against the Board and American missionaries, fueling resistance to initiatives aimed at appointing a new director and pushing Belgian congregations toward financial independence.

The overwhelming number of deputation requests received by American churches and the transatlantic tendency to view Europe as a single mission field complicated the precarious financial situation. As the prevailing 'red scare' and Cold War reinforced the belief in a limited window to evangelize Belgians before time ran out, expenses for evangelism, including a substantial investment for a mobile church, took preference over full payment of the mission's workers. Consistently adhering to the policy to give the workers wages the lowest priority was in line with Faith mission principles, where missionaries were expected to make all kinds of sacrifices for the advancement of the Gospel.

The mission's eschatological stance resulted in an ongoing short-term focus. This contributed to recurring leadership crises following the Nortons' deaths, complicated the denomination process, and the urgent search for a new director. The appointment of Homer Payne exemplified a compromise acceptable to both Americans and Europeans. We already summed up some factors that complicated the long and arduous path to denomination, such as Ralph Norton's well-intentioned policy of providing church plants from the beginning with full-time pastors and church buildings without fostering stewardship locally. Some congregations became addicted to financial support, and others were planted in areas where financial independence was unrealistic. It led to an unhealthy financial dependence of local churches on Headquarters, which was difficult to reverse unless concessions were made that would open the door for bi-vocational pastors.

Despite being officially advisory, the American Board of Trustees wielded substantial influence in the post-World War II period. Together with young George Winston, they kept the much-needed autonomization of local churches going. Whereas the Board was driven by the ongoing Cold War threat, George Winston simply found it unacceptable that congregations in a first-world country that existed for decades had become addicted to the transatlantic financial lifeline. They did not allow them to be discouraged by the frequent postponements and paralyzing the process. Forming a Free Church denomination in the Spring of 1962 was a milestone in the mission's history. It allowed the BGM to focus solely on evangelism and gradually enabled its church plants to join this new denomination within Belgian Protestantism.

The evaluation of the BGM's success is complex and multifaceted. From a quantitative perspective and an administrative angle, the answer is no. Even when the set of hard data in the archives is limited, it is clear that the mission did not emulate the success the Nortons had among the Belgian soldiers during World War I. Also, throughout the period we investigated, the mission's leadership, for various reasons that have been discussed, failed to steer the organization with a long-term perspective as a compass.

But, as Stefan Paas rightly observed, that is not the best way to evaluate the Belgian Gospel Mission as an early exponent of the American missions that turned up in force on the European continent after the Second World War.[1] Despite the Nortons' – and, by extension, most of the BGM's – resistance to contextualization and collaboration, the organization played a crucial role in the growth of Belgian Protestantism during the interwar period. Despite the BGM's stagnation, both literally and figuratively, in the post-World War II era we have researched, it remained the largest group of Evangelicals within Belgian Protestantism. Also, the mission's Bible schools trained numerous evangelists, youth workers, RE teachers, and pastors who served in Belgium and beyond, including within denominations that opposed the BGM.

Thus, while the historical record of the Belgian Gospel Mission may evoke mixed feelings regarding its successes and potential, its impact extends far beyond a mere footnote in the history of twentieth-century Belgian Protestantism.

---

[1] Paas, "Mission from Anywhere to Europe," 7.

APPENDICES

APPENDIX 1: THE BELGIAN GOSPEL MISSION'S CONFESSION OF FAITH[1]

1. I believe in one God, Creator of heaven and earth, Spirit, Light, Love and Truth; eternal, almighty, infallible and unchangeable, infinitely wise, just and holy. God reveals Himself in the Bible as Father, Son, and Holy Spirit.
2. I believe in Jesus Christ, the only begotten Son of God, the eternal Word manifested in flesh. I believe that He was conceived by the Holy Spirit, and that He was born of the Virgin Mary. I believe in His substitutionary and redeeming death, in His bodily resurrection, in His ascension and His personal return for His redeemed ones, followed by His coming in glory to judge the rebellious and to establish His millennial reign.
3. I believe in the Holy Spirit, in His personality, and in His work of regeneration and of sanctification.
4. I believe in the whole Bible (the sixty-six books of the Old and New Testaments) has proceeded from and is inspired by God and thus constitutes an inerrant revelation, the only rule of faith and life.
5. I believe that man, having been created pure and in the image of God, is by his own sin fallen from grace, and I believe that in consequence all have sinned, are guilty and lost, and absolutely incapable of saving themselves by their own works, being dead in their trespasses and sins; that for those who, in this life, will not repent the result of sin will be eternal punishment of which they will be fully conscious.
6. I believe that we are saved solely by grace, through faith in the blood sacrifice of the Son of God.
7. I believe in the personality of Satan, the author of the fall and in his judgment and in his eternal punishment.
8. I believe in the bodily resurrection of man, some to eternal life and others to judgment.
9. I believe that Jesus Christ instituted the Lord's Supper to commemorate His death till He come; and Baptism as a symbol of the believer's union with Christ in His death and in His resurrection.
10. I believe that the Church of Jesus Christ is solely composed of those who have been redeemed and washed in His blood, and regenerated and sealed by the Holy Spirit, and that they are saved to serve; that they must seek to live a holy life, to separate themselves from and forsake all that might dishonor God, or cast discredit on His cause, or even weaken their testimony.
11. In short, I believe in all that the Bible teaches.
    To the Father who has loved us,
    To the Son who has redeemed us,
    To the Holy Spirit who has regenerated us,
    Be honor, praise and glory,
    For ever and ever.
    Amen

APPENDIX 2: GUIDING PRINCIPLES TO SERVE IN THE FIXING OF WORKERS' SALARIES IN THE BELGIAN GOSPEL MISSION[2]

1. Every worker should receive sufficient remuneration to enable him or her to live respectably.
2. Whether a worker is single or married, and the number of those wholly dependent upon him for support, should be taken into consideration.
3. The importance of the post which the worker holds, the amount of responsibility devolving upon him, taken in connection with his ability, preparation, experience, or other qualifications for his task, and the length of service in the mission, should be considered.
4. In general the salaries in the B.G.M. should not be noticeably higher than salaries paid in other occupations of a similar character, in order that people may not be attracted by the emoluments offered, rather than directed by the Holy Spirit to enter the work.

---

1   ABEM, 1231: Certified Translation of the Asbl Articles.
2   ABEM, 1225: Guiding Principles to Serve the Fixing of Workers' Salaries in the Belgian Gospel Mission (1927).

Version of 15 August 1927

1. *Workers are to be divided into categories according to occupation* viz. Heads of Posts ... Colporters ... etc. and *according to length of service.*
   At the end of two years service [sic] in the mission in the mission a worker becomes a candidate for an advance in category. The number of categories in force at the present time is ten (10).
2. In any category the supplement based on family is as follows:
a) Married	33⅓%
b) One child 7-16 years	15%
c) More than one child 7-16 years	10% each
d) One child under 7 years	10%
e) More than one child under 7 years	5% each even if there is a first child between the ages of 7 and 16 years

   f) Other relatives entirely dependent on the worker for support may be considered as equivalent to a wife or child of either age indicated according to the exigencies of the case in question.

   N.B. The percentage increases for children are calculated on the basis of the married worker's salary.
3. There is a supplement based on place of residence for workers living in certain localities where prices are especially high, as follows:
a) Brussels	5%
b) Antwerp	5%
c) Province of Hainaut	3%

   Note: This percentage increase is calculated on the basis of the salary after the addition of the family supplement.
4. a. Wherever possible Mission workers are lodged free of charge in buildings owned or rented by the mission.

   b. In other cases lodging allowances are made as follows:

Persons	City	Town	Village
1	125 BEF.	125 BEF.	75 BEF.
2	175 BEF.	150 BEF.	100 BEF.
3	200 BEF.	175 BEF.	150 BEF.
4	250 BEF.	200 BEF.	175 BEF.
5 or more	300 BEF.	250 BEF.	200 BEF.

   c. Workers are expected to pay their own light, heat and water bills.
5. Where workers are staying with the tent or travelling with the roulette or doing itinerant work, a special allowance of BEF 10 per diem may be made in view of the necessity of taking meals in restaurants and out of the way places.

   When workers on duty are entertained by members of the mission they are allowed to make a charge on the expense account of the mission for the meals furnished, but in this case the worker benefited is not expected to receive the special indemnity for the days when he was so entertained. In general this special supplement is only expected to cover the difference between the actual cost of board and lodging to the worker, and what it would cost him had he stayed home.
6. a. In case of sickness the mission intervenes where necessary in doctors and hospital expenses to the amount of one-third.

   b. A worker on sick leave for an extended time is entitled to full pay during three months, and half pay for the remainder of the time up to six months.

   c. All adjustments in salaries required by change in the cost of living are made on the basis of the Index Number for the average price of living necessities in Belgium, as found in the 'Revue du Travail.'
7. No adjustment is to be made oftener than every three months, unless the variation in the Index Number amounts to more than 20% since the immediately preceding adjustment was made. In any case no adjustment is to be made unless the variation in the Index Number exeeds 10% since the immediately preceding adjustment was made.

8. The following are the sums employed as the basis of calculation in each category:
   Category 1   715.00
            2   822.25
            3   893.75
            4   953.33
            5   1,012.91
            6   1,072.50
            7   1,191.66
            8   1,310.83
            9   1,382.33
           10   1,430.00
9. All students are expected to pay BEF 150 per month toward their living expenses, and to furnish two hours per day of manual labour. Tuition is free.

APPENDIX 3: LIST OF PUBLICATIONS BY THE BGM

a) *Books*
   Blackstone, William E. *Jésus révient*. Brussels: Mission Evangélique Belge, 1957.
      Jezus komt. Brussels: Belgische Evangelische Zending, 1925.
      Jezus komt. 2nd ed. Brussels: Evangelisatiewerk in België, 1923.
   Chafer, Lewis Sperry. *L'homme spirituel*. Brussels: Mission Belge Evangélique, 1918.
      La grâce. Brussels, n.d.
      Le salut. Brussels: Mission Belge Evangélique, n.d.
      Les grandes doctrines de la Bible. Brussels: Mission Belge Evangélique, n.d.
   Collett, Sidney. *The Scripture of Truth (French Title Unknown)*. Brussels: Mission Belge Evangélique, n.d.
   Goodman, George. *Opgewekt uit de doden*. Brussels: Evangelisatiewerk in België, n.d.
   Howard Sr., Philip E. *A New Invasion of Belgium*. Philadelphia, PA: Sunday School Times, 1924.
   Lukasse, Johan. *Licht in een duistere plaats: de moderne geschiedenis van het evangelie te Genk*. Genk: Stichting Vrienden van Genk, 1960.
   McConkey, James H. *La vie livré*. Brussels: Le bon livre, 1961.
      Le Triple Secret du Saint-Esprit. Translated by O Prêtre. 4th Brussels: Le bon livre, 1961.
   Moody, D.L. *Le chemin qui mène à Dieu*. Brussels: Mission Evangélique Belge, n.d.
   Norton, Edith F. *Ralph Norton and The Belgian Gospel Mission*. New York: Fleming H Revell, 1935.
   Scofield, C.I. *Dispensant correctement la parole de la vérité (2 Tim. 2 : 15) : dix études sur les grandes divisions de l'Ecriture*. Brussels: Mission Belge Evangélique, n.d.
   Strombeck, J.F. *Ce si grand salut*. Neuchâtel: Monnier, 1946.
      Zo grote zaligheid. Brussels: Belgische Evangelische Zending, 1947.
   Torrey, R.A. *Ce que la bible enseigne : une étude complète des grandes doctrines bibliques*. Brussels: Mission Evangélique Belge, n.d.
      Hoe brengen wij zielen tot Jezus?, n.d.
   Van Dorp, Henk. *Uw woord is de waarheid: het verhaal van 100 jaar Belgische Evangelische Zending*. Zwolle: Scholten Uitgeverij BV, 2019.
   Une vie livrée ... Raymond Van Assche 1920 - 1953. Brussels: Jean Vandenbroeck, 1953.
   Wilson, Robert Dick. *La haute critique est-elle scientifique?* Brussels: Mission Evangélique Belge, n.d.

b) *Periodicals*

   De Getuige. Evangelisatiewerk in België, 1923.
   Flanders Fields. Belgian Gospel Mission, 1933-1964, continued as *Belgian Beacon*.
   La lueur du Foyer. Foyer de l'Institut Biblique, 1934-1935.
   Le Messager de la Bonne Nouvelle: Bulletin périodique d'information, pour la diffusion des Ecritures dans la Province de Namur. Auvelais: La Mission Evangélique Belge, 1944-1950.
   Limburg voor Christus. Genk: Belgische Evangelische Zending, 1954-1988, continued as *Brussels Perspectief* (1988-1997?).

Missions-Nachrichten aus Belgiën, 1943.
Notre Espérance, 1925-1963.
Onze Hoop, 1925-1963.
Opwekking. Brussels: Belgische Evangelische Zending, 1945.
The Belgian Gospel Mission. London, 1947.

c) *PR-materials*

BASEC, *Easter Under Shell Fire at the Belgian Front*, n.d.
   What Belgian Soldiers Told Us. Philadelphia, PA, n.d.
Belgian Gospel Mission, *A Million Children Waiting for the Gospel*, n.d.
   An Illustrated Letter from Belgium for Sunday School Folk. London, n.d.
   Belgian Gospel Mission, Inc. 1945th Philadelphia, PA, n.d.
   Belgium's Eagerness for the Bible. Philadelphia, PA, n.d.
   British Personnel Serving With The Belgian Gospel Mission, n.d.
   Everywhere. Philadelphia, PA, n.d.
   How They Built a Trailer Church, n.d.
   Let's Go Abroad: Introducing the Work of the Belgian Gospel Mission, n.d.
   Open Channels. Philadelphia, PA, n.d.
   Other Sheep I Have. Philadelphia, PA, n.d.
   The Belgian Gospel Mission, What It Is, n.d.
   Things That Happen. Philadelphia, PA, London, n.d.
   We Are Full of Confidence. Brussels, Philadelphia PA, n.d.
   What Is the Belgian Gospel Mission. Philadelphia, PA, 1954.
   What Is the Belgian Gospel Mission? Its Origin and Expansion, Its Field - Present and Future And Its Position Doctrinally. Brussels: Belgian Gospel Mission, 1926.
Belgische Evangelische Zending, *Na twintig jaren: een kort overzicht van de wonderdaden Gods in België*. Brussels, 1938.
   Na zeven jaren 1919 - 1926: beknopt overzicht van het ontstaan en den arbeid der Belgische Evangelische Zending. Brussels: Belgische Evangelische Zending, 1926.
Bentley, Henry K. *Seated with Christ on High: A Little Song of Christian Privilige, Power and Peace*. London, n.d.
Horsburgh, W.J.R, *The Forbidden Book*. [1948] London: Belgian Gospel Mission, n.d.
   Why Support the Belgian Gospel Mission. Brussels: Belgian Gospel Mission, n.d.
Inwood, Charles. *Belgium Revisit*Philadelphia, PA, n.d.
La Mission Belge Evangélique, *Après vingt ans: apercu des merveilles que Dieu a accomplies en Belgique, 1918-1939*. Brussels, 1938.
Lockyer, Herbert J. *A Modern Missionary Miracle*. London: Belgian Gospel Mission, n.d.
Maclean, J. Kennedy. *A Dark Land at Our Own Doors*. London, Edinburgh: Marshall, n.d.
   Building a Gospel Light House. Philadelphia, PA: Belgian Gospel Mission, n.d.
   Does Anyone Care? London, n.d.
Mission Evangélique Belge, *Après Sept Ans 1919 - 1926: Court aperçu de la fondation et du développement de l'œuvre poursuivie par la Mission Belge Evangélique*. Brussels: Mission Belge Evangélique, 1926.
Mrs. Norton, Ralph C. *Beyond the First Trench Lines*. Philadelphia, PA: Belgian Gospel Mission, n.d.
   The Belgian Farceur Who 'Didn't Mean It'. Philadelphia, PA: BASEC, n.d.
   The Moody Post Links Up With Belgium, n.d.
   The Voice of the Carillon. Marshall. London, n.d.
Norton, Edith F. *Just Himself*. Philadelphia, PA: Belgian Gospel Mission, n.d.
   New Belgium Calls Us. Brussels, Philadelphia PA, Toronto: Belgian Gospel Mission, n.d.
   Oh, That Wonderful Rich Gospel: How It Is Working in Belgium. Philadelphia, PA: Belgian Gospel Mission, n.d.
   The Beggars Wood. Philadelphia, PA: Belgian Gospel Mission, n.d.
   The Mystery of Suffering. Philadelphia, PA: Belgian Gospel Mission, n.d.
   The Notary's Story. Brussels, Philadelphia PA: Belgian Gospel Mission, 1930.
   The Story of Stefanie. Philadelphia, PA: Belgian Gospel Mission, n.d.

Three Tales From Belgium. Philadelphia, PA: Belgian Gospel Mission, n.d.
What Happened in Villeroux. Brussels: Belgian Gospel Mission, n.d.
Norton, R.C., and E.F. Norton. *Belgium*. Brussels: Belgian Gospel Mission, n.d.
Norton, Ralph C. *Belgium's New Heart Hunger for Christ*, n.d.
Feed My Lambs. Brussels: Belgian Gospel Mission, n.d.
The Coming Conflict and Victory. Brussels: Belgian Gospel Mission, n.d.
Norton, Ralph C., and Edith F. Norton. *Sowing Seed for the Master*. Philadelphia, PA: Belgian Gospel Mission, n.d.
Why Evangelize Belgium? Brussels, Philadelphia PA, n.d.
Norton, Ralph C. *Is Belgium the Key to Europe's Evangelization?* London: Belgian Gospel Mission, n.d.
Stearns, M.B. *Bible Training in the Belgian Gospel Mission Inc.* Brussels, n.d.
Vansteenberghe, C. *Edwald, A Gospel Herald in Flanders*. Philadelphia, PA: Belgian Gospel Mission, 1933.
Vansteenberghe, O. *A New Look at Belgium*. Philadelphia, PA: Belgian Gospel Mission, 1958.
Eighteen Years of Seed-Sowing in Belgium. Brussels: Belgian Gospel Mission, n.d.
The Bread of Life in a Flemish Bakery. Brussels: Belgian Gospel Mission, n.d.
The Last Night: Triumph in the Face of Death. Philadelphia, PA: Belgian Gospel Mission, n.d.
The New Dogma of the Roman Catholic Church. [1950] Belgian Gospel Mission, n.d.
Three Daniels. Brussels, Philadelphia PA: Belgian Gospel Mission, n.d.
What Is the Belgian Gospel Mission? Philadelphia, PA: Belgian Gospel Mission, n.d.
Winston, Grace W. *At the Crossroads of Europe*. Philadelphia, PA: Belgian Gospel Mission, 1948.
Belgium, Gateway to Europe Stands Open to the Gospel. Philadelphia, PA: Belgian Gospel Mission, n.d.
How Peter Vansteenberghe Triumphed over Death. Philadelphia, PA: Belgian Gospel Mission, n.d.
Peter, A Belgian Trench Apostle. Philadelphia, PA: BASEC, n.d.
Qu'est-ce-que la Mission Belge Evangélique:son origine - son expansion - son champ d'action - perspectives d'avenir - sa position doctrinale. Brussels: La Mission Belge Evangélique, 1926.
Ten Reasons for Extending the Work of the Belgian Gospel Mission, n.d.
Wat is de Belgische Evangelische Zending? Brussels: Belgische Evangelische Zending, 1926.

d) *Tracts*

Antomarchi, A. *A quoi bon vivre?* Brussels: La Mission Belge Evangélique, n.d.
Bon pour les Femmes. Brussels: La Mission Belge Evangélique, n.d.
Qui est Jésus-Christ? Brussels: Mission Belge Evangélique, n.d.
S.O.S. Brussels: Mission Belge Evangélique, n.d.
Barnhouse, Donald Grey. *Une Conversation*. Brussels: La Mission Belge Evangélique, n.d.
Belgische Evangelische Zending, *Enkele onderwerpen voor gebed voor elken dag der week*. Brussels, n.d.
Blinde Leidslieden der Blinden. Brussels, n.d.
De laatste biecht van vader Egidio. Brussels, n.d.
De onbetrouwbare Spaarpot. Brussels, n.d.
De Stervende Priester. Brussels, n.d.
De Zwaan en de Kraanvogel. Brussels, n.d.
Dood van een dokter in de geneeskunde. Brussels, n.d.
Door één lucifer. Brussels, n.d.
Een korte predikatie. Brussels, n.d.
Een ontroerend Getuigenis. Brussels, n.d.
Een ware geschiedenis. Brussels, n.d.
Een woord voor Ouders, die treuren over hun gestorven Lievelingen. Evangelisatie-Drukkerij. Brussels, n.d.
Eeuwigheid, eeuwigheid. Brussels, n.d.
Fientje Maneschijn. Brussels, n.d.
Gered aan de deur van haar huis. Evangelisatie-Drukkerij. Brussels, n.d.
God en de wees. Brussels, n.d.
God heeft gesproken. Brussels: Scripture Gift Mission, n.d.

    Handelingen der Apostelen en Brieven van den Apostel Petrus. London: Scripture Gift Mission, n.d.
    Harteleed. Brussels, n.d.
    Het eenige Fondament. Evangelisatie-Drukkerij. Brussels, n.d.
    Het Heilig Evangelie naar de beschrijving van Johannes. Brussels: Scripture Gift Mission, n.d.
    Hoe een Iersch meisje in vrede stierf. Brussels, n.d.
    Ik ben verloren en hij hebt het mij nooit gezegd. Brussels, n.d.
    Ik heb geen tijd! Evangelisatie-Drukkerij. Brussels, n.d.
    Jozef en zijn broeders. Brussels, n.d.
    Menschelijke vragen en Goddelijke antwoorden. Evangelisatie-Drukkerij. Brussels, n.d.
    Naar het Kerkhof. Brussels, n.d.
    Redding en verlossing voor allen: Gij moet gered worden van den Dood. Brussels, n.d.
    Toen eenige jaren geleden. Brussels, n.d.
    Uit goeder trouw... maar toch bedrogen... Brussels, n.d.
    Waarom vloekt gij, Vriend? Brussels, n.d.
    Waarom zijt gij Protestant geworden? Evangelisatie-Drukkerij. Brussels, n.d.
    Waren de eerste Christenen Roomsch-Katholiek? Brussels, n.d.
    Wat is de Belgische Evangelische Zending? Ontstaan en ontwikkeling - arbeidsveld - heden en toekomst - leerstellig standpunt. Brussels, n.d.
    Wat moet ik doen om verloren te gaan? Brussels, n.d.
    Weet gij wat een gift is? Evangelisatie-Drukkerij. Brussels, n.d.
    Wilt gij gezond worden? Brussels, n.d.
    Wormstekige menschen. Evangelisatie-Drukkerij. Brussels, n.d.
Bentley, H.K. *Exposé des doctrines de l'Antoinisme*. Brussels: La Mission Belge Evangélique, n.d.
    Ou allons-nous? Brussels: La Mission Belge Evangélique, n.d.
Chafer, Lewis Sperry. *L'homme spirituel*. Brussels: Mission évangélique Belge, n.d.
    Le Salut. Brussels: Mission évangélique Belge, n.d.
    Les Grandes Doctrines de la Bible. Brussels: La Mission Évangélique Belge, n.d.
D, J. *Mon Témoignage*. Brussels: Mission Belge Evangélique, n.d.
Dubois, S. *Qu'elle s'explique!* Dour, n.d.
Ellis, M. *Quand le Seigneur Jésus-Christ va revenir: Comment Le recevrez-vous?* Brussels: La Mission Belge Evangélique, n.d.
Evangelisatiewerk in België, *Betert u dan en bekeert u, opdat uwe zonden mogen uitgewischt worden*. Brussels, n.d.
    Bijbelleergang Evangelisatiewerk in België. Brussels, n.d.
    De verbaasde machinist, n.d.
    Een iegelijk, die den naam des Heeren zal aanroepen, zal zalig worden. Brussels, n.d.
    Er is niemand verstandig, er is niemand, die God zoekt. Brussels, n.d.
    Gelooft gij in droomen, n.d.
    God tevreden stellen kan een ander niet voor U doen. Brussels, n.d.
    Het Evangelie is de kracht Gods tot zaligheid. Brussels, n.d.
    Het schoone in den Bijbel, n.d.
    Hij had zijn moeder lief, n.d.
    Ik, eerste Persoon, n.d.
    Jezus Christus komt weder op de wolken des hemels. Brussels, n.d.
    Jezus Christus op aarde gekomen. Brussels, n.d.
    Jezus Christus opgestaan uit de dooden. Brussels, n.d.
    Jezus Christus voor U aan het kruis gestorven. Brussels, n.d.
    Jezus komt! Brussels, n.d.
    O alle gij dorstigen komt tot de wateren. Brussels, n.d.
    Redding en verlossing voor allen: De redding van den dood. Brussels, n.d.
    Redding en verlossing voor allen: De geheele wereld dood in zonden en misdaden. Brussels, n.d.
    Redding en verlossing voor allen: Gij moet gered worden van den Dood. Brussels, n.d.
    Twee Stierven voor mij. Brussels, n.d.
    Uit goeder trouw...maar toch bedrogen, n.d.
    Verzekerd om alle vlekken te verwijderen. Brussels, n.d.
    Voor uwe ziel zorgen kan geen mensch, maar alleen God. Brussels, n.d.

    Voorbij het reddings punt [sic]. Brussels, n.d.
    Zalig die hongeren en dorsten naar de gerechtigheid, want zij zullen verzadigd worden. Brussels, n.d.
Farr, F.W. *Dix raisons d'aimer son avènement*. Brussels: La Mission Belge Evangélique, n.d.
Flamment, J.-B. *Van het anarchisme naar het Evangelie*. Evangelisatie-Drukkerij. Brussels, n.d.
Franc, Jean. *Entre terrassiers*. Brussels: Mission Belge Evangélique, n.d.
    Le poids d'une âme. Brussels: Mission Belge Evangélique, n.d.
    Une 'Histoire à finir'. Brussels: La Mission Belge Evangélique, n.d.
Goodman, George. *Opgewekt uit de dooden*. Brussels: Evangelisatiewerk in België, n.d.
    Vivant d'entre les morts. London: Ralph and Edith Norton, 1918.
Gordon, A.J. *Sauvé en trois minutes*. Brussels: La Mission Belge Evangélique, n.d.
Gould-Shepard, H. *L'Eternel est mon berger*. Brussels: Mission Belge Evangélique, n.d.
    La gloire de Dieu et la dignité de l'homme. Brussels: Mission Belge Evangélique, n.d.
    La prophétie du Messie souffrances et mort. Brussels: Mission Belge Evangélique, n.d.
    Les beatitudes: sel et lumière: la loi et les prophètes. Brussels: Mission Belge Evangélique, n.d.
    Les Dix Commandements. Brussels: Mission Belge Evangélique, n.d.
    Un sauveur qui enlève les péchés. Brussels: Mission Belge Evangélique, n.d.
Hession, Roy and Revel. *Le chemin de la sainteté*. Liège: R Salsac, n.d.
Hitman, Thomas. *La conversion d'un communiste*. Brussels: La Mission Belge Evangélique, n.d.
I., W. *Au Congo*. Brussels: La Mission Belge Evangélique, n.d.
    Chez ces Protestants! Brussels: La Mission Belge Evangélique, n.d.
La Mission Belge Evangélique, *12 Grands Faits*. Brussels, n.d.
    Choses à Savoir. Brussels, n.d.
    Comment un assassin échappa à l'exécution capitale, n.d.
    Consolation illusoire. Brussels, n.d.
    De liefde des Vaders. Scripture Gift Mission. London, n.d.
    Een heerlyke [sic] roeping. Scripture Gift Mission. London, n.d.
    Een man die ryk [sic] werd. Scripture Gift Mission. London, n.d.
    Een vriend in nood. Scripture Gift Mission. London, n.d.
    Etes-vous sauvé? Oui? ou Non? Brussels, n.d.
    Heerlyke Vryheid [sic]. Scripture Gift Mission. London, n.d.
    Het Water des Levens. Scripture Gift Mission. London, n.d.
    Is de mensch laag gevallen? Scripture Gift Mission. London, n.d.
    La Mission Belge Evangélique. Castiaux. Brussels, 1920.
    Le démon de l'alcool. Brussels, n.d.
    Le Sabbat, est-il à observer aujourd'hui. Brussels, n.d.
    Le Sang du Christ. Brussels: La Mission Belge Evangélique, n.d.
    Le Spiritisme. Brussels, n.d.
    Mémento. Brussels, n.d.
    Qu'est-ce que la Reforme? Brussels, n.d.
    Une mort triomfante. Brussels, n.d.
    Une Réforme radicale. Brussels, n.d.
La Mission Evangéliqe Belge, *Et après?* Brussels, n.d.
    Faits que nous devons savoir et croire pour être sauvés. Brussels, n.d.
    Presque! Brussels, n.d.
Laidlaw, Robert. *De reden waarom*. Brussels: Evangelisatiewerk in België, n.d.
    Il perche'. Brussels: La Mission Belge Evangélique, n.d.
    La razón por qué. Brussels: La Mission Belge Evangélique, n.d.
L., R. *Le Pourquoi*. Brussels: Mission Belge Evangélique, n.d.
M., J.A. *De Mis en hare beteekenis: Een gesprek met een priester, bij het hoogaltaar van de R.K. Kathedraal van Westminster*. Brussels: Belgische Evangelische Zending, n.d.
Mapp, Henry. *De lievelings-brilslag*. Evangelisatie-Drukkerij. Brussels, n.d.
Mission Belge Evangélique, *Autours de la Messe*. Brussels, n.d.
    Aveugles, conducteurs d'aveugles. Brussels, n.d.
    De l'or et du pain. Brussels, n.d.
    Enlève toutes les taches! Garantie Absolue. Brussels, n.d.

Il a donné son fils. Brussels, n.d.
La réligion de nos pères. Brussels, n.d.
Le Chef africain. Brussels, n.d.
Le cinq de pique. Brussels, n.d.
Le frère Egidio, n.d.
Le petit Bohémien. Brussels, n.d.
Le remplaçant volontaire. Brussels., n.d.
Le soupir de la terre. Brussels, n.d.
Le trésor. Brussels, n.d.
Le vieux Jean est mort; Je suis le nouveau Jean. Brussels, 1922.
Les causes de la Réforme. Brussels, n.d.
Les Floralies. Brussels, 1923.
Les merveilles de Dieu dans une âme. Brussels, n.d.
Louve et louveteaux. Brussels, n.d.
Pour nous deux. Brussels, n.d.
Pourquoi Luther quitta-t-il l'Eglise de Rome? Brussels, n.d.
Pourquoi? Brussels, n.d.
Quand l'abeille piqua maman. Brussels, n.d.
Qui payera? Brussels, n.d.
Satisfait! Etes-vous? Brussels, n.d.
Sur le bateau. Brussels, n.d.
Tenez-vous là où le feu a passé. Brussels, n.d.
Tuer le temps. Brussels, n.d.
Un livre sans paroles. Brussels, n.d.
Un mot pour vous. Brussels, n.d.
Un point d'appui. Brussels, n.d.
Une bonne nouvelle. Brussels, n.d.

Mission Evangélique Belge, *L'espérance du chétien: "le Seigneur est proche."* Brussels, n.d.
Soyez prêts! "Car l'avénement du Seigneur est proche." Brussels, n.d.
Plus qu'un ami. Brussels, n.d.

N., R. *La Paysan et son Curé*. Brussels: La Mission Belge Evangélique, n.d.
Neusy, J. *La foi et l'assurance du salut*. Brussels: La Mission Evangélique Belge, n.d.
Norton, Edith F. *Rien que Lui...* Brussels: La Mission Belge Evangélique, n.d.
Norton, Ralph, and Edith F. Norton. *Qui est Jésus Christ et qu'est il vénu faire?* London, n.d.
O., J. *Tout pour rien*. Brussels: La Mission Belge Evangélique, n.d.
Une amitié rare. Brussels: La Mission Belge Evangélique, n.d.
P., F. *Un pas de plus et vous êtes perdus..!* Brussels: Mission Belge Evangélique, n.d.
Panton, D.M. *La Prière pour le retour du Seigneur*. Brussels: La Mission Belge Evangélique, n.d.
Ryle, J.C. *Etes-vous sur le bon chemin?* Brussels: Mission Belge Evangélique, n.d.
Saillens, R. *Les Fers qui tombent*. Brussels: Mission Belge Evangélique, n.d.
Sayles, Harold F. *La vérité en abrégé*. Translated by M B Parent. Brussels: La Mission Belge Evangélique, n.d.
Spurgeon, C.H. *Cette Nuit Mémorable*. Brussels: La Mission Belge Evangélique, 1922.
De Gedenkwaardige Nacht. Brussels: Evangelisatiewerk in België, n.d.
L'Histoire du Général. Translated by Chrispeels. [1920] Brussels: La Mission Belge Evangélique, n.d.
Trumbull, C G. *La Vie victorieuse*. Translated by Mme Contesse-Vernier. Brussels: La Mission Belge Evangélique, n.d.
Van W., J.-J. *Worden wij niet oud?* Brussels: Belgische Evangelische Zending, n.d.
W., M. *Le temps d'angoisse pour Jacob*. Brussels: Mission Evangélique Belge, n.d.
Wilson, Woodrow. *Ce que le Président des Etats-Unis pense de la Bible*. Brussels: La Mission Belge Evangélique, 1919.
Actes des Apôtres. Brussels: La Mission Belge Evangélique, 1930.
Brief van den Apostel Paulus aan de Romeinen. Brussels: Belgische Evangelische Zending, n.d.
Christ portant les pechés du peuple. Brussels: La Mission Belge Evangélique, n.d.
De Algemeene Brieven van den Apostel Petrus. Brussels: Belgian Gospel Mission, n.d.

Dieu a parlé. SGM. Brussels: La Mission Belge Evangélique, 1930.
Gaat de wereld vooruit? Brussels: Belgische Evangelische Zending, n.d.
Handelingen der Apostelen. SGM. Brussels: Belgische Evangelische Zending, n.d.
L'Epître aux Romains. Brussels: La Mission Belge Evangélique, n.d.
L'Evangile selon Saint Jean. SGM. Brussels: La Mission Belge Evangélique, 1930.
La mort du petit tambour. Brussels: La Mission Belge Evangélique, n.d.
Les Actes des Apôtres et les Epîtres de Saint Pierre. SGM. Brussels: Scripture Gift Mission, n.d.
Les Epîtes de Saint Pierr. Brussels: La Mission Belge Evangélique, n.d.
Maria, Moeder van Jezus. Brussels, n.d.
Réjouis-toi jeune homme! Bruyère, n.d.
Tu mourras certainement. Bruyère, n.d.
Un sûr chemin pour vous. SGM. Brussels: La Mission Belge Evangélique, n.d.
Wie kan vroolijk zijn? 1920th ed., n.d.
Ziet, Ik kom haastiglijk en mijn loon is met Mij, om een iegelijk te vergelden, gelijk Zijn loon zal zijn. Brussels, n.d.

APPENDIX 4: CHURCHES AND STATIONS FOUNDED BY THE BGM

Antwerp
Antwerp	1919-present
Boom	1938-1940
Hoboken	1922-1923
Kiel	1922
Schelle/Hemiksem	1937, 1944-present
Turnhout	1953-present
Willebroek	1928-present

Brabant
Anderlecht	1958-1962
Beaurieux	1938
Blanmont	1938
Bosvoorde	1952-1953
Bousval	1927
Brussels (Dutch)	1923-present
Brussels (French)	1919-present
Brussels (German)	1960
Couture Saint-Germain	1961
Gastuche	1957-1961
Halle	1936-1962
Herent	1922, 1924-1925
La Hulpe	1920-1922
Laeken	1932-1933
Lennik	1962
Leuven/Blauwput	1924-1948
Limal	1923
Limelette	1924
Ottignies	1937
Sart (Court-Saint-Etienne)	1922, 1925-1960
Sint-Pieters-Kapelle	1933
Stockel	1928-1937
Tienen	1934-1948
Uccle	1937
Villeroux	1933-1962
Woluwe	1952

East Flanders
Deinze	1936-1938
Eeklo	1921-1947, 1953-1962
Ghent (French)	1932
Ghent	1927-present
Ghent-Hoppestraat	1932-1933
Ghent-North	1932-1933
Hamme	1932, 1936-1938, 1953
Lembeke	1927
Lokeren	1923-1937
Maldegem	1937-1938
Moerbeke-Waas	1927- ?
Oudenaarde	1920-1921
Sint-Niklaas	1924-present
Wachtebeke	± 1938
Zele	1938-1940
Zelzate	1922-1925
Zinghem	1949

Hainaut
Antoing	1926-1932, 1936-1938
Ath	1922-1962
Basècles	1937-1938, 1953, 1958
Binche	1938-1940
Blaton	1923, 1927
Bracquegnies	1952-1955
Braine-le-Comte	1923-1962
Bray	1937, 1958-1962
Cambron-Casteau	1921-1927
Charleroi	1931-present
Châtelineau	1936-1962
Cuesmes	1920
Deux-Acren	1925-1955
Dottignies	1938, 1953
Dour	1921-1962
Elouges	1936-1937
Enghien	1926-1937
Florennes	1937-1938, 1953, 1958
Gilly	1939, 1960
Harchies	1927-1932, 1958-1962
Herseaux	1937-1948
La Chapelle St Pierre	1927-1937
La Croyère	1933, 1952-1953
La Louvière	1927-1962
La Ronce (Seneffe)	1931-1933
Leuze	1921-1932
Maffle	1925-1930
Manage	1924-1927
Marlière	1950
Maurage	1937-1938
Meslin-l'Evèque	1952-1953
Mont-a-Leux	1937
Montignies-sur-Roc	1956-1962
Montigny-sur-Sambre	1955-1958
Mouscron	1932-present
Naest	1931

Neufvilles	1936-1937, 194?
Ostiches	1933
Quevaucamps	1922
Quiévrain	1955-1962
Rebecq	1928-1929
Roisin	1922
Scoumont	1937-1940
Soignies	1923-1924, 1926-1962
Soleilmont	1960
Thulin	1934-1962
Tournai	1927-1962
Vaudignies	1937-1938
Vezon	1958
Warquignies	1921-1962
Wasmuel	1920
Wodecq	1954-1958

Liège
Ans	1949-1955
Beyne-Heusy	1927-1937
Engis	1952-1953
Fize-Fontaine	1931-1960
Hamoir	1929-1937
Hannut	1931-1932
Huy	1923-1962
Jehay Bodegnée	1948-1955
Lantin (Liège)	1934-1940
Les Gottes-Strée	1928-1932
Liège	1922-present
Miécret	1927-1945
Modave	1930
Ocquier	1928-1932
Point-du-Jour	1938
Quartier Robermont (Liège)	1936-1937
Saint-Léonard Liège	1926-1927
Saint-Nicolas	1931
Seraing	1927-1962
Stockay Saint-Georges	1927-1962
Val-Potet-Seraing	1953
Wandre	1926, 1953, 1960-1962

Limburg
Borgloon	1939-1962
Bree	1957, 1961-1962
Eisden	1952
Hasselt	1923-1937
Leopoldsburg/Beverlo	1937-1940
Mol	1953
Tongeren	1928-1962
Winterslag / Genk	1924-present

Luxembourg
Arlon	1930-present
Athus	1932-1962
Hollogne-sur-Marche	1952-1953
Neufchâteau	1954-1962

Saint Mard	1934-1962
Tintigny	1960

Namur
Andenne	1948
Auvelais	1937-1962
Buzet	1933
Ciney	1949-1962
Eghezée	1950
Fosse	1957
Hargimont	1931-1932
Jambes	1950
Jemelle	1925, 1937-1962
Maffle	1922
Marche-les-Dames	1927-1940
Noiseux	1948-1962
Saint-Hubert	1953-1954
Sarthe	1957
Verlaine	1931-1938

West Flanders
Adinkerke	1937-1952
Blankenberge	1920
Boezinge	1938
Bruges	1919-present
De Panne	1938-present
Eernegem	1960-2006
Gistel	1952-present
Heule	1938
Ichtegem	1928-present
Ieper	1921, 1945-1947
Ingelmunster	1938-1940
Izegem	1937-1940
Kachtem	1952-1953
Knokke-Heist	1937-1940, 1954
Koekelare	1933-present
Koksijde	1957-1961
Kortrijk	1923-present
Lombardsijde	1938-1940
Oostduinkerke	1939-1962?
Oostrozebeke	1922- present
Passendale	1920
Pervijze	1961
Poperinge	1925-present
Reninge	1953, 1957
Roeselare	1940
Sas-Slijkens (Ostend)	1920
Sint-Jan	1938-1940
Sint-Jans Kapelle (French Flanders)	1932
Steene	(1920) 1922-1925
Tielt	1927-1962
Vladsloo	1920
Vlamertinge	1932
Zeebrugge	1954
Zillebeke	1932
Zwevegem	1952

ABBREVIATIONS

AAMVR	Archives Van Roey
ABEM	Archives of the Belgian Evangelical Mission, Evadoc, Leuven
AC	Archives CEGESOMA
ACCC	American Council of Christian Churches
AECMB	Archives of the Église Chrétienne Missionnaire Belge
AEPA	Albert-Elisabeth Private Archives
AFCU	American Foreign Christian Union
AFPSFA	Archives FPS Foreign Affairs
AIBB	Archives Etudiants IBB 1919 - 1937
AJDPS	Archives of the Justice Department, section Public Safety
AJHS	Archives J.H. Scheps
AMCBC	Archives of the Methodist Church, Belgian Conference
APRT	Archives of Radio and Television Commissions of the Belgian Protestant Churches
AUPCB	Archives of the United Protestant Church of Belgium
AWT	Archives W. Teeuwissen
BASEC	British and Allied Soldiers Evangelistic Campaign
BBS	Belgian Bible Society BBS
BEJV	Belgisch Evangelisch Jeugd Verbond
BEM	Belgian Evangelical Mission
BFBS	British and Foreign Bible Society
BGM	Belgian Gospel Mission
BNO	Bonne Nouvelle par les Ondes
CAE	Committee of Evangelistic Activities
CAEC	Committee of Evangelistic Activities and Conference
CIM	China Inland Mission
CRB	Commission for Relief in Belgium
CUP	Comité d'Union Protestante
DGBP	Donald Grey Barnhouse Papers
EC	Executive Committee
ECMB	Église Chrétienne Missionnaire Belge
FCCC	Federal Council of Churches of Christ in America
ICCC	International Council of Christian Churches
IFMA	Interdenominational Foreign Mission Association
JWCP	John Wilbur Chapman Papers
MBI	Moody Bible Institute
NAE	National Association of Evangelicals
OAM	Open Air Mission
RE	Religious Education
REA	Records of the World Evangelical Alliance
RHKH	Records of the Howard Kelly Hospital
SGM	Scripture Gift Mission
SST	The Sunday School Times
SVM	Student Volunteer Movement
UBS	United Bible Societies
UCJG	Union Chrétienne de Jeunes Gens
UJEB	Union de la Jeunesse Evangélique Belge
UPCB	United Protestant Church of Belgium
UPECB	United Protestant Evangelical Church of Belgium
USC	United States Code
VEU	Vereeniging voor Evangelische Uitgaven
WCC	World Council of Churches
YMCA	Young Men's Christian Association
YWCA	Young Women's Christian Association

BIBLIOGRAPHY

Primary Sources

Archives
Amsterdam
   International Institute of Social History
      Archives J.H. Scheps (AJHS)
Baltimore, MD
   Johns Hopkins University
      Records of the Howard Kelly Hospital (RHKH) – Patient Records
Brussels
   Boudin-Willems Archives of the United Protestant Church in Belgium
      Archives of the Église Chrétienne Missionnaire Belge (AECBM)
      Archives of the Methodist Church, Belgian Conference (AMCBC)
      Archives of the United Protestant Church of Belgium (AUPCB)
      Archives of Radio and Television Commissions of the Belgian Protestant Churches (APRT)
   State Archives of Belgium – Archives of the Royal Palace
      Albert-Elisabeth Private Archives (AEPA)
   State Archives of Belgium
      Archives of the Justice Department, section Public Safety (AJDPS)
      Archives CEGESOMA (AC)
   Institut Biblique de Bruxelles
      Archives Etudiants IBB 1919 - 1937 (AIBB)
Leuven
   KADOC-KU Leuven, Evadoc Collection
      Archives of the Belgian Evangelical Mission (ABEM)
Mechelen
   Archives Archdiocese Mechelen
      Archives Van Roey (AAMVR)
Paris
   Archives W. Teeuwissen (AWT)
Philadelphia, PA
   Presbyterian Historical Society
      John Wilbur Chapman Papers (JWCP)
      Donald Grey Barnhouse Papers (DGBP)
Wheaton, IL
   Wheaton College, Evangelism and Mission Archives
      Records of the World Evangelical Alliance (REA)

Published Sources

1929 Yearbook of the International Bible Students Association with Daily Texts and Comments. Brooklyn, New York: International Bible Students Association, 1928.

Anet, Henri K. "Protestant Churches in Belgium; The Religious Conditions Under Military Rule." *Missionary Review of the World* 39 (1916): 33–37.

Anon. "The Battle Front." *Sunday School Times*, 1916.

Anon. "Untitled." *Sunday School Times*, 1915.

Asheville Citizen-Times. "American Evangelists Find Rockwell In French Hospital." December 4, 1915.

Bach, H. "The Soldiers' Foyers." *The American McAll Record*, 1917.

Barnhouse, Donald G. "Dynamiting Where Tyndale Was Burned." *Sunday School Times* 61, 1919.

Barnhouse, Donald G. "Training Belgians for Congo Missions." *Sunday School Times*, 1920

Barnhouse, Donald G. "The Times of the Gentiles and the War in the Light of Prophecy." *Christian Workers Magazine*, May 1916.

Blackstone, William E. *Jezus komt.* Brussels: Evangelisatiewerk in België, 1923.
Blommaert, M.E. "Our Work In Dunkirk." *Protestant Alliance Magazine*, 1916.
Bolomey, H.A. "Through Belgium in a Gospel Motor Car." *Sunday School Times*, 1925.
Boyd, Eleanor H. "The Bible Conference at Eagles Mere, Pa." *Christian Workers Magazine*, 1918.
British and Foreign Bible Society. *Hundred and Thirty-First Report of the British and Foreign Bible Society for the Year Ending March MCMXXXV*. London: The Bible House, 1935.
Buunk, H. "Post Deynze." *Onze Hoop*, 1 August 1938, sec. Uit den arbeid.
Buunk, H.S. "Herinneringen aan Ralph Norton; Bij het 30-jarig bestaan der Belgische Evangelische Zending." *De Kruisbanier, Algemeen Evangelisch Weekblad*, 1 January 1949.
Buunk, H.S. "Petegem – Deinze." *Onze Hoop*, 1 September 1939, sec. Uit den arbeid.

Chants joyeux: Recueil de cantiques pour cultes, réunions d'évangélisation, de sanctification, missions, écoles du dimanche, etc. Bureau du Réveil, 1933.
Committee for Christian Relief in France and Belgium. *An Interchurch Campaign for Protestant Relief in France and Belgium*, n.d.
Cosandey, Ulysse. *L'armée du Salut aux pays latins*. Paris: Schaeler, 1904.

De Belgische Boodschapper. "Uit het Vlaamsche land." March 1921.
De Kruisbanier. "'De Kruisbanier' doorheen 1945." 29 December 1945.
De Meyer, Des. "Deze zomer in Schelle een evangelische kerk?" *Onze Hoop* 1 May 1947, sec Uit den arbeid.
De Schepper, L.F.P. "Onze eerste reis met de Evangelisatie-automobiel." *Christelijk Volksblad*, 29 July 1922.
Dubois, S. "Bezoekt de samenkomsten." *Onze Hoop*, 1 August 1937, sec. Uit den arbeid.

Editorial. "The Heart of the Belgian Soldier." *Sunday School Times*, 1916.

Fox Norton, Edith. "A Glimpse of the Norton's at Work; Mrs. Norton Throws Open the Office Door at N° 15 Strand, and Reads a Batch of Love Letters." *Sunday School Times*, 1917.
Fox Norton, Edith. "After the War in Belgium – What?" *Missionary Review of the World*, 1918.
Fox Norton, Edith. "Christmas in the Belgian Trenches." *Sunday School Times*, 1916.
Fox Norton, Edith. "God's Hand in a Perplexing Hold-Up." *Sunday School Times*, 1917.
Fox Norton, Edith. "Our Three Weeks in Paris." *Sunday School Times*, 1916.
Fox Norton, Edith. "Taking Jesus in His Fullness." In *The Board of Managers of Princeton Conference. Victory in Christ, A Report of Princeton Conference 1916*, 226–233. [Philadelphia]: Board of Managers of Princeton Conference, 1916.
Fox Norton, Edith. "The Soldiers' Christmas in Belgian Trenches." *Sunday School Times*, 1917.
Fox Norton, Edith. "When We Actually Started for the Front; Would We Get to See Peter and the Belgian Queen?" *Sunday School Times*, 1916.

Gautier, Aloïs. "Un fait grave." *Le Chrétien Belge, revue religieuse* 66, no. 4.
Griffith Thomas, Rev. W.H. "Speaking 'by Interruption' in Belgium." *Sunday School Times*, 1922.
Grandjean, J. "La retraite spirituelle de Chexbres, du 3 au 8 may 1926." *Notre Espérance*, June 1926, 2 (6), sec. Le trait d'union.

Haesevoets, X. "Evangelisatie-Kruistocht te Luik met het team Eric Hutchings." *Onze Hoop*, 1 February 1959, sec. Uit den arbeid.
Hepp, V. "Synode – Indrukken." *De Reformatie*, 2 November 1923.
Het Zoeklicht. "Evangelisatie in België." 1920.
Het Zoeklicht. "Tijdspiegel." 1921.
Hopkins, Elsie M. "How God's Word Grows and Prevails in Belgium." *Sunday School Times*, 1923.
Hopkins, Paul. "What made the man?" in *Eternity, Memorial Issue*, March 1971.
Howard, Philip E. *A New Invasion of Belgium.* Philadelphia, PA: Sunday School Times Company, 1924.
Howard, Philip E. "Taking Bread to Belgium -Two Kinds; How the Nortons' Work Is Expanding since the Armistice." *Sunday School Times* 1919.

Institut national de statistique (Belgium), ed. *Annuaire statistique de la Belgique et du Congo belge*. Brussels: Imprimerie A. Lesigne, 1925.
Institut national de statistique (Belgium), ed. *Annuaire statistique de la Belgique et du Congo belge*. Brussels: Imprimerie A. Lesigne, 1926.
Institut national de statistique (Belgium), ed. *Annuaire statistique de la Belgique et du Congo belge*. Brussels: Imprimerie A. Lesigne, 1927.

Institut national de statistique (Belgium), ed. *Annuaire statistique de la Belgique et du Congo belge*. Brussels: Imprimerie A. Lesigne, 1928.

Inwood, Charles. "Making Christ Known in Needy Belgium." *Sunday School Times*, 1923.

'Jeruël' : (officieel orgaan der) stadsevangelisatie Jeruël te Rotterdam. Rotterdam, 1906.

Journal Militaire Officiel. Vol. 2. Brussels: Demanet, 1916.

Kennedy Maclean, J. "A Week of Wonderful Blessing, The Chapman-Alexander Mission at the Metropolitan Tabernacle and Some of Its Fruits." *Life of Faith*, October 21, 1914.

Kennedy Maclean, J. *Apostles of the Belgian Trenches*. London: Marshall Brothers, 1917.

Kennedy Maclean, J., and T. Wilkinson Riddle. *The Y.M.C.A. with the Colours: A Stirring Chapter in the History of a Great Christian Enterprise*. London: Marshall Brothers, 1914.

La Mission Belge Evangélique. *La Mission Belge Evangélique*. Castiaux. Brussels, 1920.

Lagrange, Ch. *Leçons sur la parole de Dieu : Précédées d'une lettre à S.M. Albert, roi des belges*. 2md éd. Bruxelles: Office de publicité, 1910.

McQuilkin, Robert C. *Gospel Heroes of the Belgian Trenches, How Two Young Americans Reached the Heart of the Belgian Soldier*, 1915.

Ministerie van Binnenlandsche Zaken. Koninklijk besluit betreffende de samenscholingen in open lucht, Belgisch Staatsblad § (1940).

Monsma, J.A. "Boekaankondiging: Moeten of mogen wij onze kindertjes laten dopen?" *Onze Hoop*, August 1931, 7 (15).

Mott, John R. *The Evangelization of the World in This Generation*. New York: Student Volunteer Movement for Foreign Missions, 1900.

Mott, John R. *The World-Interest in the Evangelization of France; Address at the 31st Annual Meeting of the American McAll Association at Buffalo, N.Y., April 28, 1914*. [Philadelphia]: [American McAll Association], 1914.

Na zeven jaren 1919 - 1926: beknopt overzicht van het ontstaan en den arbeid der Belgische Evangelische Zending. Brussels: Belgische Evangelische Zending, 1926.

Norton, Edith. *Ralph Norton and the Belgian Gospel Mission*. New York: Revell, 1935.

Norton, Edith F. "A Gospel Booth at a Belgian Exposition; Distributing Scriptures at a Great National Celebration." *Sunday School Times*, 1930.

Norton, Edith F. "A Place Where His Honor May Dwell." *Sunday School Times*, 1924.

Norton, Edith F. "Could the Belgians Support Our Mission? What Are the Salaries, Living Expenses and Offerings of Our Belgian Church Members?" *Sunday School Times*, 1929.

Norton, Edith F. "Counting Blessings in Belgium." *Sunday School Times*, 1925.

Norton, Edith F. "Exploring for Gospel Centers in the Belgian Ardennes; A Tour through Two Provinces by the Versailles Treaty." *Sunday School Times*, 1930.

Norton, Edith F. "Finding Peace in a Belgian Gospel Tent; When Life Really Began for a Lawless Young Man Headed for the Rocks of Spiritism." *Sunday School Times*, 1927.

Norton, Edith F. "Preaching Under Difficulties in Belgium." *Sunday School Times*, 1926.

Norton, Edith F. "Sunshine and Shadow in Belgium; As the Glorious Light of the Gospel Shines into Darkened and Troubled Hearts." *Sunday School Times*, 1927.

Norton, Edith F. "Treasure Seeking in Belgium." *Sunday School Times*, 1924.

Norton, Edith Fox. "Annexing the Fifth Division of the Belgian Army; Mrs. Norton's Diary Records the Personal Presentation of 1500 'Christmas' Boxes on Washington's Birthday." *Sunday School Times*, 1918.

Norton, Edith F. "Satan Sifts a Soldier in Two Warfares." *Sunday School Times*, 2 May 1918.

Norton, Edith F. "Spending Easter Under Shell Fire at the Front; As Belgian Soldiers Testify What the Resurrection Means to Them." *Sunday School Times*, 1918.

Norton, Edith F. "Under Fire with Belgium's Queen; Queen Elisabeth a Lady Americans Would Love." *Sunday School Times*, 1918.

Norton, Edith F. "When Service Adjourned to the Wine-Cellar!" *Sunday School Times*, 1918.

Norton, Edith F. "When the Postman Appears at the Belgian Front." *Sunday School Times*, 1917.

Norton, Mrs. Edith C. "The Nortons' Work in Belgium." *Christian Workers Magazine*, July 1919.

Norton, Mrs. Ralph C. "A Macedonian Cry from Belgian Cities; Buildings Needed for New Centers of Evangelization." *Sunday School Times*, 1922.

Norton, Mrs. Ralph C. "An Old-Fashioned Revival in Belgium's Capital; How it was advertised, who came, and what they heard." *Sunday School Times*, 1920.

Norton, Mrs. Ralph C. "Another Milestone in Belgian Evangelization, Reporting in Detail How God Has Led, and Provided." *Sunday School Times*, 1920.

Norton, Mrs. Ralph C. "Christmas with the Belgian Soldiers." *Christian Workers Magazine*, n.d.

Norton, Mrs. Ralph C. "Diplomas for Six Belgian Students; Graduating the First Class from the Bible School." *Sunday School Times*, 1921.

Norton, Mrs. Ralph C. "Evangelizing the Belgian Soldiers." *Missionary Review of the World* 40 (1917): 33–37.

Norton, Mrs. Ralph C. "How I Met Aline D'Amour of Poperinghe; Who Is No Longer Afraid of Her Testament." *Sunday School Times*, 1921.

Norton, Mrs. Ralph C. "Peter's Bold Plan to Evangelize Belgium's Army; A League for Christ in the Trenches of Death." *Sunday School Times*, 1916.

Norton, Mrs. Ralph C. "Recruiting for Apostles of the Trenches; What the Newly Commissioned 'Apostles' Do When They Return to the Front." *Sunday School Times*, 1915.

Norton, Mrs. Ralph C. "That First Sunday Service in Belgium." *Sunday School Times*, 1919.

Norton, Mrs. Ralph C. "The Apostles of the Trenches at the Belgian Front; Peter and Pierre and Jospeh Knocking at Our Door for More Testaments and Gospels." *Sunday School Times*, 1916.

Norton, Mrs. Ralph C. "The Gospel as Belgium's Hope." *Life of Faith*, 1917.

Norton, Mrs. Ralph C. "The Heart of the Belgian Soldier." In *The Board of Managers of Princeton Conference. Victory in Christ, A Report of Princeton Conference 1916*, 226. [Philadelphia]: Board of Managers of Princeton Conference, 1916.

Norton, Mrs. Ralph C. "Three Rings at the Convent Door-Bell." *Sunday School Times*, 1924.

Norton, Mrs. Ralph C. "What the Little Belgian Soldier Told Us; And What He Took Back to the Trenches." *Sunday School Times*, 1915.

Norton, Mrs. Ralph C. "When Belgians Said 'Thank You' for Gift Boxes, A Hunger for God's Word Followed War-Created Famine." *Sunday School Times*, 1919.

Norton, Mrs. Ralph C. "When I Followed Europe's Finest Orator!'." *Sunday School Times*, 1918.

Norton, Mrs. Ralph C. "When I Told the Belgian Queen a Story." *Sunday School Times*, 3 May, 1919.

Norton, Mrs. Ralph C. "When New Shoes Bring Rapture." *Sunday School Times*, 1919.

Norton, Mrs. Ralph C. "When We Dedicated the New Headquarters." *Sunday School Times*, 1927.

Norton, Mrs. Ralph C. "Why Jeanne's Face Shone on Christmas Night." *Sunday School Times*, 1919.

Norton, Mrs. Ralph C. "Why We Are Going Back to England and France; Some Reasons Why a Young American Couple, Representing The Sunday School Times, Are Giving Their Lives to Service among the Soldiers." *Sunday School Times*, 1915.

Norton, Ralph C. "Dreigende rampen." *Onze Hoop*, June 1930.

Norton, Ralph C. "Europe's Impending Disaster." *Sunday School Times*, 1930.

Norton, Ralph C. "Incidents and Experiences." In *Winona Echoes Notable Addresses Delivered at the Twenty-Second Annual Bible Conference*, 136–149. Winona Lake, Indiana: Winona Publishing Society, 1916.

Norton, Ralph C. "Is Belgium the Key to Europe's Evangelization?" *Sunday School Times*, 1924.

Norton, Ralph C. "Norton's Work in Belgium." *Christian Workers Magazine*, May 1920.

Norton, Ralph C. "Taking Soldiers Alive for Christ," In Victory in Christ. *A Report of Princeton Conference 1916*. [Philadelphia]: Board of Managers of Princeton Conference, 1916.

Norton, Ralph C. "Waarom wij naar Amerika gaan." *Onze Hoop*, 1 January 1930, 6 (2).

Norton, Ralph C. "What Hath God Wrought in Belgium?, Five Years of Miracles in the Face of Seeming Impossibilities." *Sunday School Times*, 1924.

Norton, Ralph C. and Edith F. "A Personal Interview with Mussolini; Fascism, the Bible, and the Cross." *Sunday School Times*, 1932.

Norton, Ralph C. and Edith F. "Annonces." 1 November 1926, 2 (22).

Norton, Ralph C. and Edith F. "En Suisse." 1 May 1926, 2 (9), sec. Le trait d'union 2 (5).

Norton, Ralph C. and Edith F. "Frappants exaucements de prière en 1924," 1 April 1925, sec. Le trait d'union, 2.

Norton, Ralph C. and Edith F. "La fête du 15 Août." 1 September 1929, sec. Le trait d'union, 1.

Norton, Ralph C. and Edith F. "Le Moody du Japon," 15 November 1925, 1 (23).

Norton, Ralph C. and Edith F. "Les débuts de notre Mission (suite)." March 1925, sec. Le trait d'union.

Norton, Ralph C. and Edith F. "Notes - Personalia, Etc." June 1926, 2 (11), sec. Le trait d'union 2 (6).

Norton, Ralph C. and Edith F. "Notre Institut Biblique Français." 1929, sec. Le trait d'union.

Norton, Ralph C. and Edith F. "Sujet général des Conférences." October 1925.

Norton, Ralph C. and Edith F. "Untitled." October 1925.

Norton, Ralph C. and Edith F. "Visite de 'l'Open air mission.'" June 1925, sec. Le trait d'union.

Norton, Ralph C. and Edith F. "Visite du Colonel Fermaud." 1 February 1926.

Notre Espérance. "Annonces." 1 October 1926, 2 (20).

Ons Heidewerk; Maandblad der Vereeniging Nederlandsche Landkolonisatie en inwendige zending. "Jaarverslag." November 1917.

Onze Hoop. "Bijzonder week-end in de Bethelkerk." February 1957, sec. Uit onze zending.

Onze Hoop. "Comité tot hulp aan Protestantsche vluchtelingen." 1 February 1939, sec. Uit den arbeid.

Onze Hoop. "De Tentcampagne, Tentcampagne te Mariakerke Gent." 1 August 1939, sec. Uit den arbeid.

Onze Hoop. "Dr. Pettingill te Brussel." 1 November 1938, sec. Uit den arbeid.

Onze Hoop. "Een ernstige mededeeling aan Gods kinderen in en buiten België. Een stroom van gebeden en gaven noodig om voort te kunnen gaan." 1 October 1930, 6 (20).

Onze Hoop. "Evangelisatie-arbeid in Heyst." 1 June 1938, sec. Uit den arbeid.

Onze Hoop. "Gebedsverhooring." 1 March 1925.

Onze Hoop. "Het Belgisch Evangelisch Jeugd Verbond." July 1936, 12 (13), sec. Uit den arbeid.

Onze Hoop. "Het Bijbelinstituut der Belgische Evangelische Zending." March 1927, 3 (5), sec. Berichten uit het hoofdkwartier voor de werkers en vrienden 3 (3).

Onze Hoop. "Het jeugdkamp in Genk." September 1935, 11 (17), sec. Uit den arbeid.

Onze Hoop. "Inwijding eener zaal te Gilly." 1 October 1938, sec. Uit den arbeid.

Onze Hoop. "Is dit werk waard om gedaan te worden? Is het uw gebed en steun waard? Rapport over den arbeid van de evangelisatie-auto Nr. 1 van 9 juli tot 10 september 1926." November 1, 1926, 2 (21), sec. Berichten uit het hoofdkwartier voor de werkers en vrienden 2 (11).

Onze Hoop. "Maldegem." 1 March 1938, sec. Uit den arbeid.

Onze Hoop. "Met de tent door het land." October 1925, sec. Onder ons.

Onze Hoop. "Naklanken van onze jeugddag te Brussel." September 1928, 4 (17), sec. Berichten uit het hoofdkwartier voor de werkers en vrienden 4 (9).

Onze Hoop. "Nieuws uit den Arbeid." 1 October 1939,

Onze Hoop. "Nieuws uit den Arbeid – Van een doopfeest en nog wat." 5, no. 13 (1929)

Onze Hoop. "Nieuws uit onze posten." 1 May 1929, 5 (10).

Onze Hoop. "Nieuws van onze Posten." 1 January 1928, 4 (1), sec. Berichten uit het hoofdkwartier voor de werkers en vrienden 4 (1).

Onze Hoop. "Nieuwtjes uit de Zending," October 1925, sec. Onder ons.

Onze Hoop. "Nieuwtjes uit de Zending." December 1925, sec. Onder ons.

Onze Hoop. "Onze Zending op de wereldtentoonstelling te Luik." May 1930, 6 (9).

Onze Hoop. "Personalia." April 1926, 2 (7), sec. Onder ons.

Onze Hoop. "Personalia." 1 July 1937, sec. Onder ons.

Onze Hoop. "Personeel en posten van de Belgische Evangelische Zending." 1 December 1938.

Onze Hoop. "Tentcampagne te Moeskroen." 1 July 1938, sec. Uit den arbeid.

Onze Hoop. "Voor onze Belgische geloovigen." January 1936, 12 (1), sec. Uit den arbeid.

Onze Hoop. "Zendingsberichten." 1927, 3 (13), sec. Berichten uit het Hoofdkwartier voor de werkers en vrienden 3 (7).

Popular Science. "Carrying the Gospel by Motor." June 1920.

Postma, W. "Eeclo." *Onze Hoop*, 1 October 1937, sec. Uit den arbeid.

Potma, C.T. "Revival in Belgium." *Pentecostal Evangel*, May 28, 1921.

Putnam, C.E. "Missionary Alliance Conference." *Christian Workers Magazine*, 1918.

Report of the First International Convention of the Student Volunteer Movement for Foreign Missions, Held at Cleveland, Ohio, U.S.A., February 26,27,28, and March 1, 1891. Boston, MS: T.O. Metcalf & Co, 1891.

Salvation Army. *The Salvation Army Yearbook*. London, 1929.

Secretary of the Methodist Episcopal Church, ed. *Minutes of the Fifty-Sixth Session of the North Indiana Annual Conference of the Methodist Episcopal Church Held at Decatur, Indiana, April 5-10, 1899*. Richmond, IN: Nicholsen Printing & MFG. Co., 1899.

Servaas Sr., J. "De Evangeliewagen." *Onze Hoop*, 1 July 1937, sec. Uit den arbeid.

Seymour Houghton, Louise. *Handbook of French and Belgian Protestantism*. New York: Mission Education Movement, 1919.

Smith, Florence E. "Colombia." In *The Student Missionary Appeal; Addresses at the Third International Convention of the Student Volunteer Movement for Foreign Missions*, 281–82. New York: Student Volunteer Movement for Foreign Missions, 1898.

Speer, Robert E. *South American Problems*. New York: Student Volunteer Movement for Foreign Missions, 1921.

Students and the Missionary Problem. Addresses Delivered at the International Student Missionary Conference, London, January 2-6, 1900. London: The Conference, 1900.

Student's Hand-Book 1892-1893. Greencastle, IN: Beckett, 1892.

Student's Hand-Book 1894-1895. Greencastle, IN: Beckett, 1894.

Student's Hand-Book 1895-1896. Greencastle, IN: Beckett, 1895.

Sunday School Times. "Editorial." April 1917.

The Alliance Weekly: a Journal of Christian Life and Mission. Dr. W. Leon Tucker." 30 June 1934.

The American McAll Record. "Echoes from Our Relief Work." 1917.

The American McAll Record. "Editorial." 1916.

The Atlanta Constitution. "Bravery of Atlanta Boys In French Foreign Legion Is Told of by Evangelists." 17 February 1915.

The Keswick Convention 1931. London, Glasgow: Pickering & Inglis, 1931.

The Master and The Multitude. "Wonderful Meetings in Brussels with Our Gospel Motor Wagon (From France)." October 1925.

The New York Times. "Peace Note of Germany and Her Allies." December 12, 1916." 13 December 1916.

"The Nortons in Brussels, Belgium." *Christian Workers Magazine* XX. December 1919.

The Palm Beach Post. "Evangelist Touring Country Travels in Unique Auto." 6 January 1921.

The Pittsburgh Gazette Times. "The Rev. Dr. Hugh Black, of New York, Is Here for Church Conference." 5 February 1916.

Sunday School Times. "When 10,000 Soldiers Got Their Christmas Boxes." 1917.

Sword and Trowel. "Good Work Among The Belgian Soldiers." 1918.

Two of the Workers. "Another Year in Belgium's Evangelization; From Two Stations to Twelve, and from Ten Workers to Twenty-Five." *Sunday School Times*, 1921.

Vail, William H. "The Five Points of Calvinism Historically Considered." *New Outlook* 104 (August 1913).

Valeton Jr., J.J.P. *N. de Jonge in zijn leven en werken*. Brussels: Evangelisatie-Drukkerij, 1899.

Van Belleghem, J.C. "Brugge op 4 mei." *Christelijk Volksblad* 54, no. 48 (1925): 3–4.

Van Dam, J. "Het Belgisch Evangelisch Jeugdverbond, ons Kamp te Limauges." *De Kruisbanier*, 21 July 1945.

Van Dam, J. "Verslag der tentcampagne te Boom." *Onze Hoop*, 1 September 1938, sec. Uit den arbeid.

Van de Riet, G. "Bijzondere samenkomsten in Genk 2 en 3 febr. 1936." *Onze Hoop*, April 1936, 12 (7), sec. Uit den arbeid.

Van de Riet, G. "Toen ons B.E.J.V. er nog niet was … (3)." *Jeugd*, 31 May 1965.

Van Lierop, B. "Marktevangelisatie." *Onze Hoop*, 1 June 1938, sec. Uit den arbeid.

Van Lierop, J.B.H. "De geschiedenis van ons gebouw te Gent." *Onze Hoop*, April 1928, 4 (7), sec. Berichten uit het hoofdkwartier voor de werkers en vrienden.

Van Lierop, J.B.H. "Tentvergaderingen te Gent." *Onze Hoop*, 1 September 1937, sec. Uit den arbeid.

Van Puffelen, A. "Jaarvergadering der jonge jeugdvereeniging 'Eben-Haezer' te Brussel." *Onze Hoop*, 1 March 1932, 8 (6).

Vandervelde, Lalla Speyer. *Monarchs and Millionaires*. New York: Adelphi Co, 1925.

Vansteenberghe, O. "Herinneringen VII." June 1961, sec. Bijblad, 3.

Vansteenberghe, O. *The Last Night: Triumph in the Face of Death*. Philadelphia, PA: Belgian Gospel Mission, n.d.

Victorious Life Conference, ed. *The Victorious Life, Messages From The Summer Conferences At Whittier, California, June; Princeton, New Jersey, July; Cedar Lake, Indiana, August; Including Also Some Messages From The 1917 Conference At Princeton And Other Material*. Philadelphia, PA: Board of managers of Victorious Life Conference, 1918.

Visée, W. "Tienen." May 1936, sec. Uit den arbeid, 2-3.

Watch Tower Bible and Tract Society. *1958 Yearbook of Jehovah's Witnesses*. Brooklyn, NY: Watch Tower Bible and Tract Society, 1957.

Weik, Jesse W., ed. *Alumnal Record DePauw University*. Greencastle, IN: DePauw University, 1915.

Whitson, Rolland Lewis, ed. *Centennial History of Grant County, Indiana, 1812 to 1912*. Vol. 2. Chicago, New York: Lewis Publishing Company, 1914.

Winckel, "Buitenland." *De Heraut*, 28 November 1920.

Winston, J.C. "The Religious Situation in Europe and Belgium To-Day, (A Radio Address Recently given by J.C. Winston, Co-Director of the Belgian Mission While in U.S.A.)." *The Fundamentalist*, 2 August 1937.

Yale Daily News. "Final Meetings of Convention; Important Speakers to Address Last Sessions of Religious Education Association." New Haven, CT, 7 March 1914.

"You Will Believe in This New Invasion of a Waiting Belgium," *Sunday School Times*, 1918.

Young Men's Christian Association of Minneapolis. *Religious Work Announcement, Season 1904-1905*, 1904.

Secondary Sources

Published Sources

Alexander, Helen C., J. Kennedy Maclean, *Charles M. Alexander, A Romance of Song and Soul-Winning*. London: Marshall Brothers Ltd, 1920.

Allison, Neil E. "Free Church Revivalism in the British Army during the First World War." In *The Clergy in Khaki; New Perspectives on British Army Chaplaincy in the First World War*, 41-55. Ashgate Studies in First World War History. London: Routledge, 2013.

"Associated Gospel Churches." In *Melton's Encyclopedia of American Religions*, 8th ed., 559. Detroit, MI: Gale Cengage Learning, 2009.

Austin, Alvyn J. "Blessed Adversity: Henry W. Frost and the China Inland Mission." In *Earthen Vessels: American Evangelicals and Foreign Missions*, 47-70. Grand Rapids, MI: Eerdmans, 1990.

Austin, Alvyn J. "No Solicitation: The China Inland Mission and Money." In *More Money, More Ministry: Money and Evangelicals in Recent North Amerikan History*, 207–234. Grand Rapids, MI: Eerdmans, 2000.

Baker, W.H. "Dispensation, Dispensationalism." In *Evangelical Dictionary of Biblical Theology*, 1217-1218. Grand Rapids, Carlisle, Cumbria: Baker Books, Paternoster Press, 1996.

Balmer, Randall. "American Fundamentalism: The Ideal of Femininity." In *Fundamentalism & Gender*. Oxford: Oxford University Press, 1994.

Bangura, Joseph Bosco. "A New Kind of Ministry for a New Kind of Context: The Rise of New Indigenous Churches in West Africa." In *Global Pentecostal Movements: Migration, Mission and Public Religion*, edited by Michael Wilkinson, 154-169. International Studies in Religion and Society 14. Leiden; Boston: Brill, 2017.

Bangura, Joseph Bosco. "African Christian Churches in Flanders, Belgium: People, Practices and Problems." In *Globale Christentümer*, edited by Bernhard Grümme, Claudia Jahnel, Martin Radermacher, Claudia Rammelt, Jens Schlamelcher, Mihail Comanoio, Roland Spliesgart, et al., 89–106. Brill | Schöningh, 2022.

Bangura, Joseph Bosco. "African Pentecostalism and Mediatised Self-Branding in Catholic (Flanders) Belgium." *Journal of Religion in Africa* 48, no. 3 (December 5, 2018): 297-307.

Bangura, Joseph Bosco. "Reverse Mission? *Missio Dei* and the Spread of African Pentecostalism in the West." Ecclesiology 16, no. 3 (2020): 379-499.

Barabas, Steven. *So Great Salvation: The History and Message of the Keswick Convention*. Eugene, OR: Wipf & Stock, 2005.

Baré, Sophie. *Het Wit-Gele Kruis 1937 – 2007, 70 Jaar thuis in verpleging aan huis*. Leuven: Kadoc KU Leuven, 2007.

Barton, Peter, Willem van Paassen, and Stan Verschuuren. *De slagvelden van Wereldoorlog I: van de eerste Slag om Ieper tot Passendale*. Tielt: Lannoo, 2005.

Bassett, Paul Merritt. "The Theological Identity of the North American Holiness Movement." In *The Variety of American Evangelicalism*, 72–108. Knoxville, TN: University of Tennessee Press, 1991.

Bebbington, D. *Evangelicalism in Modern Britain : A History from the 1730s to the 1980s*. Grand Rapids, MI: Baker Book House, 1989.

Bebbington, David, and David Ceri Jones. "Introduction." In *Evangelicalism and Fundamentalism in the United Kingdom during the Twentieth Century*, 1-12. Oxford: Oxford University Press, 2013.

Becker, Annette. *La guerre et la foi: de la mort à la mémoire, 1914-1930*. Une histoire contemporaine. Paris: A. Colin, 1994.

Belgia 2000, De complete geschiedenis van België. "Het ontwaken van het protestantisme in het Koninkrijk België (1830-1980)." March 1984.

Bendroth, Margaret L. "Fundamentalism." In *Encyclopedia of Women and Religion in North America*, 1:439-446. Bloomington: Indiana University Press, 2006.

Bendroth, Margaret L. "Fundamentalism and Femininity: Points of Encounter between Religious Conservatives and Women, 1919-1935." *Church History* 61, no. 2 (1992): 221-233.

Bernardo y Garcia, Luis Angel. *Le ventre des Belges: une histoire alimentaire des temps d'occupation et de sortie de guerre (1914-1921 & 1939-1948)*. Studies in Belgian history 4. Bruxelles: Archives générales du Royaume et Archives de l'État dans les Provinces, 2017.

Blocher, Jacques Emile. "Tel père, quelle fille? Un cas de succession pastorale à l'Eglise du Tabernacle." *Théologie Évangélique* 9, no. 2 (2010): 173-189.

Blocher-Saillens, Madeleine, and Jacques Blocher. *Madeleine Blocher-Saillens, féministe et fondamentaliste*. Collection d'Etudes sur le Protestantisme Évangélique. Paris: Excelsis, 2014.

Blom, J.C.H., E. Lamberts, and Ludo Milis. *Geschiedenis van de Nederlanden*. Amsterdam: Prometheus, Bert Bakker, 2014.

Boniface, Xavier. *Histoire religieuse de la Grande Guerre*. Paris: Fayard Editions, 2014.

Boudin, H.R. "1919 De Opperaalmoezenier van de Protestantse Eredienst Pierre Blommaert in opdracht in de Verenigde Staten van Amerika." In *Belgische Protestantse Biografieën*, BIO-Blom 1-32. Brussels: Prodoc, 2003.

Boudin, H.R. "De betrekkingen tussen dr. Charles Stedman MACFARLAND secretaris-generaal van de Federal Council of Christ in America en het Belgisch protestantisme." In *Belgische Protestantse Biografieën*, Mac Far1-29. BIO. Brussels, 2003.

Boudin, H.R. "Galet, Emile (1870-1940)." In *Van Leopold I tot Jean Rey; De protestanten in België van 1839 tot 1989*, 51. Brussels: Universitaire Faculteit voor Protestantse Godgeleerdheid, 1990.

Boudin, H.R. *La croix et la bannière; Les protestants et les anglicans en Belgique face à l'occupation 1940 - 1944*. Brussel: Prodoc-Promu, 2012.

Boudin, H.R. "Lesaffre, André Jules Paul (1882-1982)." In *Van Leopold I tot Jean Rey; De protestanten in België van 1839 tot 1989*, 51. Brussels: Universitaire Faculteit voor Protestantse Godgeleerdheid, 1990.

Boudin, H.R. "Protestantse burger en legeraalmoezeniers ten dienste van Belgische militairen, krijgsgevangenen en geïnterneerden tijdens de wereldoorlog 1914-1918." In *Belgische Protestantse Biografieën*, 50. L–21. Brussel: Prodoc, 1990.

Boyer, Paul S. *When Time Shall Be No More: Prophecy Belief in Modern American Culture*, Studies in Cultural History. Cambridge, MS: Belknap Press of Harvard University Press, 1992.

Braekman, Emile M., S. Simons (transl.), and F. Van den Neste (transl.). "150 jaar protestants leven in België." *Bulletin de la Société de l'Histoire du Protestantisme Belge* IX, no. 1 (1981): 2-20.

Braekman, E.M. *Histoire du Protestantisme en Belgique au XIXme siècle. Première partie - 1795-1865*. Histoire du Protestantisme en Belgique et au Congo belge 3. Flavion-Florennes: Le Phare, 1988.

Brereton, Virginia Lieson. *Training God's Army: The American Bible School, 1880-1940*. Bloomington, IN: Indiana University Press, 1990.

Broomhall, Marshall. *The Jubilee Story of the China Inland Mission*. London, Philadelphia, PA: Morgan & Scott, China Inland Mission, 1915.

Bundy, David. *Keswick: A Bibliographic Introduction to the Higher Life Movements*. Wilmore, KY: Asbury Theological Seminary, 1975.

Buyst, Eric. "De economische balans van de Eerste Wereldoorlog." In *De Groote Oorlog voorbij; België 1918-1928*, 107–14. Tielt: Lannoo, 2018.

Cahalan, Peter James. "The Treatment Of Belgian Refugees In England During The Great War." McMasters University, 1977.

Campbell, H. *Belgian Soldiers at Home in the United Kingdom*. London: Saunders and Cullingham, s.d.

Carpenter, Joel. A. *Revive Us Again, The Reawakening of American Fundamentalism*. New York: Oxford University Press, 1997.

Carpenter, Joel. A. "Propagating the Faith Once Delivered: The Fundamentalist Missionary Enterprise, 1920-1945." In *Earthen Vessels: American Evangelicals and Foreign Missions*, 92-132. Grand Rapids, MI: Eerdmans, 1990.

Clifton, Michael. *Amigo, Friend of the Poor*. Leominster: Gracewing Publishing, 2006.

Collinet, Robert. *Histoire du Protestantisme en Belgique aux xviime et xviiime siècles*. Histoire du Protestantisme en Belgique et au Congo belge 2. Bruxelles: Librairie des Eclaireurs Unionistes, 1959.

Conway, Martin. "The Christian Churches and Politics in Europe, 1914-1939." In *World Christianities c. 1914-c. 2000*, 151-178. Cambridge History of Christianity, v. 9. Cambridge, UK; New York: Cambridge University Press, 2006.

Creemers, Jelle. "All Together in One Synod? The Genesis of the Federal Synod of Protestant and Evangelical Churches in Belgium (1985-1998)." *Trajecta. Religie, cultuur en samenleving in de Nederlanden* 26, no. 2017 (2018): 275-302.

Creemers, Jelle. "Freedom of Religion or Belief in Belgium: Some Religions Are More Equal than Others." *Talk About: Law and Religion: Blog of the International Center for Law and Religion Studies* (blog), 5 January 2021.

Creemers, Jelle. "Protestanten verenigd voor of door de staat? Onderhandelingen over de afbakening van een erkende eredienst in België (1999-2002)." *Tijdschrift voor Religie, Recht en Beleid* 9, no. 2 (2018): 5-18.

Cruickshank, Joanna, and Patricia Grimshaw. *White Women, Aboriginal Missions and Australian Settler Governments: Maternal Contradictions*. Leiden: Brill, 2019.

DeBerg, Betty A. *Ungodly Women: Gender and the First Wave of American Fundamentalism*. Macon, GA: Mercer University Press, 2000.

De Clerck, K. *Chronologisch Overzicht van de Belgische Onderwijsgeschiedenis 1830-1990*. Gent: Centrum in de Studie van de Historische Pedagogiek, 1991.

De Kruisbanier, Algemeen Evangelisch Weekblad. "Advert." 9 December 1969.

De Kruisbanier, Algemeen Evangelisch Weekblad. "Telefoondienst in Brussel." 2 December 1961.

De Kruisbanier, Algemeen Evangelisch Weekblad. "Foto's van de Euro '70 Billy Graham kruistocht in Deurne bij Antwerpen." 21 April 1970.

De Maeyer, Jan, and Jan De Volder. "The Church in Belgium during and after the First World War. Cardinal Désiré-Joseph Mercier (1851/1906-1926) between Idealism and Reality.," in *Santa Sede e Cattolici Nel Mondo Postbellico (1918-1922): Raccolta Di Studi Nel Centenario Della Conclusione Della Prima Guerra Mondiale*. Citta del Vaticano: Libreria editrice vaticana, 2020.

Demart, Sarah, Joseph Tonda, and Alain Tarrius. *Les territoires de la délivrance: le réveil Congolais en situation postcoloniale (RDC et Diaspora)*. Hommes et Sociétés. Paris: Éditions Karthala, 2017.

De Paepe, Eddy. "Uit het gulden boek: Jonkvrouw Henriëtte Sarah Hartsen, geheelonthoudster en evangeliste." *Hilversums Historisch Tijdschrift Eigen Perk* 2, no. 2 (2000): 80-87.

Depasse, Henri. "Le Pasteur Ernest Charensol (1903-1945)." *Bulletin de la société de l'histoire du protestantisme belge* 140 (June 2008): 33-42.

De Raaf, A. *Een eeuw Silo*. Laken: Silogemeente [etc.], 1983.

DeRemer, Bernard R. "Thunder in the Pulpit: Howard Kelly Beloved Physician of Baltimore." *Fundamentalist Journal*, December 1988, 34-35.

De Schaepdrijver. *De Groote Oorlog; Het koninkrijk België tijdens de Eerste Wereldoorlog*. Antwerp: Atlas Contact / Hautekiet, 2013.

De Volder, Jan. "Belgium and Luxemburg." In *Christianity in Western and Northern Europe*, 75-85. Edinburgh Companions to Global Christianity. Edinburgh: Edinburgh University Press, 2024.

De Weerdt, Denise. *En de vrouwen?: vrouw, vrouwenbeweging en feminisme in België 1830-1960*. Gent: Masereelfonds, 1980.

Dheedene, Lise, Patrick Loobuyck, and Stijn Oosterlynck. "'Stretched' Postsecular Rapprochement: Evangelical Solidarities in a Local Flemish Welfare Regime." *International Journal of Religion and Spirituality in Society* 14, no. 3 (2023): 117-134.

Dixon, A.C., and R.A. Torrey, eds. *The Fundamentals: A Testimony To The Truth*. Chicago, IL: Testimony Publishing Company, 1910.

Dujardin, Vincent and Mark Van den Wijngaert. "1939 - 1950 Land zonder koning." in *Nieuwe Geschiedenis van België*, vol. II. Tielt: Lannoo, 2006.

Dumoulin, Michel. "Het ontluiken van de twintigste eeuw, 1905-1918." In *Nieuwe Geschiedenis van België*, 697-868. Tielt: Lannoo, 2006.

Dupriez, Léon H. "Les rémunérations en Belgique de 1936 à 1952." *Bulletin de l'Institut de Recherches Economiques et Sociales* 18, no. 5 (1952): 433-476.

Elisabeth, Piller. "American War Relief, Cultural Mobilization, and the Myth of Impartial Humanitarianism,1914-17." *Journal of the Gilded Age and Progressive Era* 17, no. 4 (2018): 619-635.

Ellsworth Day, Richard. *Breakfast Table Autocrat, The Life of Henry Parsons Crowell*. Chicago, IL: Moody Press, 1946.

Elsman, Domus. *Johannes de Heer: evangelist in het licht van de wederkomst*. Zoetermeer: Boekencentrum, 1995.

Evans, Richard Kent. "A New Protestantism Has Come": World War I, Premillennial Dispensationalism, and the Rise of Fundamentalism in Philadelphia." *Pennsylvania History: A Journal of Mid-Atlantic Studies* 84, no. 3 (2017): 292-312.

Fath, Sébastien. *Du ghetto au réseau : Le protestantisme évangélique en France, 1800-2005*. Genève: Labor et Fides, 2005.

Ferreira, Ignatius Wilhelm, and Joseph Bosco Bangura. "African Charismatic Movements and Urban Missiology." In *Africa Bears Witness: Mission Theology and Praxis in the 21st Century*, edited by Harvey Kwyani, 99–111. Nairobi; Accra: ATN Press, 2021.

Fiedler, Klaus. *Ganz auf Vertrauen : Geschichte und Kirchenverständnis der Glaubensmissionen*. Giessen, Basel: Brunnen, 1992.

Fiedler, Klaus. *Interdenominational Faith Missions in Africa: History and Ecclesiology*. Mzuzu [Malawi]: Mzuni Press, 2018.

Fiedler, Klaus. *The Story of Faith Missions. From Hudson Taylor to Present Day Africa*. Oxford: Regnum Books International, 1994.

Findlay, James F, and Martin E Marty. *Dwight L. Moody: American Evangelist, 1837-1899*. Eugene, OR: Wipf and Stock Publishers, 2007.

Fleming, Guy. *In the Wake of the Whirlwind, the Story of the Belgian Evangelical Mission*. Brussels: Belgian Evangelical Mission, 1973.

Foreign Evangelical Society. *Fourth Annual Report of the Foreign Evangelical Society ; Presented at the Annual Meeting, Held in the Reformed Dutch Church, Washington Square, New-York ; on Tuesday Evening, May 9, 1843*. New York: John S. Taylor & Co, 1843.

Frizen, Edwin L. *75 Years of IFMA, 1917-1992: The Nondenominational Missions Movement*. Pasadena, CA: William Carey Library, 1992.

Gerard, Emmanuel. "De binnenlandse politiek." In *België, een land in crisis, 1913-1950*, 65-120. Antwerp: Standaard Uitgeverij, 2006.

Gerard, Emmanuel. "De democratie gedroomd, begrensd en ondermijnd. 1918-1939." In *Nieuwe Geschiedenis van België*, 2: 867-1118. Tielt: Lannoo, 2006.

Gevers, Lieve. "Hoogtepunt en einde van een tijdperk (1926-1961); Het aartsbisdom onder kardinaal Van Roey." In *Het aartsbisdom Mechelen-Brussel: 450 jaar geschiedenis*, Vol. 2:173–253. Antwerpen: Halewijn, 2009.

Gevers, Lieve, Arie W. Willemsen, and Els Witte. "Geschiedenis van de Vlaamse Beweging." In *Nieuwe Encyclopedie van de Vlaamse Beweging*, 1:35–86. Tielt: Lannoo, 1998.

Gibson, Scott M. *A.J. Gordon: American Premillennialist*. Lanham, MD: University Press of America, 2001.

Glass, William R. "Transatlantic Fundamentalism: Southern Preachers in London's Pulpits during World War I." in *The U.S. South and Europe: Transatlantic Relations in the Nineteenth and Twentieth Centuries*, New Directions in Southern History. Lexington, KY: University Press of Kentucky, 2013.

Godwin, Colin. "Indigenous Church Planting in Post-Christian Europe: A Case Study of Belgian Pioneers." *Missiology*, 1 July 2011, 391-405.

Godwin, Colin. "The Recent Growth of Pentecostalism in Belgium." *International Bulletin for Missionary Research* 37, no. 2 (2013): 90-94.

Goffinet, Sylvie-Anne, and Dirk Van Damme. *Functioneel analfabetisme in België*. Brussels: Koning Boudewijnstichting, 1990.

Grubb, Norman P. *C.T. Studd: Cricketer and Pioneer*. n.p.: Home Farm Books, 2006.

Hambrick-Stowe, Charles E. "'Sanctified Business': Historical Perspectives on Financing Revivals of Religion." In *More Money, More Ministry: Money and Evangelicals in Recent North Amerikan History*, 81–103. Grand Rapids, MI: Eerdmans, 2000.

Hamilton, Michael S. "Women, Public Ministry, and American Fundamentalism, 1920-1950." *Religion and American Culture: A Journal of Interpretation* 3, no. 2 (1993): 171-196.

Hamm, Thomas D. *The Transformation of American Quakerism: Orthodox Friends, 1800-1907*. Bloomington, IN: Indiana University Press, 1992.

Handbuch der deutschen evangelischen Kirchen, 1918 bis 1949: Organe--Ämter--Verbände--Personen. Göttingen: Vandenhoeck & Ruprecht, 2010.

Hankins, Barry. *American Evangelicals: A Contemporary History of a Mainstream Religious Movement*. Critical Issues in History. Lanham: Rowman & Littlefield Publishers, 2008.

Hannah, John D. *An Uncommon Union: Dallas Theological Seminary and American Evangelicalism*. Grand Rapids, MI: Zondervan, 2009.

Harder, Ben. "The Student Volunteer Movement for Foreign Missions and Its Contribution to Overall Missionary Service." *Christian Higher Education* 10, no. 2 (March 22, 2011): 140-154.

Harris, Harriet A. *Fundamentalism and Evangelicals*. Oxford Theological Monographs. Oxford: Oxford University Press, 2008.

"History of the International Council of Christian Churches: ICCC : A World-Wide Testimony : Regional and National Councils." *Reformation Review* 15, no. 4 (1967): 217-223.

Hollinger, David A. *Protestants Abroad: How Missionaries Tried to Change the World but Changed America*. Princeton, NJ: Princeton University Press, 2017.

Horner, Norman A. "Kanamori, Tsurin ('Paul')." In *Bibliographical Dictionary of Christian Missions*, 353. New York: Macmillan Reference USA, 1998.

Howard, David M. *The Dream That Would Not Die: The Birth and Growth of the World Evangelical Fellowship, 1846-1986*. Exeter: Paternoster Press, 1986.

Hutchinson, Mark, John Wolffe. *A Short History of Global Evangelicalism*. Cambridge: Cambridge University Press, 2012.

Hutchinson, Mark. "Globalized Fundamentalismm." In *The Oxford Handbook of Christian Fundamentalism*, 683-699. New York: Oxford University Press, 2023.

Jacquemyns, Herwich. *België in de Tweede Wereldoorlog*. Vol. 2. Een bezet land. Antwerpen: Pelckmans, 1991.

Jaumotte, André. "Notice sur Charles Lagrange, membre de l'Académie." *Annuaire de l'académie royale de Belgique*, 1992, 3-44.

Jenkins, Philip. *The Great and Holy War: How World War I Became a Religious Crusade*. First Edition. San Francisco: Harper One, 2014.

Johnson, Todd M., Gina A. Zurlo, Becky Yang Hsu, David B. Barrett, and George Thomas Kurian. *World Christian Encyclopedia*. Third edition. Edinburgh: Edinburgh University Press, 2020.

Joiner, Theckla Ellen. *Sin in the City: Chicago and Revivalism; 1880 – 1920*. Columbia: University of Missouri Press, 2007.

Judt, Tony. *Postwar: A History of Europe since 1945*. London: Pimlico, 2007.

Kaastra, Jelle. *Nederlands Verbond van Jeugdbonden 'Eén in Christus': Christian Endeavour Nederland*. Self-published, 2010.

Kahn, Elizabeth Louise. *The Neglected Majority : "Les Camoufleurs," Art History, and World War I*. Lanham, MD: University Press of America, 1984.

Koops, Enne. "Dutch Calvinist and Catholic War Sermons," *Trajecta : Tijdschrift voor de geschiedenis van het katholiek leven in de Nederlanden* 23, no. 2, (2014): 275-290.

Koppel, Gert. *Untergetaucht: eine Flucht aus Deutschland*. Würzburg: Arena, 1997.

Kostlevy, William. *Historical Dictionary of the Holiness Movement*. Lanham, MD: Scarecrow Press, 2009.

Krabbendam, Hans. *Saving the Overlooked Continent: American Protestant Missions in Western Europe, 1940-1975*. Leuven: Leuven University Press, 2020.

Laveille, Eugène. *Au service des blessés, 1914-1918*. Gembloux: J Duculot, 1921.

Leconte, Jacques-Robert. *Aumôniers militaires belges de la guerre 1914-1918*. Vol. 5. Travaux / Centre d'histoire militaire. Brussels: Koninklijk Museum van het Leger en van Krijgsgeschiedenis, 1969.

Lutjeharms, W. *De Vlaamse Opleidingsschool van Nicolaas de Jonge en zijn opvolgers (1875-1926)*. Historische studies 6. Brussel: Vereniging voor de Geschiedenis van het Belgisch Protestantisme, 1978.

Maes, Jan. *De ster en het kruis: De Gereformeerde Jodenzending in Antwerpen en Brussel (1931-1948)*. Brussels: Stichting voor de Eigentijdse Herinnering, 2020.

Maiden, John. "Fundamentalism and Anti-Catholicism in Inter-War English Evangelicalism." In *Evangelicalism & Fundamentalism in the United Kingdom during the Twentieth Century*, 151-170. Oxford: Oxford University Press, 2013.

Marinello, Thomas J. *New Brethren in Flanders: The Origins and Development of the Evangelische Christengemeenten Vlaanderen, 1971-2008*. Eugene, OR: Pickwick Publications, 2013.

Marquette, Arthur F. *Brands, Trademarks, and Good Will, the Story of Quaker Oats Company*. New York: McGraw-Hill, 1967.

Marsden, George M. *Fundamentalism and American Culture : The Shaping of Twentieth Century Evangelicalism, 1870-1925*. New York: Oxford University Press, 1980, 2006, 2022.

Marsden, George M. *Reforming Fundamentalism: Fuller Seminary and the New Evangelicalism*. Grand Rapids, MI: W.B. Eerdmans, 1987.

Marsden, George M. "The Rise of Fundamentalism." In *Turning Points in the History of American Evangelicalism*, 133-153. Grand Rapids, MI: Eerdmans, 2017.

Martin, Roger. *R.A. Torrey: Apostle of Certainty*. Mursfreeboro, TN: Sword of the Lord Publishers, 1976.

Maskens, Maïté. "Migration et pentecôtisme à Bruxelles. Expériences croisées." *Archives de sciences sociales des religions* 143, no. 3 (2008): 49-68.

Matthäus, Jürgen. *Jewish Responses to Persecution. Documenting Life and Destruction*. Lanham MD, Washington DC: AltaMira Press, 2010.

Matthews, Arthur H. *Standing Up, Standing Together: The Emergence of the National Association of Evangelicals*. Carol Stream, Ill: National Association of Evangelicals, 1992.

McAlister, Melani. *The Kingdom of God Has No Borders: A Global History of American Evangelicals*. New York: Oxford University Press, 2018.

McIntire, C. *What Is the Difference between Fundamentalism and New Evangelicalism*. Collingswood, NJ: 20th Century Reformation, s. d.

"McQuilkin, Robert C., JR." In *The Evangelicals: A Historical, Thematic, and Biographical Guide*, 274-275. Westport, CT: Greenwood Press, 1999.

Meersman, Levi, ed. *Gods werk gaat door. 70 jaar Evangeliewerk Oostrozebeke 1922-1992*, n.d.

Mietes, P.J. *Hij reisde zijn weg met blijdschap*. Doorn: Het Zoeklicht, 1985.

Moreau, A. Scott. "Evangelical Missions Development 1910 to 2010 in the North American Setting: Reaction and Emergence." In *Evangelical and Frontier Mission: Perspectives on the Global Progress of the Gospel*, 3-46. Fortress Press, 2011.

Muukkonen, Martti. *Ecumenism of the Laity : Continuity and Change in the Mission View of the World's Alliance of Young Men's Christian Associations, 1855-1955*. Joensuu: University of Joensuu, 2002.

Newnham-Davis, Nathaniel. *The Gourmet's Guide to London*. London: Grant Richards, 1914.

Ottman, Ford C. *J. Wilbur Chapman, A Biography*. New York: Doubleday, Page & Company, 1920.

Overbeeke, J.K., ed. *Jaarboek der evangelische kerken*. Antwerp: J.K. Overbeeke, 1947.

Overbeeke, J.K., ed. *Jaarboek der evangelische kerken in België 1950*. Hoboken: J.K. Overbeeke, 1950.

Overbeeke, J.K., ed. *Jaarboek der evangelische kerken in België 1954*. Hoboken: J.K. Overbeeke, 1954.

Overbeeke, J.K., ed. *Jaarboek der evangelische kerken in België 1963*. Antwerpen: J.K. Overbeeke, 1963.

Overbeeke, J.K., ed. *Jaarboek voor de protestantse kerken in België 1966*. Berchem: J.K. Overbeeke, 1966.

Overbeeke, J.K., ed. *Jaarboek van de protestantse kerken in België 1972*. Antwerp: Fa. Overbeeke, 1972.

Overbeeke, J.K., ed. "The Making of a Mission Field: Paradigms of Evangelistic Mission in Europe," *Exchange* 41, no. 1 (2012): 44-67.

Paas, Stefan. "Mission from Anywhere to Europe." *Mission Studies* 32, no. 1 (April 10, 2015): 4-31.

Paldiel, Mordecai. *Churches and the Holocaust: Unholy Teaching, Good Samaritans, and Reconciliation*. Jersey City, NJ: Ktav, 2006.

Parker, Michael. *The Kingdom of Character: The Student Volunteer Movement for Foreign Missions (1886-1926)*. Lanham, MD: American Society of Missiology ; University Press of America, 1998

Passmore, Kevin. "Politics." In *Europe 1900-1945*, 77-115. Short Oxford History of Europe. Oxford: Oxford University Press, 2002.

Penton, M. James *Jehovah's Witnesses and the Third Reich: sectarian politics under persecution.* Toronto: University of Toronto Press, 2004.

Phillips, Clifton Jackson, and John J. Baughman. *DePauw: A Pictorial History.* Greencastle, IN: DePauw University, 1987.

Pocock, Michael. "The Influence of Premillennial Eschatology on Evangelical Missionary Theory and Praxis from the Late Nineteenth Century to the Present." *International Bulletin for Missionary Research* 33, no. 3 (2009): 129-136.

Polasky, Janet L. *The Democratic Socialism of Emile Vandervelde: Between Reform and Revolution.* Oxford: Berg, 1995.

Pollock, John Charles. *The Keswick Story: The Authorized History of the Keswick Convention-- Updated!* Rev. ed. Fort Washington, PA: CLC Publications, 2006.

Poujol, Geneviève. *Un féminisme sous tutelle: les protestantes françaises, 1810-1960.* Editions de Paris, 2003.

Prins, Aaldert. "De protestants-evangelische kerken en de Anglicaanse kerk," in *Bronnen voor de studie van het hedendaagse België, 19e-21e eeuw,* ed. Patricia Van den Eeckhout and Guy Vanthemsche. Brussels: Koninklijke Commissie voor Geschiedenis, 2017.

Pylyser, Jean-Marie. *Verzwegen schuld: Het "drama" Irma Laplasse; Finale overzicht en analyse met nieuwste onthullingen.* Middelkerke: J.P.M. Trends, 2009.

Reynebeau, Marc. "Mensen zonder eigenschappen." In *De massa in verleiding: De jaren '30 in België,* 12-73. Brussels: Ludion, 1994.

Reynolds, Amber Thomas. "Fundamentalist Magazine Publishing." In *The Oxford Handbook of Christian Fundamentalism,* 198-216. Oxford: Oxford University Press, 2023.

Robert, Dana Lee. *American Women in Mission: A Social History of Their Thought and Practice.* Macon, GA: Mercer University Press, 1996.

Robert, Dana Lee. "From Missions to Mission to Beyond Missions: The Historiography of American Protestant Foreign Missions Since World War II." *International Bulletin of Missionary Research* 18, no. 4 (1994): 146-162.

Robert, Dana Lee. "'The Crisis of Missions': Premillennial Mission Theory and the Origins of Independent Evangelical Missions." In *Earthen Vessels: American Evangelicals and Foreign Missions,* 29-46. Grand Rapids, MI: Eerdmans, 1990.

Robinson, G.L. *Autobiography of George L. Robinson, a Short Story of a Long Life.* Grand Rapids, MI: Baker Book House, 1957.

Rosenberg, Emily S., and Eric Foner. *Spreading the American Dream: American Economic and Cultural Expansion, 1890-1945.* 1st ed. American Century Series. New York: Hill and Wang, 1982.

Ruotsila, Markku. *Fighting Fundamentalist: Carl McIntire and the Politicization of American Fundamentalism.* London: Oxford University Press, 2016

Russell, C. Allyn. "Donald Grey Barnhouse: Fundamentalist Who Changed." *Journal of Presbyterian History* 59, no. 1 (1981): 33–57.

Ruthven, J.M. "New Folding Church Trailer." *The Pentecostal Evangel,* 1 July 1950.

Sandeen, Ernest R. *The Roots of Fundamentalism; British and American Millenniarism 1800-1930.* Grand Rapids, MI: Baker Book House, 1978.

Sauer, Christof, and Hans Ulrich Reifler. "The Relevance of Transnational Networking in the Global Ministry of Fredrik Franson." *Missionalia* 48, no. 1 (2020): 58-80.

Scheps. *Weersta vanaf het begin maar alleen met het geesteszwaard: Het verzetswerk van J.H. Scheps 1940-1945.* Amsterdam: Aksant, 2010.

Schuler, Ulrike. "Crisis, Collapse, and Hope: Methodism in 1945 Europe." *Methodist History* 51, no. 1-2 (2012-203): 5-27.

Schweitzer, Richard. *The Cross and the Trenches: Religious Faith and Doubt among British and American Great War Soldiers.* Contributions in Military Studies, no. 225. Westport, CT: Praeger Publishers, 2003.

Séguy, Jean. *Les assemblées anabaptistes-mennonites de France.* Société, mouvements sociaux et idéologies : 1. sér., Études 17. Paris: Mouton, 1977.

Setran, David P. *The College "Y": Student Religion in the Era of Secularization.* Basingstoke: Palgrave Macmillan, 2007.

Sharpe, Eric E. "Reflections on Missionary Historiography." *International Bulletin for Missionary Research* 13, no. 2 (1989): 76-81.

Shepard, Lansing. *The 150 Year Commemorative Celebration - YMCA of Greater Saint Paul 1856-2006.* Minneapolis, MN: YMCA of Greater Saint Paul, 2006.

Silo-Vereeniging: stads-evangelisatie in Brussel en lands-evangelisatie in Vlaanderen: na 50 Jaren, 1874-10 Mei 1924. Brussels: Silo-Vereeniging, 1925.

Sittser, Gerald L. "Protestant Missionary Biography as Written Icon." *Christian Scholar's Review* 36, no. 303-321 (2007).

Slagter, W. "Heer, Johannes de (1866-1961)." In *Biografisch Woordenboek van Nederland*. Kampen: Kok, 2002.

Smith, Timothy Lawrence. *Called Unto Holiness: The Story of the Nazarenes, the Formative Years*. Kansas City, MO: Nazarene Publishing House, 1962.

Snape, M.F. *God and the British Soldier: Religion and the British Army in the First and Second World Wars*. Christianity and Society in the Modern World. London: Routledge, 2005.

Stanley, Brian. "Global Mission." In *Oxford Handbook of Christian Fundamentalism*, 495-510. New York: Oxford University Press, 2023.

Stark, Rodney. "Efforts to Christianize Europe, 400-2000." *Journal of Contemporary Religion* 16, no. 1 (2001): 105-123.

Steuer, Kenneth. "Key Figures YMCA Secretaries." In *Pursuit of an "Unparalleled Opportunity" The American YMCA and Prisoner of War Diplomacy among the Central Power Nations during World War I, 1914-1923*. New York: Columbia University Press, 2009.

Stevenson, David. "International Relations" In *Europe 1900-1945*, 26-47. Short Oxford History of Europe. Oxford: Oxford University Press, 2012.

Streiff, Patrick. *Der Methodismus in Europa im 19. und 20. Jahrhundert*. Stuttgart: Medienwerk der Evangelisch-methodistischen Kirche, 2003.

Sutton, Matthew Avery. *American Apocalypse: A History of Modern Evangelicalism*. Cambridge, MA: Belknap Press of Harvard University Press, 2014.

Sweetnam, Mark S. "Defining Dispensationalism: A Cultural Studies Perspective." *Journal of Religious History* 34, no. 2 (2010): 191–212.

Synan, Vinson. *The Holiness-Pentecostal Tradition: Charismatic Movements in the Twentieth Century*. 2nd ed. Grand Rapids, MI: Eerdmans, 1997.

Tatford, Frederick. *West European Evangel*. Bath: Echoes of Service, 1985.

Terry, John Mark and Robert L. Gallagher. *Encountering the History of Missions: From the Early Church to Today*, Encountering Mission. Grand Rapids, MI: Baker Academic, 2017.

Thompson, Michael Glenn. *For God and Globe: Christian Internationalism in the United States between the Great War and the Cold War*. The United States in the World. Ithaca, NY: Cornell University Press, 2015.

Thompson, Phyllis. *Firebrand of Flanders : The Gospel in Belgium Seen in the Life of Odilon Vansteenberghe*. Lutterworth, Leicester: Belgian Evangelical Mission, 1983.

Torrey, R.A. *How to Work for Christ: A Compendium of Effective Methods*. Chicago: Fleming H. Revell, 1901.

Treloar, Geoffrey R. *The Disruption of Evangelicalism: The Age of Torrey, Mott, Mcpherson and Hammond*. A History of Evangelicalism, Vol. 4. Downers Grove, IL: IVP Academic, 2017.

Trogh, Pieter, Dominiek Dendooven, and Ivan Couttenier. *Amerikanen in Flanders Fields*. De Namenlijst 4. Ieper: In Flanders Fields Museum, 2024.

Van den Berg, K.H.M. "Protestantisme in België, Wat is de B.E.Z.? – De Bijbelschool in Brussel - Strijd en zegen." *Nieuwe Utrechtsche Courant*, February 1936, sec. Zondagsblad.

Van der Laan, P. and Cornelius van der Laan. *Pinksteren in beweging: vijfenzeventig jaar pinkstergeschiedenis in Nederland en Vlaanderen*. Kampen: Kok, 1982.

Van Isacker, Karel. *De zaak Irma Laplasse: stukken voor een dossier ingeleid door K. van Isacker*. Antwerp: Nederlandsche Boekhandel, 1970.

Vanlandschoot, Romain, Nico Van Campenhout, and Aragorn Fuhrmann. "Verschaeve, Cyriel." In *Digitale Encyclopedie van de Vlaamse Beweging*, 2024. https://encyclopedievlaamsebeweging.be/nl/verschaeve-cyriel.

Van Rijn, Henk. *100 Jaar Adventkerk in België*, s.d.

Van Rompaey, Lies. *Strijd Voor Waardering: Het COV van 1893 Tot 1983*. Antwerpen: Garant, 2003.

Van Wageningen, D. *Gedenk de dagen; geschiedenis van de Protestantse kerk te Ronse*. Vol. 2. Ronse: Protestants Aktiekomitee, 1988.

Veraghtert, K. "Het economische leven – 1918-1940." In *Algemene geschiedenis der Nederlanden*, 14:79–101. Haarlem: Fibula-Van Dishoeck, 1979.

Verleyen, Misjoe. *Mei 1940: België op de vlucht*. Antwerp: Manteau, 2010.

Vernette, Jean, and Claire Moncelon. *Dictionnaire des groupes religieux aujourd'hui: religions, églises, sectes, nouveaux mouvements religieux, mouvements spiritualistes.* Paris: Presses universitaires de France, 2001.

Walls, Andrew. "The American Dimension in the History of the Missionary Movement." In *Earthen Vessels: American Evangelicals and Foreign Missions*, 1-25. Grand Rapids, MI: Eerdmans, 1990.

Walls, Andrew. *The Missionary Movement in Christian History: Studies in the Transmission of Faith*. Maryknoll, NY, Edinburgh: Orbis Books; T&T Clark, 1996.

Wargenau - Saillens, M. *Ruben et Jeanne Saillens, Evangélistes*. Paris: Les Bons Semeurs, 1947.

Weber, Timothy P. *Living in the Shadow of the Second Coming: American Premillennialism, 1875-1982*. Grand Rapids, MI: Zondervan, 1983.

Wiley, S. Wirt, and Florence Lehmann. *Builders of Men: A History of the Minneapolis Young Men's Christian Association: 1866-1936*. Minneapolis, MN, 1938.

Willequet, Jacques. "Het politiek en sociaal leven." In *De dolle jaren in België 1920-1930: 29 Oktober 1981-24 Januari 1982 Galerij ASLK*, 17-22. Brussels: ASLK, 1981.

Witte, E. "Vrijdenkersbeweging 1873-1914." In *Algemene Geschiedenis der Nederlanden*, 13:102-105. Haarlem: Fibula-Van Dishoeck, 1978.

Wos, Jan Wladislaw, Wiktor Jacewicz, and Akademia teologii katolickiej (Varsovie). *Martyrologium polskiego duchowienstwa rzymskokatolickiego po okupacja hitlerowska w latach: 1939-1945*. 5 vols. Warszawa: ATK, 1977.

W.P. "Charles Inwood." In *Historical Dictionary of the Holiness Movement*. Scarecrow Press, 2009.

Yaakov, Ariel. *Evangelizing the Chosen People: Missions to the Jews in America, 1880-2000*. Chapel Hill NC: University of North Carolina Press, 2000.

Yapp, Arthur Keysall. *The Romance of the Red Triangle; The Story of the Coming of the Red Triangle and the Service Rendered by the Y.M.C.A. to the Sailors and Soldiers of the British Empire.* London: Hodder and Stoughton, 1918.

Zdanowski, Jerzy. "Protestant Millennialism and Missions at the Turn of the 20th Century," *Hemispheres. Studies on Cultures and Societies* 33. 2018.

Internet and Unpublished Sources

Ars Moriendi.be, ed. "De CEUNINCK, Baron Armand, L.-T.," accessed 10 May 2014, http://www.ars-moriendi.be/DE_CEUNINCK_FR.html.

Berrus, Albert , "Brigade et Brigadette," Chrétienne évangélique," 7 December 2009, accessed 8 November 2012, http://chretienneevangelique.centerblog.net/rub-t-.html.

Blommers, B., "Evert van Dalen," acessed 20 October 2013, http://members.tele2.nl/bblommers/cgpred.htm#D.

Boersema, Pieter R. "De evangelische beweging in de samenleving : een antropologisch onderzoek naar religieuze veranderingen in de evangelische beweging in Vlaanderen en Nederland gedurende de periode 1972 - 2002." PhD diss., KU Leuven, 2004.

Bogaert, Nele, and Hannelore Decoodt, "School van de Koningin," 2004, accessed 12 December 2018, https://id.erfgoed.net/teksten/196126.

Brandt-Bessire, Daniel. "Considérations historiques: théologiques et bibliographiques concernant directement ou indirectement le mouvement de pentecôte Francophone belge (1928-1982)." Licentiate Thesis, Faculté Universitaire de Theologie Protestante de Bruxelles, 1987.

Christmas Letters to Prisoners, "A Potted History of Our Work and Ministry," accessed 17 January 2013, http://www.christmasletters.plus.com/Short%20History.html.

Creemers, Jelle, "The Flemish Draft Law on Religious Communities: A Critical Analysis." *Bitter Winter* (blog), 6 March 2021, accessed 20 June 2021, https://bitterwinter.org/the-flemish-draft-law-on-religious-communities-a-critical-analysis/.

Dale, Olive. "Aperçu sur l'évangélisation en Belgique pendant l'entre-Deux-Guerres." Licentiate's thesis, Faculté Libre de Théologie Evangélique, 1976.

Delhove, Frans. "Histoire du protestantisme belge depuis la création de l'état belge jusqu'au début de la Seconde Guerre Mondiale, 1830 – 1939." Licentiate's thesis, Faculté de Théologie de l'Eglise évangélique libre du Canton de Vaud, 1953.

Demaerel, Ignace. "Tachtig jaar Pinksterbeweging in Vlaanderen (1909-1989); Een historisch onderzoek met korte theologische en sociologische analyse." Licentiate's thesis, Universitaire Faculteit voor Protestantse Godgeleerdheid, 1990.

Demart, Sarah. "Les territoires de la délivrance : mises en perspectives historique et plurilocalisée du réveil congolais (Bruxelles, Kinshasa, Paris, Toulouse)." PhD diss., Université Catholique de Louvain, 2010.

Demasure, Brecht, "Het Nationaal Hulp- en Voedingscomité redt de bevolking." *Boter bij de vis: Landbouw, Voeding en Eerste Wereldoorlog* (blog). Accessed 2 December 2018. https://www.boterbijdeviswo1.be/verhalen/maatschappij/het-nationaal-hulp-en-voedingscomite-redt-de-bevolking/.

Goldsborough, Gordon and Jamie Howison, "Memorable Manitobans: Sidney Thomas Smith (1878-1947)," The Manitoba Historical Society, 2010. Accessed 1 July 2010, http://www.mhs.mb.ca/docs/people/smith_st.shtml.

Graves, MSL, Dan. "Walter L. Wilson Converted," 2007, accessed 17 January 2013, http://www.christianity.com/church/church-history/timeline/1801-1900/walter-l-wilson-converted-11630649.html.

"History of OFM International," accessed 4 June 2014, http://www.omf.org/omf/cambodia/about_omf/history_of_omf_international.

Jourdain, Virginie. "L'hôtellerie bruxelloise 1880-1940. Acteurs, structures et logiques spatiales d'un secteur multiforme." PhD diss, Université Libre de Bruxelles, 2012.

Kind en Gezin, ed., "Geschiedenis," accessed 22 January 2013, http://www.kindengezin.be/over-kind-en-gezin/geschiedenis/.

Laan, P.H. van der. "Gemeentestichtende evangelisatie in Vlaanderen: een onderzoek naar de stichting van gemeenten in Vlaanderen door zowel de Belgische Evangelische Zending als Richard Haverkamp en zijn medewerkers van 1972 tot 1988." 1991.

Marinello, Thomas J., "A History of the Evangelische Christengemeenten Vlaanderen: Its Origins and Development, 1971-1980." PhD diss, Evangelical Theological Faculty Leuven, 2009.

Meul, Mieke ,"De oorlogsmeters van de Belgische soldaten tijdens de Eerste Wereldoorlog (1914-1918)." KU Leuven, accessed 10 April 2009, http://www.ethesis.net/oorlogsmeters/oorlogsmeters_corpus.htm#HOOFDSTUK%203:%20DE%20OORLOGSMETERS.

Militärbefehlshabers in Belgien und Nord-Frankreich, ed., "Verordnungsblatt Nr. 8, 25/7/1940." 25 July 1940.

Moody Bible Institute, ed., "James M. Gray," accessed 20 February 2014, http://mmm.moody.edu/GenMoody/default.asp?SectionID=13F805882ACF4020AE62F6133C4848D8.

National Association of Evangelicals. "History," accessed 1 February 2013, http://www.nae.org.

Omon, Klazina, "Voor het hoogste het beste; De Angelsaksische invloed op de verspreiding van religieuze traktaten in Nederland (1913-1959)." PhD diss, Free University Amsterdam, 2014.

Prins, Aaldert, "The History of the Belgian Gospel Mission from 1918 to 1962." PhD diss., Evangelical Theological Faculty Leuven, 2015.

Reich, Joy. "Elisabeth Lemière Shannon; Missionary to the Belgian Congo and to Quebec, Canada, Based on and Including Passages from the Memoir She Wrote for Her Family and Excerpts from Her e-Mails to Family Members." 2012.

Rosier, Mariel, "De houding van de Belgische katholieken tegenover het protestantisme (1830-1865)." Licentiate's thesis, KU Leuven, 1989.

Sagan, Sean Geoffrey, "Only a Tract: The Production and Distribution of Evangelical Gospel Literature and the Construction of Social Boundaries," PhD diss., University of California, 2017.

Smelne's Erfskip, ed., "Houtigehage Ds. Visscherwei 71," accessed 21 March 2013, http://www.smelneserfskip.nl/monumenten/gemeentelijke-monumenten/194-houtigehage-ds-visscherwei-71.

Strobbe, Karel, "Een verre vijand: Enkele Belgische katholieke periodieken over protestanten en het protestantisme (1884-1914)." Licentiate's thesis, Ghent University, 2006.

Superintendent Methodist Central Hall Westminster, "Ministers of Central Hall," accessed 13 September 2012, http://www.methodist-central-hall.org.uk/history/Archives/SuperintendentMinisters.pdf.

"The Righteous Among The Nations: Phebade Family." Yad Vashem, accessed 19 November 2014, http://db.yadvashem.org/righteous/family.html?language=en&itemId=4066223.

United States Code (USC) 50, 53. Trading with the enemy, https://uscode.house.gov/, accessed December 2020.

Van Dongen, Hildegard, "Winterhulp 1940-1944 : aspekten van de voedselvoorziening en de hulpverlening in de bezettingstijd." Licentiate's thesis, Ghent University, 1983.

Van Marcke, Eva, "Het Leger des Heils in België." Master's thesis, KU Leuven, 1991.

Wong, Hoover, "Wang Zai (Leland Wang) 1898 ~ 1975," accessed 17 January 2013, http://www.bdcconline.net/en/stories/w/wang-zai.php.

INDEX OF PERSONS

Albert I 77
Alexander, Charles M. 20, 27, 79, 81, 83
Anderson, Robert 40, 62
Andries, André 160
Antomarchi, Antonio 66, 82
Arnold, Eberhard, 60
Atkinson, Ralph 66

Baert (Mrs.) 97
Baird, Robert 12
Banks, Howard A. 47
Barbezat, Edouard 105, 131, 151
Barnhouse, Donald 58, 68, 81, 83, 86, 97-98
Barton, J. Harvey 82
Bauwens, Charles 160
Bell (secretary) 42, 97
Bendroth, Margaret 88
Bentley, Henry K. 81, 88, 105, 119
Bergman, Harvey 18
Bertiaux, Zéphirin 159
Besselaar, Gerrit 124
Bingham, Rowland V. 66, 124, 152
Bivort, Joannes 143
Blackstone, William E. 61-62, 68
Blocher, Arthur 40
Blocher, Jacques 187
Blommaert, Karel 80, 97
Blommaert, Pierre 33-34, 37, 42, 148
Bolomey, Henry 73, 81
Bordon, Mary 47, 88
Bradbury, John W. 124
Brading, Francis C. 120
Brockhaus, Carl 48
Brons, Jane 92
Brookes, James H. 61
Brucks, George 185
Buchman, Frank 77
Buunk, Herman 168, 172-173, 183

Cailleaux, Jules 92
Carey, William 12
Castiaux, Fernand 80, 168, 183
Chafer, Lewis Sperry 67-68, 143

Chapman, J. Wilbur 20, 22, 25, 27-29, 79, 81
Charensol, Ernest 141, 163
Châtelain, Léon 129
Claude, Raoul 159
Cleaver, John Martin 37
Cockburn, J. Hutchinson 171
Cockrem, Frank 83
Cohn, Joseph Hoffman 146
Collet, Sidney 68
Collinet, G. 100
Contesse-Vernier, H. 83
Cornet, Pieter 141
Cosandey, Ulysse 49, 67, 124, 145
Crowell, Henry P. 29, 35, 118, 188

Darby, John Nelson 61
Daumerie, Elisée 80
Dawe, Freda 181
Dawe, Stanley 181
De Backer, Jules 181
de Broqueville, Charles 33, 35, 41
De Ceuninck, Armand L.T. 41
de Heer, Johannes 66, 83, 92, 124
de Jonge, Nicolaas 48, 61, 68, 87
De Kerpel, Théophile 163
Delacroix, Léon 52, 55-56, 64
Denecker, Valentine 86, 89
Dentan, Charles 66
de Perrot, Bernard 124
De Pooter, Anne-Marie 92
Dequenne, Jean 163
De Smidt, Jannis 166, 168
Diriken, Pierre 173
Dobbelaere, René 150
Dubois, Samuel 112, 119, 138, 158
Du Meunier, Jean 164
du Val de Beaulieu, Raymond 77
Duvanel (evangelist) 71

Eicher, Benjamin 124
Elleman, Johannes 108, 151
Elliott, Elisabeth 81

Fermaud, Charles 67, 83
Frank, Christian Arnold 146
Freundler, Ch. 67, 119
Freytag, Alexander 143
Frost, Henry W. 44

Galet, Emile 77
Gaudibert, Casimir 48-49
Gaudibert, George F. 49
Gillain, Cyriaque 54
Glegg, Alexander Lindsay 120
Glover, Archibald E. 135
Goley (evangelist) 72
Gordon, Adoniram J. 61
Gordon, Samuel D. 124
Graham, Billy 185-186
Grandjean, Charles 83
Gray, James M. 29

Haines, R.B. Jr. 47, 88
Haldeman, I.M. 39
Harford-Battersby, T.D. 10
Harrison, Leonard Sale 145
Hartsen, Henriëtte 92
Hepp, Valentijn 58
Hilberinck, Berend 112
Hoekendijk, Christiaan J. 124
Hoffman, Julius 58
Houghton, William E. 124
Howard, Catherine 195
Howard, Philip E. 47, 66, 70, 82, 88
Howard, Philip Jr. 71, 81, 147, 195
Hoyt, Esther 143, 147, 161
Hunter, James 69
Hutchings, Eric 185
Huyghe, Joseph 162

Inwood, Charles 66, 124

Jaeger, Harry 195-196
Johnston, Howard Agnew 35
Joseph II 15
Jung, Walter 83, 105

Kanamori, Paul 67
Keller, Henri 107, 110, 119
Kelly, Howard 39
Kensit, John Alfred 120, 124
Key, Joseph S. 219
Knecht, Jan Sr. 84, 87, 196
Krauer, Willy 124
Krik, Arthur 86

Lagrange, Charles 77
Laidlaw, Robert 170

Langston, E.L 120
Laplasse, Irma 162
Lauwers, A. 104
Laveille, Eugène 33
Lemière, Elisabeth 109
Leprince, Joseph 120
Lesaffre (Lieutenant-General) 77
L'Hermenault 160
Louwage, F.E. 173
Luc, Jeanne 90
Luteijn, Jacob 168

Macartney, Clarence E.N. 124
Macfarland, Charles S. 50-51
Maclean, J. Kennedy 72
Macors (colporteur) 69
Mangold, Jörg 124
Marchandise, Armand 51
Massinon (colonel) 40
Masson, Fulgence 53
Max, Adolphe 72
McAfee, Cleland Boyd 39
McAll, Robert Whitaker 40, 57
McGhie, Anna E. 124
McIntire, Carl 11, 181
Meersman, Remy 80, 160
Meijer, Daniël 84, 100-101, 108
Meima (pastor) 170
Mercier, Désiré 55
Meyhoffer, Jean 58-59
Michiels, Jules 74, 109
Mietes (colporteur) 69
Monsma, Jan Arnold 80, 101, 105, 122
Moody, Dwight L. 10, 19, 31
Mott, John 21, 25
Mouchet, H. 119, 124
Mouchet, Walther 72
Müller, George 49
Muller, Joseph 145
Mussolini, Benito 63

Neusy, Jules 161
Nock, Mary 57
Nock, William 49, 57
Norton, Edith 9, 15-18, 20, 24-47, 51-68, 72, 76, 79-82, 85, 89, 92, 94-95, 97-98, 100-105, 112, 118-119, 134, 137, 139, 145, 201-202, 204-205
Norton, Elisabeth Louise 23-24
Norton, Ralph 9, 15-47, 51-72, 76, 79-82, 88-89, 91, 93-95, 97-98, 100-105, 117-119, 121-124, 131-134, 136-137, 145, 153, 189, 197, 200-202, 204-205

Pache, René 124, 145
Parmentier, August 80, 103-104
Payne, Homer 190, 204
Pettingill, William L. 145

Pius XI 127
Postma, Willem 148-149
Potma, Cornelis 70

Quaedpeerds, Jean 110
Quenon, Herman 75
Quenon, Herman (Mrs.) 149, 159, 166-167

Racine, Gaston 185
Rambaud, Jules 40
Reddish, Mary 49
Revell, Fleming H. 185
Rey, Jean 188
Riley, W.B. 124
Rinehart, Mary Roberts 35
Robinson, George L. 39
Rottier, Lina 91
Roy-Tophel, J.B. 145
Ruthven, J.M. 184

Saillens, Ruben 58, 65-66, 72, 82, 85, 185
Salsac, Robert 178
Samuel, Otto 146-147, 160
Scheps, Johannes H. 103-104
Schyns, Matthieu 130
Scofield, Cyrus I. 39, 62, 68, 146
Scott, Eleanor 92-93
Servaas Sr., Jacob 76, 108
Sikkema, Heinze 173
Smith, Alli Pierce 18
Smith, Robert Pearsall 10
Smith, Thomas 118
Sommers, Lulu 143, 147, 161
Spaak, Paul Henri 173
Speer, Robert Elliot 44
Stearns, Miner Daniel 39, 88, 99, 144, 164, 166, 180, 186-187
Stewart, Lyman 11, 47, 68, 88
Stewart, Milton 68, 88
Stewart, Priscilla 37
Stordeur, Désiré 163
Strong, August H. 39
Studd, Charles Thomas 37

Teeuwissen, Walter 71, 81, 105, 129, 161
Thonger, William 76
.H. Gritffith
Thys, Robert 34
Tissot, Paul 119, 124
Torrey, Reuben Archer , 20, 35, 62, 68
Trumbull, Charles G. 10, 29, 43, 47, 82, 88
Trumbull, Henry Clay 81
Tucker, Leon 66

Valet, Deborah 89
Vandenbroeck, Jean 143, 178, 184

Van Den Wyngaert, Frank 86
van der Beek, Daniel 108-109, 170-171
van de Riet, Gerrit 147, 159, 168, 172
Van der Kneipen, Victor 86
Van Der Smissen, Aloysius 48
Vandervelde, Emile 33, 35, 40, 42, 64
Vandervelde, Lalla 33, 35, 37
Van Doorne, Maurice 148, 163, 166
Van Goethem, Robert 106, 170
Van Koeckhoven, Peter 26, 32, 35, 86
van Lierop, Johan 105, 113, 123, 141, 160-161
van Puffelen, Abraham C. 81, 87, 114, 123
Van Roey, Ernest 126-127
Vansteenberghe, Odilon 37, 44, 58, 80-81, 84, 91, 94, 98, 100, 105-106, 108, 110, 112, 114, 119, 134-137, 139-140, 142, 147, 150-151, 153, 160, 162-163, 168-173, 175-176, 185-186, 188-191, 195, 203
Vansteenberghe, Paul 163
Vansteenberghe, Pierre 163
Verdickt (baker) 168
Verschaeve, Cyriel 32
Verton, Jeanne 93
Visée, Willem 126
Visser 't Hooft, Willem 171
Voorhoeve, H.C. 48
Vuilleumier, André 109, 166

Walschaert (Mrs.) 97
Walters, William G. 120
Wälti, Jean 82, 105, 129, 133, 159
Wang, Leland 145
Wauters, Joseph 56
Wesley, John 10
Wharton, Edith 35
Whitall Smith, Hannah Tatum 10
White, May B. 42, 91, 93, 97-98
Wielenga, Bastiaan 124
Williams, Grace 173
Williams, Milan B. 20
Wilson, Robert 10
Wilson, Walter L. 145
Wilson, Woodrow 13, 63
Winston, George 174, 194-197
Winston, John Jr. 184, 190, 196
Winston, John C. Sr. 81, 94-95, 100, 105, 107, 110-112, 120, 123, 126, 131, 134, 136-137, 139-142, 146-147, 151-154, 159-162, 164-165, 173, 175, 178, 180, 182-183, 185, 189-190, 196, 199-200, 202-203

Young, Dinsdale T. 120

COLOPHON

FINAL EDITING
Luc Vints

LAY-OUT
Alexis Vermeylen

KADOC-KU Leuven
Documentation and Research Centre on Religion, Culture and Society
Vlamingenstraat 39
B - 3000 Leuven
www.kadoc.kuleuven.be

Leuven University Press
Minderbroedersstraat 4
B - 3000 Leuven
www.lup.be

www.ingramcontent.com/pod-product-compliance
Lightning Source LLC
LaVergne TN
LVHW081917240725
817018LV00038B/838